Ty Beanies Tracker

Third Edition

Karen Holmes

Editor

Ty® Beanies Tracker
Third Edition

MANAGING EDITOR
Karen Holmes

BUSINESS AND PRODUCTION
Leatrice Sherry - Production Director
Sharen Forsyth - Operations Manager
Chuck Barnard - Sales and Service Manager

SPECIAL THANKS

Marlene Seuffert, VA
Karen Boeker, TX
Becky Estenssoro, IL
Janie Daniels, VA
Olive Bopp, WI

Arlene Nance
Jon Phillips, NC
Jennifer Wood, NJ
Debi Rice, TX
Tony Holmes & family

ACKNOWLEDGEMENTS (in alphabetical order)

Ashley Mueller, MO
Jenny Borman, IL
Beanie Friends World Wide Members
Carolyn Carpenter
Cliff Nebel, NY
Dorothy Marino
Dottie Wofford, TX
Jenni Wilson-Neasom, Cornwall, UK
Kathy Evans, DE
Kathy in TN
Marie Dyson, CA

Marilyn Whalen, WI
Morley Lester, Ty UK
Nikki Benson, PA
RodeoQueen
Sakurako, Japan
Shirley Gerken, WI
Susan Green, TX
Tradefair Members
Vinnie Stevens, Canada
Winkies, Whitefish Bay, WI

Library of Congress Control Number: 2007929018

ISBN 978-0-97790995-7 Copyright © 2007 by Bangzoom Software, Inc. All rights reserved. No part of this book may be reproduced or transmitted in any form or by any means, electronic or mechanical, including photocopying, record-ing, or by any information storage or retrieval system, without the written permission of the publisher. Printed in China

Bangzoom Publishers
(A Division of Bangzoom Software, Inc.)
14 Storrs Avenue Braintree, MA 02184
www.bangzoom.com

Table of Contents

Editorials

Welcome to the 3rd Edition

Bangzoom's commitment to provide quality books for collectors is demonstrated in their decision to include all of Ty's product lines. Ty has certainly been active in the last 11 years so the book is double the size of the 2nd edition which was already double the size of the 1st edition!

Enjoy revisiting older product lines, learning more about recent releases, and all that came in between. Exciting things have happened in the Beanie world since the last book — new web sites have emerged, old web sites have new looks, new product lines have been launched and new collectors have come on board.

The values in the book are to be used as a guideline and many factors come into play when determining them. More is written about how the prices are arrived at later in the book. However, values should never be the motivating factor when collecting, rather, the appeal of the product should be the deciding factor.

We have strived to provide a book that is accurate and informative. Whether you are a collector of Beanie Babies, Classics, or a variety of Ty products, there is something for everyone in this book.

Letter from the Editor

When Bangzoom contacted me for help with the Third Edition book and said they were going to include ALL Ty products, I was both excited and panicked. I collect all Ty Beanie Babies and some other lines but not all of every product line. However, I have always wanted detailed information about the various lines, in one place, in print form.

Where to start? I had my work from the 2nd Edition book to build on and my latest Update Booklet but was venturing into unknown territories when it came to Pillow Pals, Baby Ty, Attic Treasures, Plush/Classics…23 different lines in total. Wowee!! It has been an incredible learning experience and I could not have done it alone, no one could. There was an incredible amount of research to do, style numbers, birthdays, introduction dates, retirement dates, not forgetting hang tag details, generations, and photographs…on over 4,000 products and values!

There were several deciding factors that made it feasible to embark on such a huge project. I have an incredible network of friends in the Beanie community and when I don't know the answers, they do. Many are happy to contribute their years of experience and knowledge. Also, Jon Phillips, with Dave Ferrance, launched a web site — Stashmatic.com — in December 2006, which provides a forum for collectors to pool their information and the database that Jennifer, myself and others have been building was a considerable help.

Marlene Seuffert and Karen Boeker have been with me every step of the way and their contributions can be seen on every page. Marlene is an avid Ty collector and, having been a proofreader in the past, pays attention to detail. She has worked with me over the last few years to keep an accurate database. We record copyright years, pellets, origins, as well as the other relevant information. Karen has been a collector since the beginning of Ty and is a respected, active seller of Ty products. Karen and Marlene, with the input of other active sellers, both online and offline, did the research on the values. Pricing is one area that I do not get involved in so needed help from those who have kept records over time because some products are rarely up for sale on auction, instead they go directly to customers on wait lists.

Gathering together all the photographs needed was another obstacle overcome with the help of many. Arlene has an extensive collection of Attic Treasures, Marlene also has a vast amount of Attic Treasures and Pluffies. Olive opened up her home to allow Tony (my husband) to photograph her huge Classic collection and complete Pillow Pal collection. Debi willingly photographed what she had of the Classics that I still needed. Marilyn provided the NASCAR® beanie hang tags photographs. Ty allowed us to use photographs from their site and I spent countless hours scanning photographs from the Ty retailer's catalogues to be able to provide a picture rather than have a missing image. Jennifer allowed me to use whatever photographs I wished to use that she had uploaded onto Stashmatic.com and others who had contributed to that site joined in the quest to help me, too. Ms. Janie allowed me to take information and photographs from her web site and Marie had the one missing image I wanted to complete the Attic Treasures Collection — Woolie Brown — from her visit to TyRiffic Store in Chicago. Becky allowed us to use any information or photographs she had which were of immense value.

There have been many others on standby to offer help and moral support, Dorothy, Jenni, Scott & others at Ty Inc. and so many more. Cliff Nebel allowed me to use his fun Beanie Daffynitions that he posted recently on BeanieUK web site. Anyone who has ever shared information, be it directly or indirectly through a website, has played a part in this book, too. A big thank you to all, and not forgetting Lee at Bangzoom who made it possible to get this book ready for printing in record time by giving 120% percent of herself. Enjoy the book.

Love,
Karen

About the Book and Prices

We list asking prices in this guide for items in mint condition. We observe prices at auctions, on the Internet, at retail stores, and in "buy-sell" sections in collector magazines. We list all prices gathered, then arrive at a concensus.

Occasionally, a dealer will sell inventory at below cost. We dismiss these prices. Why? Because these prices are temporary. As soon as the inventory is gone, prices will rise. This is similar with auction prices but usually in reverse. High prices, spurred on by the emotion of the moment, do not make a market!

Older retired Beanies are extremely hard to find in museum quality condition, especially 1st generation Beanies. The true value of the 1st generation Beanies has often been overlooked and undervalued because these Beanies are easily found in the common version. For example, a 1st generation Blackie is one of the rarest Beanies ever made by Ty. Many collectors are happy with just having the 4th generation version of this Beanie so they will never know how hard it is to find it in the 1st generation version. The prices listed in our guide reflect the values of what collectors pay or could expect to pay if they could actually find one of these Beanies in museum quality condition.

We urge the reader to remember that this is a guide, and the actual selling price will always depend on a number of factors, including the motivation of the buyer and seller, the location, and the economic climate. The skills of the buyer at bargaining and the seller at promoting also affect the price. It is impossible to combine all of these factors and arrive at one definitive price. This is why we call this book a "guide."

Abbreviations

The 3rd Edition index format has been changed and is now a true alphabetical index. The following abbreviations are used after the item's name to identify the Ty product line.

ANG	Angeline	JB	Jingle Beanies
AT	Attic Treasures	PK	Pinky's Beanie Babies
BB	Beanie Babies	PKO	Pinkys Others
BK	Beanie Kids	PL	Pluffies
BOP	Beanie Boppers	PP	Pillow Pals
BSK	Basket Beanies	PU	Punkies
BT	Baby Ty	TBB	Teenie Beanie Babies
BU	Beanie Buddies	TBOP	Teenie Boppers
BW	Bow Wow Beanies	TGIR	Ty Girlz
CL	Ty Classic/Plush	TGR	Ty Gear
HB	Halloweenie Beanies	VB	Valenteenie Beanies

All Ty's Creatures

by Olive Bopp & Karen Holmes

Ty Warner established his company in 1986, launching a line of plush cats. The line was eventually renamed Ty Classic and was extended to include a wider variety of plush animals.

In 1993, Attic Treasures, a delightful nostalgic product line, appeared. Fully jointed bears and rabbits from six to twelve inches debuted this first year. During the period of 1995 to 1998, they were called Ty Collectibles before returning as Attic Treasures.

Ty's best known product line — Beanie Babies — started with the showing of Brownie and deep fuchsia Patti at the Gatlinberg show in 1993, where attendees placed orders for the January 1994 official introduction of the original nine Ty Beanie Babies. The little cuddly, soft and poseable

Woolie Gold
Attic Treasure

toys appealed to gift stores owners because the products were affordable to children and, being under stuffed with soft pellets, they could easily be held in small hands or carried in pockets.

In 1995, Pillow Pals, the predecessors to today's Baby Ty, made the scene. More and more retailers outside the Chicago area started demanding Ty products. A few products were removed from the order forms, later to be known as "retirements".

Antlers
Pillow Pal

In 1996 a combination of events started to get the attention of collectors of all ages. To everyone's delight, Beanie Babies hang tags saw the addition of birthdays and poems (see 4th Generation hang tags). Ty launched his web site, which made more information available and retirements public. As more people started using the internet, trading and selling sites were launched. A secondary market was developing for those who were having trouble finding the products, which had them flying off the shelves even faster. Shipping was not keeping up with demand, making them scarcer yet.

Beanie frenzy was in full swing in 1997. In addition, a surprise McDonald's promotion brought Ty's first Teenie Beanies, delighting children and keeping collectors hopping each year through 2000. In the years since the first Teenie Beanie Babies were introduced in the USA, McDonald's in several other countries have promoted their own exclusive Teenie Beanies. In 2006, Malaysia received a completely new line of My Ty Bears.

Beanie Buddies, a larger version of Beanie Babies and even more huggable, due to the creation of Ty's new fabric, Tylon, premiered in the year 2000. Beanie Kids also appeared this year. Most notable were the wide eyes and the realistic belly buttons. A line of Ty Gear was subsequently introduced for the Beanie Kids, clothing them for all occasions and imaginations.

SCARED-e
Halloweenie Beanie

Since the year 2000, Ty has continued to create lines for all to enjoy, even BowWow Beanies for dogs! Ty holiday ornaments came along in 2001 with Jingle Beanies, and more lines have been added — Basket Beanies, Halloweenies, Valenteenies — for special occasions.

2001 was the year of the Beanie Boppers, trendy dolls with the "tween" look. Of special interest were their Ty site stories - their birthdays, families, hometowns and interests. Teenie Beanie Boppers, smaller poseable versions, followed.

Punkies made us smile, with their bright colors and spiky hair. Introduced in 2002, they are still Ty-soft, despite their comically disheveled appearance.

The precious Pluffies followed in 2004 and are gentle enough for newborns' first cuddles! The year 2005 brought us three new lines. The new Ty Key-clips can now adorn many a child's backpack. Pinkys in several sizes were created especially for all the little girls who love the color pink. Angeline, a sweet little doll in several sizes and variations, is a companion to the poignant children's book, A Story of Love. In the last few years Ty has been licensed to create several cartoon character Beanie Babies for younger collectors around the world.

Angeline

Ty's latest venture has been his new product, Ty Girlz. Launched in 2007 at the New York Toy Fair, the Girlz are the latest in teenage fashion dolls, created with great attention to detail. Ty Girlz are 14" soft-sculpt dolls that are dressed in the latest trend-setting fashions that can be mixed and matched, and each outfit is completed with complimentary earrings, necklaces and bracelets. Ty Girlz have soft realistic hair that can be easily combed and made into many different styles. Each doll has its own signature color. Their clothes, hair and makeup are coordinated in monochromatic hues that give them a distinctive look and singular appeal.

Never before has a realistic type hair been created on a plush doll. In the past, plush or "soft sculpt" dolls generally had hair made of yarn or other fabrics that could neither be combed nor styled in any way. And unlike other fashion dolls, Ty Girlz is 100% handmade with a Super Velboa fabric that feels skin-soft. There are no plastics, vinyls or injection molds used in the creation of Ty Girlz.

Another unique and compelling component of the Ty Girlz is the Ty Girlz website. Ty Girlz dolls each come with her own secret code, which will give girls access to the Ty Girlz website. Here Ty has created a whole world for the girls and their dolls to visit.

It is completely interactive! Ty has designed a virtual world for girls where they can decorate their virtual bedroom, play games, do makeovers, chat, learn about the world they live in, and just "hang out" in a forum that's both fun and safe for kids.

Girls will earn points for playing games, or learning new things, and those points are converted into "money" for their savings account. They can withdraw money from their account to buy virtual accessories for their bedrooms, gifts for their cyber friends, clothes for their virtual Ty Girlz counterpart. They'll be able to "interact" with their friends and girls from all over the world in this safe cyber-environment. The games, which continue to be updated and improved, are great for sharpening the senses and exercising the memory.

Before we could say,"What's next?", Ty has expanded his Beanie Baby line to include NASCAR® beanies. What little boy wouldn't want a set of these? There's one thing we never doubt. Ty's creative process will keep us coming back for more – again and again!

NASCAR® No. 3
Beanie Baby

6

▼▼▼ Ty and NASCAR® ▼▼▼
A Winning Combination
by Janie Daniels

NASCAR (National Association for Stock Car Auto Racing) was created in 1948 and has become one of the hottest spectator sports in the world. Initially, southern boys were drawn into the sport and enjoyed the fender-bending action, high speeds and heart pounding excitement. Today's sport includes drivers from different locations of the country and beyond.

A defining moment in NASCAR would be in 1959 when the first Daytona 500 race would be run. This race would set the stage for what is now defined as speed weeks at Daytona. In 1979 the Daytona race would receive its first flag to flag coverage on CBS. Very few races would be televised until 1981 when ESPN brought limelight to NASCAR. Their ongoing coverage of the sport brought it notoriety and more important, fans; the rest is history.

Millions of NASCAR fans pile into tracks across the country to view their favorite driver and watch this exciting form of motor sport.

#1 Mark Martin

#2 Kurt Busch

#5 Kyle Busch

#7 Clint Bowyer

#9 Kasey Kahne

#11 Denny Hamlin

#12 Ryan Newman

#16 Greg Biffle

#17 Matt Kenseth

Matt Kenseth #17
Roush Fenway Racing
DATE OF BIRTH: March 10, 1972
CHECKERED FLAG: Kenseth was the 2000 Cup Rookie of the Year and the 2003 Cup Champion !
HORSEPOWER: Matt is a huge fan of the NFL Green Bay Packers !

#18 J.J. Yeley

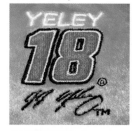

J.J. Yeley #18
Joe Gibbs Racing
DATE OF BIRTH: October 5, 1976
CHECKERED FLAG: One of Yeley's best NEXTEL Cup finishes of 2006 came at the California Speedway where he finished 8th !
HORSEPOWER: J.J. was born Christopher Beltram Hernandez Yeley !

#19 Elliot Sadler

Elliott Sadler #19
Evernham Motorsports
DATE OF BIRTH: April 30, 1975
CHECKERED FLAG: In 2004, Sadler was one of only four drivers to stay in the top 10 in points the entire year !
HORSEPOWER: Elliott started racing with go-carts, and racked up more than 200 go-kart victories since age 7 !

#20 Tony Stewart

Tony Stewart #20
Joe Gibbs Racing
DATE OF BIRTH: May 20, 1971
CHECKERED FLAG: Stewart has won championships in sprint cars, Indy cars, and stock cars !
HORSEPOWER: A devoted philanthropist, Tony created his own charity in 2003 !

#24 Jeff Gordon

Jeff Gordon® #24
Hendrick Motorsports
DATE OF BIRTH: August 4, 1971
CHECKERED FLAG: Gordon is a four-time NASCAR Cup Series Champion !
HORSEPOWER: Jeff is a three-time Daytona 500 winner and four-time Brickyard 400 winner !

#25 Casey Mears

#29 Kevin Harvick

#31 Jeff Burton

#48 Jimmie Johnson

#99 Carl Edwards

Ty on the Web

by Karen Holmes

About Ms. Janie

MsJanie.com is the longest running Beanie-related web site on the net. Past articles, as news happened, are interesting to read. Ms. Janie keeps collectors up-to-date and members share news of 'Beanie sightings', their displays, ideas, interesting facts and so much more. It is a very interactive web site and fun to belong to. Membership is free! There is a message board for all to join in and you can receive breaking news by email or go directly to the web site to view it. You can read more about Ms. Janie and her accomplishments on her web site. As a note of interest, Ms. Janie's son, David, is the first driver to be sponsored by Ty — visit www.dancoracing.com for more news about this and photographs. Ms. Janie has been very generous sharing her information to help make this book what it is. She is a good friend and highly regarded and appreciated by all collectors.

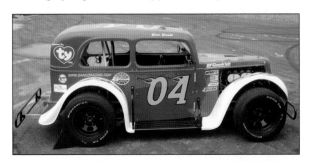

Becky Estenssoro, Authenticator

Becky Estenssoro, owner of True Blue Beans, Inc. has devoted an incredible amount of time to researching Ty Products. Being the co-author/publisher/ editor of the BEANIE MANIA books, magazine and newsletter, she continues to share this information with others.

Becky has been an inspiration and with the help of her publications, phone calls, emails, her web site and archived photographs, so much more information has been included. Thank you, Becky!

Becky, together with Karen Boeker and Mary Kay Williams, devote a lot of time to educating collectors on counterfeits and are actively involved in alerting collectors to counterfeit beanies being sold. A link is on TrueBlue-Beans website for Clean Up The Beans (http://truebluebeans.forumup.org/) and collectors are grateful to all those who help keep this hobby safe and fun. Many 'Beanie angels' work in the background alerting of auctions and you will see familiar 'faces' there: BeanieLogic, Mags, Lizzy, MaryAnne, Wladzia, Lightsgo, Rhonab, Milkbugdug & Loopycards and others.

Becky is a well-respected authenticator in the industry. Collectors know that if Becky has authenticated a Ty product as Museum Quality then both the tag and item are in mint condition. This greatly affects the price of an item and many sellers/collectors choose her service because of the accuracy in her grading. She also sonically seals her cases so they are tamper-resistant. For more details about authenticating and her services, please visit her web site, www.truebluebeans.com.

The Ultimate Online Community Database

stashmatic Track Your Stuff

Jon Phillips and Dave Ferrance had the exciting idea of creating an online database where collectors could actively participate and share their information. From that community database of collectibles, you can create your own personal checklist with photographs included. Stashmatic isn't limited to Beanie Collectors — it is for any collector or hobbyist to organize, track and share information about their collections.

The advantages of getting involved are numerous. From a Beanie collector's point of view, it means that you can record what you have and if you don't have all the information about an item, chances are that it is there. At any time you can go to "My Stash," view your whole collection(s) and make your own checklists.

PattiBuddy, myself and others have expanded the database to include all Ty products. Everyone is welcome to join in. Follow the format example on the site and make sure the item you're adding isn't already listed to avoid duplicate listings. If you see some missing information, feel free to enter it after double-checking for accuracy.

The possibilities are endless as to the details that can be recorded. Multiple images can be uploaded so hang tags can be added or other interesting items such as commemorative cards or ticket stubs. There is also a place where you can 'add a link' to another website.

KuddleKitty, as the name implies, helped provide some older cat Classic photographs. Scott10 has actively been listing Teenie Beanies and Marilyn in Wisconsin has added her wonderful photographs. It is so enjoyable to meet other collectors and the site is free to join.

Letter From a Webmaster

Ty remains a driving force in the plush industry! Ty products continue to thrive in today's market and are collected by many who appreciate fine quality at reasonable prices.

The late 90's would bring scrambling collectors trying to locate their desired styles, long lines and quick retirements! Today's market can be summed up in one word 'change'. Ty has changed with the industry and has adapted their products to keep up with the latest trend. The introduction of the Ty Girlz interactive 3-D virtual website has delighted many who appreciate a safe haven for kids on the Internet. The Ty Girlz website offers a variety of games, chat, music and interactive activities.

Ty's NASCAR Beanie line is a welcome sight for all race fans. Boys will especially enjoy this line as sponsor logo's should be familiar and collectible. The entire line is made up of Ty bears, which are without a doubt their most popular style. The NASCAR Beanies are bold in color and should enhance any race theme collectors may currently have.

Cartoon Beanies have taken center stage and Ty's younger collectors enjoy characters such as Garfield and Friends, SpongeBob, Charlotte's Web, Blue's Clues, Boblins, Dora the Explorer and Diego. Although SpongeBob has always been a favorite in various locations, his popularity soared in the UK and Japan. The original SpongeBob Squarepants has sold up to $25.00 in Japan. The Boblins line offers colors of the rainbow, different personalities and moods to match their color. Children can relate to characters who demonstrate excitability, such as Yam Yam. Gully is practical, Pi uses his imagination, while Ruddle is moody and grumpy at times. Boblins are a great inspiration to kids of all ages and sought out pieces will probably be collected based on individual moods, wants and needs.

Leave it to Ty to continually stay on top of their game and be willing to adapt to industry change. With new product lines such as the Ty Girlz, NASCAR Beanies and cartoon Beanies, the sky's the limit!

Janie Daniels
MsJanie.com

Beanie Websites

www.ty.com

www.DoodlesPage.com

http://groups.msn.com/BeanieUK

www.metaexchange.com

www.aboutbeanies.com

www.PBBAGS.com

www.addiesattic.com

www.planetbeans.com

www.beanieuniverse.com

www.SimSys.com

www.beanwatcher.com

www.TraderList.com

www.tygirlz.com

Hang Tags

A "hang tag" (a.k.a. heart tag or swing tag) is attached to an ear or appendage. Tags are referred to by their generation, which is identifiable from the front of the tag. When reference is made to a 3rd generation Beanie, it means the hang tag is 3rd generation but the tush tag could be 1st or 2nd generation.

There are multiple versions of each tag generation. This occurs when the information or the typeface has had changes made. The following covers the different generations of hang tags and special hang tags but not the different versions of each generation because there are over 80 different versions.

Beanie Babies®

Employee Bear is the only Beanie Baby issued without a hang tag. In 1996 birth dates and poems were added to hang tags and Ty is the only product line with both.

PRE-1ST GENERATION UK HANG TAG

This is the rarest of all hang tags. Ty, Inc.'s very first shipment of "Original 9" Beanies to the UK, had the regular 1st generation hang tags and did not have the required "CE" mark on them (Conformite Europeenne). This mark appears on products that meet the safety standards required to enter the country. These tags were put on those Beanies to meet the CE regulations. Immediately after this requirement was recognized, the rare UK stickers were made for 1st generation hang tags. It is easy to make fake copies of these, so buy with caution.

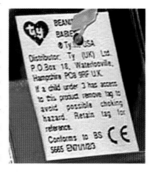

1ST GENERATION - 1993

This is the only hang tag that is "single" – it doesn't open. It only has a front and back. The 'ty' letters are skinny and edged in gold. Some say, "For ages 5 and up," and later changed to "For ages 3 and up." Some have stickers with new information on them. The earliest copyright date is 1993.
Seen with 1st Generation Tush Tag.

14

2ND GENERATION - SPRING 1994 TO SPRING 1995

The first of the "double" (book style) hang tags that open. It is the same size as 1G, but the left side is straight on the fold. The back has a bar code. WIth 2G UK hang tag, the "Ltd" is written with just the L capitalized. Almost all fake UK hang tags have "Ltd" all capitalized and on the right side, a lot say 1983 instead of 1993.

Seen with 1st Generation Tush Tag.

3RD GENERATION - SPRING 1995 TO SPRING 1996

The "Ty" became "fatter" letters. This was the start of the rounder hang tags.
Seen with 1st and 2nd Generation Tush Tags.

Rare 3rd Generation Hang Tag

4TH GENERATION - SPRING 1996 TO LATE 1997

These have a yellow star on the front and are similar to 5G hang tags but are easily differentiated by the "i's" in "Beanie" and "Original". The "i's" do not have a cross at the top or bottom, they are just a straight line. Inside the hang tag the date of birth is written in numbers only and the syle number is next to name.

Seen with 3rd, 4th, and 5th Generation Tush Tags.

Some 4G tags have the name in all capital letters. This is referred to as "All Caps".

5TH GENERATION - EARLY 1998 TO EARLY 2000

Similar to 4G, but the "i" in the word "Beanie" and "Original" has been crossed at the top and bottom of the line. In the date-of-birth the month is written out, it is no longer just a number. The style number was removed from the inside of the tag.

Seen with 6th, 7th, and 8th Generation Tush Tags.

Special 5G Tags:

Princess

Princess has exceptional tags. It is a 4G hang tag on the front, but 5G inside, with a comic sans font and the style number removed. The tush tag is 6G, which only goes with a 5G hang tag. This is the only hang tag classified as 5G that was issued in late 1997. All other 5G hang tags were issued early 1998.

6TH GENERATION - MARCH 2000 TO EARLY 2001

The year 2000 is written across a holographic star.

Seen with 9th Generation Tush Tag.

7TH GENERATION - MARCH 2000 TO EARLY 2004

This has BEANIES across a holographic star. This hang tag is only on European Beanies.

Seen with 9th, 10th, 11th, and 12th Generation Tush Tags.

8TH GENERATION - EARLY 2001 TO JULY 2001

This tag has BEANIE above star and BABY below the star.

Seen with 10th Generation Tush Tag.

9TH GENERATION - JULY 2001 TO DECEMBER 2001

The tag now says BABIES below star instead of BABY.

Seen with 10th Generation Tush Tag.

10TH GENERATION - JANUARY 2002 TO JANUARY 2003

The design now has 5 little stars over the word BEANIE.

Seen with 11th Generation Tush Tag.

11TH GENERATION - EARLY 2003 TO EARLY 2004

The stars have been changed to "10 yrs" to commemorate a decade of Beanies and the font used for BEANIE BABIES has been changed.
Seen with 12th and 13th Generation Tush Tags.

12TH GENERATION - EARLY 2004 TO DECEMBER 2004

ORIGINAL has been added over the word BEANIE (over BEANIES in European version) and a comet underneath. This is the first change in the European tags since March 2000.
Seen with 13th Generation Tush Tag.

Ty Europe [12EU]

13TH GENERATION - JANUARY 2005 TO DECEMBER 2005

The comet has been removed and a star added next to the BEANIES.
Seen with 13th Generation Tush Tag.

NOTE: Due to changes of ownership from Ty Europe to Ty UK, their hang tags changed during the year.

Ty Europe [13EU] - January 2005 through August 2005
Aware released August 31, 2005 still has 13EU hang tag.

Ty UK [13UK] - September 4, 2005 through December 2005
Y Ddraig Goch has both 13EU and 13UK hang tags.

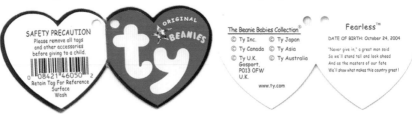

14TH GENERATION - JANUARY 2006 TO DECEMBER 2006
The star has been turned yellow and placed behind the word "original."
Seen with 13th Generation Tush Tag.

Ty UK [14UK]

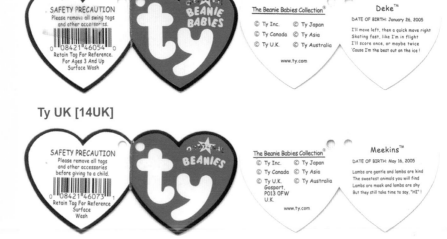

15TH GENERATION - JANUARY 2007 to Present

The star has been removed and a slash placed below the "original."
Seen with 13th Generation Tush Tag.

Ty UK [15UK]

CANADIAN EXTRA TAG

In 2003 Canadian Beanies were supplied by the USA and were given an extra hang tag instead of an extra tush tag.

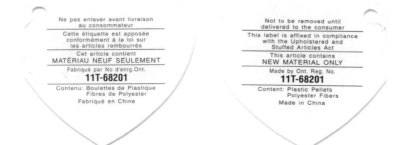

EUROPEAN EXTRA TAG

In 2004 European Beanies were shipped with an extra hang tag.

SPECIAL BEANIE BABY TAGS

Birthday Bear (pot bellied)

Birthday Bear (new face)

Beanie Baby of the Month (BBOM)

Champion

Attic Treasures®

This is a brief sampling of Attic Treasures' hang tags for quick reference.

1ST GENERATION

Single, does not open book style. Complete heart shape. Skinny "ty" letters.

2ND GENERATION

Skinny 'ty' letters, straight left side at the fold. Should say The Attic Treasures Collection,but some mistakenly have The Beanie Babies Collection inside.

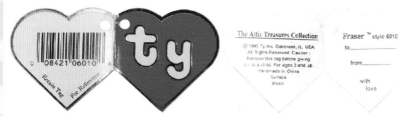

3RD GENERATION

Red tag, fat/bubble 'ty' letters.

4TH GENERATION

Green COLLECTIBLE line on the front, and Ty Collectibles inside.

5TH GENERATION

Beige with maroon writing and paw prints. Ty Collectibles inside and style #. The safety precaution mentions removing "buttons" before giving to a child. Ty UK andTy Deutschland are listed separately, but no Ty Canada.

6TH GENERATION

Beige with maroon writing and paw prints. This generation saw the change from Ty Collectibles back to The Attic Treasures Collection, so can say either. Safety precautions do not specify buttons, just accessories in general. Now has UK and Deutschland together as Ty Europe, and Ty Canada is added.

7TH GENERATION

Back to the red tag with bubble letters. Addition of a phrase instead of to___from___with love.

Beanie Buddies®

1ST GENERATION

Ty Europe have Fareham address.

2ND GENERATION
Ty Europe have Gasport (incorrect spelling) address.

3RD GENERATION
Ty Europe have Gosport (correct spelling) address.

4TH GENERATION
4th generation has multi-colored star on front.

Special Tags:
Champion

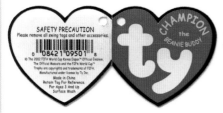

Buddy (extra large)

24

Ty Classic®/Plush

1ST GENERATION

This is the only hang tag that is 'single' – it doesn't open. There are many variations of it, some maroon and some red.

The first generation plush animals had a hard plastic heart shaped tag, in addition to the Ty hang tag. This "charm" was put on the neck, tail or ear. Later on these plastic tags were excluded to comply with child safety regulations.

2ND GENERATION

These are the first of 'double' (book-style) hang tags that open and therefore are straight on the left side on the fold.

3RD GENERATION

These are similar to Ty's tags in other product lines. Their insides can vary.

4TH GENERATION

This marked the change of the name of the Plush line to "Classic" line.

Other Hang Tags

The hang tags of Alphabet Beanies, Basket Beanies, Halloweenie Beanies, Jingle Beanies, Key-clip Beanies, Teenie Beanie Boppers and Valenteenies are all smaller than a regular sized Beanie Baby's hang tag.

ALPHABET BEANIES®

ANGELINE®

BABY TY®

BASKET BEANIES®

BEANIE BOPPERS®

BEANIE KIDS®

1st Generation

2nd Generation

BOW WOW BEANIES®

To:

From:

www.ty.com

GIRLZ®

UK

HALLOWEENIES®

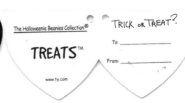

27

JINGLE BEANIES®

PILLOW PALS®
1st GENERATION 1995
There are 3 versions of what is classed as 1st Generation Pillow Pal tags:
1st version was larger than a beanie baby hang tag, red with puffed 'ty' letters and edged in gold, On the left inside are Ty offices and addresses and age suitability. On the right inside: to___ from___ with love.
2nd version is the same size as a beanie baby hang tag. Age suitability is now on the back.
3rd version the style number is not written in, only the barcode on the back has the numbers.
2nd GENERATION 1998
They now have prayer poems inside.

PINKYS®

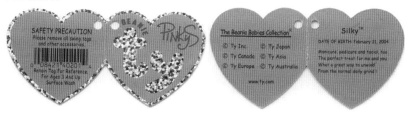

PLUFFIES®

PUNKIES®

TEENIE BEANIE BABIES®

1997 - 1999

2000 - 2007

TEENIE BEANIE BOPPERS®

VALENTEENIES®

Tush Tags

Beanie Babies®

A "tush tag" is sewn into the seam, usually on its bottom.

1ST GENERATION

Original black and white tag. Some say, "For Ages 3 And Up." Tag will say either "HAND MADE IN CHINA" or "HAND MADE IN KOREA." Name is not on tag. 1993 or 1995 date. *Seen with Hang Tag Generations 1, 2, and 3.*

© 1993 TY INC., OAKBROOK IL.U.S.A. ALL RIGHTS RESERVED HANDMADE IN CHINA SURFACE WASHABLE	ALL NEW MATERIAL POLYESTER FIBER & P.V.C. PELLETS PA. REG #1965 FOR AGES 3 AND UP

German Tush Tag

2ND GENERATION

Wider tag with red Ty heart logo. "HAND MADE IN CHINA." Some say, "For Ages 3 And Up." No Beanie name on tag. 1993 or 1995 date.
Seen with Hang Tag Generation 3.

3RD GENERATION

Added "The Beanie Babies Collection" above heart logo and the name of the piece below. No star next to heart. Some seen with "sufrace." "HAND MADE IN CHINA" or "HAND MADE IN KOREA."
1993, 1995, or 1996 date.
Seen with Hang Tag Generation 4.

4TH GENERATION

Same as 3rd generation but with a small star to the upper left of the Ty heart logo. Some have temporary stickers with a star. "HAND MADE IN CHINA." 1993, 1995, or 1996 date.
Seen with Hang Tag Generation 4.

5TH GENERATION

The word "Beanie Babies" is registered (®) and the item name is trademarked (™). "HAND MADE IN CHINA" or "HAND MADE IN INDONESIA." 1993, 1995, or 1996 date.
Seen with Hang Tag Generation 4.

6TH GENERATION

Tags may say either "PE" or "PVC." Some also have red stamp inside indicating factory of origin. Watermark added. Shows registered symbol after the word "Collection." May have ""HAND MADE IN CHINA" or "HAND MADE IN INDONESIA." 1993, 1995, 1996, 1997, or 1998 date.
Seen with Hang Tag Generation 5.

Billionaire 5 has a special 6G tush tag. The copyright date is 2000, ® after collection but no star or stamp.

7TH GENERATION

Biggest change: hologram with heart. "The Beanie Babies Collection" inside above item name and a heat-activated heart image was added. Placing finger on heart will cause heart disappear but it will return.
1999 date.
Seen with Hang Tag Generation 5.

8TH GENERATION

Only change: this is no longer a loop tag. Single sheet, printed on two sides. 1999 date.
Seen with Hang Tag Generation 5.

HANDMADE IN CHINA
© 1999 TY INC.,
OAKBROOK, IL. U.S.A.
SURFACE WASHABLE
ALL NEW MATERIAL
POLYESTER FIBER
& P.E. PELLETS
REG.NO PA. 1965(KR) (€

9TH GENERATION

Return to loop format. New eight digit code on inner surface. Hologram images alternate between star and "Ty." "Beanie" appears above star and "Babies" below. 2000 date.
Seen with Hang Tag Generations 6 and 7.

China™
HANDMADE IN CHINA
© 2000 TY INC.,
OAKBROOK, IL. U.S.A.
SURFACE WASHABLE
ALL NEW MATERIAL
POLYESTER FIBER
& P.E. PELLETS (€
REG.NO PA. 1965(KR)

China™
HANDMADE IN CHINA
© 2000 TY INC.,
OAKBROOK, IL. U.S.A.
SURFACE WASHABLE

4M197TSS

10TH GENERATION

Hologram is more intricate, showing diagonal lines, hearts, stars. 2001 date.
Seen with Hang Tag Generations 7, 8, and 9.

Classy™
HANDMADE IN CHINA
© 2001 TY INC.,
OAKBROOK, IL. U.S.A.
SURFACE WASHABLE
ALL NEW MATERIAL
POLYESTER FIBER
& P.E. PELLETS (€
REG.NO PA. 1965(KR)

4961NKB1

11TH GENERATION

Hologram shows image of a bear hugging the heart. 2001 or 2002 date.
Seen with Hang Tag Generations 7 and 10.

Champion™
HANDMADE IN CHINA
© 2002 TY INC.,
OAKBROOK, IL. U.S.A.
SURFACE WASHABLE
ALL NEW MATERIAL
POLYESTER FIBER
& P.E. PELLETS (€
REG.NO PA. 1965(KR)

4SB7NG1R

12TH GENERATION

Decade™
HANDMADE IN CHINA
© 2002 TY INC.,
OAKBROOK, IL. U.S.A.
SURFACE WASHABLE
ALL NEW MATERIAL
POLYESTER FIBER
& P.E. PELLETS
REG.NO PA. 1965(KR)

Hologram has heart logo in middle and hearts and stars around it. Hearts and star are angled, not centered. 2002 or 2003 date.
Seen with Hang Tag Generation 11.

4MI97TSS

13TH GENERATION

True™
HANDMADE IN CHINA
© 2003 TY INC.,
OAKBROOK, IL. U.S.A.
SURFACE WASHABLE
ALL NEW MATERIAL
POLYESTER FIBER
& P.E. PELLETS
$C\,E$
REG.NO PA. 1965(KR)

Scrappy™
HANDMADE IN CHINA
© 2004 TY INC.,
OAKBROOK, IL. U.S.A.
SURFACE WASHABLE
ALL NEW MATERIAL
POLYESTER FIBER
& P.E. PELLETS
$C\,E$
REG.NO PA. 1965(KR)

Metallic heart with "ty" in white letters replaces hologram. CE is moved to its own line. Some July 2004 releases have "ty" written in gold. 2003, 2004, 2005, 2006 or 2007 date.
Seen with Hang Tag Generations 11, 12, 13, 14 and 15.

• Ronald McDonald Beanie Baby, available at the McDonald's Convention, has a 'cut' tush tag. It is thought that perhaps the printing was done the wrong way, so rather than the ends being inside the seam, the fold is inside.

OTHER TAGS

• Canadian product has an additional tush tag to meet Canadian toy import standards. The tag is written in English and French.
• A very small amount of 2nd generation Canadian Beanies have been

found to also have an embroidered tush tag with a 1994 copyright date. The embroidered tag had primarily been used for other Ty products and was accidentaly attached to some limited styles of the rare 2G Canadian Beanies. On the secondary market, these Beanies are referred to as Embroidered Tush Beanies and are extremely rare and valuable. It has been confirmed by authenticators that this tag is found on Bones, Blackie, Chilly, Chocolate, Cubbie, Goldie, Pinchers, Quacker, Spot, Nip (white belly), Peking, colored Teddies (new face), Ally, Daisy, and Zip (white belly).

BEANIE BABIES®

Beanie Babies staying power since their introduction in 1993 is a tribute to Ty's creative genius with plush animals. Just the right size to fit in a child's hand or pocket and just the right price to fit a child's allowance, these soft and cuddly plush creatures are still listed among the top children's toys, after nearly a decade and a half. Beanies contain pellets which are distributed in just the right proportion and weight to allow them to be easily posed. Each Beanie has its own name and, excluding a few released in the early days, each has its own birthday and special poem. Unknown production numbers and surprise early retirements have kept Beanie fans and collectors on their toes, trying to find their favorites before they are gone.

#1 Bear™
No Style #

Birthday: None
Introduced: 12/12/1998
Retired: 12/12/1998
In appreciation of selling over several Billion dollars during 1998 and achieving the industry ranking of #1 in Gift sales, #1 in Collectable sales, #1 in Cash register area sales #1 in Markup % I present to you This signed and Numbered Bear!
253 produced. Ty Rep exclusive.
5G - $5,500

#1 Teacher™
#44054

Birthday: 5/3/2005
Introduced: 7/13/2005
Retired: 12/27/2005
Always patient, always kind
With no student left behind
And the best lesson you taught me
Was how much fun learning can be!
Ty Store exclusive.
13G - $7

123's™
#40655

Birthday: 8/22/2006
Introduced: 6/29/2007
Current
1-2-3 and A-B-C
Learning is such fun, you see
You might find out it isn't hard
To get A's on your report card!
15G - Current Retail Value

1997 Holiday Teddy™
#4200

Birthday: 12/25/1996
Introduced: 10/1/1997
Retired: 12/31/1997
Beanie Babies are special no doubt
All filled with love - inside and out
Wishes for fun times filled with joy
Ty's holiday teddy is a magical toy!
4G - $10

1998 Holiday Teddy™
#4204

Birthday: 12/25/1998
Introduced: 9/30/1998
Retired: 12/31/1998
Dressed in his PJ's, and ready for bed
Hugs given, good nights said
This little Beanie will stay close at night
Ready for a hug at first morning light!
5G - $12

1999 Holiday Teddy™
#4257

Birthday: 12/25/1999
Introduced: 8/31/1999
Retired: 12/23/1999
Peace on Earth as the holidays grow near
The season is all about giving good cheer
With love and joy in your hearts
Let's all be friends as the century starts!
5G - $8

1999 Signature Bear™
#4228

Birthday: None
Introduced: 1/1/1999
Retired: 12/23/1999
Signature Bears are issued without poems.
5G - $7

2000 Holiday Teddy™
#4332

Birthday: 12/24/2000
Introduced: 9/28/2000
Retired: 12/12/2000
When you're tucked in bed tonight
Hug Holiday Teddy really tight
He'll bring you much joy and cheer
and lots of love throughout the year!
6G - $7 ♥ 7G - $7

2000 Signature Bear™
#4266

Birthday: None
Introduced: 3/1/2000
Retired: 5/16/2000
Signature Bears are issued without poems.
6G - $7 ♥ 7G - $10

2001 Holiday Teddy™
#4395

Birthday: 12/24/2000
Introduced: 10/1/2001
Retired: 12/19/2001
This year has flown by very fast
It's hard to believe 2001 has passed
Time to look forward to a brand new year
We hope it brings you joy and cheer!
7G - $7 ♥ 9G - $7

2001 Signature Bear™
#4375

Birthday: None
Introduced: 7/31/2001
Retired: 11/19/2001
Signature Bears are issued without poems.
7G - $7 ♥ 9G - $7

2002 Holiday Teddy™
#4564

Birthday: 12/20/2001
Introduced: 9/30/2002
Retired: 11/8/2002
The other bears make fun of me
They say I'm just a wanna-be
But Santa, if you let me try
I know for sure that I can fly!
7G - $10 ♥ 10G - $7

2002 Signature Bear™
#4565

Birthday: None
Introduced: 9/30/2002
Retired: 12/27/2002
Signature Bears are issued without poems.
7G - $7 ♥ 10G - $7

2003 Holiday Teddy™
#40028

Birthday: 12/25/2003
Introduced: 9/30/2003
Retired: 12/26/2003
The holidays are a special time
And so I have a special rhyme
May your holidays be filled with cheer
And have a wonderful New Year!
7G - $7 ♥ 11G - $7

2003 Signature Bear™
#40011

Birthday: None
Introduced: 6/30/2003
Retired: 12/26/2003
Signature Bears are issued without poems.
7G - $7 ♥ 11G - $7

2004 Holiday Teddy™
#40139

Birthday: 12/25/2004
Introduced: 9/30/2004
Retired: 11/24/2004
The holidays go by so fast
Try to slow down and make it last
Take time this year to spread some joy
To each and every girl and boy!
12G/12EU - $7

2004 Signature Bear™
#40158

Birthday: None
Introduced: 10/29/2004
Retired: 12/29/2004
Signature Bears are issued without poems.
12G/12EU - $7

2005 Holiday Teddy™
#40274

Birthday: 12/24/2004
Introduced: 9/30/2005
Retired: 12/29/2005
At this festive time of year
Take the time to spread good cheer
Spend some time with those you love
Send tidings to those you're thinking of!
13G/13UK - $7

2005 Signature Bear™
#40285

Birthday: None
Introduced: 10/31/2005
Retired: 12/29/2005
Signature Bears are issued without poems.
13G/13UK - $7

2006™ (New Year)
#44064

Birthday: 1/1/2006
Introduced: 11/29/2005
Retired: 1/9/2006
Grab a hat and toot your horn
Cause the New Year's 'bout to be born
We laugh and dance and get our kicks
Here's to a great 2006!
Ty Store exclusive.
13G - $12

2006 Holiday Teddy™
#40443

Birthday: 12/25/2006
Introduced: 9/29/2006
Retired: 12/21/2006
'Tis the season for good cheer
To those you love both far and near
For young and old, tall and the small
Happy holidays to one and all!
14G/14UK - $7

2006 Signature Bear™
#40458

Birthday: None
Introduced: 10/31/2006
Retired: 3/27/2007
Signature Bears are issued without poems.
14G/14UK - $7

2006 Zodiac Dog™
#46051

Birthday: 1/29/2006
Introduced: 12/1/2005
Current
Dogs are loyal and honest to all
So full of spirit and there when you call
Leading their lives full of love and of fire
Our many qualities we know you'll admire!
Asian-Pacific exclusive.
13G - Current Retail Value

2007™
#44096

Birthday: 1/1/2007
Introduced: 11/29/2006
Retired: 12/21/2006
The magic hour's drawing near
It's time to ring in the New Year
Watch that clock so you don't miss
Giving loved ones the year's first kiss!
Ty Store exclusive.
14G - $25

2007 Zodiac Pig™
#46088

Birthday: 2/18/2007
Introduced: 11/30/2006
Current
Pigs are chivalrous, noble and true
And they will always be there for you
A desire for knowledge that can be strong
With friends like this, you'll always belong!
Asian-Pacific exclusive.
14G - $20

4-H™
#40278

Birthday: 10/2/2004
Introduced: 7/29/2005
Retired: 3/27/2006
Better than glory, fame and wealth
Use your head, heart, hands, and health
To help make the best even better
That's why "H" is our favorite letter!
USA exclusive.
13G - $12

A™
#40501

Birthday: None
Introduced: 6/30/2005
Current
Alphabet Bears are issued without poems.
AB - Current Retail Value

ABC's™
#40655

Birthday: 8/22/2006
Introduced: 6/29/2007
Current
ABC's and 123's
Learning can be quite a breeze
Just study to raise your IQ
You're sure to go far if you do!
15G - Current Retail Value

Aces™
#40380

Birthday: 1/8/2006
Introduced: 5/31/2006
Retired: 6/11/06
When in Vegas you have a shot
To try to win a big jackpot
Whether or not you like to play
With me it's still your lucky day!
Knotts Berry Farm exclusive.
14G - $25

Aces™
#40380

Birthday: 1/8/2006
Introduced: 5/31/2006
Current
When in Vegas you have a shot
To try to win a big jackpot
Whether or not you like to play
With me it's still your lucky day!
Las Vegas and Carlton Cards exclusive.
14G - Current Retail Value

Addison™
#4362

Birthday: 5/20/2001
Introduced: 6/18/2001
Retired: 6/20/2001
In the bleachers we see all
Hope we'll catch a long fly ball
When the day is finally done
Hopefully, our team has won!
8G - $7

Addison™
#4362 · with commemorative card

Birthday: 5/20/2001
Introduced: 5/20/2001
Retired: 5/20/2001
In the bleachers we see all
Hope we'll catch a long fly ball
When the day is finally done
Hopefully, our team has won!
Promotion at Chicago Cubs games.
One day only.
8G - $40

Admiral™
#40392

Birthday: 12/28/2005
Introduced: 6/30/2006
Current
When you are under my command
Here in this frozen, arctic land
One simple rule, as I decree
The first snow cone belongs to me!
14G - Current Retail Value

Admiral™
#40392

Birthday: 12/28/2005
Introduced: 7/17/2006
Current
When you are under my command
Here in this frozen, arctic land
One simple rule, as I decree
The first snow cone belongs to me!
Santa Barbara Zoo exclusive.
14G - $15

Adonis™
#48409

Birthday: 2/00/2005
Introduced: 2/1/2005
Retired: 3/1/2005
Need help with that romantic fluff?
Ask me, because I know my stuff
Start with a gift sure to impress
What could that be? Just take a guess!
February 2005
Beanie Baby of the Month.
BBOM - $7

Adore™
#44043

Birthday: 2/14/2005
Introduced: 1/12/2005
Retired: 3/18/2005
I've been thinking night and day
Of all the things I want to say
About how much you mean to me
With one look it's easy to see!
Ty Store exclusive.
13G - $7

Ai™
#4628

Birthday: 2/11/2003
Introduced: 4/28/2003
Retired: 1/20/2005
From the island of Japan
Ai came to bring you a love
She will sing with joy
To make this land peace forever
Japan exclusive.
11G - $20

Ai™
#4628 • Motomachi

Birthday: 2/11/2003
Introduced: 2/1/2004
Retired: 2/1/2004
From the island of Japan
Ai came to bring you a love
She will sing with joy
To make this land peace forever
Ty Store Japan exclusive.
11G - $150

Alabama™
#40318

Birthday: None
Introduced: 9/9/2005
Retired: 5/24/2006
In memory of those who lost their homes,
their loved ones, or their lives, as a result of
Hurricane Katrina
We extend our deepest sympathies
Together we're a stronger nation
$1 of sale donated to American Red
Cross Disaster Fund.
13G/13UK - $7

Alabama™
#44077

Birthday: None
Introduced: 9/6/2005
Retired: 5/24/2006
In memory of those who lost their homes,
their loved ones, or their lives, as a result of
Hurricane Katrina
We extend our deepest sympathies
Together we're a stronger nation
$2 of sale donated to American Red
Cross Disaster Fund. Ty Store exclusive.
13G - $7

Alana™
#40368

Birthday: 3/27/2006
Introduced: 4/28/2006
Current
The ocean air so fresh and clean
Some of the best sights to be seen
With sun and sand and mountains, too
The best wonders of nature you can view!
14G/14UK - Current Retail Value

Alani™
#48402

Birthday: 7/00/2004
Introduced: 7/1/2004
Retired: 8/1/2004
I love a tropical paradise
The warm breeze feels oh-so nice
We'll watch the waves break on the sand
As we walk together hand in hand!
July 2004 Beanie Baby of the Month.
BBOM - $7

Alberta Wild Rose™
#46035

Birthday: None
Introduced: 8/14/2005
Retired: 12/29/2005
OFFICIAL FLOWER SINCE 1930
A rose is just a rose, you see
Or is it? Take a look at me
My flower opens to the sun
I am a rose - but much more fun!
Trade Show exclusive.
13G - $20

Allegro™
#40341

Birthday: 7/14/2005
Introduced: 1/31/2006
Retired: 3/27/2007
I love things that are frou-frou
Especially my pink tutu
With pretty shoes upon my feet
I'll dance the Nutcracker Suite!
14G/14UK - $7

All-Star Dad™
#40359

Birthday: 6/18/2006
Introduced: 3/31/2006
Retired: 7/25/2006
Father, you are the best to me
An All-Star Dad, it's plain to see
If there were a place then I'd proclaim
You'd be in the Dad Hall of Fame!
14G/14UK - $8

Ally™
#4032

Birthday: 3/14/1994
Introduced: 6/25/1994
Retired: 10/1/1997
When Ally gets out of classes
He wears a hat and dark glasses
He plays bass in a street band
He's the coolest gator in the land!
1G - $1,800 ♥ 2G - $325 ♥ 3G - $50 ♥
4G - $12

Almond™
#4246

Birthday: 4/14/1999
Introduced: 4/14/1999
Retired: 12/23/1999
Leaving her den in early spring
So very hungry, she'll eat anything
Nuts, fruits, berries and fish
Mixed together makes a great dish!
5G - $7

Alpha™ Key-clip
#46063

Birthday: None
Introduced: 6/16/2006
Retired: 8/21/2006
Alpha Key-clip was issued without a poem.
Australia exclusive.
14sm - $7

Alps™
#48404

Birthday: 9/00/2004
Introduced: 9/1/2004
Retired: 10/1/2004
If you are lost or just feel blue
I'll be right there to comfort you
I promise I will never stray
Right by your side is where I'll stay!
*September 2004
Beanie Baby of the Month.*
BBOM - $7

Always™
#40161

Birthday: 2/14/2004
Introduced: 11/30/2004
Retired: 4/28/2005
I'll get down on bended knee
To give this perfect rose to thee
A symbol that my love is true
And my heart belongs to you!
12G/12EU - $7

Always™
#40161

Birthday: 2/14/2004
Introduced: 7/22/2005
Retired: 7/22/2005
I'll get down on bended knee
To give this perfect rose to thee
A symbol that my love is true
And my heart belongs to you!
FTD convention exclusive.
12G - $130

Amber™
#4243

Birthday: 2/21/1999
Introduced: 4/20/1999
Retired: 12/23/1999
Sleeping all day and up all night
Waiting to pounce and give you a fright
She means no harm, just playing a game
She's very lovable and quite tame!
5G - $7

America™
#4506 · blue body

Birthday: None
Introduced: 9/13/2001
Retired: 3/20/2002
In memory of those who lost their
lives in the national catastrophe that
took place on September 11, 2001.
We mourn for them and express our
deepest sympathy to their families.
God Bless America
Also with Japanese writing - $40.
7G - $7 ♥ 9G - $7

America™
#4412 · red with blue right ear

Birthday: None
Introduced: 3/22/2002
Retired: 4/3/2002
In memory of those who lost their
lives in the national catastrophe that
took place on September 11, 2001.
We mourn for them and express our
deepest sympathy to their families.
God Bless America
Ty Store exclusive.
10G - $10

America™
#4412 · red with reversed ears

Birthday: None
Introduced: 3/22/2002
Retired: 4/3/2002
In memory of those who lost their
lives in the national catastrophe that
took place on September 11, 2001.
We mourn for them and express our
deepest sympathy to their families.
God Bless America
Ty Store exclusive.
10G - $185

America™
#4409 · white with blue right ear

Birthday: None
Introduced: 2/25/2002
Retired: 7/4/2002
In memory of those who lost their
lives in the national catastrophe that
took place on September 11, 2001.
We mourn for them and express our
deepest sympathy to their families.
God Bless America
Ty Store exclusive.
10G - $7

America™
#4409 · white with reversed ears

Birthday: None
Introduced: 2/25/2002
Retired: 7/4/2002
In memory of those who lost their
lives in the national catastrophe that
took place on September 11, 2001.
We mourn for them and express our
deepest sympathy to their families.
God Bless America
Ty Store exclusive.
10G - $7

American™
#40624

Birthday: 6/14/2006
Introduced: 4/30/2007
Current
A symbol for this land so free
I proudly stand for all to see
And since the U.S. first began
I'm glad I'm an American!
15G - Current Retail Value

American Blessing™
#40238

Birthday: 12/2/2004
Introduced: 4/29/2005
Retired: 12/29/2005
As I sit on bended knee
These simple words I say to thee
Watch over those who everyday
Stand proudly for the U.S.A.!
13G/13EU - $7

American Blessing™
#40238

Birthday: 12/2/2004
Introduced: 5/27/2006
Retired: 5/29/2006
As I sit on bended knee
These simple words I say to thee
Watch over those who everyday
Stand proudly for the U.S.A.!
Knott's Berry Farm exclusive.
13G - $20

Amigo™
#4422

Birthday: 8/3/2003
Introduced: 7/15/2003
Retired: 9/8/2003
I'm always loyal and so true
And I'll be there to talk to you
Someone on whom you can depend
Forever yours, the best of friends!
Ty Store exclusive.
11G - $10

Anchor™
#40395

Birthday: 3/22/2006
Introduced: 6/30/2006
Current
Swimming through the waves and surf
The briny sea is my own turf
On the horizon I think I see
A brand new friend to swim with me!
14G/14UK - Current Retail Value

Ants™
#4195

Birthday: 11/7/1997
Introduced: 5/30/1998
Retired: 12/31/1998
Most anteaters love to eat bugs
But this little fellow gives big hugs
He'd rather dine on apple pie
Than eat an ant or harm a fly!
5G - $7

Aotearoa™
#46044 · black nose

Birthday: 5/23/2005
Introduced: 9/12/2005
Retired: 6/15/2006
New Zealand's flag, it flies so high
Just look around and you'll see why
Natural wonders from mountains to sea
So much beauty for you and me!
Asian-Pacific exclusive.
13G - $20

Aotearoa™
#46044 · flag nose

Birthday: 5/23/2005
Introduced: 10/15/2005
Retired: 6/15/2006
New Zealand's flag, it flies so high
Just look around and you'll see why
Natural wonders from mountains to sea
So much beauty for you and me!
New Zealand exclusive.
13G - $675

April™
#4391

Birthday: None
Introduced: 3/1/2002
Retired: 5/24/2002
My nose is the color of my birthstone.
Diamond - It brings intelligence
and non-stop adventure!
Birthday - $7

April 2003™
#4555

Birthday: None
Introduced: 2/28/2003
Retired: 7/29/2003
Charlie Chaplin - April 16
William Shakespeare - April 23
Jet'Li - April 26
Birthday - $7

April Fool™
#44102

Birthday: 4/1/2007
Introduced: 2/26/2007
Retired: 7/12/2007
I'd never play a trick on you
That's something I would never do
Do you believe that? Then let me say
The joke's on you . . . April Fool's Day!
Ty Store exclusive..
15G - $7

Arabesque™
#40339

Birthday: 9/13/2005
Introduced: 1/31/2006
Current
The curtain lifts and I begin
I'll leap and twirl, balance and spin
And when the crowd all cheers out loud
My family will be so proud!
14G/14UK - Current Retail Value

Aria™
#40092

Birthday: 7/30/2003
Introduced: 6/30/2004
Retired: 3/24/2005
A kitten curled up in your lap
Just taking a little nap
Makes you feel so warm and snug
When she wakes up give her a hug!
12G - $7

Ariel™
#4288

Birthday: None
Introduced: 6/1/2000
Retired: 12/31/2001
In Memory: 1981-1988
May little children everywhere
Remember that we'll always care
And Ariel's dreams will all come true
Because she'll share them all with you!
6G - $7 ♥ 7G - $7

Ariel™
#4288 · boxed with certificate

Birthday: None
Introduced: 6/1/2000
Retired: 12/31/2001
In Memory: 1981-1988
May little children everywhere
Remember that we'll always care
And Ariel's dreams will all come true
Because she'll share them all with you!
Ty Trade auction.
**6G/7G - Value varies depending on
celebrity signature.**

Arizona™
#40300

Birthday: None
Introduced: 11/30/2005
Retired: 7/25/2006
STATE MOTTO: "Ditat Deus" (God enriches)
NICKNAME: Grand Canyon State
FACT: Arizona produces more copper than
anywhere else in the nation!
Sold only in Arizona.
13G - $7

Aruba™
#4314

Birthday: 4/8/2000
Introduced: 7/8/2000
Retired: 4/11/2001
If you wander by the sea
And want to take a look at me
I'm swimming in the water blue
And want to throw a kiss to you!
6G - $7 ♥ 7G - $7

Astra™
#48406

Birthday: 11/00/2004
Introduced: 10/26/2004
Retired: 12/1/2004
See that star up in the sky
Make a wish and don't ask why
Let no one know but me and you
And your wish will soon come true!
*November 2004
Beanie Baby of the Month.*
BBOM - $15

Atlanta™
#40090

Birthday: 12/29/2003
Introduced: 7/9/2004
Retired: 8/11/2004
On those hot Atlanta nights
You might want to see the sights
The perfect mix of old and new
You're sure to love it like I do!
Trade Show exclusive.
12G - $7

August™
#4371

Birthday: None
Introduced: 7/3/2001
Retired: 9/14/2001
My nose is the color of my birthstone.
Peridot - It brings romance, loyalty
and laughter!
Birthday - $7

August 2002™
#4547

Birthday: None
Introduced: 6/28/2002
Retired: 10/29/2002
Jeff Gordon - August 4th
Madonna - August 16th
Li'l Romeo - August 19th
Birthday - $7

Aurora™
#4271

Birthday: 2/3/2000
Introduced: 3/1/2000
Retired: 5/21/2001
The midnight sun puts on a show
For all the polar bears below
Under ribbons of shining light
Aurora hugs you and says goodnight!
6G - $7 ♥ 7G - $7

Aussiebear™
#4626

Birthday: 1/25/2003
Introduced: 4/28/2003
Retired: 11/7/2003
My home is called the land "Down Under"
Filled with beauty, awe and wonder
From the Outback to the Great Barrier Reef
The experience here is beyond belief!
Australia exclusive.
11G - $20

Australia™
#46025

Birthday: 1/12/2005
Introduced: 2/28/2005
Retired: 4/15/2006
I love Australia, it's true
With all our crocs and kangaroo
You see why we are quite unique
So come down under and take a peek!
Australia exclusive.
13G - $20

Avalon™
#40095

Birthday: 2/5/2004
Introduced: 6/30/2004
Retired: 12/29/2004
In a land far, far away
Near the hills where dragons play
Come with me to this place of laughter
and we'll live happily ever after!
12G - $7

Aware™
#40271

Birthday: 10/10/2004
Introduced: 8/31/2005
Retired: 12/29/2005
To raise awareness is my plight
Hand in hand we'll stand and fight
Keep the faith, we will endure
Rest assured, we'll find a cure!
13G/13EU - $7

Awareness™
#40422

Birthday: 10/27/2006
Introduced: 8/31/2006
Current
Mothers, sisters, daughters, wives
The special women in our lives
Let's all join hands and do what's right
For them, let's try to win this fight!
14G/14UK - Current Retail Value

B™
#40502

Birthday: None
Introduced: 6/30/2005
Current
Alphabet Bears are issued without poems.
AB - Current Retail Value

BBOC™ Original 9 Sets
Set of 9

Birthday: None
Introduced: 10/3/2005
Retired: 3/9/2006
The sets were as follows,
and the rarer beanie in them:
Assortment 1 49012 Patti Maroon
(magenta/raspberry)
Assortment 2 49013 Spot without a Spot
Assortment 3 49014 Brownie
Assortment 4 49015 Punchers
Assortment 5 49016 Patti Deep Fuschia

All sets included Chocolate, Flash, Legs, Splash
and Squealer. If the set didn't have a rarer
Patti in it, then it had the light pink Patti with
a poem, representing the Fuschia common Patti,
although it was a lighter pink than Fuschia
Patti. If it didn't have the rarer Brownie,
Punchers, Spot without a Spot, then it had
Cubbie, Pinchers, Spot with a Spot.

Beanie Baby Official Club exclusive.
Assortment Number:
#1 - $90 ♥ #2 - $180 ♥ #3 - $180 ♥
#4 - $180 ♥ #5 - $75

B.B. Bear™
#4253

Birthday: None
Introduced: 7/14/1999
Retired: 12/23/1999
This birthday Beanie was made for you
Hope your wishes and dreams come true
Be happy today and tomorrow too
Let's all celebrate the whole year through!
5G - $7

Baaabsy™
#40376

Birthday: 4/7/2006
Introduced: 5/31/2006
Current
Sometimes I try to run real fast
Wind in my wool, it's such a blast
But sometimes when I lag behind
My long legs get all intertwined!
14G/14UK - Current Retail Value

Baaabsy Baaag™
#40448

Birthday: None
Introduced: 1/31/2007
Retired: 6/25/2007
Baaabsy Baaag was issued without a poem.
15G - $7

Baby Boy™
#4534

Birthday: 3/3/2002
Introduced: 5/31/2002
Retired: 8/8/2003
Ten little fingers, ten little toes
A tuft of hair, a button nose
This healthy, bouncing baby boy
Will bring you love and lots of joy!
7G - $7 ♥ 10G - $7

Baby Boy™
#40223

Birthday: None
Introduced: 3/31/2005
Retired: 8/25/2006
Baby Boy was issued without a poem.
13G/13EU - $7

Baby Boy™
#40424

Birthday: None
Introduced: 8/31/2006
Current
Baby Boy was issued without a poem.
14G/14UK - Current Retail Value

Baby Girl™
#4535

Birthday: 1/19/2002
Introduced: 5/31/2002
Retired: 8/8/2003
A daughter's joy can warm your heart
She's got you from the very start
With dress-up clothes, and hair to curl
Congratulations, it's a girl!
7G - $7 ♥ 10G - $7

Baby Girl™
#40222

Birthday: None
Introduced: 3/31/2005
Retired: 8/25/2006
Baby Girl was issued without a poem.
13G/13EU - $7

Baby Girl™
#40425

Birthday: None
Introduced: 8/31/2006
Current
Baby Girl was issued without a poem.
14G/14UK - Current Retail Value

The Backyardigans™ Austin™
#40404

Birthday: None
Introduced: 8/31/2006
Current
Austin was issued without a poem.
Also available at Ty Store.
14G/14UK - Current Retail Value

The Backyardigans™ Pablo™
#40412

Birthday: None
Introduced: 11/30/2005
Current
Pablo was issued without a poem.
Also available at Ty Store.
13G - Current Retail Value

The Backyardigans™ Tasha™
#40405

Birthday: None
Introduced: 8/31/2006
Current
Tasha was issued without a poem.
Also available at Ty Store.
14G/14UK - Current Retail Value

The Backyardigans™ Tyrone™
#40313

Birthday: None
Introduced: 11/30/2005
Current
Tyrone was issued without a poem.
Also available at Ty Store.
13G - Current Retail Value

The Backyardigans™ Uniqua™
#40311

Birthday: None
Introduced: 11/30/2005
Current
Uniqua was issued without a poem.
Also available at Ty Store.
13G - Current Retail Value

Badges™
#40177

Birthday: 12/1/2004
Introduced: 12/30/2004
Retired: 11/23/2005
A puppy's job is just to play
So I will do my job today
I'll jump and run, and when I'm through
I'll come and snuggle up with you!
13G/13EU - $7

Bahati™
#44024

Birthday: None
Introduced: 10/4/2004
Retired: 1/2/2007
FACT: African elephant populations are
on the increase since a global ban on
ivory sales was imposed, a measure
WWF worked hard to secure!
Ty Store/World Wildlife Fund exclusive.
12G - $7

Baldy™
#4074

Birthday: 2/17/1996
Introduced: 5/11/1997
Retired: 5/1/1998
Hair on his head is quite scant
We suggest Baldy get a transplant
Watching over the land of the free
Hair in his eyes would make it hard to see!
4G - $10 ♥ 5G - $7

Bali™
#40187

Birthday: 8/8/2004
Introduced: 12/30/2004
Retired: 2/24/2005
An Indonesian island home
Is where Komodo dragons roam
But take me home and I will be
The happiest lizard you'll ever see!
13G/13EU - $7

Bali™
#40385

Birthday: 8/8/2004
Introduced: 5/31/2006
Retired: 6/23/2006
An Indonesian island home
Is where Komodo dragons roam
But take me home and I will be
The happiest lizard you'll ever see!
USA exclusive.
14G - $9

Bali™
#47029

Birthday: 8/8/2004
Introduced: 5/31/2006
Retired: 7/25/2006
An Indonesian island home
Is where Komodo dragons roam
But take me home and I will be
The happiest lizard you'll ever see!
Shedd Aquarium exclusive.
14Gsp - $25

Bali™ Key-clip
#47030

Birthday: None
Introduced: 5/1/2006
Current
Bali Key-clip was issued without a poem.
Pizza Hut promotional item.
14sm - $20

Bam™
#4544

Birthday: 11/25/2001
Introduced: 6/28/2002
Retired: 12/27/2002
I like to bang my head it's true
'Cause it's the ram-like thing to do
I like to bang it in the yard
Good thing my head is so hard!
7G - $7 ♥ 10G - $7

Bananas™
#4316

Birthday: 6/30/2000
Introduced: 7/8/2000
Retired: 6/20/2001
If you'll come and play with me
We will swing from tree to tree
Then we'll go and have some lunch
We'll eat bananas by the bunch!
6G - $7 ♥ 7G - $7

Bandage™
#40221

Birthday: 12/3/2004
Introduced: 3/31/2005
Current
Feel under the weather today?
I'll help chase your blues away
A smile's the best medicine, it's true
And that's my get well wish to you!
13G/13EU - Current Retail Value

Bandito™
#4543

Birthday: 11/2/2001
Introduced: 6/28/2002
Retired: 2/24/2003
You might wonder enough to ask
Just why it is I wear a mask
An outlaw's life I can't deny
But I'm really just kinda shy!
7G - $7 ♥ 10G - $7

Banjo™
#40085

Birthday: 10/1/2003
Introduced: 6/30/2004
Retired: 10/27/2004
Searching for the perfect treat
Something that is not too sweet
Great big bones will suit me fine
Now I can hardly wait to dine!
12G - $7

Barbaro™
#40464

Birthday: 4/29/2003
Introduced: 10/31/2006
Current
Birthdate: April 29, 2003
Winning time: 2:01.36
Owners: Roy & Gretchen Jackson
A portion of the profits from the original sale
of this Beanie Baby will be donated to the
Barbaro Fund University of Pennsylvania School
of Veterinary Medicine
2006 Kentucky Derby Winner.
USA exclusive.
14G - Current Retail Value

Barbaro™
#40464

Birthday: 4/29/2003
Introduced: 10/31/2006
Current
Birthdate: April 29, 2003
Winning time: 2:01.36
Owners: Roy & Gretchen Jackson
A portion of the profits from the original sale
of this Beanie Baby will be donated to the
Barbaro Fund University of Pennsylvania School
of Veterinary Medicine
2006 Kentucky Derby Winner.
Kentucky Derby exclusive.
14G - $30

Barklowe™
#48428

Birthday: 9/00/2006
Introduced: 9/1/2006
Retired: 10/2/2006
It starts out with a deep, low rumble
That sort of sounds just like a grumble
Next thing I know, I bark out loud
So strong and bold, it makes me proud!
September 2006
Beanie Baby of the Month.
BBOM - $12

Barley™
#40613

Birthday: 9/25/2006
Introduced: 3/30/2007
Current
When I've got something I must say
I may mutter a simple "neigh"
But then sometimes that just won't do
And so I'll stomp all my hooves, too!
15G - Current Retail Value

Basilico™
#46062

Birthday: 6/9/2006
Introduced: 4/28/2006
Retired: 5/26/2006
I'm the king of pizzas
Spaghetti and sauces
Carry me with you
Wherever you go and you'll always enjoy
Europe exclusive.
14UK - $20

BAT-e™
#4429

Birthday: 10/31/2003
Introduced: 10/7/2003
Retired: 10/31/2003
Sometimes I feel a bit loony
When I see the full moony
But I'm not BAT-e through and through
I'm simply crazy about you!
Ty Store exclusive.
11G - $10

Batty™
#4035 · brown body

Birthday: 10/29/1996
Introduced: 10/1/1997
Retired: 3/31/1999
Bats may make some people jitter
People don't be scared of this critter
If you're lonely or have nothing to do
This Beanie Baby would love to hug you!
4G - $7 ♥ 5G - $7

Batty™
#4035 · ty-dye body

Birthday: 10/29/1996
Introduced: 1/1/1999
Retired: 3/31/1999
Bats may make some people jitter
People don't be scared of this critter
If you're lonely or have nothing to do
This Beanie Baby would love to hug you!
5G - $7

BayStars™
#46072

Birthday: 11/11/1992
Introduced: 7/13/2006
Current
NICKNAME: YB (Yokohama BayStars)
Near the harbour, the wind is on our side.
The shining stars are watching over
the vitality players.
What a cool team!
Japan exclusive.
14G - $25

Beak™
#4211

Birthday: 2/3/1998
Introduced: 9/30/1998
Retired: 12/23/1999
Isn't this just the funniest bird?
When we saw her, we said "how absurd"
Looks aren't everything, this we know
Her love for you, she's sure to show!
5G - $7

Beani™
#4397

Birthday: 7/26/2000
Introduced: 10/1/2001
Retired: 5/24/2002
Why is my name Beani the cat?
It's funny you should ask me that
My owner loves her Beanies so
She wanted the whole world to know!
7G - $7 ♥ 9G - $7

Bearon™
#40039 · brown body

Birthday: 12/17/2003
Introduced: 11/12/2003
Retired: 4/6/2004
Bearon is here to celebrate
A special and historic date
To mark 100 years of flight
And to honor the brothers Wright!
7G - $20 ♥ 11G - $20

Bearon™
#40039 · brown body

Birthday: 12/17/2003
Introduced: 11/20/2003
Retired: 12/17/2003
Bearon is here to celebrate
A special and historic date
To mark 100 years of flight
And to honor the brothers Wright!
Midwest Airlines exclusive.
11G - $165

Bearon™
#40039 · red body

Birthday: 12/17/2003
Introduced: 11/12/2003
Retired: 4/6/2004
Bearon is here to celebrate
A special and historic date
To mark 100 years of flight
And to honor the brothers Wright!
7G - $12 ♥ 11G - $12

Bearon™
#40039 · red body

Birthday: 12/17/2003
Introduced: 11/20/2003
Retired: 12/17/2003
Bearon is here to celebrate
A special and historic date
To mark 100 years of flight
And to honor the brothers Wright!
Midwest Airlines exclusive.
11G - $125

Beary Bag™
#40489

Birthday: None
Introduced: 1/31/2007
Current
Beary Bag was issued without a poem.
15G - Current Retail Value

Beary Much™
#44100

Birthday: None
Introduced: 12/27/2006
Current
A Gift To You From Me!
To show I care so Beary Much
Or to be sure we stay in touch
Perhaps because you are so kind
Want you to know you're on my mind!
Ty Store exclusive.
15G - Current Retail Value

Beatrix Potter
Jemima Puddle-duck™
#46069 · gold letters

Birthday: None
Introduced: 9/29/2006
Current
First Published: 1908
Jemima Puddle-duck was a real Hill Top
duck who wasn't good at hatching eggs. Kep,
who was based on Beatrix Potter's favourite
sheep dog, rescues Jemima from the sandy-
whiskered gentleman.
UK exclusive.
14UK - Current Retail Value

Beatrix Potter
Jemima Puddle-duck™
#46069 · red letters

Birthday: None
Introduced: 9/29/2006
Current
First Published: 1908
Same phrase..
UK exclusive.
14UK - Current Retail Value

Beatrix Potter
Mr. Jeremy Fisher™
#46066 · gold letters

Birthday:
Introduced: 6/5/2006
Current
First Published: 1906
Mr. Jeremy Fisher had existed in Beatrix
Potter's imagination for many years before his
story was eventually published in 1906. He first
appeared in a picture letter to a young child.
UK exclusive.
14UK - Current Retail Value

Beatrix Potter
Mr. Jeremy Fisher™
#46066 · green letters

Birthday: None
Introduced: 6/5/2006
Current
First Published: 1906
Same phrase.
UK exclusive.
14UK - Current Retail Value

Beatrix Potter
Mr. Tod™
#46068 · black letters

Birthday: None
Introduced: 9/29/2006
Current
First Published: 1912
Mr. Tod returns to his home only to find
Tommy Brook has taken up residence which
results in a fearful fight.
UK exclusive.
14UK - Current Retail Value

Beatrix Potter
Mr. Tod™
#46068 · gold letters

Birthday: None
Introduced: 9/29/2006
Current
First Published: 1912
Same phrase.
UK exclusive.
14UK - Current Retail Value

Beatrix Potter
Peter Rabbit™
#46064 · blue letters

Birthday: None
Introduced: 6/5/2006
Current
First Published: 1902
The Tale of Peter Rabbit was Beatrix Potter's
first book, expanded from an illustrated letter
sent to a young friend who was ill.
UK exclusive.
14UK - Current Retail Value

Beatrix Potter
Peter Rabbit™
#46064 · gold letters

Birthday: None
Introduced: 6/5/2006
Current
First Published: 1902
SAme phrase.
UK exclusive.
14UK - Current Retail Value

Beatrix Potter
Pigling Bland™
#46067 · blue letters

Birthday: None
Introduced: 6/5/2006
Current
First Published: 1913
The Tale of Pigling Bland was published in
1913, the year Beatrix Potter married and
settled down to farming life for good. But
she had already been keeping pigs and
sketched them for this story.
UK exclusive.
14UK - Current Retail Value

Beatrix Potter
Pigling Bland™
#46067 · gold letters

Birthday: None
Introduced: 6/5/2006
Current
First Published: 1913
SAme phrase.
UK exclusive.
14UK - Current Retail Value

Beatrix Potter
Tom Kitten™
#46065 · gold letters

Birthday: None
Introduced: 9/29/2006
Current
First Published: 1907
The story of Tom Kitten and his sisters
takes place in Hill Top, the first farm Beatrix
Potter bought in the Lake District.
UK exclusive.
14UK - Current Retail Value

Beatrix Potter
Tom Kitten™
#46065 · white letters

Birthday: None
Introduced: 9/29/2006
Current
First Published: 1907
Same phrase.
UK exclusive.
14UK - Current Retail Value

Benjamin™
#40239

Birthday: 1/17/1706
Introduced: 4/29/2005
Retired: 8/26/2005
" . . . that they are endowed by their Creator
with certain unalienable rights . . ."
13G/13EU - $7

Bernie™
#4109

Birthday: 10/3/1996
Introduced: 1/1/1997
Retired: 9/22/1998
This little dog can't wait to grow
To rescue people lost in the snow
Don't let him out-keep him on your shelf
He doesn't know how to rescue himself!
4G - $7 ♥ 5G - $7

Berry Ice™
#40678

Birthday: 6/23/2007
Introduced: 6/29/2007
Current
Ready for a summer treat?
Something cool and oh-so sweet?
Sit back . . . relax . . . try one of these
A Berry Ice is sure to please!
Trade Show exclusive.
15G - Current Retail Value

Bessie™
#4009

Birthday: 6/27/1995
Introduced: 6/3/1995
Retired: 10/1/1997
Bessie the cow likes to dance and sing
Because music is her favorite thing
Every night when you are counting sheep
She'll sing you a song to help you sleep!
3G - $55 ♥ 4G - $12

Bianca™
#40156

Birthday: 9/15/2004
Introduced: 10/29/2004
Retired: 5/26/2005
Some cats like to come and go
But that's just not my style, you know
I'd rather hang around the house
Than go outside and catch a mouse!
12G/12EU - $7

Bidder™
#4980

Birthday: 9/24/2003
Introduced: 11/7/2003
Current
Shopping with us is easy to do
Especially if you have this card with you
Just make your purchase; don't delay
It's one more reason to shop on eBay!
Ty MBNA exclusive.
12G - $30

Big Apple™
#40120

Birthday: 2/2/2004
Introduced: 8/15/2004
Retired: 12/29/2005
As the city's lights shine bright
New York City is such a sight
The apple of our nation's eye
Once you're there you won't ask why!
Trade Show exclusive.
12G - $7

Bijoux™
#40104

Birthday: 7/21/2004
Introduced: 7/30/2004
Retired: 8/26/2004
In France we say things differently
Instead of night we say, "Nuit"
"Je t'aime," is what I'd say to you
And you'd reply, "I love you, too"!
12G - $7

Billingham™
#48422

Birthday: 3/00/2006
Introduced: 3/1/2006
Retired: 4/3/2006
If you splash in the tubby
At times when you are feeling grubby
Please just keep one thing in mind
I'm a duck, but not the rubber kind!
March 2006 Beanie Baby of the Month.
BBOM - $7

Billionaire Bear™
No Style #

Birthday: None
Introduced: 9/26/1998
Retired: 9/26/1998
In recognition of value and
contributions in shipping over
a billion dollars since Jan '98,
I present to you this exclusive signed bear
*Signed by Ty. Estimated 1400
produced. Ty Employee exclusive.*
5G - $750

Billionaire Bear 2™
No Style #

Birthday: None
Introduced: 9/12/1999
Retired: 9/12/1999
Ty is the company that can't be beat
Mattel and Hasbro can take a back seat
We did it again and it was fun
In the toy biz, we're #1!
*Signed by Ty. 475 produced.
Ty Employee exclusive.*
5G - $1,800

Billionaire Bear 3™
No Style #

Birthday: None
Introduced: 9/23/2000
Retired: 9/23/2000
With openings of Ty Singapore,
Ty Malaysia, Ty India and Ty Trade,
our brand is #1 in global sales, profits
and awareness. Thank you for your
support and hard work!
*Signed by Ty. 650 produced.
Ty Employee exclusive.*
6G - $900

Billionaire Bear 4™
No Style #

Birthday: None
Introduced: 9/8/2001
Retired: 9/8/2001
A special gift from Ty to you
This worldwide bear makes his debut
A billion plus in sales we've done
So again this year, we're #1!
*Signed by Ty. 762 produced.
Ty Employee exclusive.*
9G - $800

Billionaire Bear 5™
No Style #

Birthday: None
Introduced: 6/28/2002
Retired: 6/30/2002
Thank you for all your support
throughout this past year.
Please accept this bear as
a token of my appreciation.
*Signed by Ty. 769 produced.
Ty Employee exclusive.*
7G - $875 ♥ 10G - $800

Billionaire Bear 6™
No Style #

Birthday: None
Introduced: 9/13/2003
Retired: 9/13/2003
In gratitude and appreciation
For your hard work and dedication
Billionaire 6 makes a special debut
A thanks from me for all you do!
*Signed by Ty. 696 produced.
Ty Employee exclusive.*
7G - $700 ♥ 11G - $700

Billionaire Bear 7™
No Style #

Birthday: None
Introduced: 10/2/2004
Retired: 10/2/2004
Danke, gracias, grazie, merci
I want to thank you most sincerely
Our brand is known all the world through
I couldn't have done it without all of you!
*Signed by Ty. 612 produced.
Ty Employee exclusive.*
12G - $800

Billionaire Bear 8™
No Style #

Birthday: None
Introduced: 9/23/2005
Retired: 10/12/2005
I know there is no better way
To say just what I want to say
To thank you all for being so great
I give to you Billionaire 8!
*Signed by Ty. 480 produced.
Ty Employee exclusive.*
13G - $800

Billionaire Bear 9™
No Style #

Birthday: None
Introduced: 11/29/2006
Retired: 12/15/2006
Join together and give three cheers
To celebrate our 20 years
I'm grateful for your helping hand
In making Ty the finest brand!
*Signed by Ty. 480 produced.
Ty Employee exclusive.*
14G - $800

Binksy™
#40186

Birthday: 6/4/2004
Introduced: 12/30/2004
Retired: 9/23/2005
Hopping down the bunny trail
With my little cotton tail
Minksy and Winksy by my side
Follow me! I'll be your guide!
13G/13EU - $7

Bits™
#49009

Birthday: 3/4/2004
Introduced: 1/31/2005
Retired: 7/27/2005
Bits of color here and there
Decorate to keep or share
Scrapbooking is fun to do
Especially with a friend like you!
*Beanie Baby Offcial Club
retailers exclusive.*
12G - $7

Bits™
#49009 · boxed

Birthday: 3/4/2004
Introduced: 1/31/2005
Retired: 7/27/2005
Bits of color here and there
Decorate to keep or share
Scrapbooking is fun to do
Especially with a friend like you!
*Beanie Baby Offcial Club
retailers exclusive.*
12G - $16

Bixby™
#40151

Birthday: 9/30/2004
Introduced: 9/30/2004
Retired: 12/29/2004
I'm a nice brown bear, it's true
Won't you take me home with you
I'll show I care, in a special way
With big bear hugs most every day!
12G/12EU - $7

Blackie™
#4011

Birthday: 7/15/1994
Introduced: 6/25/1994
Retired: 9/15/1998
Living in a national park
He only played after dark
Then he met his friend Cubbie
Now they play when it's sunny!
*1G Blackies are extremely rare
and value cannot be determined.*
**1G - N/E ♥ 2G - $300 ♥ 3G - $50 ♥
4G - $10 ♥ 5G - $7**

BLARN-e™
#4436

Birthday: 3/17/2004
Introduced: 2/19/2004
Retired: 3/19/2004
When you can't think of what to say
To a special friend on St. Patty's Day
Give me a kiss an you will see
Just how poetic you can be!
Ty Store exclusive.
12G - $10

Blessed™
#40010

Birthday: 10/11/2002
Introduced: 6/30/2003
Retired: 7/28/2004
When it's time to go to bed
Right before you rest your head
Say a prayer for you and me
For the morning light to see!
7G - $7 ♥ 11G - $7

Blessed™
#40010

Birthday: 10/11/2002
Introduced: 6/30/2003
Retired: 7/28/2004
When it's time to go to bed
Right before you rest your head
Say a prayer for you and me
For the morning light to see!
Bon-Ton and Elder-Beerman exclusive.
11G - $50

Blissful™
#40628

Birthday: None
Introduced: 4/30/2007
Current
Blissful was issued without a poem.
15G - Current Retail Value

Blitz™
#40248

Birthday: 2/6/2005
Introduced: 8/31/2005
Current
Punts are kicked and passes thrown
Trying to get to the end zone
Move the ball; try to advance
So I can do my touchdown dance!
13G/13EU - Current Retail Value

Blizzard™
#4163

Birthday: 12/12/1996
Introduced: 5/11/1997
Retired: 5/1/1998
In the mountains, where it's snowy and cold
Lives a beautiful tiger, I've been told
Black and white, she's hard to compare
Of all the tigers, she is most rare!
4G - $7 ♥ 5G - $7

Bloom™
#4596

Birthday: 4/29/2003
Introduced: 4/30/2003
Retired: 6/13/2003
When pretty flowers are in bloom
It helps to erase winter's gloom
Beautiful flowers everywhere
Are sure to bring you lots of cheer!
7G - $ ♥ 11G - $7

Bloom™
#4596

Birthday: 4/29/2003
Introduced: 7/18/2003
Retired: 7/20/2003
When pretty flowers are in bloom
It helps to erase winter's gloom
Beautiful flowers everywhere
Are sure to bring you lots of cheer!
Given at the Florida Convention.
FTD exclusive.
11G - $150

Bloomfield™
#40343

Birthday: 5/7/2005
Introduced: 1/31/2006
Current
For all the special things you do
I give this little gift to you
Because you brighten up my day
With everything you do and say!
14G/14UK - Current Retail Value

Blue™
#4424

Birthday: 1/17/2003
Introduced: 6/17/2003
Retired: 6/21/2003
A symbol of the U.S.A.
Americans proudly display
My color means justice for all
Under our flag we all stand tall!
Ty Store exclusive.
11G - $7

Bluebonnet™
#40351

Birthday: 6/22/2005
Introduced: 2/28/2006
Current
Because I would like you to be
Just as happy as you make me
I bought you this pretty bouquet
So it will brighten up your day!
14G/14UK - Current Retail Value

Blues Clues™
Blue™
#40344

Birthday: None
Introduced: 1/31/2006
Current
My name is Blue.
What's yours?
Also available at Ty Store.
14G - Current Retail Value

Blues Clues™
Blue™
#48324

Birthday: None
Introduced: 1/31/2006
Current
My name is Blue.
What's yours?
USPS exclusive.
14G - Current Retail Value

Blues Clues™ Magenta™
#40346

Birthday: None
Introduced: 1/31/2006
Current
My name is Magenta.
What's yours?
Also available at Ty Store.
14G - Current Retail Value

Blues Clues™ Magenta™
#48325

Birthday: None
Introduced: 1/31/2006
Current
My name is Magenta.
What's yours?
USPS exclusive.
14G - Current Retail Value

Blues Clues™ Periwinkle™
#40345

Birthday: None
Introduced: 1/31/2006
Current
My name is Periwinkle.
What's yours?
Also available at Ty Store.
14G - Current Retail Value

Blues Clues™ Periwinkle™
#48236

Birthday: None
Introduced: 1/31/2006
Current
My name is Periwinkle.
What's yours?
USPS exclusive.
14G - Current Retail Value

Bo™
#4595

Birthday: 10/8/2002
Introduced: 4/30/2003
Retired: 4/6/2004
Unlike all my Dalmatian friends
I do not follow all the trends
My spots are different from the rest
I think that brown spots are the best!
7G - $7 ♥ 11G - $7

Boblins™ Gimmy™
#40608

Birthday: None
Introduced: 3/30/2007
Current
My name is Gully.
I love talking to animals and taking
care of them!
Sweden exclusive. Also available in UK.
15UK - Current Retail Value

Boblins™ Gully™
#40608

Birthday: None
Introduced: 3/30/2007
Current
My name is Gully.
I love talking to animals and
taking care of them!
Canada/Australia/New Zealand exclusive.
Also available at Ty Store.
15G - Current Retail Value

Boblins™ Pi™
#40609

Birthday: Bone
Introduced: 3/30/2007
Current
My name is Pi.
I am a very clever inventor and
I love math and science!
*Canada/UK/Australia/New Zealand
exclusive. Also available at Ty Store.*
15G - Current Retail Value

Boblins™ Ruddle™
#40610

Birthday: None
Introduced: 3/30/2007
Current
My name is Ruddle.
With my trusty tool kit,
I can fix or build anything!
*Canada/UK/Australia/New Zealand
exclusive. Also available at Ty Store.*
15G - Current Retail Value

Boblins™ Yam Yam™
#40611

Birthday: None
Introduced: 3/30/2007
Current
My name is Yam Yam.
I love to bounce and have fun!
Canada/UK/Australia/New Zealand
exclusive. Also available at Ty Store.
14G - Current Retail Value

Bones™
#4001

Birthday: 1/18/1994
Introduced: 6/25/1994
Retired: 5/1/1998
Bones is a dog that loves to chew
Chairs and tables and a smelly old shoe
"You're so destructive" all would shout
But that all stopped, when his teeth fell out!
1G - $2,500 ♥ 2G - $235 ♥ 3G - $50 ♥
4G - $7 ♥ 5G - $7

Bongo™
#4067 · brown tail

Birthday: 8/17/1995
Introduced: 2/1/1996
Retired: 2/6/1997
Bongo the monkey lives in a tree
The happiest monkey you'll ever see
In his spare time he plays the guitar
One of these days he will be a big star!
3G - $50 ♥ 4G - $10

Bongo™
#4067 · tan tail

Birthday: 8/17/1995
Introduced: 6/3/1995
Retired: 12/31/1998
Bongo the monkey lives in a tree
The happiest monkey you'll ever see
In his spare time he plays the guitar
One of these days he will be a big star!
3G - $65 ♥ 4G - $7 ♥ 5G - $7

Bonnet™
#44046

Birthday: 3/27/2005
Introduced: 2/22/2005
Retired: 4/5/2005
When springtime comes around each year
That's when I wear my bunny ears
I'll put them on then hop around
Up and down, all over town!
Harrods UK exclusive.
13EU - $20

Bonnet™
#44046

Birthday: 3/27/2005
Introduced: 2/22/2005
Retired: 4/5/2005
When springtime comes around each year
That's when I wear my bunny ears
I'll put them on then hop around
Up and down, all over town!
Ty Store exclusive.
13G - $7

Bonsai™
#4567

Birthday: 11/5/2001
Introduced: 9/30/2002
Retired: 12/27/2002
I am Bonsai the chimpanzee
I like to swing from tree to tree
Come with me and we will play
Chatting in the trees all day!
7G - $7 ♥ 10G - $7

Bonzer™
#40022

Birthday: 7/28/2003
Introduced: 7/31/2003
Retired: 10/8/2003
I think my name is really cool
It's a word you won't learn in school
It means, "awesome" and you'll agree
That this name fits me perfectly!
7G - $12 ♥ 11G - $12

Books™
#40266 · blue

Birthday: 8/15/2004
Introduced: 6/30/2005
Retired: 8/26/2005
Reading and arithmetic
Fun when you get the hang of it
Study hard and go to class
And I know you're sure to pass!
13G/13EU - $9

Books™
#40266 • purple

Birthday: 8/15/2004
Introduced: 6/30/2005
Retired: 8/26/2005
Reading and arithmetic
Fun when you get the hang of it
Study hard and go to class
And I know you're sure to pass!
13G/13EU - $9

Books™
#40266 • red

Birthday: 8/15/2004
Introduced: 6/30/2005
Retired: 8/26/2005
Reading and arithmetic
Fun when you get the hang of it
Study hard and go to class
And I know you're sure to pass!
13G/13EU - $9

Booties™
#4536

Birthday: 3/26/2002
Introduced: 5/31/2002
Retired: 2/26/2004
Even when the cold wind blows
I don't fret about frozen toes
My feet are never cold because
I wear warm booties on my paws!
7G - $7 ♥ 10G - $7

Boston™
#40124

Birthday: 12/16/2003
Introduced: 9/11/2004
Retired: 10/14/2004
You can walk the Freedom Trail
Or go watch as the ships set sail
Boston Common's a must see
There's more here than the Tea Party!
Trade Show exclusive.
12G - $12

Bounds™
#40653

Birthday: 2/23/2007
Introduced: 5/31/2007
Current
Won't you take me to the park
So I can run and jump and bark
We'll have such fun today and then
Tomorrow we'll do it again!
15G - Current Retail Value

Bravo™ Key-clip
#46087

Birthday: None
Introduced: 10/31/2006
Current
Bravo Key-clip was issued without a poem.
Australia exclusive.
14sm - Current Retail Value

Breadcrumbs™
#48412

Birthday: 5/00/2005
Introduced: 5/1/2005
Retired: 6/1/2005
I won't make a single sound
So that I will not be found
You won't even hear a "squeak"
And no one will shout, "A mouse . . . eek"!
May 2005 Beanie Baby of the Month.
BBOM - $7

Bride™
#4528

Birthday: None
Introduced: 4/30/2002
Retired: 7/28/2004
Gliding slowly down the aisle
With a happy, blissful smile
Today's the day we join as one
'Cause our new life has just begun!
7G - $7 ♥ 10G - $7

Brigitte™
#4374

Birthday: 4/20/2000
Introduced: 7/3/2001
Retired: 12/12/2001
A girl must always look her best
You can tell by how she's dressed
Pretty bows, pink poofy hair
Brigitte is full of charm and flair!
7G - $10 ♥ 9G - $10

56

Britannia™
#4601 · china with embroidered flag

Birthday: 12/15/1997
Introduced: 12/31/1997
Retired: 7/26/1999
Britannia the bear will sail the sea
So she can be with you and me
She's always sure to catch the tide
And wear the Union Jack with pride
UK exclusive.
5G - $30

Britannia™
#4601 · indonesia with embroidered flag

Birthday: 12/15/1997
Introduced: 12/31/1997
Retired: 7/26/1999
Britannia the bear will sail the sea
So she can be with you and me
She's always sure to catch the tide
And wear the Union Flag with pride
UK exclusive.
5G - $50

Britannia™
#4601 · patch flag

Birthday: 12/15/1997
Introduced: 12/31/1997
Retired: 7/26/1999
Britannia the bear will sail the sea
So she can be with you and me
She's always sure to catch the tide
And wear the Union Flag with pride
UK exclusive.
5G - $125

British Columbia Pacific Dogwood™
#46038

Birthday: None
Introduced: 9/11/2005
Retired: 1/27/2006
OFFICIAL FLOWER SINCE 1956
Pacific dogwood is a tree
That really grows quite tall you see
With unique flowers; berries, too
No other simple bloom will do!
Canadian Show exclusive.
13G - $20

Bronty™
#4085

Birthday: 11/22/1994
Introduced: 6/3/1995
Retired: 6/15/1996
Bronty was issued without a poem.
3G - $400

Brownie™
#4010

Birthday: None
Introduced: 1/8/1993
Retired: 1993
Brownie was issued without a poem.
1G - $2,800

Brownie™
#49030

Birthday: None
Introduced: 10/3/2005
Retired: 3/9/2006
Brownie was issued without a poem.
Available in BBOC Original 9 Assortment 3.
Beanie Baby Offcial Club exclusive.
BBOC2 - $125

Bruno™
#4183

Birthday: 9/9/1997
Introduced: 12/31/1997
Retired: 9/18/1998
Bruno the dog thinks he's a brute
But all the other Beanies think he's cute
He growls at his tail and runs in a ring
And everyone says, "Oh, how darling!"
5G - $7

Brutus™
#40482

Birthday: 9/9/2006
Introduced: 12/29/2006
Current
Just because I'm big and tough
That doesn't mean that I am gruff
So please don't think that I'm a brute
Just look at me . . . aren't I too cute?!
15G/15UK - Current Retail Value

Bubbles™
#4078

Birthday: 7/2/1995
Introduced: 6/3/1995
Retired: 5/11/1997
All day long Bubbles likes to swim
She never gets tired of flapping her fins
Bubbles lived in a sea of blue
Now she is ready to come home with you!
3G - $75 ♥ 4G - $35

Bubbly™
#4985

Birthday: 2/16/2003
Introduced: 8/9/2003
Retired: 11/25/2003
The Beanie Babies celebrate
To mark this most auspicious date
Lift your glass and raise it high
10 years of Beanies...here's to Ty!
Trade Show exclusive.
11G - $7

Buckingham™
#4603

Birthday: 10/16/2000
Introduced: 9/3/2000
Retired: 1/31/2001
Buckingham the bear has a little secret
He wants to tell you and hopes you'll keep it
He's taking his friend Britannia to see
Someone special for crumpets and tea!
UK exclusive.
7G - $75

Bucky™
#4016

Birthday: 6/8/1995
Introduced: 1/7/1996
Retired: 12/31/1997
Bucky's teeth are as shiny as can be
Often used for cutting trees
He hides in his dam night and day
Maybe for you he will come out and play!
3G - $50 ♥ 4G - $7

Bumble™
#4045

Birthday: 10/16/1995
Introduced: 6/3/1995
Retired: 6/15/1996
Bumble the bee will not sting you
It is only love that this bee will bring you
So don't be afraid to give this bee a hug
Because Bumble the bee is a love-bug.
3G - $260 ♥ 4G - $325

Bunga-Raya™
#4615

Birthday: 2/1/2002
Introduced: 1/29/2002
Retired: 8/31/2002
Hibiscus, the national flower
Decorate the gathering attractively/brightly
Bringing glory and peace
Symbol to our multi racial people/citizen
Malaysia exclusive.
10G - $20

Busby™
#40456

Birthday: 3/7/2006
Introduced: 10/31/2006
Current
Busby is a bear with style
And he can certainly beguile
So elegant and with such flair
He's a sophisticated bear!
14G/14UK - Current Retail Value

Bushy™
#4285

Birthday: 1/27/2000
Introduced: 3/1/2000
Retired: 6/11/2001
I won't roar - I'll purr instead
So always pat me on the head
A cuddly kitten I promise to be
If you'll come over and play with me!
6G - $7 ♥ 7G - $7

Butch™
#4227

Birthday: 10/2/1998
Introduced: 1/1/1999
Retired: 12/23/1999
Going to the pet shop to buy dog food
I ran into Butch in a good mood
"Come to the pet shop down the street"
"Be a good dog, I'll buy you a treat!"
5G - $7

Buttercream™
#4803

Birthday: 4/00/2003
Introduced: 2/2/2003
Retired: 5/19/2003
When people meet me, they all say
I'm nicer than a summer's day
And sweeter than the sweetest dream
And that's why I'm named Buttercream!
April 2003 Beanie Baby of the Month.
BBOM - $7

Buzzie™
#4354

Birthday: 10/20/2000
Introduced: 4/1/2001
Retired: 12/31/2001
Buzzing through the pretty flowers
She could frolic there for hours
The nectar that smells so sweet
Is her favorite tasty treat!
7G - $7 ♥ 8G - $7

Buzzy™
#4308

Birthday: 7/6/2000
Introduced: 7/8/2000
Retired: 3/23/2001
Up in the sky is where I fly
I love to soar way up high
When I swoop down, don't run away
Cause all I want to do is play!
6G - $7 ♥ 7G - $7

C™
#40503

Birthday: None
Introduced: 6/30/2005
Current
Alphabet Bears are issued without poems.
AB - Current Retail Value

Cabaret™
#40415

Birthday: 7/19/2006
Introduced: 7/31/2006
Current
I'll sing a peppy, jazzy tune
Outside under the big full moon
You'll hear the shouts from all my fans
As they bang on their pots and pans!
14G/14UK - Current Retail Value

Caipora™
#44206

Birthday: None
Introduced: 10/6/2005
Retired: 1/2/2007
FACT: Golden lion tamarins live in the heavily
populated coastal area of Brazil, where less
than 2% of the rainforest remains, causing a
definite threat to this primate!
Ty Store/World Wildlife Fund exclusive.
13G - $10

California™
#40083

Birthday: None
Introduced: 8/30/2004
Retired: 12/29/2005
STATE MOTTO: "Eureka: (I have found it)
NICKNAME: Golden State
FACT: Death Valley, California is
282 feet below sea level!
Sold only in California.
12G - $7

California™
#40083

Birthday: None
Introduced: 6/10/2006
Retired: 6/11/2006
STATE MOTTO: "Eureka: (I have found it)
NICKNAME: Golden State
FACT: Death Valley, California is
282 feet below sea level!
Knott's Berry Farm exclusive.
12G - $25

California Poppy™
#40292

Birthday: None
Introduced: 7/22/2005
Retired: 12/29/2005
OFFICIAL FLOWER SINCE 1903
I wake up with the morning sun
And close again when day is done
In California, blooming bright
Our poppy is such a delight!
Trade Show exclusive.
13G - $7

California Poppy™
#40292

Birthday: None
Introduced: 6/17/2006
Retired: 6/18/2006
OFFICIAL FLOWER SINCE 1903
I wake up with the morning sun
And close again when day is done
In California, blooming bright
Our poppy is such a delight!
Knott's Berry Farm exclusive.
13G - $25

Canada™
#46017

Birthday: None
Introduced: 10/29/2004
Retired: 5/26/2005
CAPITOL CITY: Ottawa
NATIONAL ANTHEM: "O Canada"
FACT: The official ceremony inaugurating
the Canadian Flag was held in Ottawa on
February 15, 1965!
Canada exclusive.
12G - $15

Canada™ Key-clip
#46075

Birthday: None
Introduced: 7/31/2006
Retired: 4/26/2007
Vast, Strong and Free!
Canada exclusive.
14sm - $8

CAND-e™
#4417

Birthday: 12/13/2001
Introduced: 11/29/2002
Retired: 12/31/2002
Winter is my favorite season
I bet you can guess the reason
Candy canes are my favorite treat
That's why I wear them, head to feet!
Ty Store exclusive.
10G - $7

Canters™
#48423

Birthday: 4/00/2006
Introduced: 4/1/2006
Retired: 5/1/2006
Mirror, mirror that I see
Who's this looking back at me?
With bright eyes and a mane of pink
I'll smile and give her a wink!
April 2006 Beanie Baby of the Month.
BBOM - $7

Canyon™
#4212

Birthday: 5/29/1998
Introduced: 9/30/1998
Retired: 8/16/1999
I climb rocks and really run fast
Try to catch me, it's a blast
Through the mountains, I used to roam
Now in your room, I'll call home!
5G - $7

Cappuccino™
#4804

Birthday: 5/00/2003
Introduced: 3/2/2003
Retired: 6/3/2003
I am a very social cat
Who loves to sit around and chat
Meeting new friends sure makes me smile
So please sit down and stay awhile!
May 2003 Beanie Baby of the Month.
BBOM - $7

Captain™
#40245

Birthday: 1/24/2005
Introduced: 5/31/2005
Retired: 6/25/07
Let me give you a little tip
As Captain, I run a tight ship
Sailing across the ocean blue
So won't you come and join my crew!
13G/13EU - $7

Carnation™
#4575

Birthday: 6/22/2002
Introduced: 12/27/2002
Retired: 9/10/2004
I'm pink, I'm pink, imagine that
A funny color for a cat
My favorite flower in Creation
Is a pretty pink carnation!
7G - $7 ♥ 11G - $7

60

Carrots™
#4512

Birthday: 9/13/2001
Introduced: 12/27/2001
Retired: 4/16/2002
Of all the things I love to eat
A carrot is my favorite treat
I'll eat them raw or in a stew
But either way I'll share with you!
7G - $7 ♥ 10G - $7

Casanova™
#40476

Birthday: 2/14/2006
Introduced: 11/30/2006
Retired: 2/27/2007
Dinner, dancing and romance
A moonlit stroll, then a slow dance
This night was made for you and me
You're in my arms where you should be!
14G/14UK - $8

Cashew™
#4292

Birthday: 4/22/2000
Introduced: 6/24/2000
Retired: 6/12/2001
I like to swim and climb in trees
I like to visit with the bees
But what I really want to do
Is be your friend and play with you!
6G - $7 ♥ 7G - $7

Cassie™
#4340

Birthday: 7/12/2000
Introduced: 3/1/2001
Retired: 7/25/2001
This loyal Collie will stay by your side
When you're lost, she'll be your guide
If you need her, wherever she roams
Just call out, "Cassie Come Home!"
7G - $7 ♥ 8G - $7

Catsby™
#40361

Birthday: 7/24/2005
Introduced: 3/31/2006
Current
Angoras, Calicos, Siamese
Persians, Tabbies and Maltese
And just what type of cat am I?
I couldn't guess. Why don't you try!
14G/14UK - Current Retail Value

Caw™
#4071

Birthday: None
Introduced: 6/3/1995
Retired: 6/15/1996
Caw was issued without a poem
3G - $320

Celebrate™
#4385

Birthday: 3/13/2001
Introduced: 6/23/2001
Retired: 10/11/2001
I'm the 15th birthday bear
With a wish I'd like to share
Many more years full of fun
Let's keep Ty #1!
Issued for 15th Year Anniversary.
7G - $7 ♥ 9G - $7

Celebrations™
#4620

Birthday: None
Introduced: 4/16/2002
Retired: 8/9/2002
50th Anniversary: June 3, 2002
Her Majesty, Queen Elizabeth, celebrates
her Golden Jubilee this year, making
her the fifth-longest reigning Monarch.
*UK/Canada/Australia/New
Zealand exclusive.*
7G - $18 ♥ 10G - $18

ChariTee™
#40080

Birthday: 3/25/2004
Introduced: 5/28/2004
Retired: 9/23/2005
The PGA Tour is here to say
There's more to life than tournament play
What's better than a hole-in-one?
It's giving back . . . and we're not done!
USA exclusive.
12G - $9

Charles™
#46085

Birthday: 11/4/2006
Introduced: 11/4/2006
Retired: 1/24/2007
Although I'm very small in size
I am the finest merchandise
Which Ty and Harrods bring to you
Take me home; I'll love you too!
Harrods UK exclusive.
14UK - $25

Charles™
#46085 · boxed with certificate

Birthday: 11/4/2006
Introduced: 11/4/2006
Retired: 1/24/2007
Although I'm very small in size
I am the finest merchandise
Which Ty and Harrods bring to you
Take me home; I'll love you too!
Harrods UK exclusive.
14UK - $115

Charlie™
#40403

Birthday: 4/23/2006
Introduced: 6/30/2006
Current
From vine to vine and through the trees
So fast my fur blows in the breeze
I'll take a break...it's time to eat
Bananas! They're my favorite treat!
14G/14UK - Current Retail Value

Charlotte's Web™ Gussy™
#40450

Birthday: None
Introduced: 10/31/2006
Current
Gussy always, always, always
has a lot to say, say, say!
Also available at Ty Store.
14G/14UK - Current Retail Value

Charlotte's Web™ Gussy™ (with DVD)
#47062

Birthday: None
Introduced: 4/3/2007
Current
Gussy always, always, always
has a lot to say, say, say!
Boxed with DVD. Walmart exclusive.
15G - Current Retail Value

Charlotte's Web™ Wilbur™
#40449

Birthday: None
Introduced: 10/31/2006
Current
Wilbur may be the runt of the litter, but he
has a huge heart!
Also available at Ty Store.
14G/14UK - Current Retail Value

Charlotte's Web™ Wilbur™ (with DVD)
#47061

Birthday: None
Introduced: 4/3/2007
Current
Wilbur may be the runt of the litter, but he
has a huge heart!
Boxed with DVD. Walmart exclusive.
15G - Current Retail Value

Charm™
#40349

Birthday: 9/27/2005
Introduced: 2/28/2006
Retired: 5/24/2006
What will happen when you kiss me?
Am I a prince? Just wait and see
If your smooch will break the spell
But I will never kiss and tell!
14G/14UK - $7

Charmer™
#4568

Birthday: 9/10/2002
Introduced: 10/30/2002
Retired: 1/9/2003
Some people may think I'm a horse
Until they see my horn, of course
Not to fear, though, for I am sweet
Being your pal would be so neat!
7G - $7 ♥ 10G - $7

Charming™
#40314

Birthday: 1/17/2005
Introduced: 10/31/2005
Retired: 8/25/2006
In a castle near the sea
Up in the tower's where I'll be
I'll listen closely 'til I hear
My charming, handsome prince draw near!
13G/13UK - $7

Chaser™
#40654

Birthday: 1/11/2007
Introduced: 5/31/2007
Current
On your mark, get set, then go
I'll chase you, hope you're not slow
So when you see me you should scat
Even if you're not a cat!
15G - Current Retail Value

Cheddar™
#4525 · blue undertone

Birthday: 3/24/2002
Introduced: 4/30/2002
Retired: 5/24/2002
I love to munch a piece of cheddar
To me there's nothing that tastes better
But I'm not picky or hard to please
'Cause I'll eat any kind of cheese!
7G - $7 ♥ 10G - $7

Cheddar™
#4525 · tan body

Birthday: 3/24/2002
Introduced: 4/30/2002
Retired: 5/24/2002
I love to munch a piece of cheddar
To me there's nothing that tastes better
But I'm not picky or hard to please
'Cause I'll eat any kind of cheese!
7G - $7 ♥ 10G - $7

Cheek to Cheek™
#40472

Birthday: 10/21/2006
Introduced: 11/30/2006
Retired: 2/27/2007
As melodic as your favorite tune
As romantic as the stars and moon
My love for you makes my knees weak
So hold me closely; cheek to cheek!
14G/14UK - $7

Cheeks™
#4250

Birthday: 5/18/1999
Introduced: 4/17/1999
Retired: 12/23/1999
Don't confuse me with an ape
I have a most unusual shape
My cheeks are round and ty-dyed red
On my behind as well as my head!
5G - $7

Cheery™
#4359 · dark blue clouds

Birthday: 8/18/2000
Introduced: 5/1/2001
Retired: 8/31/2001
If you're feeling sad and blue
Cheery wants to be with you
Hug him and he'll make you smile
You'll feel better in a while!
7G - $7 ♥ 8G - $7

Cheery™
#4359 · light blue clouds

Birthday: 8/18/2000
Introduced: 5/1/2001
Retired: 8/31/2001
If you're feeling sad and blue
Cheery wants to be with you
Hug him and he'll make you smile
You'll feel better in a while!
7G - $7 ♥ 8G - $7

Cheesly™
#40240

Birthday: 11/15/2004
Introduced: 4/29/2005
Retired: 12/29/2005
Hoping not to make a creak
As this cheddar, I bravely sneak
A bite of cheese is what I long
Now I ask you can that be wrong?
13G/13EU - $7

Cheezer™
#4301

Birthday: 5/9/2000
Introduced: 6/24/2000
Retired: 6/12/2001
I hide in holes throughout the day
But when night falls I want to play
I sneak around and look for cheese
So be my friend and help me please!
6G - $7 ♥ 7G - $7

Chef Robuchon™
#47045

Birthday: 9/18/2006
Introduced: 8/9/2006
Retired: 9/5/2006
If there is no love more
sincere than the love of food
you'll find your soul mate in
Chef Robuchon's cuisine.
*Limited to opening of NY Four
Seasons L'Atelier restaurant.*
14G - $4,000

Cherry Ice™
#40678

Birthday: 6/23/2007
Introduced: 6/29/2007
Current
Ready for a summer treat?
Something cool and oh-so sweet?
How 'bout something that sure is great
A Cherry Ice would be first rate!
Trade Show exclusive.
15G - Current Retail Price

Chessie™
#40660

Birthday: 6/2/2007
Introduced: 6/29/2007
Current
Across the plains so sleek and fast
Just like a blur when I streak past
You won't have time to get away
It's Hug Your Favorite Cheetah Day!
15G - Current Retail Value

Chicago™
#40089

Birthday: 8/12/2003
Introduced: 7/22/2004
Retired: 7/26/2004
In Chicago there's so much to do
The theater, art and culture, too
Great food, great people and so much fun
The Windy City's second to none!
Trade Show exclusive.
12G - $7

Chickie™
#4509

Birthday: 9/20/2001
Introduced: 12/27/2001
Retired: 4/23/2002
When it was time to break my shell
My little beak worked really well
It took some time, but now I'm free
So come on out and play with me!
7G - $7 ♥ 10G - $7

Chili™
#40088

Birthday: 12/12/2003
Introduced: 6/30/2004
Retired: 11/24/2004
I must be a sight to behold
A polar bear that dislikes cold
I just don't care for a snow storm
I'd rather be where it is warm!
12G - $7

Chillin'™
#40025

Birthday: 1/12/2003
Introduced: 9/30/2003
Retired: 12/26/2003
This snowman is really cool
Knows where it's at; he's no fool
If you are ready, also willin'
Let's hang out with our friend Chillin'!
7G - $7 ♥ 11G - $7

Chillingsly™
#40446

Birthday: 1/21/2006
Introduced: 9/29/2006
Retired: 12/21/2006
Way up where the cold wind blows
And people wear their winter clothes
I'll be there playing on my sled
With my warm knit cap on my head!
14G/14UK - $7

Chillton™
#48432

Birthday: 1/00/2007
Introduced: 1/1/2007
Retired: 2/1/2007
You might think that I like the snow
'Cause where I'm from it's cold, you know
I really don't, so I will plan
To go where I can get a tan!
January 2007 Beanie Baby of the Month.
BBOM - $7

Chilly™
#4012

Birthday: 2/22/1994
Introduced: 6/25/1994
Retired: 1/7/1996
Chilly was issued without a poem.
1G - $2,750 ♥ 2G - $1,000 ♥ 3G - $900

China™
#4315

Birthday: 9/4/2000
Introduced: 7/8/2000
Retired: 4/19/2001
In the mountains you'll find me
Sitting near a bamboo tree
You'll laugh at such a funny sight
I only dress in black and white!
6G - $7 ♥ 7G - $7

Chinook™
#4604

Birthday: 5/24/2000
Introduced: 8/14/2000
Retired: 2/15/2001
From this great land I'll never roam
Beloved Canada is my home
Her maple leaf I proudly wear
To show the world how much I care!
Canada exclusive.
6G - $20

Chip™
#4121

Birthday: 1/25/1996
Introduced: 5/11/1997
Retired: 3/31/1999
Black and gold, brown and white
The shades of her coat are quite a sight
At mixing her colors she was a master
On anyone else it would be a disaster!
4G - $7 ♥ 5G - $7

Chipper™
#4259

Birthday: 4/21/1999
Introduced: 8/31/1999
Retired: 12/23/1999
I'm quick, I'm fast, I don't make a peep
But I love to snuggle when I sleep
Take me along when you go play
And I'll make sure you have a nice day!
5G - $7

Chitraka™
#44207

Birthday: None
Introduced: 12/14/2005
Retired: 4/17/2006
FACT: WWF supports the 'Women in
Conservation' initiative, in which many women
around the world dedicate themselves to
conservation projects like the Cheetah
Conservation Fund in Namibia, Africa!
Ty Store/World Wildlife Fund exclusive.
13G - $10

Chocolate™
#4015

Birthday: 4/27/1993
Introduced: 1/8/1994
Retired: 12/31/1998
Licorice, gum and peppermint candy
This moose always has these handy
There is one more thing he likes to eat
Can you guess his favorite sweet?
1G - $2,400 ♥ 2G - $300 ♥ 3G - $60 ♥
4G - $7 ♥ 5G - $7

Chocolate™
#49021

Birthday: 4/27/1993
Introduced: 10/3/2005
Retired: 3/9/2006
Licorice, gum and peppermint candy
This moose always has these handy
There is one more thing he likes to eat
Can you guess his favorite sweet?
*Available in BBOC Original 9
Assortments 1-5.*
Beanie Baby Offcial Club exclusive.
BBOC2 - $7

Chocolate Chip™
#47042

Birthday: 6/11/2006
Introduced: 8/31/2006
Current
Smooth landings make for one happy bear
I'm friendly and I've got cookies to share
I fly with an airline that's unique and so rare
Its fans call it, "The best care in the air"!
Midwest Airlines exclusive.
14G - $18

Chompers™
#48403

Birthday: 8/00/2004
Introduced: 8/1/2004
Retired: 8/31/2004
With an awesome smile like mine
You can see how my teeth shine
I brush each day and every night
So my toothy grin is bright!
August 2004 Beanie Baby of the Month.
BBOM - $8

Chops™
#4019

Birthday: 5/3/1996
Introduced: 1/7/1996
Retired: 1/1/1997
Chops is a little lamb
This lamb you'll surely know
Because every path that you may take
This lamb is sure to go!
3G - $75 ♥ 4G - $40

Chopstix™
#40047

Birthday: 1/22/2003
Introduced: 12/30/2003
Retired: 7/16/2004
I use chopsticks when I eat
But I admit I have to cheat
If I don't hold the sticks just right
It can be a messy sight!
12G - $7

Chuckles™
#40172

Birthday: 10/23/2004
Introduced: 12/30/2004
Retired: 1/28/2005
What's a hedgehog - don't you know?
I'm a cute and furry fellow
I sleep all day and play all night
But I will greet you at first light!
13G/13EU - $7

Cinders™
#4295

Birthday: 4/30/2000
Introduced: 6/24/2000
Retired: 5/9/2001
I sleep in caves and in the snow
A mountain life is all I know
In the spring I wake again
And look around for my best friend!
6G - $7 ♥ 7G - $7

Cinta™
#46005

Birthday: 11/25/2003
Introduced: 2/9/2004
Retired: 3/15/2006
It's famous islandwide
With a joyious face day and night
Bunga Raya, the name it's given
In high spirit at all times!
Asian-Pacific exclusive.
12G - $18

Class of 2004™
#40066

Birthday: 3/15/2004
Introduced: 3/30/2004
Retired: 7/16/2004
You worked hard and did your best
It all paid off, you've passed the test
Now here's what you've been waiting for
Congrats Class of 2004!
12G - $8

Classy™
#4373

Birthday: 4/30/2001
Introduced: 4/30/2001
Retired: 9/7/2001
I'm proud to be the Beanie you chose
I know for sure my happiness shows
Thanks so much for creating me
It's great to be the People's Beanie!
The People's Beanie. Ty Store exclusive.
8G - $7

Claude™
#4083

Birthday: 9/3/1996
Introduced: 5/11/1997
Retired: 12/31/1998
Claude the crab paints by the sea
A famous artist he hopes to be
But the tide came in and his paints fell
Now his art is on his shell!
4G - $7 ♥ 5G - $7

Clover™
#4503

Birthday: 3/17/2001
Introduced: 12/27/2001
Retired: 5/24/2002
A bit o' good luck I will bring
If you believe in such a thing
Fortune will follow everywhere
As long as you have friends that care!
7G - $7 ♥ 9G - $7

Clover™
#47012

Birthday: 10/2/2004
Introduced: 7/29/2005
Current
Heads together to think things through
Hands that will work hard for you
Healthy living that we share
Hearts that show how much we care!
4-H Club exclusive.
13G - $13

Clubby™
#4991

Birthday: 7/7/1998
Introduced: 5/1/1998
Retired: 3/15/1999
Wearing his club pin for all to see
He's a proud member like you and me
Made especially with you in mind
Clubby the bear is one of a kind!
Beanie Baby Offcial Club exclusive.
5G - $10

Clubby II™
#4992

Birthday: 3/9/1999
Introduced: 5/1/1999
Retired: 12/23/1999
A proud club member, named Clubby II
My color is special, a purplish hue
Take me along to your favorite place
Carry me in my platinum case!
Beanie Baby Offcial Club exclusive.
Comes with BBOC Platinum
membership kit.
5G - $7

Clubby II™ Kit
#4992

Birthday: 3/9/1999
Introduced: 5/1/1999
Retired: 12/23/1999
A proud club member, named Clubby II
My color is special, a purplish hue
Take me along to your favorite place
Carry me in my platinum case!
Beanie Baby Offcial Club exclusive.
BBOC Platinum membership kit.
5G - $15

Clubby III™
#4993

Birthday: 6/30/2000
Introduced: 9/18/2000
Retired: 12/10/2000
I'm as happy as can be
Because I joined BBOC
We'll play games, have lots of fun
Because this club is number 1!
Beanie Baby Offcial Club exclusive.
6G - $10 ♥ 7G - $10

Clubby IV™
#4996 · gold button

Birthday: 8/4/2001
Introduced: 9/24/2001
Retired: 1/23/2002
Which button do you think you'll get
A gold, a silver, or the whole set
Clubby IV has a surprise for you
Ty Warner autographed a few!
Beanie Baby Offcial Club exclusive.
9G - $20

Clubby IV™
#4996 · rainbow button

Birthday: 8/4/2001
Introduced: 9/24/2001
Retired: 1/23/2002
Which button do you think you'll get
A gold, a silver, or the whole set
Clubby IV has a surprise for you
Ty Warner autographed a few!
Beanie Baby Offcial Club exclusive.
9G - $7

Clubby IV™
#4996 · silver button

Birthday: 8/4/2001
Introduced: 9/24/2001
Retired: 1/23/2002
Which button do you think you'll get
A gold, a silver, or the whole set
Clubby IV has a surprise for you
Ty Warner autographed a few!
Beanie Baby Offcial Club exclusive.
9G - $12

Clubby V™
#4998

Birthday: 6/20/2002
Introduced: 9/16/2002
Retired: 1/2/2003
Five years ago we made some plans
To make a club for Beanie fans
We introduce this new Clubby
To thank you for your loyalty!
Beanie Baby Offcial Club exclusive.
7G - $10 ♥ 10G - $10

Clubby VI™
#49000 · blue with potbelly

Birthday: 4/9/2003
Introduced: 10/1/2003
Retired: 12/15/2003
Some say that good things come in threes
That's why this Clubby's sure to please
With Clubby VI you'll always be
So glad you joined the BBOC!
Beanie Baby Offcial Club exclusive.
7G - $12 ♥ 11G - $12

Clubby VI™
#49000 · purple with potbelly

Birthday: 4/9/2003
Introduced: 10/1/2003
Retired: 12/15/2003
Some say that good things come in threes
That's why this Clubby's sure to please
With Clubby VI you'll always be
So glad you joined the BBOC!
Beanie Baby Offcial Club exclusive.
7G - $12 ♥ 11G - $12

Clubby VI™
#49000 · rainbow with new face

Birthday: 4/9/2003
Introduced: 10/1/2003
Retired: 12/15/2003
Some say that good things come in threes
That's why this Clubby's sure to please
With Clubby VI you'll always be
So glad you joined the BBOC!
Beanie Baby Offcial Club exclusive.
7G - $12 ♥ 11G - $12

Clubby VII™
#49035

Birthday: 9/17/2006
Introduced: 10/2/2006
Retired: 3/30/2007
Club members from both here and there
Love each and every Clubby bear
And as I'm sure you could have guessed
Our Clubby VII is the best!
Beanie Baby Offcial Club exclusive.
14G - $10

Clucky™
#48427

Birthday: 8/00/2006
Introduced: 8/1/2006
Retired: 9/1/2006
If you'd like to come visit me
I'm on the farm, in henhouse three
But I won't let you near my coop
If you're hungry for chicken soup!
August 2006 Beanie Baby of the Month.
BBOM - $7

Coastline™
#40630

Birthday: 8/7/2006
Introduced: 4/30/2007
Current
I'm so glad I came to the coast
I can't decide what I like most
Although I like sun, sand and breeze
I love to ride on water skis!
15G - Current Retail Value

Coco Presley™
#47075 · brown

Birthday: 1/8/2007
Introduced: 7/24/2007
Current
C'mon put on your blue suede shoes
Join us in helping spread the news
We've got a rockin', rollin' treat
Coco Presley is just too sweet!
*2 different hang tag pictures - Elvis
with microphone and accoustic Elvis.*
15G - Current Retail Value

Coco Presley™
#47074 · orange

Birthday: 1/8/2007
Introduced: 7/24/2007
Current
C'mon put on your blue suede shoes
Join us in helping spread the new
We've got a rockin', rollin' treat
Coco Presley is just too sweet!
*2 different hang tag pictures –
Hawaiian Elvis and 1970s Elvis.*
15G - Current Retail Value

Cocoa Bean™
#47046

Birthday: 7/7/2007
Introduced: 12/21/2006
Current
To celebrate the hundredth year
Since Hershey's® Kisses® did appear
You will enjoy this little treat
It's cuddly, cute, and oh-so sweet!
*In honor of the 100th anniversary of the
Hershey's Kiss. Sold only at Walgreens.*
14G - $11

Color Me Beanie™
#4989 · bear

Birthday: 12/11/2001
Introduced: 8/29/2002
Retired: 12/27/2002
Use some markers to color me
Be as creative as you can be
Send photos in when you are done
We know you will have loads of fun!
*Variations: red, yellow, blue, green,
orange, and pink ribbons*
7G - $10 ♥ 10G - $10

Color Me Beanie™
#4988 · bunny

Birthday: 7/24/2002
Introduced: 2/6/2003
Retired: 7/29/2003
Coloring eggs is fun to do
With that in mind, try something new
Time to design your own creation
Use a little imagination!
*Variations ribbon & egg: yellow,
purple, blue, gold, pink, green.*
7G - $10 ♥ 11G - $10

Color Me Beanie
Birthday Kit™
#4901 · cat

Birthday: None
Introduced: 9/2/2003
Retired: 7/16/2004
CMB Kits are issued without poems.
7G - $10 ♥ 11G - $10

Color Me Beanie
Birthday Kit™
#4902 · dog

Birthday: None
Introduced: 9/2/2003
Retired: 7/16/2004
CMB Kits are issued without poems.
7G - $10 ♥ 11G - $10

Color Me Beanie
Birthday Kit™
#4903 · bear

Birthday: None
Introduced: 9/2/2003
Retired: 7/16/2004
CMB Kits are issued without poems.
*Variations ribbon: red, yellow,
blue, green and orange.*
7G - $10 ♥ 11G - $10

Color Me Beanie
Birthday Kit™
#4904 · unicorn

Birthday: None
Introduced: 9/2/2003
Retired: 7/16/2004
CMB Kits are issued without poems.
7G - $10 ♥ 11G - $10

Colorado™
#40123

Birthday: None
Introduced: 8/30/2004
Retired: 4/28/2005
STATE MOTTO: "Nil Sine Numine"
(Nothing Without the Deity)
NICKNAME: Centennial State
FACT: Colorado has over 200 state
wildlife areas!
Sold only in Colorado.
12G - $7

Colorado Columbine™
#40298

Birthday: None
Introduced: 8/27/2005
Retired: 10/21/2005
OFFICIAL FLOWER SINCE 1899
In Latin, Columbine means "dove"
A flower everyone will love
Wait till I open, then you'll see
How beautiful this dove can be!
Trade Show exclusive.
13G - $12

Colosso™
#40002

Birthday: 9/6/2002
Introduced: 5/29/2003
Retired: 6/24/2004
When I walk by, the buildings shake
And sometimes people shout,
"EARTHQUAKE"
But I don't mind because, you see
I'm very happy just being me!
7G - $7 ♥ 11G - $7

Columbus™
#40134

Birthday: 3/3/2003
Introduced: 8/23/2004
Retired: 9/10/2004
Capitol of the Buckeye State
Variety's what makes us great
History, art, sports, fashion, too
Midwestern style that's right for you!
Trade Show exclusive.
12G - $10

Comet™
#4810

Birthday: 11/00/2003
Introduced: 11/3/2003
Retired: 12/1/2003
In the darkness of the night
When the stars are shining bright
You know you'll never feel alone
With a friend like me to call your own!
November 2003
Beanie Baby of the Month.
BBOM - $20

Congo™
#4160

Birthday: 11/9/1996
Introduced: 6/15/1996
Retired: 12/31/1998
Black as the night and fierce is he
On the ground or in a tree
Strong and mighty as the Congo
He's related to our Bongo!
4G - $7 ♥ 5G - $7

Cool Chick™
#40335

Birthday: None
Introduced: 12/30/2005
Retired: 5/24/2006
ReIntroduced: 2/1/2007
ReRetired: 3/27/2007
Cool Chick was issued without a poem.
14G/14UK - $7

Cool Clutch™
#40390

Birthday: None
Introduced: 6/30/2006
Current
Cool Clutch was issued without a poem.
14G - Current Retail Value

Cool Teacher ™
#40356

Birthday: 5/3/2006
Introduced: 3/31/2006
Current
Teacher, you're better than the rest
You rock! You really are the best
With all your guidance and concern
You've taught me that it's fun to learn!
14G/14UK - Current Retail Value

Coop™
#40493

Birthday: 7/12/2006
Introduced: 1/31/2007
Retired: 5/25/2007
I love my mom, but when I'm grown
I'll finally move out on my own
I'll shout out a joyful, "WHOOP"
Because I've finally flown the coop!
15G - $7

Coral™
#4079

Birthday: 3/2/1995
Introduced: 6/3/1995
Retired: 1/1/1997
Coral is beautiful, as you know
Made of colors in the rainbow
Whether it's pink, yellow or blue
These colors were chosen just for you!
3G - $90 ♥ 4G - $40

Coral Casino™
No Style #

Birthday: None
Introduced: 12/9/2001
Retired: 12/9/2001
Kissed by the sun
Caressed by the sea
Rich with beauty and memories
Forever you'll always mean so much to me
Signed by Ty. 588 produced.
Coral Casino exclusive.
9G - $4,000

Coreana™
#4629

Birthday: 10/3/2002
Introduced: 4/28/2003
Retired: 11/7/2003
Made it to the worldcup semifinals
My country is Daehanminguk
Pride of Asia
It is where your dreams come true
Korea exclusive.
11G - $20

Cornbread™
#4704

Birthday: 7/3/2003
Introduced: 9/29/2003
Retired: 12/26/2003
No matter how near or far you roam
You'll always find a taste of home
So stop on by and take a rest
This cornbread is the very best!
Cracker Barrel exclusive.
11G - $7

Cornstalk™
#40614

Birthday: 11/10/2006
Introduced: 3/30/2007
Current
Both on the cob or from a can
I'll eat it right out of the pan
I love corn, what can I say
To me it's tastier than hay!
15G - Current Retail Value

Corsage™
#40046

Birthday: 4/12/2003
Introduced: 12/30/2003
Retired: 7/16/2004
I thought to brighten up your day
I'd give to you a nice bouquet
Something to wear on your wrist
I'm the corsage you can't resist!
12G - $7

Cottonball™
#4511

Birthday: 8/30/2001
Introduced: 12/27/2001
Retired: 4/8/2002
Most bunnies like to hop around
They like to leap and love to bound
But the thing that I love best
Is lying back to take a rest!
7G - $7 ♥ 10G - $7

Count™
#40116

Birthday: 9/8/2003
Introduced: 8/30/2004
Retired: 10/27/2004
When the Halloween fun ends
I like to gather with my friends
Into a pile we'll put our sweets
So we can count up all our treats!
12G - $7

Countdown™ (10, 9, 8)
#44027

Birthday: 1/1/2005
Introduced: 12/2/2004
Retired: 1/31/2005
As we count down to the New Year
Come on, join in, begin to cheer
We'll start it off with 10, 9, 8
2005 will sure be great!
Ty Store exclusive.
12G - $10

Countdown™ (7, 6, 5, 4)
#44027

Birthday: 1/1/2005
Introduced: 12/2/2004
Retired: 1/31/2005
As we count down to the New Year
Come on, join in, begin to cheer
We're down to 7, 6, 5, and 4
2005 has good things in store!
Ty Store exclusive.
12G - $10

Countdown™ (3, 2, 1)
#44027

Birthday: 1/1/2005
Introduced: 12/2/2004
Retired: 1/31/2005
As we count down to the New Year
Come on, join in, begin to cheer
Nothing left but 3, 2, 1
2005 will be great fun!
Ty Store exclusive.
12G - $35

Countess™
#48401

Birthday: 6/00/2006
Introduced: 6/1/2004
Retired: 7/1/2004
I am a lady, quite refined
Very gentle and very kind
A Countess has great grace and style
Join me for tea and chat awhile!
June 2004 Beanie Baby of the Month.
BBOM - $7

Courage™
#4515 · flag on right or left leg

Birthday: None
Introduced: 10/12/2001
Retired: 7/25/2002
To honor our heroes who lost their lives in the
national catastrophe that
took place on September 11, 2001.
We mourn for them and express our deepest
sympathy to their families.
God Bless America
*Available in Japan with Japanese
writing on hang tag.*
9G - $8

Courage™
#4515 · flag on right leg

Birthday: None
Introduced: 10/12/2001
Retired: 7/25/2002
To honor our heroes who lost their lives in the
national catastrophe that
took place on September 11, 2001.
We mourn for them and express our deepest
sympathy to their families.
God Bless America
Ty Store exclusive.
9G - $7

Courageous™
#46083

Birthday: None
Introduced: 10/31/2006
Current
Let me win,
but if I cannot win,
let me be brave in the attempt!
Canada exclusive.
14G - $18

Courageous™
#47043

Birthday: None
Introduced: 10/10/2006
Current
Let me win,
but if I cannot win,
let me be brave in the attempt!
Limited to 1000.
Special Olympics Canada exclusive.
14G - $150

Courageous™
#47043

Birthday: None
Introduced: 12/6/2006
Current
Let me win,
but if I cannot win,
let me be brave in the attempt!
*Limited to 500. Special Olympics
Canada 1st Annual Festival exclusive*
14G - $80

Courageously™
#46083

Birthday: None
Introduced: 10/31/2006
Current
Let me win,
but if I cannot win,
let me be brave in the attempt!
Canada exclusive.
14G - $18

Courageously™
#47043

Birthday: None
Introduced: 10/10/2006
Current
Let me win,
but if I cannot win,
let me be brave in the attempt!
imited to 1000.
Special Olympics Canada exclusive
14G - $150

Courageously™
#47043

Birthday: None
Introduced: 12/6/2006
Current
Let me win,
but if I cannot win,
let me be brave in the attempt!
Limited to 500. Special Olympics
Canada 1st Annual Festival exclusive
14G - $80

Courageousness™
#46083

Birthday: None
Introduced: 10/31/2006
Current
Let me win,
but if I cannot win,
let me be brave in the attempt!
Canada exclusive.
14G - $18

Courageousness™
#46043

Birthday: None
Introduced: 10/10/2006
Current
Let me win,
but if I cannot win,
let me be brave in the attempt!
Simited to 1000.
Special Olympics Canada exclusive
14G - $150

Courageousness™
#46043

Birthday: None
Introduced: 12/6/2006
Current
Let me win,
but if I cannot win,
let me be brave in the attempt!
Limited to 500. Special Olympics
Canada 1st Annual Festival exclusive.
14G - $80

Creepers™
#4376

Birthday: 10/18/2000
Introduced: 9/3/2001
Retired: 11/12/2001
In your closet I will hide
Until the door is opened wide
You may think that I'll shout "BOO!"
But I just want to play with you!
7G - $7 ♥ 9G - $7

Crinkles™
#40151

Birthday: 10/7/2003
Introduced: 9/30/2004
Retired: 3/24/2005
You can see some by my nose
And also right down near my toes
But, if you please, don't call them wrinkles
I prefer you call them crinkles!
12G/12EU - $7

Croaks™
#40178

Birthday: 12/8/2004
Introduced: 12/30/2004
Retired: 2/24/2005
You will laugh and I will croak
When I tell you this funny joke
What happens when two frogs collide?
What do you think? They get tongue tied!
13G/13EU - $7

Crunch™
#4130

Birthday: 1/13/1996
Introduced: 1/1/1997
Retired: 9/24/1998
What's for breakfast? What's for lunch?
Yum! Delicious! Munch, munch, munch!
He's eating everything by the bunch
That's the reason we named him Crunch!
4G - $7 ♥ 5G - $7

Cubbie™
#4010

Birthday: 11/14/1993
Introduced: 1/8/1994
Retired: 12/31/1997
Cubbie used to eat crackers and honey
And what happened to him was funny
He was stung by fourteen bees
Now Cubbie eats broccoli and cheese!
1G - $2,700 ♥ 2G - $300 ♥ 3G - $60 ♥
4G - $7 ♥ 5G - $7

Cubbie™
#49029

Birthday: 11/14/1993
Introduced: 10/5/2005
Retired: 3/9/2006
Cubbie used to eat crackers and honey
And what happened to him was funny
He was stung by fourteen bees
Now Cubbie eats broccoli and cheese!
*Available in BBOC Original 9
Assortments 1, 2, 4 and 5.
Beanie Baby Official Club exclusive.*
BBOC2 - $10

Cupid™
#4501 · patch on right eye

Birthday: 2/14/2001
Introduced: 2/9/2002
Retired: 3/18/2002
This puppy has a special look
You'll never find him in a book
He'll lick your face, it's very sweet
His kisses are a Valentine treat!
7G - $7 ♥ 9G - $7

Cupid™
#4501 · patch on left eye

Birthday: 2/14/2001
Introduced: 11/30/2001
Retired: 3/18/2002
This puppy has a special look
You'll never find him in a book
He'll lick your face, it's very sweet
His kisses are a Valentine treat!
7G - $7 ♥ 9G - $7

Cure™
#40027

Birthday: 10/1/2003
Introduced: 10/1/2003
Retired: 10/21/2005
To those we've lost and those we love
Our promise is to rise above
We know we'll beat this, that's for sure
Support the cause, help find a cure!
7G - $7 ♥ 11G - $7

Curls™
#40172

Birthday: 8/26/2004
Introduced: 12/30/2004
Retired: 12/29/2005
If you're feeling sad or blue
I know something you can do
With just one little hug from me
You'll feel better instantly!
13G/13EU - $7

Curly™
#4052

Birthday: 4/12/1996
Introduced: 6/15/1996
Retired: 12/31/1998
A bear so cute with hair that's Curly
You will love and want him surely
To this bear always be true
He will be a friend to you!
4G - $7 ♥ 5G - $7

Curtsy™
#40627

Birthday: 11/11/2006
Introduced: 5/31/2007
Current
When I start my movie career
And I'm at my first big premier
I'll cross my legs; bend at the knee
And gracefully do a curtsy!
15G - Current Retail Value

Cutesy™
#40149

Birthday: 4/10/2004
Introduced: 9/30/2004
Retired: 6/29/2005
People try to take care of me
Because I am so small, you see
But I won't always be a pup
Boy, I can't wait 'til I grow up!
12G/12EU - $7

74

D™
#40504

Birthday: None
Introduced: 6/30/2005
Current
Alphabet Bears are issued without poems.
AB - Current Retail Value

Dabbles™
#48424

Birthday: 5/00/2006
Introduced: 5/1/2006
Retired: 6/1/2006
A purple colored bear like me
Surely is a sight to see
But you won't find me in a zoo!
'Cause I would rather live with you!
May 2006 Beanie Baby of the Month.
BBOM - $7

Dad™
#40230 • yellow "A"

Birthday: 6/21/2004
Introduced: 4/29/2005
Retired: 7/27/2005
He'll hug me when I have a fright
Read bedtime stories late at night
He'll make me smile when I am sad
That's why I'm happy he's my dad!
13G/13EU - $7

Dad™
#44051• purple "A"

Birthday: 6/19/2005
Introduced: 5/10/2005
Retired: 6/23/2005
Dad, you are the best there is
At games and sports you are a whiz
You're also kind, and caring, too
I hope you know that I love you!
Ty Store exclusive.
13G - $7

Dad 2006™
#44087

Birthday: 6/18/2006
Introduced: 5/2/2006
Retired: 6/19/2006
My dad's the coolest guy I know
We'll play catch or just go see a show
He helps me with my homework, too
For that and more I say, "Thank you"!
Ty Store exclusive.
14G - $7

Dad 2007™
#44105

Birthday: 6/17/2007
Introduced: 5/9/2007
Current
As dad's go you rate #1
It's true you are second to none
And with your smile and warm embrace
There's no one who can take your place!
Ty Store exclusive.
15G - Current Retail Value

DAD-e™
#4413

Birthday: 6/16/2002
Introduced: 5/17/2002
Retired: 5/18/2002
Dad, you've always been my guide
Through ups and downs you're by my side
This bear is for that "extra mile"
To say, "I love you, Dad" with style!
Ty Store exclusive.
10G - $20

DAD-e 2003™
#4421

Birthday: 6/15/2003
Introduced: 5/12/2003
Retired: 5/14/2003
This is a special teddy bear
To show you, Dad, how much I care
That's why today I give to you
This gift to show my love is true!
Ty Store exclusive.
11G - $10

DAD-e 2004™
#44012

Birthday: 6/20/2004
Introduced: 5/19/2004
Retired: 7/15/2004
You're a super dad, it's true
I know you love me through and through
One day each year we observe
You get the recognition you deserve!
Ty Store exclusive.
12G - $9

Daffodil™
#4624

Birthday: 3/1/2002
Introduced: 10/18/2002
Retired: 1/3/2003
You will find me on the hills
Gathering up daffodils
I will sing my country's song
Every day and all night long!
UK exclusive.
7G - $25

Daichi™
#46090

Birthday: 4/19/2006
Introduced: 1/31/2007
Current
From east to west, from north to south
Sping, summer, autumn, winter
Beautiful country, Japan
That is my daichi!
Japan map. Asian-Pacific exclusive.
15G - $20

Daisy™
#4006

Birthday: 5/10/1994
Introduced: 6/25/1994
Retired: 9/15/1998
Daisy drinks milk each night
So her coat is shiny and bright
Milk is good for your hair and skin
What a way for your day to begin!
1G - $2,500 ♥ 2G - $275 ♥ 3G - $50 ♥
4G - $7 ♥ 5G - $7

Daisy™
#4006 · Harry Caray

Birthday: None
Introduced: 5/3/1998
Retired: 5/3/1998
A friend to many. A legend to all,
The most popular figure in all of baseball,
Crowds would cheer when hearing his name,
Without you Harry, it won't be the same
In memory of Harry Caray
Ty presents Daisy at Wrigley Field,
May 3, 1998
6G - $150

Dancy™
#44113

Birthday: 7/27/2007
Introduced: 7/19/2007
Current
Pretty as flowers in bloom
Sweeter than the best perfume
The perfect gift that you can share
Dancy, the purple panda bear!
Ty Store exclusive.
15G - Current Retail Value

Darling™
#4368

Birthday: 8/22/2000
Introduced: 7/3/2001
Retired: 9/10/2001
How cute can a puppy be?
Pick me up and you will see
I'm soft and cuddly, this is true
Won't you take me home with you?
7G - $7 ♥ 9G - $7

Dart™
#4352

Birthday: 11/22/2000
Introduced: 4/1/2001
Retired: 7/25/2001
In the rainforest you will find
A special frog that's one of a kind
His bright blue color warns a stranger
That his poison could be danger!
7G - $7 ♥ 8G - $7

Dear™
#4706

Birthday: 5/1/2004
Introduced: 4/1/2004
Retired: 4/26/2004
There is no one who can compare
You always show how much you care
For all the things you say and do
With love, I give this gift to you!
Hallmark Gold Crown exclusive.
12G - $7

Dear Dad™
#47051

Birthday: 6/23/2006
Introduced: 3/30/2007
Current
Dear Dad, through thick and also thin
Good times or bad, and lose or win
You're there for me and I'm so glad
I love you and you're my Dear Dad!
Hallmark Gold Crown exclusive.
15G - Current Retail Value

Dear Grandma™
#47050

Birthday: 5/9/2006
Introduced: 3/1/2007
Retired: 5/25/2007
Dear Grandma all the things you do
Tell me how much I mean to you
You're kind and have a gentle touch
Dear Grandma, I love you so much!
Hallmark Gold Crown exclusive.
15G - $9

Dear Grandpa™
#47052

Birthday: 6/26/2006
Introduced: 3/30/2007
Retired:
Current
Dear Grandpa when it's you and me
I'm just as happy as can be
Those fun and silly things you do
Are why, Dear Grandpa, I love you!
Hallmark Gold Crown exclusive.
15G - Current Retail Value

Dear Heart™
#47024

Birthday: 5/12/2005
Introduced: 2/28/2006
Retired: 5/25/2007
Whether she's young, or young at heart
Grandmothers play a special part
Her loving smile's a special treat
A grandma's love is very sweet!
Hallmark Gold Crown exclusive.
14G - $10

Dear Mom™
#47049

Birthday: 5/27/2007
Introduced: 3/1/2007
Retired: 5/25/2007
Dear Mom, I know you're there for me
Helping me be, all I can be
Good times and bad, with grace and calm
That's why I love you my Dear Mom!
Hallmark Gold Crown exclusive.
15G - $7

Dear One™
#47023

Birthday: 5/8/2005
Introduced: 2/28/2006
Retired: 7/25/2006
A mother's love's a precious thing
Such joy and laughter it can bring
For all the many gifts she'll share
Let her know how much you care!
Hallmark Gold Crown exclusive.
14G - $10

Dearest™
#4350

Birthday: 5/8/2000
Introduced: 4/1/2001
Retired: 6/17/2001
You cheer me up when I am blue
You make sure I know what to do
Your gentle words and your sweet touch
Are why I love you very much!
7G - $7 ♥ 8G - $7

Dearly™
#47008

Birthday: 4/14/2004
Introduced: 3/1/2005
Retired: 5/26/2005
This gift was chosen just for you
With love and care that's pure and true
And in my life you'll always be
Someone who means so much to me!
Hallmark Gold Crown exclusive.
13G - $10

Decade™
#4585 · light blue body

Birthday: 1/22/2003
Introduced: 3/14/2003
Retired: 5/19/2003
Ten years ago a toy was created
Around the world, people were elated
Across all ages, colors and races
Beanies would put a smile on their faces!
7G - $10 ♥ 11G - $10

Decade™
#4585 · red body

Birthday: 1/22/2003
Introduced: 3/14/2003
Retired: 10/1/2003
Ten years ago a toy was created
Around the world, people were elated
Across all ages, colors and races
Beanies would put a smile on their faces!
7G - $10 ♥ 11G - $10

Decade™
#4585 · white body

Birthday: 1/22/2003
Introduced: 3/14/2003
Retired: 10/1/2003
Ten years ago a toy was created
Around the world, people were elated
Across all ages, colors and races
Beanies would put a smile on their faces!
7G - $10 ♥ 11G - $10

Decade™
#4585 · dark blue body

Birthday: 1/22/2003
Introduced: 5/29/2003
Retired: 10/1/2003
Ten years ago a toy was created
Around the world, people were elated
Across all ages, colors and races
Beanies would put a smile on their faces!
7G - $10 ♥ 11G - $10

Decade™
#4806 · hot pink body

Birthday: 7/00/2003
Introduced: 7/1/2003
Retired: 8/1/2003
Ten years ago a toy was created
Around the world, people were elated
Across all ages, colors and races
Beanies would put a smile on their faces!
July 2003 Beanie Baby of the Month.
BBOM - $25

Decade™
#4585 · orange body

Birthday: 1/22/2003
Introduced: 8/1/2003
Retired: 11/8/2003
Ten years ago a toy was created
Around the world, people were elated
Across all ages, colors and races
Beanies would put a smile on their faces!
7G - $10 ♥ 11G - $10

Decade™
#4585 · purple body

Birthday: 1/22/2003
Introduced: 9/3/2003
Retired: 11/8/2003
Ten years ago a toy was created
Around the world, people were elated
Across all ages, colors and races
Beanies would put a smile on their faces!
7G - $10 ♥ 11G - $10

Decade™
#4585 · green body

Birthday: 1/22/2003
Introduced: 10/1/2003
Retired: 11/8/2003
Ten years ago a toy was created
Around the world, people were elated
Across all ages, colors and races
Beanies would put a smile on their faces!
7G - $10 ♥ 11G - $10

Decade™
#4585 · gold body

Birthday: 1/22/2003
Introduced: 10/30/2003
Retired: 12/26/2003
Ten years ago a toy was created
Around the world, people were elated
Across all ages, colors and races
Beanies would put a smile on their faces!
7G - $10 ♥ 11G - $10

Decade™
#4585 · brown body

Birthday: 1/22/2003
Introduced: 12/15/2003
Retired: 2/6/2004
Ten years ago a toy was created
Around the world, people were elated
Across all ages, colors and races
Beanies would put a smile on their faces!
Ty Store exclusive.
11G - $10

December™
#4387

Birthday: None
Introduced: 11/1/2001
Retired: 12/31/2001
My nose is the color of my birthstone.
Turquoise - It brings happiness,
creativity and success!
Birthday - $7

December 2002™
#4551

Birthday: None
Introduced: 10/30/2002
Retired: 3/27/2003
Britney Spears - Dec 2
Sir Isaac Newton - Dec 25
Tiger Woods - Dec 30
Birthday - $7

Deke™
#46054

Birthday: 1/26/2004
Introduced: 1/31/2006
Current
I'll move left, then a quick move right
Skating fast, like I'm in flight
I'll score once, or maybe twice
'Cause I'm the best out on the ice!
Canada exclusive.
14G - $15

Deke™ Key-clip
#46077

Birthday: None
Introduced: 7/31/2006
Current
He shoots . . . He scores!
Canada exclusive.
14sm - Current Retail Value

Delights™
#44049

Birthday: 6/7/2004
Introduced: 5/5/2005
Retired: 8/25/2005
Ice cream, cookies, all kinds of sweets
These are my most favorite treats
But these delights cannot compare
To having friends with whom to share!
Pinky shipped with Beanie tag.
Ty Store exclusive.
13G - $150

Delilah™
#40176

Birthday: 7/13/2004
Introduced: 12/30/2004
Retired: 7/27/2005
Some say I have a regal air
You might call it panache or flair
I think that it's just what makes me
The happy cat I love to be!
13G/13EU - $7

Demure™
#40043

Birthday: 7/11/2003
Introduced: 12/30/2003
Retired: 6/29/2005
Sometimes when people look at me
They think I'm bold and fancy free
Despite my beauty and allure
You'll find I'm shy and quite demure!
12G - $7

Denver™
#40135

Birthday: 11/7/2003
Introduced: 8/28/2004
Retired: 10/14/2004
The Mountains almost touch the sky
That's why we call it "Mile High"
There's more to do here than just ski
Making Denver a great city!
Trade Show exclusive.
12G - $35

Deputy™
#40626

Birthday: 2/6/2007
Introduced: 3/30/2007
Current
Around these parts I am the law
I don't rule with an iron paw
Don't worry while I'm on the force
Unless you are a cat, of course!
15G - Current Retail Value

Derby™
#4008 · fine mane with no star

Birthday: None
Introduced: 6/3/1995
Retired: 10/31/1995
Derby was issued without a poem.
3G - $900

Derby™
#4008 · coarse mane with no star

Birthday: 9/16/1995
Introduced: 6/3/1995
Retired: 12/15/1997
All the other horses used to tattle
Because Derby never wore his saddle
He left the stables, and the horses too
Just so Derby can be with you!
3G - $125 ♥ 4G - $10 ♥ 5G - $10

Derby™
#4008 · coarse mane with star

Birthday: 9/16/1995
Introduced: 12/15/1997
Retired: 12/31/1998
All the other horses used to tattle
Because Derby never wore his saddle
He left the stables, and the horses too
Just so Derby can be with you!
5G - $7

Derby™
#4008 · fur mane with star

Birthday: 9/16/1995
Introduced: 1/1/1999
Retired: 5/26/1999
All the other horses used to tattle
Because Derby never wore his saddle
He left the stables, and the horses too
Just so Derby can be with you!
5G - $7

Derby 132™
#40374

Birthday: 5/6/2006
Introduced: 3/31/2006
Retired: 4/27/2006
The stands erupt with cheers and cries
Thoroughbred's most prestigious prize
Run for the Roses; win, place or show
At the starting gate . . . and off they go!
USA exclusive.
14G - $10

Derby 132™
#40374

Birthday: 5/6/2006
Introduced: 3/31/2006
Retired: 4/27/2006
The stands erupt with cheers and cries
Thoroughbred's most prestigious prize
Run for the Roses; win, place or show
At the starting gate . . . and off they go!
Kentucky Derby exclusive.
14G - $25

Derby 133™
#40479

Birthday: 5/5/2007
Introduced: 12/29/2006
Current
Thoroughbreds at the starting gate
With bated breath the crowd will wait
The Run for the Roses will soon begin
Just can't wait to see who'll win!
USA exclusive.
15G - Current Retail Value

Derby 133™
#40479

Birthday: 5/5/2007
Introduced: 1/12/2007
Current
Thoroughbreds at the starting gate
With bated breath the crowd will wait
The Run for the Roses will soon begin
Just can't wait to see who'll win!
Kentucky Derby exclusive.
15G - $18

Deuce™
#40417

Birthday: 8/28/2006
Introduced: 7/31/2006
Retired: 12/21/2006
As soon as I step on the court
I'm grateful tennis is my sport
Serve and volley; in bounds or out
Best game in town, without a doubt!
USA exclusive.
14G - $7

Deuce™
#47034

Birthday: 8/28/2006
Introduced: 7/31/2006
Retired: 10/25/2006
As soon as I step on the court
I'm grateful tennis is my sport
Serve and volley; in bounds or out
Best game in town, without a doubt!
US Open exclusive.
14G - $45

Deutschland™
#40091 · black nose

Birthday: 5/9/2003
Introduced: 6/30/2004
Retired: 10/27/2004
Black, red, gold is my color
I was born to be cared for
I come from the country
of poets and thinkers
You may collect me or make me a gift!
12G - $9

Deutschland™
#4639 · flag nose

Birthday: 5/9/2003
Introduced: 2/9/2004
Retired: 10/27/2004
"Kloß" and "Soß", "Kassler"- meat and
"Sauerkraut", traditional German beer
German specialties are loved
by everybody here in Germany
and in other countries!
German exclusive.
12G - $15

Diddley™
#4383

Birthday: 7/25/2000
Introduced: 7/31/2001
Retired: 4/8/2002
Whenever I go anywhere
People always stop and stare
They're not trying to be mean
They've never seen a dog that's green!
7G - $7 ♥ 9G - $7

Diego™ (Go Diego Go)
#40423

Birthday: None
Introduced: 10/31/2006
Current
¡Hola! ¡Soy Diego!
Do you want to be an Animal Rescuer with me?
To the rescue!
¡Al rescate!
Also available at Ty Store.
14G - Current Retail Value

Digger™
#4027 · orange body

Birthday: None
Introduced: 6/25/1994
Retired: 6/3/1995
Digger was issued without a poem.
1G - $2,500 ♥ 2G - $650 ♥ 3G - $350

Digger™
#4027 · red body

Birthday: 8/23/1995
Introduced: 6/3/1995
Retired: 5/11/1997
Digging in the sand and walking sideways
That's how Digger spends her days
Hard on the outside but sweet deep inside
Basking in the sun and riding the tide!
3G - $150 ♥ 4G - $40

Diggidy™
#40652

Birthday: 3/18/2007
Introduced: 5/31/2007
Current
I dig a hole so I can hide
All my treasures right inside
And then maybe when I am done
I will dig holes just for fun!
15G - Current Retail Value

Diggs™
#40142

Birthday: 10/17/2003
Introduced: 9/30/2004
Retired: 2/24/2005
I can't find my bone anywhere
Did I bury it here or there?
I think a map would help a lot
Then I'd use X to mark the spot!
12G/12EU - $7

Dimples™
#44061

Birthday: 7/10/2005
Introduced: 10/12/2005
Retired: 11/30/2005
You learned to ride a bike today
The doctor said you're a-okay
You've got your license and straight A's, too
Whatever the reason, I'm happy for you!
Ty Store exclusive.
13G - $7

Dinky™
#4341

Birthday: 9/25/2000
Introduced: 1/1/2001
Retired: 12/31/2001
Alright I know, I'm a little small
But what's so great about being tall?
Soon I'll grow up and you will see
Just how beautiful I will be!
7G - $7 ♥ 8G - $7

Dippy™
#4583 · blue tummy

Birthday: 4/24/2002
Introduced: 1/30/2003
Retired: 5/29/2003
Coloring eggs is so much fun
They look so pretty when you're done
What colors do you like the best?
I like them all; you might have guessed!
7G - $7 ♥ 11G - $7

Dippy™
#4583 · pink tummy

Birthday: 4/24/2002
Introduced: 1/30/2003
Retired: 5/29/2003
Coloring eggs is so much fun
They look so pretty when you're done
What colors do you like the best?
I like them all; you might have guessed!
7G - $7 ♥ 11G - $7

Dippy™
#4583 · yellow tummy

Birthday: 4/24/2002
Introduced: 1/30/2003
Retired: 5/29/2003
Coloring eggs is so much fun
They look so pretty when you're done
What colors do you like the best?
I like them all; you might have guessed!
7G - $7 ♥ 11G - $7

Discover™
#46007

Birthday: 6/20/2004
Introduced: 8/15/2004
Retired: 1/4/2005
Canada, so proud and true
I pledge my loyalty to you
Land of the north, so brave and free
There's no place that I'd rather be!
Canada Show exclusive.
12G - $50

Discover™
#47035 · blue

Birthday: 7/22/2006
Introduced: 7/25/2006
Current
Discover what the future holds
For those who have hopes, dreams and goals
I bring you opportunity
To build a lasting legacy!
Northwestern Mutual exclusive.
14G - $30

Discover™
#47036 · gold

Birthday: 7/22/2006
Introduced: 7/25/2006
Current
Discover what the future holds
For those who have hopes, dreams and goals
I bring you opportunity
To build a lasting legacy!
Northwestern Mutual exclusive.
14G - $30

Divalectable™
#40409

Birthday: 7/7/2006
Introduced: 7/31/2006
Current
When you're a diva, just like me
You dress so everyone can see
You're hip and trendy as can be
I'm just too cute; don't you agree?!
14G - Current Retail Value

Divalectable™ Key-clip
#40670

Birthday: None
Introduced: 6/29/2007
Current
Hot Diva Dog!
15Gsm - Current Retail Value

82

Divalightful™
#40410

Birthday: 11/6/2005
Introduced: 7/31/2006
Current
Divas come and divas go
The best, like me, will always show
The trends and tips to help you glow
So you'll be cute like me, you know!
14G - Current Retail Value

Dizzy™
#4365 · black ears with black spots

Birthday: 10/7/2000
Introduced: 5/31/2001
Retired: 8/8/2001
Black and white is just a bore
I can't stand it anymore
Purple, green or maybe blue
Think I'll see what I can do!
7G - $8 ♥ 8G - $7

Dizzy™
#4365 · black ears with colored spots

Birthday: 10/7/2000
Introduced: 6/19/2001
Retired: 8/8/2001
Black and white is just a bore
I can't stand it anymore
Purple, green or maybe blue
Think I'll see what I can do!
7G - $7 ♥ 8G - $7

Dizzy™
#4365 · black spots, ears, and tail

Birthday: 10/7/2000
Introduced: 12/1/2001
Retired: 8/8/2001
Black and white is just a bore
I can't stand it anymore
Purple, green or maybe blue
Think I'll see what I can do!
Canada exclusive.
8G - $125

Dizzy™
#4365 · colored ears with black spots

Birthday: 10/7/2000
Introduced: 10/9/2001
Retired: 8/8/2001
Black and white is just a bore
I can't stand it anymore
Purple, green or maybe blue
Think I'll see what I can do!
UK exclusive.
7G - $25

Dizzy™
#4365 · colored ears with colored spots

Birthday: 10/7/2000
Introduced: 7/19/2001
Retired: 8/8/2001
Black and white is just a bore
I can't stand it anymore
Purple, green or maybe blue
Think I'll see what I can do!
7G - $8 ♥ 8G - $9

Dizzy™ Key-clip
#40401

Birthday: None
Introduced: 6/30/2006
Current
I'm Seeing Spots!
14sm - Current Retail Value

Doby™
#4110

Birthday: 10/9/1996
Introduced: 1/1/1997
Retired: 12/31/1998
The dog is little but he has might
Keep him close when you sleep at night
He lays around with nothing to do
Until he sees it's time to protect you!
4G - $7 ♥ 5G - $7

Docks™
#40552

Birthday: 9/12/2006
Introduced: 2/28/2007
Current
Swimming in the warm lagoon
Underneath the summer moon
My friends and I will zig and zag
And play a game of water-tag!
15G - Current Retail Value

Docks™ Key-clip
#40559

Birthday: None
Introduced: 3/30/2007
Current
Time for a swim!
15sm - Current Retail Value

Dominion™
#44016

Birthday: 7/1/2004
Introduced: 6/2/2004
Retired: 8/2/2004
Everyone will be invited
In honor of our land united
Won't you join us as we say
Have a nice Canada Day!
Ty Store exclusive.
12G - $15

Doodle™
#4171

Birthday: 3/8/1996
Introduced: 5/11/1997
Retired: 7/12/1997
Listen closely to "cock-a-doodle-doo"
What's the rooster saying to you?
Hurry, wake up sleepy head
We have lots to do, get out of bed!
4G - $12

Doogie™
#40362

Birthday: 8/12/2005
Introduced: 3/31/2006
Current
You could look but you won't see
A better trained dog than Doogie
Any command and he'll obey
Especially if it's "sit" or "stay"!
14G/14UK - Current Retail Value

Dooley™
#40387

Birthday: 6/1/2006
Introduced: 6/30/2006
Retired: 2/27/2007
Please throw that rubber ball to me
And I will catch it...watch and see
Then I will bring it back to you
Playing catch is fun to do!
14G/14UK - $7

Dora™ (China)
#40451

Birthday: None
Introduced: 10/31/2006
Current
Hello from China!
Nee-how!
Let's explore China!
¡ Vamos a explorar a China!
Also available at Ty Store.
14G - Current Retail Value

Dora™ (Dora the Explorer™)
#40327

Birthday: None
Introduced: 2/28/2006
Current
Hi, I'm Dora!
¡ Hola, soy Dora!
Let's explore together!
¡ Vamos a explorar juntos!
Also available at Ty Store.
14G/14UK - Current Retail Value

Dora™ (France)
#40454

Birthday: None
Introduced: 10/31/2006
Current
Greetings from France!
Bonjour!
Let's explore France!
¡ Vamos a explorar a Francia!
Also available at Ty Store.
14G - Current Retail Value

Dora™ (Holiday)
#40445

Birthday: None
Introduced: 9/29/2006
Retired: 12/21/2006
Hi, I'm Dora!
¡Hola, soy Dora!
Merry Christmas!
¡Feliz Navidad!
14G/14UK - $8

Dora™ (Russia)
#40453

Birthday: None
Introduced: 10/31/2006
Current
Hello from Russia!
Preev-yet!
Let's explore Russia!
¡ Vamos a explorar a Rusia!
Also available at Ty Store.
14G - Current Retail Value

Dora™ (Tanzania)
#40452

Birthday: None
Introduced: 10/31/2006
Current
Hello from Tanzania!
Jambo!
Let's explore Africa!
¡ Vamos a explorar a Africa!
Also available at Ty Store.
14G - Current Retail Value

Dora Del Tenis™
#40393

Birthday: None
Introduced: 6/30/2006
Current
Hi, I'm Dora!
¡ Hola, soy Dora!
Let's play tennis together!
¡ Vamos jugar al tenis juntos!
Also available at Ty Store.
14G/14UK - Current Retail Value

Dora Del Tenis™
#47039

Birthday: None
Introduced: 7/21/2006
Retired: 10/25/2006
Hi, I'm Dora!
¡ Hola, soy Dora!
Let's play tennis together!
¡ Vamos jugar al tenis juntos!
US Open exclusive.
14G - $10

Dotson™
#40153

Birthday: 9/2/2004
Introduced: 9/30/2004
Retired: 10/27/2004
People think they're seeing spots
Just look at me and you'll see lots
When running, I look like a blur
Because of the dots on my fur!
12G/12EU - $20

Dotty™
#4100

Birthday: 10/17/1996
Introduced: 5/11/1997
Retired: 12/31/1998
The Beanies all thought it was a big joke
While writing her tag, their ink pen broke
She got in the way, and got all spotty
So now the Beanies call her Dotty!
4G - $7 ♥ 5G - $7

Down Under™
#46093

Birthday: 11/8/2006
Introduced: 1/31/2007
Current
Where kangaroos and emus roam free
An Opera House that looks over the sea
So many things that you won't believe
When you visit won't want to leave
Australian map. Asian-Pacific exclusive.
15G - $20

Dreamer™
#4802

Birthday: 3/00/2003
Introduced: 1/1/2003
Retired: 4/1/2003
Lay your head down and close your eyes
And I'll give you a great surprise
The sweetest dreams I'll give to you
In hopes that they will all come true!
March 2003 Beanie Baby of the Month.
BBOM - $14

Drumstick™
#44026

Birthday: 11/25/2004
Introduced: 11/1/2004
Retired: 12/20/2004
A Thanksgiving treat I'd like to share
Just to show you that I care
A friend like you I do adore
That's what I'm most thankful for!
Ty Store exclusive.
12G - $10

Dublin™
#4576

Birthday: 3/16/2002
Introduced: 12/27/2002
Retired: 5/29/2003
If you found a four-leaf clover
Your days of bad luck would be over
So how long will your luck hold true?
It will as long as I'm with you!
7G - $7 ♥ 11G - $7

DUCK-e™
#4425

Birthday: 6/21/2002
Introduced: 3/24/2003
Retired: 4/28/2003
There is no better way to play
Than splashing in a pond all day
Imagine if you had my luck
That's why I'm such a happy duck!
Ty Store exclusive.
11G - $10

Dundee™
#40190

Birthday: 9/19/2004
Introduced: 12/30/2004
Retired: 12/29/2005
When the Scots dress to the hilt
They will wear a tartan kilt
But I don't, it's no surprise
'Cause they don't make one in my size!
13G/13EU - $12

Durango™
#40087

Birthday: 6/3/2004
Introduced: 6/30/2004
Retired: 12/29/2004
Saddle me up, we'll go for a ride
We'll travel across the countryside
I'll run all day and into the night
I gallop fast so please hold on tight!
12G - $7

Dusty™
#4702

Birthday: 5/4/2003
Introduced: 5/4/2003
Retired: 5/4/2003
Dusty makes his hometown debut
As he proudly wears Cubby blue
A brand new era has begun
And this year will be so much fun!
Promotion at Chicago Cubs games.
With commemorative card - $200.
11G - $185

E™
#40505

Birthday: None
Introduced: 6/30/2005
Current
Alphabet Bears are issued without poems.
AB - Current Retail Value

Early™
#4190

Birthday: 3/20/1997
Introduced: 5/30/1998
Retired: 12/23/1999
Early is a red breasted robin
For a worm he'll soon be bobbin'
Always known as a sign of spring
This happy robin loves to sing!
5G - $7

Ears™
#4018

Birthday: 4/18/1995
Introduced: 1/7/1996
Retired: 5/1/1998
He's been eating carrots so long
Didn't understand what was wrong
Couldn't see the board during classes
Until the doctor gave him glasses!
3G - $50 ♥ 4G - $7 ♥ 5G - $7

Echo™
#4180

Birthday: 12/21/1996
Introduced: 5/11/1997
Retired: 5/1/1998
Echo the dolphin lives in the sea
Playing with her friends, like you and me
Through the waves she echoes the sound
"I'm so glad to have you around!"
4G - $8 ♥ 5G - $7

Echo™
#4180 · "Waves" tush tag

Birthday: 12/21/1996
Introduced: 5/11/1997
Retired: 5/1/1998
Echo the dolphin lives in the sea
Playing with her friends, like you and me
Through the waves she echoes the sound
"I'm so glad to have you around!"
4G - $10

Eggbeart™
#4437

Birthday: 4/11/2004
Introduced: 3/16/2004
Retired: 4/19/2004
This brightly colored egg you see
Is a special gift from me
But just who will I give it to?
Happy Easter...it's for you!
Ty Store exclusive.
12G - $10

Eggbert™
#4232

Birthday: 4/10/1998
Introduced: 1/1/1999
Retired: 7/28/1999
Cracking her shell taking a peek
Look, she's playing hide and seek
Ready or not, here I come
Take me home and have some fun!
5G - $7

Eggerton™
#40048

Birthday: 3/30/2003
Introduced: 1/30/2004
Retired: 4/16/2004
An egg for me, an egg for you
All colored brightly, pink and blue
I think it's really fun to share
I guess I'm just a giving hare!
12G - $9

Eggnog™
#44097

Birthday: 12/25/2006
Introduced: 11/16/2006
Retired: 7/12/2007
By the fireplace, warm and snug
We'll drink some eggnog from a mug
Let's give a toast of holiday cheer
To friends and family, far and near!
Ty Store exclusive.
14G - $8

Eggs™
#4337

Birthday: 4/23/2000
Introduced: 1/1/2001
Retired: 3/23/2001
Decorating eggs is fun to do
Coloring them with pink and blue
Hiding them is lots of fun
Make sure you find every one!
7G - $8 ♥ 8G - $7

Eggs II™
#4510

Birthday: 8/15/2001
Introduced: 12/27/2001
Retired: 4/16/2002
When hiding eggs around the yard
You shouldn't make it very hard
It won't be funny, you'll agree
If one of the eggs you lose is me!
7G - $7 ♥ 10G - $7

Eggs III™
#4581

Birthday: 4/2/2002
Introduced: 1/30/2003
Retired: 4/28/2003
If in your basket you should see
Some chocolate candy and Eggs III
'Though chocolate is a tasty treat
With Eggs III, sweets cannot compete!
7G - $7 ♥ 11G - $7

Eggs 2004™
#40052

Birthday: 4/6/2003
Introduced: 1/30/2004
Retired: 4/16/2004
You can pick which color dye
Just dip the egg and let it dry
We'll color them for you and me
And share them with our family!
12G - $7

Eggs 2005™
#40184

Birthday: 3/31/2004
Introduced: 12/30/2004
Retired: 3/24/2005
It's almost time, I just can't wait
Let's get some eggs to decorate
And when the decorating's done
We can dress up and have more fun!
13G/13EU - $7

Eggs 2006™
#40323

Birthday: 4/16/2006
Introduced: 12/30/2005
Retired: 3/27/2006
Bunnies hopping to and fro
This way, that way, off they go
They've an important Easter task
I'd love to help if they would ask!
14G/14UK - $7

Eggs 2007™
#40496

Birthday: 4/8/2007
Introduced: 1/31/2007
Retired: 5/25/2007
Coloring eggs is what I do
I'll paint them almost any hue
And when I'm done we'll have a treat
Something chocolaty and sweet!
15G - $7

Elfis™
#47058

Birthday: 3/13/2006
Introduced: 11/6/2006
Retired: 3/27/2007
If you are good both day and night
Then you might see this little sprite
Who will bring you good luck and cheer
All throughout the coming year!
Learning Express exclusive.
14G - $9

Employee Bear™
No Style #

Birthday: None
Introduced: 9/13/1997
Retired: 9/13/1997
Employee Bear was issued without
a hang tag and a 2G tush tag.
Variations: red or green ribbon.
Ty Employee exclusive.
2G - $3,000

Enchanting™
#40315

Birthday: 8/6/2005
Introduced: 11/30/2005
Current
A horse as beautiful as me
Enchanting everyone I see
With charm that cannot be denied
Can't help but want me by your side
13G/13UK - Current Retail Value

England™
#4608

Birthday: 10/5/2001
Introduced: 2/3/2002
Retired: 7/8/2002
England is surrounded by the sea
For many, there's no other place to be
It looks quaint and small for its size
Traditionally, that's been its best disguise!
England exclusive.
7G - $20

England™
#46014

Birthday: 6/25/2004
Introduced: 9/5/2004
Retired: 10/8/2004
England's the place that's home to me
From hills, to forest, and to the sea
It's a place from which I do not roam
My beautiful green and pleasant home!
UK exclusive.
12G - $20

Enigma™
#46096

Birthday: 6/15/2006
Introduced: 2/16/2007
Current
Enigma is my name but where is my home
Under the water, is that where I roam?
Do you believe in the myth of Loch Ness
Do I exist, that's anyone's guess!
Loch Ness Shop exclusive.
15UK - $30

Erin™
#4186

Birthday: 3/17/1997
Introduced: 1/31/1998
Retired: 5/21/1999
Named after the beautiful Emerald Isle
This Beanie Baby will make you smile,
A bit of luck, a pot of gold,
Light up the faces, both young and old!
5G - $7

Erin™ Key-clip
#40334

Birthday: None
Introduced: 12/30/2005
Retired: 3/27/2006
Luck O' The Irish!
14sm - $6

Eucalyptus™
#4240

Birthday: 4/28/1999
Introduced: 4/8/1999
Retired: 10/27/1999
Koalas climb with grace and ease
To the top branches of the trees
Sleeping by day under a gentle breeze
Feeding at night on two pounds of leaves!
5G - $7

Ewey™
#4219 · frowning

Birthday: 3/1/1998
Introduced: 1/1/1999
Retired: 7/19/1999
Needles and yarn, Ewey loves to knit
Making sweaters with perfect fit
Happy to make one for you and me
Showing off hers, for all to see!
5G - $7

Ewey™
#4219 · smiling

Birthday: 3/1/1998
Introduced: 1/1/1999
Retired: 7/19/1999
Needles and yarn, Ewey loves to knit
Making sweaters with perfect fit
Happy to make one for you and me
Showing off hers, for all to see!
5G - $7

F™
#40506

Birthday: None
Introduced: 6/30/2005
Current
Alphabet Bears are issued without poems.
AB - Current Retail Value

Fairydust™
#40357

Birthday: 3/24/2006
Introduced: 3/31/2006
Current
I'll spread a bit of fairy dust
Then wave a wand, now that's a must
And with a "POOF," what do you see?
A brand new friend for you . . . that's me!
14G - Current Retail Value

Fairytale™
#40189

Birthday: 11/22/2004
Introduced: 12/30/2004
Retired: 3/24/2005
First I'll give a little wink
Then I'll flip my braid of pink
Next I'll simply spin and twirl
I really love being a girl!
13G/13EU - $7

Fancy™
#40003

Birthday: 12/4/2002
Introduced: 5/29/2003
Retired: 6/24/2004
I have a certain savoir faire
And a sophisticated air
But more than just a pampered pet
I'll be the friend you won't forget!
7G - $7 ♥ 11G - $7

Farley™
#40460

Birthday: 2/15/2006
Introduced: 10/31/2006
Current
Over bonnie hill and dale
I'll run and romp and wag my tail
Outdoors is where I long to be
C'mon with me and we'll run free!
14G/14UK - Current Retail Value

Fauna
#40648

Birthday: 5/19/2007
Introduced: 5/19/2007
Current
All the creatures big and small
I can't help but love them all
In the forest or in the zoo
Let's go and see them, just us two!
15G - Current Retail Value

Fearless™
#46050

Birthday: 10/24/2004
Introduced: 9/4/2005
Retired: 1/24/2007
"Never give in," a great man said
So we'll stand tall and look ahead
And as the masters of our fate
We'll show what makes this country great!
UK exclusive.
13UK - $15

February™
#4389

Birthday: None
Introduced: 12/27/2001
Retired: 4/23/2002
My nose is the color of my birthstone.
Amethyst - It brings prosperity,
excitement and joy!
Birthday - $7

February 2003™
#4553

Birthday: None
Introduced: 12/27/2002
Retired: 4/28/2003
Charles Dickens - Feb 7
Michael Jordan - Feb 17
Jennifer Love-Hewitt - Feb 21
Birthday - $7

Feder -bear™
#40480

Birthday: 8/8/1981
Introduced: 12/29/2006
Current
In tennis, ranked as number one
Playing with skill, but having fun
So try your best and you'll soon see
You'll be the best that you can be!
14G - Current Retail Value

Feder -bear™
#40480

Birthday: 8/8/1981
Introduced: 11/27/2006
Current
ROGER FEDERER
Born August 8, 1981
FEDER-RANK: Roger has been ranked ATP
World No. 1 since February 2004
FEDER-FACT: Roger was appointed Goodwill
Ambassador to UNICEF on April 3, 2006!
Ty Store ATP/Unicef for ACE exclusive.
14G - Current Retail Value

Feder -bear™
#40480

Birthday: 8/8/1981
Introduced: 12/29/2006
Current
In tennis, ranked as number one
Playing with skill, but having fun
So try your best and you'll soon see
You'll be the best that you can be!
Racquet sewn at both ends. UK exclusive.
14UK - $15

Ferny™
#4618

Birthday: 2/6/2002
Introduced: 1/29/2002
Retired: 9/16/2002
I am New Zealand's cute bear
The silver fern I'm proud to wear
Here you will never be far from the sea
Won't you come and join me?
New Zealand exclusive.
10G - $20

Fetch™
#4189

Birthday: 2/4/1997
Introduced: 5/30/1998
Retired: 12/31/1998
Fetch is alert at the crack of dawn
Walking through dew drops on the lawn
Always golden, loyal and true
This little puppy is the one for you!
5G - $7

Fetcher™
#4289

Birthday: 4/27/2000
Introduced: 6/24/2000
Retired: 6/12/2001
Through the house I love to dash
Then I'm back in a flash
Please don't fret, I won't go far
I'm only happy where you are!
6G - $7 ♥ **7G - $7**

Fiddler™
#48408

Birthday: 1/00/2005
Introduced: 1/1/2005
Retired: 2/1/2005
Ever since I was quite little
I wished that I could play the fiddle
I'd practice 'til I got it right
Fiddling all day and night!
January 2005 Beanie Baby of the Month.
BBOM - $12

Fidget™
#40005

Birthday: 1/20/2003
Introduced: 6/30/2003
Retired: 9/5/2003
Can't sit still, just got to move
And keep on dancin' to the groove
I'll keep on shakin' to the beat
I just can't stop my happy feet!
7G - $7 ♥ **11G - $7**

FIFA Champion™
#4408 · Argentina

Birthday: None
Introduced: 4/4/2002
Retired: 6/7/2002
Argentina has participated in twelve of
the sixteen FIFA World Cup
tournaments; 1930-1934,1958-1966, 1974-
1998. Argentina hosted and won the finals
in 1978. They won again in 1986 and
placed second in 1930 and 1990.
7G - $7 ♥ **10G - $7**

FIFA Champion™
#4408 · Belgium

Birthday: None
Introduced: 4/4/2002
Retired: 6/17/2002
Belgium has taken part in ten FIFA World
Cup tournaments: 1930-1938, 1954, 1970,
1982-1998. Belgium was one of hte FIFA's
founding members.
7G - $7 ♥ **10G - $7**

FIFA Champion™
#4408 · Brazil

Birthday: None
Introduced: 4/4/2002
Retired: 6/30/2002
Brazil has more success than any other
nation in the FIFA World Cup , qualifying
for all 16 (1930-1998). Brazil was the first
country to win 3 FIFA World Cup Trophies;
1958, 1962, 1970 & was the runner-up in 1950.
7G - $7 ♥ **10G - $7**

FIFA Champion™
#4408 · Cameroon

Birthday: None
Introduced: 4/4/2002
Retired: 6/11/2002
Cameroon has qualified for four
FIFA World Cup Tournaments.
1982, 1990, 1994, 1998
7G - $7 ♥ **10G - $7**

FIFA Champion™
#4408 · China PR

Birthday: None
Introduced: 4/4/2002
Retired: 6/4/2002
China, the world's most populous nation,
capped the most significant year in its
sporting history when the national soccer
team reached the FIFA World Cup Finals for
the first time.
7G - $7 ♥ **10G - $7**

FIFA Champion™
#4408 · Costa Rica

Birthday: None
Introduced: 4/4/2002
Retired: 6/13/2002
Costa Rica clinched its first FIFA
World Cup berth since 1990,
totally outplaying a U.S. team that
only twice came close to scoring.
7G - $7 ♥ 10G - $7

FIFA Champion™
#4408 · Croatia

Birthday: None
Introduced: 4/4/2002
Retired: 6/3/2002
Croatia finished third in the 1998 FIFA
World Cup held in France. Davor Suker
won the title of Best Scorer at World
Cup '98 in France.
7G - $7 ♥ 10G - $7

FIFA Champion™
#4408 · Denmark

Birthday: None
Introduced: 4/4/2002
Retired: 6/15/2001
Denmark has qualified for the FIFA
World Cup twice before; in 1986
and 1998, reaching the quarter finals
in France where they lost 3-2 Brazil.
7G - $7 ♥ 10G - $7

FIFA Champion™
#4408 · Ecuador

Birthday: None
Introduced: 4/4/2002
Retired: 6/3/2002
Ecuador has never played at a FIFA
World Cup and they have never beaten
Brazil. Ecuador produced a stunning upset
when they beat four-time champions Brazil 1-0
in a FIFA World Cup qualifier.
7G - $7 ♥ 10G - $7

FIFA Champion™
#4408 · England

Birthday: None
Introduced: 4/4/2002
Retired: 6/21/2002
England won the FIFA World Cup Title in
1966 on their home soil and is currently
ranked 9th in the FIFA World Rankings.
7G - $7 ♥ 10G - $7

FIFA Champion™
#4408 · France

Birthday: None
Introduced: 4/4/2002
Retired: 5/31/2002
France made football history as the
host country when they beat the
defending champions Brazil 3-0 to
win the 1998 FIFA World Cup.
7G - $7 ♥ 10G - $7

FIFA Champion™
#4408 · Germany

Birthday: None
Introduced: 4/4/2002
Retired: 6/30/2002
Germany appeared in 14 of the 16 FIFA
World Cup tournaments (1934-1938,1954-
1998). Germany is one of the only three
countries to win three FIFA World Cup Trophies (1954, 1974, 1990). The other 2
countries are Brazil & Italy.
7G - $7 ♥ 10G - $7

FIFA Champion™
#4408 · Republic of Ireland

Birthday: None
Introduced: 4/4/2002
Retired: 6/16/2002
Ireland qualified for their first FIFA World
Cup final,traveling to Italy in 1990. Ireland
qualified for the 1994 FIFA World Cup with a
1-1 draw to Northern Ireland.
7G - $7 ♥ 10G - $7

FIFA Champion™
#4408 · Italy

Birthday: None
Introduced: 4/4/2002
Retired: 6/8/2002
Founded in 1898, Italy is one of the
three countries known as one of the
FIFA World Cup tournaments most
honored nations. The other two
countries are Brazil and Germany.
7G - $7 ♥ 10G - $7

FIFA Champion™
#4408 · Japan

Birthday: None
Introduced: 4/4/2002
Retired: 6/18/2002
As host to the 2002 FIFA World Cup along with Korea, Japan is a relative newcomer to the competition. The country first qualified for a FIFA World Cup berth in the 1998 games in France.
7G - $7 ♥ 10G - $7

FIFA Champion™
#4408 · Japan with Japanese writing

Birthday: None
Introduced: 4/4/2002
Retired: 6/18/2002
Same phrase written in Japanese.
10G - $18

FIFA Champion™
#4408 · Republic of Korea

Birthday: None
Introduced: 4/4/2002
Retired: 6/25/2002
The 2002 FIFA World Cup will make the sixth appearance at the finals for the year's co-host. The Korea Republic set an Asian record when they reached the finals five times in a row.
7G - $7 ♥ 10G - $7

FIFA Champion™
#4408 · Republic of Korea with Korean writing

Birthday: None
Introduced: 4/4/2002
Retired: 6/25/2002
Same phrase written in Korean.
10G - $18

FIFA Champion™
#4408 · Mexico

Birthday: None
Introduced: 4/4/2002
Retired: 6/17/2002
Turkey reaches their first ever UEFA European Championship in 1996 & made it to the quarter-final stage of the corresponding tournament in 2000. Turkey now seems set to make a mark on the world stage
7G - $7 ♥ 10G - $7

FIFA Champion™
#4408 · Nigeria

Birthday: None
Introduced: 4/4/2002
Retired: 6/2/2002
The Super Eagles have long been regarded as Africa's best hope for FIFA World Cup success. On both previous appearances in the finals, they have made it to the last round before having their hopes thwarted
.7G - $7 ♥ 10G - $7

FIFA Champion™
#4408 · Paraguay

Birthday: None
Introduced: 4/4/2002
Retired: 6/7/2002
France 1998 was Paraguay's first return to the FIFA World Cup since 1986. In the early stages of qualifying they went 9 games without defeat after an initial loss against Columbia
.7G - $7 ♥ 10G - $7

FIFA Champion™
#4408 · Poland

Birthday: None
Introduced: 4/4/2002
Retired: 6/4/2002
Poland has made it to their first FIFA World Cup in 16 years, last qualifying for the finals in 1986. Poland received 13 FIFA World Cup qualifying points. They scored 13 goals. The player who scored the 13th goal was #13 and he was born the 13th day of the month.
7G - $7 ♥ 10G - $7

FIFA Champion™
#4408 · Portugal

Birthday: None
Introduced: 4/4/2002
Retired: 6/5/2002
Portugal was the second team to qualify for the FIFA World Cup tournament. This will be Portugal's third time competing in the FIFA World Cup. Portugal last qualified last in 1986
.7G - $7 ♥ 10G - $7

FIFA Champion™
#4408 · Russia

Birthday: None
Introduced: 4/4/2002
Retired: 6/9/2002
As Russia, this team has not competed in the FIFA World Cup although as part of the Soviet Union it had a hand in 7 finals.
7G - $7 ♥ 10G - $7

FIFA Champion™
#4408 · Saudi Arabia

Birthday: None
Introduced: 4/4/2002
Retired: 6/1/2002
Saudi Arabia first attempted to qualify for the FIFA World Cup in 1978. It lost to Iran and was eliminated. Qualification for the 1994 FIFA World Cup came when Saudi Arabia beat Iran 4-2. Saudi Arabia took part in 2 FIFA World Cup tournaments (1994, 1998).
7G - $7 ♥ 10G - $7

FIFA Champion™
#4408 · Senegal

Birthday: None
Introduced: 4/4/2002
Retired: 6/22/2002
Qualifying for the first time by beating Namibia 5-0, Senegal now becomes the fourth African country to clinch a spot in this FIFA World Cup tournament.
7G - $7 ♥ 10G - $7

FIFA Champion™
#4408 · Slovenia

Birthday: None
Introduced: 4/4/2002
Retired: 6/2/2002
A nation still in the infancy of it's independence, Slovenia was admitted as a member of UEFA and FIFA in 1992, one year after declaring its independence from Yugoslavia.
7G - $7 ♥ 10G - $7

FIFA Champion™
#4408 · South Africa

Birthday: None
Introduced: 4/4/2002
Retired: 6/12/2002
In the past 10 years, the country has emerged as a strong power on the African continent. South Africa qualified for the last FIFA World Cup finals in France.
7G - $7 ♥ 10G - $7

FIFA Champion™
#4408 · Spain

Birthday: None
Introduced: 4/4/2002
Retired: 6/22/2002
Spain served as host for the 1982 FIFA World Cup and has participated in ten FIFA World Cup tournaments: 1934, 1950, 1962-1966, 1978-1990, 1994,1998.
7G - $7 ♥ 10G - $7

FIFA Champion™
#4408 · Sweden

Birthday: None
Introduced: 4/4/2002
Retired: 6/16/2002
In 1958 Sweden hosted the first FIFA World Cup to receive international television coverage. Sweden has taken part in 8 FIFA World Cup tournaments; 1934-1950, 1958, 170-1978, 1990.
7G - $7 ♥ 10G - $7

FIFA Champion™
#4408 · Tunisia

Birthday: None
Introduced: 4/4/2002
Retired: 6/5/2002
Tunisia reached the 2002 FIFA World Cup finals with a 3-0 win over the Democratic Republic of Congo in Kinshasa and the failure of the Ivory Coast to beat Congo.
7G - $7 ♥ 10G - $7

FIFA Champion™
#4408 · Turkey

Birthday: None
Introduced: 4/4/2002
Retired: 6/3/2002
Turkey reaches their first ever UEFA European Championship in 1996 & made it to the quarter-final stage of the corresponding tournament in 2000. Turkey now seems set to make a mark on the world stage
7G - $7 ♥ 10G - $7

FIFA Champion™
#4408 · Uruguay

Birthday: None
Introduced: 4/4/2002
Retired: 6/1/2002
In 1930 in Uruguay, 13 countries participated in the first FIFA World Cup. The So. American final was between Uruguay & Argentina. Uruguay was down 2-1 at half time but scored 3 goals in the second half, ending the game with a 4-2 victory.
7G - $7 ♥ 10G - $7

FIFA Champion™
#4408 · USA

Birthday: None
Introduced: 4/4/2002
Retired: 6/14/2002
The United States has participated in 5 FIFA World CupTM tournaments (1930, 1934,1950 1990 and 1994). The best finish by a US team in the FIFA World Cup play was third place in the 1930 tournament. In 1950, the US enjoyed its most celebrated FIFA World CupTM moment with a 1-0 upset win over England. And, in 1994, many people were surprised when the US was asked to host the 15th FIFA World Cup.
7G - $7 ♥ 10G - $7

Filly™
#4592

Birthday: 7/16/2002
Introduced: 3/31/2003
Retired: 6/24/2004
I love to run across the plain
With the wind blowing through my mane
Hop on my back and ride with me
It's fun running wild and free!
7G - $7 ♥ 11G - $7

Finn™
#40394

Birthday: 5/14/2006
Introduced: 6/30/2006
Current
If you should see that tell-tale fin
Soon followed by a toothy grin
Then black eyes and a pointed snout
Be careful! There are sharks about!
14G/14UK - Current Retail Value

Finn™
#40394

Birthday: 5/14/2006
Introduced: 7/1/2006
Retired: 10/25/2006
If you should see that tell-tale fin
Soon followed by a toothy grin
Then black eyes and a pointed snout
Be careful! There are sharks about!
Sold out on August 20th.
Ty Store/Sea Center exclusive.
14G - $10

Fins™
#40033

Birthday: 3/4/2003
Introduced: 10/30/2003
Retired: 7/16/2004
My playground is the artic sea
There is no place I'd rather be
I'll sunbathe on the rocky shore
And then dive in and swim some more!
7G - $7 ♥ 11G - $7

Fireplug™
#48405

Birthday: 10/00/2004
Introduced: 9/28/2004
Retired: 11/1/2004
The fire engine is my post
A dog like me is unlike most
My friends will always save the day
And keep you out of harm's way!
October 2004 Beanie Baby of the Month.
BBOM - $7

Fireworks™
#43438

Birthday: 7/00/2007
Introduced: 7/1/2007
Current
Across our nation's countryside
Americans all show their pride
When fireworks light up the sky
Each year on the Fourth of July!
July 2007 Beanie Baby of the Month.
BBOM - $10

First Dog™
#44088

Birthday: 7/4/2006
Introduced: 6/5/2006
Retired: 1/16/2007
I'll sit up tall, paw on my heart
Then I will proudly say my part
As First Dog join me to say
Happy Birthday U.S.A.!
Ty Store exclusive.
14G - $7

Fitz™
#40097

Birthday: 1/10/2004
Introduced: 6/30/2004
Retired: 10/27/2004
My fur is colored chestnut red
But what if I was blonde instead
Or brunette might me really cool
No, not for me, 'cause redheads rule!
12G - $7

Fizz™
#4983

Birthday: 2/16/2003
Introduced: 8/9/2003
Retired: 11/25/2003
The Beanie Babies celebrate
Ty marks this most auspicious date
Lift your glass and raise it high
10 years of Beanies . . . Here's to Ty!
Trade Show exclusive.
11G - $7

Flaky™
#4572

Birthday: 1/31/2002
Introduced: 11/27/2002
Retired: 1/9/2003
The falling snow has just begun
It's wintertime, and it's such fun
Snowball fights, snow angels, too
Outdoors all day 'til I am blue!
7G - $7 ♥ 10G - $7

Flash™
#4021

Birthday: 5/13/1993
Introduced: 1/8/1994
Retired: 5/11/1997
You know dolphins are a smart breed
Our friend Flash knows how to read
Splash the whale is the one who taught her
Although reading is difficult under the water!
**1G - $2,300 ♥ 2G - $285 ♥
3G - $70 ♥ 4G - $35**

Flash™
#49019

Birthday: 5/13/1993
Introduced: 10/3/2005
Retired: 3/9/2006
You know dolphins are a smart breed
Our friend Flash knows how to read
Splash the whale is the one who taught her
Although reading is difficult under the water!
*Available in BBOC Original 9
Assortments 1-5.
Beanie Baby Offcial Club exclusive.*
BBOC2 - $10

Flashy™
#4339

Birthday: 12/30/2000
Introduced: 1/1/2001
Retired: 3/27/2001
More colorful than the rest of the crowd
It's easy to see why he's so proud
He struts his stuff for all to see
It's like he's saying, "Look At Me!"
7G - $7 ♥ 8G - $7

Fleece™
#4125

Birthday: 3/21/1996
Introduced: 1/1/1997
Retired: 12/31/1998
Fleece would like to sing a lullaby
But please be patient, she's rather shy
When you sleep, keep her by your ear
Her song will leave you nothing to fear.
4G - $7 ♥ 5G - $7

Fleecie™
#4279

Birthday: 1/26/2000
Introduced: 3/1/2000
Retired: 7/14/2000
Fleecie is cuddly and soft as can be
Give her a hug and then you will see
When you hold her close to your ear
You'll hear her whisper "I love you, dear!"
6G - $7 ♥ 7G - $7

Fleur™
#40143

Birthday: 5/28/2004
Introduced: 9/30/2004
Retired: 12/29/2005
I love to smell the pretty flowers
When they bloom after spring showers
Guess that's how I got my name
'Cause Fleur and flower are the same!
12G/12EU - $7

Flicker™
#48419

Birthday: 12/00/2005
Introduced: 12/1/2005
Retired: 1/3/2006
At night when everyone's asleep
I'll get up; won't make a peep
I'll wait by flickering candlelight
To see if Santa comes tonight!
December 2005
Beanie Baby of the Month.
BBOM - $7

Flip™
#4012

Birthday: 2/28/1995
Introduced: 1/7/1996
Retired: 10/1/1997
Flip the cat is an acrobat
She loves playing on her mat
This cat flips with such grace and flair
She can somersault in mid air!
3G - $60 ♥ 4G - $9

Flitter™
#4255

Birthday: 6/2/1999
Introduced: 7/14/1999
Retired: 12/23/1999
I did not know what I was to be
Covered in fuzz, it was hard to see
Now a butterfly, what a beautiful sight
On silken wings I take to flight!
5G - $7

Float™
#4343

Birthday: 11/12/2000
Introduced: 3/1/2001
Retired: 4/11/2001
She flitters and flies and floats around
Graceful and lovely, not making a sound
Although she flies both near and far
She'll always return to where you are!
7G - $7 ♥ 8G - $7

Floppity™
#4118

Birthday: 5/28/1996
Introduced: 1/1/1997
Retired: 5/1/1998
Floppity hops from here to there
Searching for eggs without a care
Lavender coat from head to toe
All dressed up and nowhere to go!
4G - $7 ♥ 5G - $7

Flora™
#40647

Birthday: 3/9/2007
Introduced: 5/31/2007
Current
I love the green leaves on the trees
When flowers bloom and buzzing bees
There's so much beauty you can see
Come take a nature walk with me!
15G - Current Retail Value

Florida™
#40147

Birthday: None
Introduced: 8/30/2004
Retired: 12/29/2005
STATE MOTTO: "In God We Trust"
NICKNAME: Sunshine State
FACT: The St. John's River is 1 of only 3
rivers in the U.S. that flows north
instead of south!
Sold only in Florida.
12G - $7

Floxy™
#40498

Birthday: 1/11/2007
Introduced: 1/31/2007
Current
The other sheep will all attest
This lamb is unlike all the rest
Strong, determined, full of moxie
That's the one we all call Floxy!
15G - Current Retail Value

Fluff™
#40236

Birthday: 11/20/2005
Introduced: 12/30/2005
Retired: 1/27/2006
Get some string or a toy mouse
And we can play around the house
We can do tons of cool stuff
With my best friends, Muff & Pluff!
14G/14UK - $7

Flurry™
#47015

Birthday: 12/2/2005
Introduced: 10/24/2005
Retired: 12/29/2005
When snow flurries fall during the day
It's time to go outside and play
Grab your scarf so we don't get chilly
Let's go sledding and act real silly!
Learning Express exclusive.
13G - $7

Flutter™
#4043

Birthday: None
Introduced: 6/3/1995
Retired: 6/15/1996
Flutter was issued without a poem
3G - $395

Forever Friends™
#40530

Birthday: None
Introduced: 4/28/2006
Current
Greetings Bears are issued without poems.
14G - Current Retail Value

Fortress™
#40650

Birthday: 5/22/2007
Introduced: 5/31/2007
Current
Pixies, elves and fairy dust
Of course, a princess is a must
A gallant knight will soon appear
My life's a fairy tale here!
15G - Current Retail Value

Fortune™
#4196

Birthday: 12/6/1997
Introduced: 5/30/1998
Retired: 8/24/1999
Nibbling on a bamboo tree
This little panda is hard to see
You're so lucky with this one you found
Only a few are still around!
5G - $7

Founders™
#48414

Birthday: 7/00/2005
Introduced: 7/1/2005
Retired: 8/1/2005
The founding fathers did agree
Americans should all be free
And so we have a special day
To honor the U.S. of A.!
July 2005 Beanie Baby of the Month.
BBOM - $7

Fraidy™
#4379

Birthday: 10/13/2000
Introduced: 9/3/2001
Retired: 11/12/2001
Superstitious people fear
I'll bring bad luck if I am near
But I'm not into all of that
I'm really just a happy cat!
7G - $7 ♥ 9G - $7

Frankenteddy™
#4562 · blue left and orange right foot

Birthday: 10/31/2001
Introduced: 8/29/2002
Retired: 10/24/2002
It's Halloween-that scary night
When Jack-O-Lanterns glow with light
Come with us and Trick or Treat
Let's see how many friends we meet!
7G - $7 ♥ 10G - $7

Frankenteddy™
#4562 · blue left and purple right foot

Birthday: 10/31/2001
Introduced: 8/29/2002
Retired: 10/24/2002
It's Halloween-that scary night
When Jack-O-Lanterns glow with light
Come with us and Trick or Treat
Let's see how many friends we meet!
7G - $7 ♥ 10G - $7

Frankenteddy™
#4562 · blue left and red right foot

Birthday: 10/31/2001
Introduced: 8/29/2002
Retired: 10/24/2002
It's Halloween-that scary night
When Jack-O-Lanterns glow with light
Come with us and Trick or Treat
Let's see how many friends we meet!
7G - $7 ♥ 10G - $7

Frankenteddy™
#4562 · green left and blue right foot

Birthday: 10/31/2001
Introduced: 8/29/2002
Retired: 10/24/2002
It's Halloween-that scary night
When Jack-O-Lanterns glow with light
Come with us and Trick or Treat
Let's see how many friends we meet!
7G - $7 ♥ 10G - $7

Frankenteddy™
#4562 · purple left and green right foot

Birthday: 10/31/2001
Introduced: 8/29/2002
Retired: 10/24/2002
It's Halloween-that scary night
When Jack-O-Lanterns glow with light
Come with us and Trick or Treat
Let's see how many friends we meet!
7G - $7 ♥ 10G - $7

Frankenteddy™
#4562 · purple left and red right foot

Birthday: 10/31/2001
Introduced: 8/29/2002
Retired: 10/24/2002
It's Halloween-that scary night
When Jack-O-Lanterns glow with light
Come with us and Trick or Treat
Let's see how many friends we meet!
7G - $7 ♥ 10G - $7

Freckles™
#4066

Birthday: 6/3/1996
Introduced: 6/15/1996
Retired: 12/31/1998
From the trees he hunts prey
In the night and in the day
He's the king of camouflage
Look real close, he's no mirage!
Also has birthday of July 28, 1996.
4G - $7 ♥ 5G - $7

Free™
#40237

Birthday: 6/20/2004
Introduced: 4/29/2005
Retired: 10/21/2005
If you gaze high up in the sky
Then you might see me flying by
Its quite a feeling to be so free
Something we are grateful to be!
13G/13EU - $7

Free™
#44052

Birthday: 7/4/2005
Introduced: 6/2/2005
Retired: 9/27/2005
Over the hills and through the valleys
Across the city streets and alleys
From city to town and sea to sea
Home of the brave and land of the free!
Ty Store exclusive.
13G - $10

Freezie™
#40439

Birthday: 12/20/2005
Introduced: 9/29/2006
Retired: 12/21/2006
When the temps all drop down low
And there's lots of ice and snow
That's when you'll see me appear
And you'll know that winter's here!
14G - $7

Freiherr von Schwarz™
#4611

Birthday: 6/17/2001
Introduced: 1/31/2002
Retired: 5/3/2002
In the dark night
Baron von Schwarz is protecting you.
The luminous morning will then come
And all your sorrows will be gone.
German exclusive.
7G - $35

Fridge™
#4579

Birthday: 11/10/2002
Introduced: 12/27/2002
Retired: 5/25/2004
Way out among the iceberg caps
Is where I love to make my naps
I won't be cold out in the snow
My coat will keep me warm, you know!
7G - $7 ♥ 11G - $7

Fridge™
#4579

Birthday: 11/10/2002
Introduced: 7/31/2004
Retired: 8/1/2004
Way out among the iceberg caps
Is where I love to make my naps
I won't be cold out in the snow
My coat will keep me warm, you know!
Brookfield Zoo promotional item.
11G - $75

Friedrich™
#46033

Birthday: 12/1/2004
Introduced: 5/31/2005
Retired: 9/23/2005
From the Alps to the Ostseestrand,
historic cities known worldwide.
A Land - romantic and modern,
we love Football and poetry.
13EU - $20

Friends™
#44109

Birthday: None
Introduced: 7/5/2007
Current
This gift is just for you, you see
Because you mean so much to me
Through thick and thin, until the end
I know you'll always be my friend!
Ty Store exclusive.
15G - Current Retail Value

Frightful™
#47031

Birthday: 9/1/2006
Introduced: 9/1/2006
Retired: 10/25/2006
Though ghosts and ghouls might lurk about
And make you want to shriek or shout
This Halloween you shouldn't fear
Because Frightful the cat is here!
Borders/Walden exclusive.
14G - $7

Frigid™
#4270

Birthday: 1/23/2000
Introduced: 3/1/2000
Retired: 12/15/2000
Waddling on the slippery ice
Frigid thinks the cold is nice
He jumps into the water below
Then does it again, he loves it so!
6G - $7 ♥ 7G - $7

Frills™
#4367

Birthday: 3/5/2001
Introduced: 5/31/2001
Retired: 6/18/2001
I wear a frill upon my head
Soft and fuzzy, it's very red
Don't know what it's there to do
No one seems to know, do you?
7G - $7 ♥ 8G - $7

Frisbee™
#4508

Birthday: 6/29/2001
Introduced: 1/29/2002
Retired: 12/27/2002
Throw the disc and watch me go
I'll always bring it back, you know
To me this game is always new
You'll get tired before I do!
7G - $7 ♥ 10G - $7

Frisbee™
#4508 · Wham-O hang tag

Birthday: 6/29/2001
Introduced: 1/29/2002
Retired: 12/27/2002
Throw the Frisbee and watch me go
I'll always bring it back, you know
To me this game is always new
You'll get tired before I do!
10G - $150

Frisco™
#4586

Birthday: 9/7/2002
Introduced: 2/28/2003
Retired: 6/24/2004
A squeaky toy or ball of string
I'll play with almost anything
But my favorite thing to do
Is snuggle up and nap with you!
7G - $7 ♥ 11G - $7

Frisky™
#48416

Birthday: 9/00/2005
Introduced: 9/1/2005
Retired: 10/3/2005
I'm so eager to greet the day
Because I just can't wait to play
I'm full of life and energy
Guess that's why I'm named Frisky!
September 2005
Beanie Baby of the Month.
BBOM - $10

Fritters™
#48410

Birthday: 3/00/2005
Introduced: 3/1/2005
Retired: 4/1/2005
As I hop down your street or lane
What is my goal? Well, it's quite plain
Delivering treats to all I see
I think I'll save one just for me!
March 2005 Beanie Baby of the Month.
BBOM - $7

Frolic™
#4519

Birthday: 6/28/2001
Introduced: 3/1/2002
Retired: 6/25/2002
Please take me to the park today
Where I can run and jump and play
It's so much fun to be with you
I hope you feel the same way too!
7G - $7 ♥ 10G - $7

Frosty™
#40009

Birthday: 12/7/2002
Introduced: 6/30/2003
Retired: 5/25/2004
In Arizona, riding high
You might just see me passing by
Walking along with my Ty friends
In Scottsdale the fun never ends!
7G - $7 ♥ 11G - $7

Fuddle™
#40625

Birthday: 2/25/2007
Introduced: 4/30/2007
Current
Sometimes I get a little muddled
Confused and even quite befuddled
But even still I always try
It helps to have a friend nearby!
15G - Current Retail Value

Fumbles™
#40171

Birthday: 9/1/2004
Introduced: 12/30/2004
Retired: 12/29/2005
Through the jungle, high and low
Up and down and around I go
Look at me swing from tree to tree
Won't you come and play with me?
13G/13EU - $7

Fun™
#40383

Birthday: 2/12/2006
Introduced: 4/28/2006
Retired: 6/23/2006
20 years of laughter and smiles
From coast to coast, across the miles
20 years of hugs and such fun
C'mon . . . join in! We've just begun!
20th Anniversary Bear.
14G/14UK - $10

Fun™ Key-clip
No Style

Birthday: None
Introduced: 8/23/2006
Retired: 1/24/2007
20 years of fun from our hearts to yours
NY Show 2/12-2/15/06 and
Dallas Show 6/23-6/26/06.
14sm - $25

Funky™
#40413

Birthday: 1/30/2006
Introduced: 7/31/2006
Current
Some people think I'm out of sight
Because my colors are so bright
I think I'm funky as can be
One look at me and you'll agree!
14G - Current Retail Value

Furston™
#40434

Birthday: 11/18/2005
Introduced: 8/31/2006
Current
When I get older I will be
The best sheepdog you'll ever see
We'll play and laugh and jump and leap
Until I have to herd some sheep!
14G/14UK - Current Retail Value

Fussy™
#40086

Birthday: 2/15/2004
Introduced: 6/30/2004
Retired: 10/27/2004
I'm fussy about what I wear
And the bows I put in my hair
I really liket o look just right
I think that I am quite a sight!
12G - $7

Fuzz™
#4237

Birthday: 7/23/1998
Introduced: 1/1/1999
Retired: 12/23/1999
Look closely at this handsome bear
His texture is really quite rare.
With golden highlights in his hair
He has class, style and flair!
5G - $7

G™
#40507

Birthday: None
Introduced: 6/30/2005
Current
Alphabet Bears are issued without poems.
AB - Current Retail Value

Garcia™
#4051

Birthday: 8/1/1995
Introduced: 1/7/1996
Retired: 5/11/1997
The Beanies used to follow him around
Because Garcia traveled from town to town
He's pretty popular as you can see
Some even say he's legendary!
3G - $175 ♥ 4G - $80

Garfield™
#40114

Birthday: None
Introduced: 5/28/2004
Retired: 10/27/2004
SOMETHING TO SNACK ON: The
Garfield Comic Strip originally debuted
on June 19, 1978!
GARFIELD MORSEL: Garfield's favorite food
is lasagna and his favorite toy
is his teddy bear, POOKY!
Also available at Ty Store.
12G - $8

Garfield™ (with DVD)
No Style

Birthday: None
Introduced: 12/5/2006
Current
I love being me!!
Mini Garfield in box with DVD.
15single - Current Retail Value

Garfield 4-H™
#47037

Birthday: None
Introduced: 8/9/2006
Retired: 12/29/2006
An apple a day . . .
. . . keeps the vet away!
4-H Club exclusive.
14G - $15

Garfield™ Key-clip
#40603

Birthday: None
Introduced: 2/28/2007
Current
Got Lasagna?
Also available at Ty Store.
15sm - Current Retail Value

Garfield™ Arlene™
#40110

Birthday: None
Introduced: 5/28/2004
Retired: 12/29/2004
SOMETHING TO SNACK ON: Arlene joined
the Garfield comic-strip family on
December 17, 1980!
ARLENE MORSEL: Arlene is Garfield's
on again, off again girlfriend!
12G - $8

Garfield™ Cool Cat™
#40215

Birthday: None
Introduced: 4/29/2005
Current
SOMETHING TO SNACK ON: Garfield the
Movie premiered on June 11, 2004!
GARFIELD MORSEL: Garfield's favorite
cologne smells like tuna!
Also available at Ty Store.
13G - Current Retail Value

Garfield™ Goodnight Garfield™
#40316

Birthday: None
Introduced: 11/30/2005
Retired: 5/25/2007
Goodnight Garfield was issued
without comments.
13G - $8

Garfield™ Happy Holidays™
#40305

Birthday: None
Introduced: 10/31/2005
Retired: 12/29/2005
Happy Holidays Garfield was issued
without comments.
13G/13UK - $8

Garfield™ Happy Valentines Day™
#40317

Birthday: None
Introduced: 11/30/2005
Retired: 2/24/2006
Happy Valentines Day was issued
without comments.
13G - $8

Garfield™ His Majesty™
#40397

Birthday: None
Introduced: 6/12/2006
Current
"Cats rule . . .dogs drool."
Or "It's good to be king!"
Or "My kingdom. My rules."
3 variations of comment.
Also available at Ty Store.
14G - Current Retail Value

Garfield™ I don't do perky™
#40668

Birthday: None
Introduced: 6/29/2007
Current
But I will do nap time!
15G - Current Retail Value

Garfield™ Louis™
#40113

Birthday: None
Introduced: 5/28/2004
Retired: 11/24/2004
SOMETHING TO SNACK ON: On June 11,
2004 Louis first ran across Garfield's path
in "GARFIELD THE MOVIE"
LOUIS MORSEL: Louis would take care of
Garfield for a macadamia nut cookie!
12G - $8

Garfield™ Luca™
#40111

Birthday: None
Introduced: 5/28/2004
Retired: 12/29/2004
SOMETHING TO SNACK ON: Luca came
face to face with Garfield June 11, 2004 in
"GARFIELD THE MOVIE"
LUCA MORSEL: Luca is always trying
to take a bite out of Garfield!
12G - $8

Garfield™ Nermal™
#40109

Birthday: None
Introduced: 5/28/2004
Retired: 12/29/2004
SOMETHING TO SNACK ON: On
September 3, 1979, Nermal, "the world's
cutest kitten," made his debut!
NERMAL MORSEL: Nermal's
favorite pastime is taunting Garfield
about his age and looks!
12G - $8

Garfield™ Odie™
#40112

Birthday: None
Introduced: 5/28/2004
Retired: 12/29/2004
SOMETHING TO SNACK ON: Odie first
met Garfield on August 8, 1978!
ODIE MORSEL: Odie wasn't always
Jon Arbuckel's dog. He was originally
owned by Jon's friend, Lyman!
12G - $8

Garfield™ Odie™ (with DVD)
No Style #

Birthday: None
Introduced: 5/28/2004
Retired: 12/29/2004
An Ode to Odie
Mini Odie in box with DVD.
12G - $15

Garfield™ Perfectly Lovable™
#40629

Birthday: None
Introduced: 4/30/2007
Current
Garfield — Perfectly Lovable was issued
without comments.
Also available at Ty Store.
15G - Current Retail Value

Garfield™ Pooky™
#40155

Birthday: None
Introduced: 8/16/2004
Retired: 9/28/2004
SOMETHING TO SNACK ON: Pooky
and Garfield became inseparable
on October 23, 1978!
POOKY MORSEL: Garfield found Pooky in a
dresser drawer and adopted him as his own!
12G - $8

Garfield™ Pooky™ Key-clip
#40672

Birthday: None
Introduced: 6/29/2007
Current
Lovable and Huggable
15Gsm - Current Retail Value

Garfield™ Season's Greetings™
#40447

Birthday: None
Introduced: 9/29/2006
Retired: 11/22/2006
Season's Greetings!
14G/14UK - $8

Garfield™ Stuck On You™
#40487

Birthday: None
Introduced: 12/29/2006
Current
I'm stuck on you!
Also available at Ty Store.
14G - Current Retail Value

George™
#46059

Birthday: 6/9/2006
Introduced: 4/28/2006
Retired: 5/18/2006
Let's raise the spirit of '66
And show us all your football tricks
Now everyone, let's cheer out loud
Come on England and make us proud!
Europe exclusive.
14UK - $20

Georgia™
#40128

Birthday: None
Introduced: 8/30/2004
Retired: 12/29/2005
STATE MOTTO: "Wisdom, Justice,
and Moderation"
NICKNAME: Peach State
FACT: 4th state to ratify the
U.S. Constitution!
Sold only in Georgia.
12G - $7

Georgia Cherokee Rose™
#40291

Birthday: None
Introduced: 7/15/2005
Retired: 12/29/2005
OFFICIAL FLOWER SINCE 1916
They say I grew from mothers' tears
That's been the tale for many years
I'm bright and sunny and you'll see
The Georgia rose called Cherokee
Trade Show exclusive.
13G - $10

Germania™
#4236 • German-English tag

Birthday: 10/3/1990
Introduced: 1/1/1999
Retired: 12/23/1999
Unity and Justice and Freedom
Is the song of German unity.
All good little girls and boys
Should love this little German bear.
German exclusive.
5G - $10

Germania™
#4236 • tag in German

Birthday: 10/3/1990
Introduced: 1/1/1999
Retired: 12/23/1999
Einigkeit und Recht und Freiheit
ist der Deutschen Einheitslied.
Allen Kindern brav und fein
soll dieser Bär der Liebste sein!
German exclusive.
5G - $40

Germany™
#46034

Birthday: 2/20/2004
Introduced: 5/31/2005
Retired: 9/23/2005
My land was two but now is one
A land of love is where I'm from
Hiding in the verdant trees
Come visit me I'm sure to please!
German exclusive.
13EU - $20

Ghoul™
#40260

Birthday: 11/1/2004
Introduced: 8/31/2005
Retired: 11/23/2005
Ghosts and ghouls and goblins, too
Strange noises and loud shouts of, "BOO"
Spookiest things you've ever seen
That's why I love Halloween!
13G/13EU - $7

Ghoulianne™
#40260

Birthday: 11/1/2004
Introduced: 8/31/2005
Retired: 11/23/2005
Things that go bump in the night
Creaks and shrieks that cause a fright
Spookiest things you've ever seen
That's why I love Halloween!
13G/13EU - $7

Ghoulish™
#40421

Birthday: 8/23/2006
Introduced: 8/31/2006
Retired: 10/25/2006
I really want to make the scene
When I go out for Halloween
Was so anxious to get some treats
That I took the wrong set of sheets!
14G - $7

Giblets™
#44060

Birthday: 11/24/2005
Introduced: 10/19/2005
Retired: 11/28/2005
On Thanksgiving most every year
People give thanks for what is dear
So what would I be thankful for?
If you'd prefer roast chicken more!
Ty Store exclusive.
13G - $10

Gift™ (Joy)
#47003

Birthday: 11/7/2003
Introduced: 10/1/2004
Retired: 12/29/2004
A special gift that's just for you
Comes from a heart that's pure and true
And as the holiday bells ring
The gift of joy is what I bring!
Hallmark exclusive.
12G - $10

Gift™ (Love)
#47005

Birthday: 11/7/2003
Introduced: 10/1/2004
Retired: 12/29/2004
A special gift that's just for you
Comes from a heart that's pure and true
And as the holiday bells ring
The gift of love is what I bring!
Hallmark exclusive.
12G - $10

Gift™ (Peace)
#47004

Birthday: 11/7/2003
Introduced: 10/1/2004
Retired: 12/29/2004
A special gift that's just for you
Comes from a heart that's pure and true
And as the holiday bells ring
The gift of peace is what I bring!
Hallmark exclusive.
12G - $10

Giganto™
#4384

Birthday: 12/17/2000
Introduced: 7/31/2001
Retired: 6/25/2002
When you see me, be prepared
I'm really big, so don't be scared
All that matters in the end
Is that I want to be your friend!
7G - $7 ♥ 9G - $7

GiGi™
#4191

Birthday: 4/7/1997
Introduced: 5/30/1998
Retired: 12/23/1999
Prancing and dancing all down the street
Thinking her hairdo is oh so neat
Always so careful in the wind and rain
She's a dog that is anything but plain!
5G - $7

Giraffiti™
#40060

Birthday: 8/31/2003
Introduced: 2/26/2004
Retired: 7/28/2004
If I stand on tippy toes
The leaves almost touch my nose
I'm still to small to reach the trees
Would you help me . . .pretty please?!
12G - $7

Gizmo™
#4541

Birthday: 8/21/2001
Introduced: 6/28/2002
Retired: 8/29/2002
What kind of creature can I be
With big, red eyes so I can see
I sleep all day and play all night
If you guessed a lemur...you were right!
7G - $7 ♥ 10G - $7

Glam Bag™
#40391

Birthday: None
Introduced: 6/30/2006
Current
Glam Bag was issued without a poem.
14G - Current Retail Value

Glider™
#4574

Birthday: 10/4/2001
Introduced: 11/27/2002
Retired: 3/17/2003
Some people think I look absurd
Because I'm a strange-looking bird
"You're not like other birds," they shriek
But I am proud to be unique!
7G - $7 ♥ 10G - $7

Glory™
#4188

Birthday: 7/4/1997
Introduced: 5/30/1998
Retired: 12/31/1998
Wearing the flag for all to see
Symbol of freedom for you and me
Red white and blue - Independence Day
Happy Birthday USA!
5G - $7

Glow™
#4283

Birthday: 1/4/2002
Introduced: 3/1/2000
Retired: 3/27/2001
To find me when you want to play
Look for my light to guide the way
I'll be the brightest in the park
I'm the Beanie that glows in the dark!
6G/6EU - $7 ♥ 7G - $7

Goatee™
#4235

Birthday: 11/4/1998
Introduced: 1/1/1999
Retired: 12/23/1999
Though she's hungry, she's in a good mood
Searching through garbage,
tin cans for food
For Goatee the goat, it's not a big deal
Anything at all makes a fine meal!
5G - $7

Gobbles™
#4034

Birthday: 11/27/1996
Introduced: 10/1/1997
Retired: 3/31/1999
Gobbles the turkey loves to eat
Once a year she has a feast
I have a secret I'd like to divulge
If she eats too much her tummy will bulge!
4G - $7 ♥ 5G - $7

Goddess™
#40054

Birthday: 5/27/2003
Introduced: 1/30/2004
Retired: 6/24/2004
It must come as no surprise
That my best feature is my eyes
I'll bat my lashes, long and lush
Then bow my head as my cheeks blush!
12G - $7

Goldie™
#4023

Birthday: 11/14/1994
Introduced: 6/25/1994
Retired: 12/31/1997
She's got rhythm, she's got soul
What more to like in a fish bowl?
Through sound waves Goldie swam
Because this goldfish likes to jam!
1G - $1,800 ♥ 2G - $250 ♥ 3G - $60 ♥
4G - $9 ♥ 5G - $7

Goochy™
#4230 · light green body

Birthday: 11/18/1998
Introduced: 1/1/1999
Retired: 12/23/1999
Swirl, swish, squirm and wiggle
Listen closely, hear him giggle
The most ticklish jellyfish you'll ever meet
Even though he has no feet!
5G - $7

Goochy™
#4230 · pink body

Birthday: 11/18/1998
Introduced: 1/1/1999
Retired: 12/23/1999
Swirl, swish, squirm and wiggle
Listen closely, hear him giggle
The most ticklish jellyfish you'll ever meet
Even though he has no feet!
5G - $7

Goody™
#40275 · center

Birthday: 9/6/2005
Introduced: 9/30/2005
Retired: 12/29/2005
Cookies, cakes, and any sweets
These are my most favorite treats
In my stocking, hope I see
A candy cane that's just for me!
13G - $9

Goody™
#40275 · left

Birthday: 9/6/2005
Introduced: 9/30/2005
Retired: 12/29/2005
Cookies, cakes, and any sweets
These are my most favorite treats
In my stocking, hope I see
A candy cane that's just for me!
13G - $9

Goody™
#40275 · right

Birthday: 9/6/2005
Introduced: 9/30/2005
Retired: 12/29/2005
Cookies, cakes, and any sweets
These are my most favorite treats
In my stocking, hope I see
A candy cane that's just for me!
13G - $9

Grace™
#4274

Birthday: 2/10/2000
Introduced: 3/1/2000
Retired: 6/11/2001
Please watch over me night and day
When I sleep and when I pray
Keep me safe from up above
With special blessings of your love!
6G - $7 ♥ 7G - $7

Gracie™
#4126

Birthday: 6/17/1996
Introduced: 1/1/1997
Retired: 5/1/1998
As a duckling, she was confused,
Birds on the lake were quite amused.
Poking fun until she would cry,
Now the most beautiful swan at Ty!
4G - $7 ♥ 5G - $7

Graf von Rot™
#4612

Birthday: 11/9/2001
Introduced: 3/1/2002
Retired: 7/8/2002
Love, Happiness, Satisfaction
Wishes you Graf von Rot forever
That all people living in Germany
Take care of each other.
German exclusive.
7G - $30

Gramps™
#44058

Birthday: 9/11/2005
Introduced: 8/15/2005
Retired: 11/4/2005
You have a kind and gentle touch
You spoil me, but not too much
So, Gramps, I just want to say
Love you! Happy Grandparents Day!
Ty Store exclusive.
13G - $10

Grams™
#44057

Birthday: 9/11/2005
Introduced: 8/15/2005
Retired: 11/4/2005
Grams, you're always there for me
You love me unconditionally
It brings a smile to my face
When I'm in your warm embrace!
Ty Store exclusive.
13G - $10

Grandfather™
#44019

Birthday: 9/12/2004
Introduced: 8/3/2004
Retired: 9/8/2004
My grandfather is brave and strong
He teaches me what's right and wrong
I hope someday that I can be
Just half as wonderful as he!
Ty Store exclusive.
12G - $15

Grandmother™
#44018

Birthday: 9/12/2004
Introduced: 8/3/2004
Retired: 9/8/2004
When your grandmother hugs you tight
You know that everything's alright
And for that sweet and loving touch
Tell her you love her very much!
Ty Store exclusive.
12G - $15

Grape Ice™
#40678

Birthday: 6/23/2007
Introduced: 6/29/2007
Current
Ready for a summer treat?
Something cool and oh-so sweet?
After a long day in the sun
A Grape Ice is second to none!
Trade Show exclusive.
15G - Current Retail Value

Greetings™
#48407

Birthday: 12/00/2004
Introduced: 12/1/2004
Retired: 1/3/2005
Seasons greetings from you to me
Make the holidays bright and merry
Seasons greetings from me to you
May your holiday wishes all come true!
December 2004
Beanie Baby of the Month.
BBOM - $7

Grizzwald™
#40101

Birthday: 3/26/2004
Introduced: 6/30/2004
Retired: 7/7/2004
A hug for me, a hug for you
One for mommy and daddy, too
A hug for you, a hug for me
I love hugs because they're free!
12G - $7

Groom™
#4529

Birthday: None
Introduced: 4/30/2002
Retired: 7/28/2004
With a love that's pure and true
I will give my heart to you
I can't wait to hear you say
That you will be my wife today!
7G - $7 ♥ 10G - $7

Groovey™
#40412

Birthday: 7/22/2006
Introduced: 7/31/2006
Current
Some people think I'm out of sight
Because my colors are so bright
I think I'm groovey as can be
And so footloose and fancy free!
14G - Current Retail Value

Groovy™
#4256

Birthday: 1/10/1999
Introduced: 8/31/1999
Retired: 12/23/1999
Wearing colors of the rainbow
Making good friends wherever I go
Take me with you, don't let me stay
I need your love all night and day!
5G - $7

Groowwl™
#40440

Birthday: 8/28/2006
Introduced: 9/29/2006
Current
In the kitchen, on the prowl
Because I heard my tummy growl
I'll pounce just when I spy my prey
A thick and juicy rare filet!
14G/14UK - Current Retail Value

Grumbles ™
#48425

Birthday: 6/00/2006
Introduced: 6/1/2006
Retired: 7/1/2006
There's one thing that I must explain
Now, I don't normally complain
Although I am a crab, you see
That doesn't mean that I'm crabby!
June 2006 Beanie Baby of the Month.
BBOM - $7

Grunt™
#4092

Birthday: 7/19/1995
Introduced: 1/7/1996
Retired: 5/11/1997
Some Beanies think Grunt is tough
No surprise, he's scary enough
But if you take him home you'll see
Grunt is the sweetest Beanie Baby!
3G - $75 ♥ 4G - $40

Gypsy™
#40094

Birthday: 8/24/2003
Introduced: 6/30/2004
Retired: 10/27/2004
I like to go out at night
When the moon is full and bright
And sing a song to all my friends
I hope the evening never ends!
12G - $7

H™
#40508

Birthday: None
Introduced: 6/30/2005
Current
Alphabet Bears are issued without poems.
AB - Current Retail Value

Hairy™
#4336

Birthday: 10/6/2000
Introduced: 1/1/2001
Retired: 1/26/2001
Hairy the spider hangs from a thread
Looking at you from overhead
Hanging around is his favorite way
Of spending each and every day!
7G - $7 ♥ 8G - $7

Halo™
#4208

Birthday: 8/31/1998
Introduced: 9/30/1998
Retired: 11/19/1999
When you sleep, I'm always here
Don't be afraid, I am near
Watching over you with lots of love
Your guardian angel from above!
5G - $7

Halo II™
#4269

Birthday: 1/14/2000
Introduced: 3/1/2000
Retired: 4/6/2001
Little angel up above
Guard me with your special love
Make sure that you will always be
By my side and close to me!
6G - $7 ♥ 7G - $7

Hamish™
#46082

Birthday: 11/30/2006
Introduced: 9/29/2006
Current
Hamish is a bonny beast
Who thinks that heather makes a feast
In the snow he loves to play
Will you take him home today?
UK exclusive.
14UK - $16

Hamlet™
#40016

Birthday: 11/13/2002
Introduced: 8/28/2003
Retired: 11/25/2003
I'm not too neat, I must confess
My friends all think my home's a mess
But I think it suits me just fine
'Cause, after all, I am a swine!
7G - $7 ♥ 11G - $7

Hamley™
#46080

Birthday: 9/1/2006
Introduced: 9/16/2006
Retired: 10/25/2006
In 1760 the first Hamley's store
Was opened and filled up with toys galore
The best in the world he desired it to be
And achieve the he did, to all of our glee!
Hamley's UK exclusive.
14UK - $25

Hannah™
#46002

Birthday: 3/20/2003
Introduced: 2/9/2004
Retired: 3/15/2006
Stop and see
Many flowers are blooming.
May the blessing from God
Will reach abundantly
Like a large bouquet!
Japan exclusive.
12G - $15

Happily™
#47020

Birthday: 2/25/2006
Introduced: 1/13/2006
Retired: 4/21/2006
My friends and I have a neat job to do
Coloring eggs in pink, yellow, and blue
Once that is finished our job isn't done
We have to deliver them to everyone!
Hallmark exclusive.
14G - $7

Happy™
#4061 · gray body

Birthday: None
Introduced: 6/25/1994
Retired: 6/3/1995
Happy was issued without a poem.
1G - $2,300 ♥ 2G - $450 ♥ 3G - $300

Happy™
#4061 · lavender body

Birthday: 2/25/1994
Introduced: 6/3/1995
Retired: 5/1/1998
Happy the Hippo loves to wade
In the river and in the shade
When Happy shoots water out of his snout
You know he's happy without a doubt!
3G - $100 ♥ 4G - $7 ♥ 5G - $7

Happy Birthday™
#40058 · orange

Birthday: None
Introduced: 7/30/2004
Retired 1/12/2005
Happy Birthday was issued without a poem.
12G - $7

Happy Birthday™
#40198 · red

Birthday: None
Introduced: 12/30/2004
Retired: 2/24/2006
Happy Birthday was issued without a poem.
13G/13EU - $7

Happy Birthday™
#40234 · brown

Birthday: None
Introduced: 3/31/2005
Current
Happy Birthday was issued without a poem.
Retired 4/21/06 then Current 4/28/06.
Birthday - Current Retail Value

Happy Birthday™
#40224 · yellow

Birthday: None
Introduced: 5/31/2005
Retired: 4/21/2006
Happy Birthday was issued without a poem.
13G - $7

Happy Birthday™
#40259 · orange

Birthday: None
Introduced: 8/31/2005
Retired: 12/21/2006
Happy Birthday was issued without a poem.
13G/13EU - $7

Happy Birthday™
#40328 · tan

Birthday: None
Introduced: 12/30/2005
Current
Happy Birthday was issued without a poem.
14G/14UK - Current Retail Value

Happy Birthday™
#40532 · brown

Birthday: None
Introduced: 4/28/2006
Current
Greetings Bears are issued without poems.
14G - Current Retail Value

Happy Birthday™
#40483 · orange

Birthday: None
Introduced: 12/29/2006
Current
Happy Birthday was issued without a poem.
15G/15UK - Current Retail Value

Happy Birthday!™
#40617 · blue

Birthday: None
Introduced: 3/30/2007
Current
Happy Birthday was issued without a poem.
15G - Current Retail Value

Happy Birthday!™
#40616 · red

Birthday: None
Introduced: 3/30/2007
Current
Happy Birthday was issued without a poem.
15G - Current Retail Value

Happy Hanukkah™
#40279 · menorah

Birthday: 12/25/2005
Introduced: 9/30/2005
Retired: 12/29/2005
Happy Hanukkah can be heard
For the miracle that occurred
And so we gather for eight nights
To mark the festival of lights!
13G - $8

Happy Hanukkah™
#44053 · dreidel

Birthday: 12/25/2005
Introduced: 11/17/2005
Retired: 1/3/2006
Happy Hanukkah can be heard
For the miracle that occurred
Letters on the dreidel declare
"A great miracle happened there"!
Ty Store exclusive.
13G - $8

Happy Holidays™
#47009

Birthday: 12/26/2004
Introduced: 10/26/2005
Retired: 12/29/2005
You should take the time each year
To spread some joy and peace and cheer
So when you meet someone just say
"I wish you a HAPPY HOLIDAY"!
Hallmark Gold Crown exclusive.
13G - $8

Happy Holidays™
#40537

Birthday: None
Introduced: 9/29/2006
Retired: 12/21/2006
Greetings Bears are issued without poems.
14G - $8

Harrison™
#40194

Birthday: 5/2/2004
Introduced: 12/30/2004
Retired: 6/29/2005
My floppy ears get in the way
Whenever I might try and play
There must be something I can do
Because I want to play with you!
13G/13EU - $7

Harry™
#4546

Birthday: 12/9/2001
Introduced: 6/28/2002
Retired: 11/26/2002
"Your hair's too long!" some people say
"You should get it cut today!"
But I like it this way, you see
It's the thing that makes me, me!
7G - $7 ♥ 10G - $7

Haunt™
#4377

Birthday: 10/27/2000
Introduced: 9/3/2001
Retired: 11/12/2001
My favorite time is Halloween
When ghosts and goblins can be seen
It's so much fun to trick-or-treat
I hope you'll give me something sweet!
7G - $7 ♥ 9G - $7

Haunts™
#47032

Birthday: 9/1/2006
Introduced: 9/1/2006
Retired: 10/25/2006
Shhh . . . now did you hear that sound?
Do you think there are ghosts around?
Oh no! I think I heard a creak
Please hold my paw so I don't SHRIEK!
Borders/Walden exclusive.
14G - $7

Hawaii™
#40166

Birthday: None
Introduced: 12/7/2004
Current
STATE MOTTO: "The life of the land is
perpetuated in righteousness"
NICKNAME: Aloha State
FACT: Under-sea volcanoes that erupted
thousands of years ago formed the Hawaiian
Islands!
Sold only in Hawaii.
12G - $20

Hawthorne™
#40154

Birthday: 5/18/2004
Introduced: 9/30/2004
Retired: 2/24/2005
I'll write a story just for you
But first there's one thing I must do
I'll proofread it once or even twice
To make sure everything's precise!
12G/12EU - $7

Heartthrob™
#4813

Birthday: 2/00/2004
Introduced: 2/1/2004
Retired: 3/1/2004
I'm all heart some people say
Especially this Valentines Day
I share my love with one and all
No matter if you're big or small!
*February 2004
Beanie Baby of the Month.*
BBOM - $7

Heiress™
#40079

Birthday: 4/20/2004
Introduced: 6/30/2004
Retired: 10/25/2006
We'll do our hair and paint our toes
And then change in to dress up clothes
Next we can dance and skip and twirl
It's so much fun to be a girl!
12G - $7

Henry™
#46084

Birthday: 11/4/2006
Introduced: 11/4/2006
Retired: 1/24/2007
Although I'm very small in size
I am the finest merchandise
Which Ty and Harrods bring to you
Take me home; I'll love you too!
Harrods UK exclusive.
14UK - $25

Henry™
#46084 · boxed with certificate

Birthday: 11/4/2006
Introduced: 11/4/2006
Retired: 1/24/2007
Although I'm very small in size
I am the finest merchandise
Which Ty and Harrods bring to you
Take me home; I'll love you too!
Harrods UK exclusive.
14UK - $90

Herald™
#4570

Birthday: 1/7/2002
Introduced: 10/30/2002
Retired: 12/27/2002
I'm an angel from up above
I bring you thoughts of peace and love
With a prayer and a wish I'll fly
Beyond the beautiful blue sky!
7G - $7 ♥ 10G - $7

Herder™
#4524

Birthday: 8/29/2001
Introduced: 4/1/2002
Retired: 12/27/2002
My job each day is herding sheep
The days are long, there's little sleep
But when my day is finally through
I'm happy to come home to you!
7G - $7 ♥ 10G - $7

Hero™
#4351

Birthday: 6/18/2000
Introduced: 4/1/2001
Retired: 5/9/2001
You give me hugs when I am sad
You love me if I'm good or bad
Thank you for all you do
I can always count on you!
7G - $7 ♥ 8G - $7

HERO™
#40012 · USA flag on chest

Birthday: 3/12/2003
Introduced: 4/10/2003
Retired: 12/29/2005
We all pray
When day is done
That freedom comes
To everyone!
11G - $7

HERO™
#40012 · USA flag with stars front

Birthday: 3/12/2003
Introduced: 4/10/2003
Retired: 12/29/2005
We all pray
When day is done
That freedom comes
To everyone!
11G - $7

HERO™
#40012 · USA flag with stripes front

Birthday: 3/12/2003
Introduced: 4/10/2003
Retired: 12/29/2005
We all pray
When day is done
That freedom comes
To everyone!
11G - $7

HERO™
#40012 · Cody Banks 2

Birthday: 3/12/2003
Introduced: 3/6/2004
Retired: 3/6/2004
We all pray
When day is done
That freedom comes
To everyone!
Only available at movie premiere.
11G - $150

HERO 2003™
#40013 · UK flag

Birthday: 3/12/2003
Introduced: 4/10/2003
Retired: 6/13/2003
We all pray
When day is done
That freedom comes
To everyone!
11G - $7

HERO 2003™
#40014 · AUS flag

Birthday: 3/12/2003
Introduced: 5/27/2003
Retired: 6/13/2003
We all pray
When day is done
That freedom comes
To everyone!
Ty Store & Australia exclusive.
11G - $7

Hers™
#44013

Birthday: None
Introduced: 5/6/2004
Retired: 12/27/2005
Standing proudly at his side
Wife-to-be; the blushing bride
Today's the day you say, "I do"
And your life begins anew!
Ty Store exclusive.
12G - $7

Herschel™
#4700

Birthday: 4/26/2002
Introduced: 11/25/2002
Retired: 1/10/2003
I'm Herschel the Cracker Barrel bear
You'll love my down-home country flair
Please stop by and stay awhile
My friends and I will make you smile!
Cracker Barrel exclusive.
10G - $7

Hikari™
#46041 · black nose

Birthday: 8/6/2005
Introduced: 9/12/2005
Retired: 6/15/2006
When the round sun shines
the land in the morning
It is the time to wake up
Shine the country and
Bless my homeland forever!
Asian-Pacific exclusive.
13G - $25

Hikari™
#46049 · flag nose

Birthday: 8/6/2005
Introduced: 10/15/2005
Retired: 6/15/2006
When the round sun shines
the land in the morning
It is the time to wake up
Shine the country and
Bless my homeland forever!
Japan exclusive.
13G - $60

Hippie™
#4218

Birthday: 5/4/1998
Introduced: 1/1/1999
Retired: 7/12/1999
Hippie fell into the dye, they say
While coloring eggs, one spring day
From the tips of his ears, down to his toe
Colors of springtime, he proudly shows!
5G - $7

Hippily™
#47020

Birthday: 2/25/2006
Introduced: 1/13/2006
Retired: 4/21/2006
My friends and I have a great job, I think
Coloring eggs in blue, yellow, and pink
Once that is finished our job isn't done
We have to deliver them to everyone!
Hallmark exclusive.
14G - $7

Hippity™
#4119

Birthday: 6/1/1996
Introduced: 1/1/1997
Retired: 5/1/1998
Hippity is a cute little bunny
Dressed in green, he looks quite funny
Twitching his nose in the air
Sniffing a flower here and there!
4G - $7 ♥ 5G - $7

His™
#44014

Birthday: None
Introduced: 5/6/2004
Retired: 12/27/2005
On this very special day
To your new wife you must say
That you will love her and be true
With these two simple words, "I do"
Ty Store exclusive.
12G - $7

Hissy™
#4185

Birthday: 4/4/1997
Introduced: 12/31/1997
Retired: 3/31/1999
Curled and coiled and ready to play
He waits for you patiently every day
He'll keep his best friend, but not his skin
And stay with you through thick and thin.
5G - $7

Ho Ho Ho™
#40538

Birthday: None
Introduced: 9/29/2006
Retired: 12/21/2006
Ho Ho Ho was issued without a poem.
14G/14UK - $7

Hobo™
#40231

Birthday: 10/11/2004
Introduced: 3/31/2005
Retired: 3/27/2006
Around my neck or on my head
Tied in a knot or bow instead
My bandana is so cool you see
It's my favorite accessory!
13G/13EU - $10

Hocus™
#40262

Birthday: 10/29/2004
Introduced: 8/31/2005
Retired: 11/23/2005
I have a pet that I love so
I take him everywhere I go
Upon my head . . . the perfect seat
For us to go and "Trick or Treat"!
13G/13EU - $7

Hodge-Podge™
#4569 · blue front paws

Birthday: 7/27/2002
Introduced: 10/30/2002
Retired: 3/27/2003
So many patterns, styles and prints
In different colors, shades and tints
I need a friend who loves to play
And won't mind my colorful way!
7G - $7 ♥ 10G - $7

Hodge-Podge™
#4569 · pink front paws

Birthday: 7/27/2002
Introduced: 10/30/2002
Retired: 3/27/2003
So many patterns, styles and prints
In different colors, shades and tints
I need a friend who loves to play
And won't mind my colorful way!
7G - $7 ♥ 10G - $7

Hodges™
#40651

Birthday: 5/17/2007
Introduced: 5/31/2007
Current
If it's a special pet you seek
I know a cat that's quite unique
With feline grace and such beauty
Who is this cat? Who else but me!
15G - Current Retail Value

Hollydays™
#40273

Birthday: 12/15/2004
Introduced: 9/30/2005
Retired: 12/29/2005
Stringing popcorn for the tree
Twinkling lights for all to see
A pretty wreath upon the door
I love my holiday decor!
13G/13UK - $7

Hollyhorse™
#40444

Birthday: 12/4/2005
Introduced: 9/29/2006
Retired: 11/22/2006
My wish is that this holiday
I will get to lead the sleigh
And take you on a special ride
All across the countryside!
14G/14UK - $7

116

Holmes™
#4801

Birthday: 2/00/2003
Introduced: 12/2/2002
Retired: 2/24/2003
I can sniff out most any clue
Just like the real detectives do
I will search high and then search low
Finding friends wherever I go!
February 2003
Beanie Baby of the Month.
BBOM - $12

Holy Father™
#40265

Birthday: None
Introduced: 4/20/2005
Retired: 8/26/2005
Teacher, writer, Father, friend
Your love for us will never end
Throughout your life a light did shine
On acts of kindness to all mankind!
13G/13EU - $7

Homeland™
#40364

Birthday: 6/14/2006
Introduced: 4/28/2006
Retired: 6/23/2006
I just cannot help but crow
About this great land that I know
Where everyone can all be free
The U.S.A.'s the best to me!
14G - $7

Honey-Bun™
#40159

Birthday: 6/25/2004
Introduced: 11/30/2004
Retired: 1/28/2005
A little pup so cute and sweet
Bringing you a special treat
Some love and cuddles just for you
Maybe even a kiss or two!
12G/12EU - $7

Honks™
#4258

Birthday: 3/11/1999
Introduced: 8/31/1999
Retired: 12/23/1999
Honks the goose likes to fly away
South for winter he will stay
When spring comes back, north he will fly
And swim in ponds and lakes nearby!
5G - $7

Honor Roll™
#44106

Birthday: 4/22/2007
Introduced: 5/1/2007
Current
A celebration is drawing near
Let's all gather 'round and cheer
I'll move my tassel to the right
My future certainly seems bright!
Ty Store exclusive.
15G - Current Retail Value

Honors™
#40358

Birthday: 5/31/2006
Introduced: 3/31/2006
Retired: 7/25/2006
You've done well, in fact, just great
And today you graduate
It's quite a feat, you should be proud
So toss your hat and shout out loud!
The Graduation Bear
14G - $7

Hoodwink™
#40499

Birthday: 3/9/2006
Introduced: 1/31/2007
Current
No matter where it is I go
It seems that trouble will follow
I just love a good prank, you see
Even if the joke's on me!
15G - Current Retail Value

Hoofer™
#4518

Birthday: 11/17/2001
Introduced: 3/1/2002
Retired: 12/27/2002
Marching proudly, stepping high
People wave as I walk by
Parades are so much fun for me
There's just no place I'd rather be!
7G - $7 ♥ 10G - $7

Hoops™
#40286

Birthday: 3/6/2005
Introduced: 10/31/2005
Current
Running up and down the court
Poised for a layup; then stop short
Release the ball, it's good for three
At the buzzer, we've won . . . Yipee!
13G/13UK - Current Retail Value

Hoot™
#4073

Birthday: 8/9/1995
Introduced: 1/7/1996
Retired: 10/1/1997
Late to bed, late to rise
Nevertheless, Hoot's quite wise
Studies by candlelight, nothing new
Like a president, do you know Whooo?
3G - $50 ♥ 4G - $9

Hope™
#4213

Birthday: 3/23/1998
Introduced: 1/1/1999
Retired: 12/23/1999
Every night when it's time for bed
Fold you hands and bow your head
An angelic face, a heart that's true
You have a friend to pray with you!
5G - $7

Hopper™
#4342

Birthday: 8/7/2000
Introduced: 1/1/2001
Retired: 4/4/2001
He hops around from place to place
To put a smile upon your face
Bringing baskets and good cheer
It's his favorite time of year!
7G - $7 ♥ 8G - $7

Hoppily™
#47020

Birthday: 2/25/2006
Introduced: 1/13/2006
Retired: 4/21/2006
My friends and I have a fun job, you know
Coloring eggs in pink, blue, and yellow
Once that is finished our job isn't done
We have to deliver them to everyone!
Hallmark exclusive.
14G - $7

Hoppity™
#4117

Birthday: 4/3/1996
Introduced: 1/1/1997
Retired: 5/1/1998
Hopscotch is what she likes to play
If you don't join in, she'll hop away
So play a game if you have the time,
She likes to play, rain or shine!
4G - $7 ♥ 5G - $7

Hopson™
#40495

Birthday: 2/23/2006
Introduced: 1/31/2007
Retired: 5/25/2007
Over the hills to the meadow
Along the winding trail I go
All the way home until I see
My happy, hoppy family!
15G - $7

Hornsly™
#4345

Birthday: 8/24/2000
Introduced: 3/1/2001
Retired: 8/8/2001
I have horns, I'm quite a sight
Some people run away in fright
But I don't want to scare you away
All I want to do is play!
7G - $7 ♥ 8G - $7

Houston™
#40388

Birthday: 11/17/2005
Introduced: 6/30/2006
Retired: 2/27/2007
I just got some brand new toys
And they make different kinds of noise
The best thing 'bout these toys I see
Is that they all are just for me!
14G/14UK - $7

Howl™
#4310

Birthday: 5/23/2000
Introduced: 7/8/2000
Retired: 4/24/2001
When the moon is round and bright
I howl and howl all through the night
But don't be scared and run away
I'm calling out, "Who wants to play?"
6G - $9 ♥ 7G - $9

Huggins™
#40077

Birthday: 10/18/2003
Introduced: 5/28/2004
Retired: 10/27/2004
I'd like to give a little kiss
To the person that I miss
And then I'll give a big hug, too
Just so you'll know that I like you!
12G - $7

Hug-hug™
#40310

Birthday: 2/15/2005
Introduced: 11/30/2005
Retired: 1/27/2006
To me you're unlike any other
So here's a kiss and then another
Next I'll give you a hug or two
Just so you know that I love you!
13G/13UK - $7

Huggy™
#4306

Birthday: 8/20/2000
Introduced: 7/8/2000
Retired: 6/18/2001
I'd love to be your special friend
I'll stick right by you to the end
So hold me close next to your heart
And from your side I'll never part!
6G - $7 ♥ 7G - $7

Hugsy™
#47047

Birthday: 7/7/2007
Introduced: 12/21/2006
Current
To celebrate the hundredth year
Since Hershey's® did appear
Here's a treat you will adore
Not only sweet but so much more!
In honor of the 100th anniversary of the
Hershey's Kiss. Sold only at Walgreens.
14G - Current Retail Value

Humphrey™
#4060

Birthday: 5/19/1994
Introduced: 6/25/1994
Retired: 6/15/1995
Humphrey was issued without a poem
1G - $2,800 ♥ 2G - $1,000 ♥ 3G - $78

Huntley™
#40107

Birthday: 7/16/2003
Introduced: 6/30/2004
Retired: 12/29/2004
As you know a hug takes two
So won't you bring me home with you?
We can cuddle all day long
In your arms, where I belong!
12G - $7

Hutch Clutch™
#40336

Birthday: None
Introduced: 12/30/2005
Current
Hutch Clutch was issued without a poem.
Retired 5/24/06. ReIntroduced 2/1/2007.
14G/14UK - Current Retail Value

I™
#40509

Birthday: None
Introduced: 6/30/2005
Current
Alphabet Bears are issued without poems.
AB - Current Retail Value

I ♥ You™
#40307

Birthday: 2/19/2005
Introduced: 11/30/2005
Retired: 2/24/2006
My dear, my partner, my best friend
My love for you, it knows no end
Forever you and I will be
Together for eternity!
13G - $10

Icecubes™
#48420

Birthday: 1/00/2006
Introduced: 1/1/2006
Retired: 2/1/2006
I really love the cold and snow
"The colder the better" is my motto
'Cause of the gloves and scarf I wear
I am one warm and toasty bear!
January 2006
Beanie Baby of the Month.
BBOM - $20

Icepack™
#44205

Birthday: None
Introduced: 11/2/2005
Retired: 3/16/2006
FACT: Global warming, which poses a great
threat to the polar bears' natural habitat, and
hunting have both contributed to declines in
polar bear populations!
Ty Store/World Wildlife Fund exclusive.
13G - $10

Icing™
#40241

Birthday: 12/18/2004
Introduced: 10/31/2005
Current
I'll slip a bit and then I'll slide
Across the ice; I love to glide
Then I will do a figure eight
Gosh, I simply love to skate!
13G/13EU - Current Retail Value

Iggy™
#4038 · tie-dyed with no tongue

Birthday: 8/12/1997
Introduced: 12/31/1997
Retired: 10/1/1998
Sitting on a rock, basking in the sun
Is this iguana's idea of fun
Towel and glasses, book and beach chair
His life is so perfect without a care!
1st Variation has hang tag on foot.
2nd Variation has hang tag on spine.
Both can have PVC or PE pellets.
5G - $7

Iggy™
#4038 · pastel with tongue

Birthday: 8/12/1997
Introduced: 6/15/1998
Retired: 1/1/1999
Sitting on a rock, basking in the sun
Is this iguana's idea of fun
Towel and glasses, book and beach chair
His life is so perfect without a care!
3rd Variation-1 Pastel Color Stamp
inside tush tag is perpendicular to writ-
ing on outside of tush tag. PE pellets.
5G - $7

Iggy™
#4038 · neon with tongue

Birthday: 8/12/1997
Introduced: 6/15/1998
Retired: 1/1/1999
Sitting on a rock, basking in the sun
Is this iguana's idea of fun
Towel and glasses, book and beach chair
His life is so perfect without a care!
3rd Variation-2 Sherbet/Neon Color
Stamp inside tush tag is parallel to
writing on outside of tush tag.
5G - $7

Iggy™
#4038 · blue with no tongue

Birthday: 8/12/1997
Introduced: 8/15/1998
Retired: 3/31/1999
Sitting on a rock, basking in the sun
Is this iguana's idea of fun
Towel and glasses, book and beach chair
His life is so perfect without a care!
4th Variation: Hang tag is on spine.
5th Variation: Hang tag is on foot.
5G - $7

Illinois™
#40127

Birthday: None
Introduced: 8/30/2004
Retired: 12/29/2005
STATE MOTTO: State Sovereignty,
National Union
NICKNAME: Prairie State
FACT: 40th President Ronald Reagan
was born in Illinois!
Sold only in Illinois.
12G - $10

Illinois Violet™
#40293

Birthday: None
Introduced: 7/23/2005
Retired: 12/29/2005
OFFICIAL FLOWER SINCE 1908
The state of Illinois agrees
This pretty flower's sure to please
It's simple beauty you can't forget
That's why we love the violet!
Trade Show exclusive.
13G - $10

Inch™
#4044 · felt antennas

Birthday: 9/3/1995
Introduced: 6/3/1995
Retired: 10/15/1997
Inch the worm is a friend of mine
He goes so slow all the time
Inching around from here to there
Traveling the world without a care!
3G - $90 ♥ 4G - $80

Inch™
#4044 · yarn antennas

Birthday: 9/3/1995
Introduced: 10/15/1997
Retired: 5/1/1998
Inch the worm is a friend of mine
He goes so slow all the time
Inching around from here to there
Traveling the world without a care!
4G - $7 ♥ 5G - $7

Independence™
#40366 · blue

Birthday: 7/4/2006
Introduced: 4/28/2006
Retired: 10/25/2006
Every Independence Day
I stand tall and proudly say
Let's join together, hand in hand
For America, our great homeland!
14G - $7

Independence™
#40366 · red

Birthday: 7/4/2006
Introduced: 4/28/2006
Retired: 10/25/2006
Every Independence Day
With head held high I proudly say
I pledge allegiance to this land
And for the freedom which we stand!
14G - $7

Independence™
#40366 · white

Birthday: 7/4/2006
Introduced: 4/28/2006
Retired: 10/25/2006
Every Independence Day
Hand on heart I proudly say
Freedom and liberty are grand
That's why I love this, my homeland!
14G - $7

India™
#4291

Birthday: 5/26/2000
Introduced: 6/24/2000
Retired: 6/12/2001
Through jungle shadows I will prowl
Don't be afraid, sometimes I growl
I'm not fierce, don't run away
We'll be best friends and play all day!
6G - $7 ♥ 7G - $7

Inky™
#4028 · tan with no mouth

Birthday: None
Introduced: 6/25/1994
Retired: 9/12/1994
Inky was issued without a poem.
1G - $2,900 ♥ 2G - $1,500

Inky™
#4028 · tan with mouth

Birthday: None
Introduced: 9/12/1994
Retired: 6/3/1995
Inky was issued without a poem.
2G - $600 ♥ 3G - $390

Inky™
#4028 · pink with mouth

Birthday: 11/29/1994
Introduced: 6/3/1995
Retired: 5/1/1998
Inky's head is big and round
As he swims he makes no sound
If you need a hand, don't hesitate
Inky can help because he has eight!
3G - $125 ♥ 4G - $7 ♥ 5G - $7

Ireland™
#46019

Birthday: 12/17/2004
Introduced: 12/30/2004
Retired: 3/27/2006
With the Blarney Stone to make a wish
And Irish stew, a tasty dish
An Irish jig to dance with glee
Ireland's a great place to be!
UK exclusive.
13G - $18

Issy™
#4404

Birthday: None
Retired
See Issy Appendix for Poem, Introduced
dates, Retired dates, and a complete
listing of the 63 locations that are printed
on the hang tags.

It's A Boy™
#40056

Birthday: None
Introduced: 1/30/2004
Retired: 3/30/2005
It's A Boy was issued without a poem.
12G - $9

It's A Girl™
#40055

Birthday: None
Introduced: 1/30/2004
Retired: 3/30/2005
It's A Girl was issued without a poem.
12G - $9

J™
#40510

Birthday: None
Introduced: 6/30/2005
Current
Alphabet Bears are issued without poems.
AB - Current Retail Value

Jabber™
#4197

Birthday: 10/10/1997
Introduced: 5/30/1998
Retired: 12/23/1999
Teaching Jabber to move his beak
A large vocabulary he now can speak
Jabber will repeat what you say
Teach him a new word everyday!
5G - $7

Jack™
#40071 · black nose

Birthday: 6/14/2003
Introduced: 4/29/2004
Retired: 9/10/2004
The Union Jack flies across the land
With Saints combined, so we understand
That this great land will always be
The United Kingdom for you and me!
12G - $8

Jack™
#4634 · UK flag nose

Birthday: 6/14/2003
Introduced: 2/1/2004
Retired: 3/5/2004
The Union Jack flies across the land
With Saints combined, so we understand
That this great land will always be
The United Kingdom for you and me!
UK exclusive.
12G - $12

Jake™
#4199

Birthday: 4/17/1997
Introduced: 5/30/1998
Retired: 12/23/1999
Jake the drake likes to splash in a puddle
Take him home and give him a cuddle
Quack, Quack, Quack, he will say
He's so glad you're here to play!
5G - $7

Janglemouse™
#40437

Birthday: 11/28/2005
Introduced: 9/29/2006
Retired: 12/21/2006
Swiftly I'll creep through the house
'Cause after all, I am a mouse
Bringing morsels of peace and joy
This Christmas for each girl and boy!
14G/14UK - $7

January™
#4388

Birthday: None
Introduced: 11/30/2001
Retired: 3/22/2002
My nose is the color of my birthstone.
Garnet - It brings good health and
a wealth of knowledge!
Birthday - $7

January 2003™
#4552

Birthday: None
Introduced: 11/27/2002
Retired: 4/28/2003
Dr. Martin Luther King, Jr. - Jan 15
Muhammad Ali - Jan 17
Oprah Winfrey - Jan 29
Birthday - $7

Japan™
#46022

Birthday: 2/11/2004
Introduced: 2/28/2005
Retired: 4/15/2006
Surrounded by the sea, God gave the land
Four seasons with full blessings
Mt Fuji, sakura, hot springs and sashimi
This is why I love Japan!
Japan exclusive.
Also available Asian-Pacific.
13G - $25

Jaz™
#40074

Birthday: 4/25/2004
Introduced: 5/28/2004
Retired: 9/10/2004
When I hear that jazzy beat
I can't help but tap my feet
That sweet sound of "ba-ba-de-bop"
My dancing paws will never stop!
12G - $7

Jersey™
#48012

Birthday: 1/00/2004
Introduced: 12/31/2003
Retired: 2/6/2004
Most cows will give a hearty, "MOO"
Because that is what most cows do
But as far as greetings go
I prefer to say "HELLO"!
January 2004
Beanie Baby of the Month.
BBOM - $7

Jester™
#4349

Birthday: 9/30/2000
Introduced: 4/1/2001
Retired: 12/31/2001
He loves to play in the sea
With his friend the anemone
Dancing is their favorite way
Of spending each and every day!
7G - $7 ♥ 8G - $7

Jimbo™
#40064

Birthday: 10/2/2003
Introduced: 2/26/2004
Retired: 7/28/2004
No matter where it is I go
I bring my trunk with me, you know
I'd never forget it at home you see
'Cause I have a great memory!
12G - $7

Jinglemouse™
#40436

Birthday: 11/28/2005
Introduced: 9/29/2006
Retired: 12/21/2006
Swiftly I'll creep through the house
'Cause after all, I am a mouse
Bringing crumbs of Christmas cheer
To all of those that you hold dear!
14G/14UK - $7

Jinglepup™
#4394 · green hat with green tail

Birthday: 12/3/2000
Introduced: 10/11/2001
Retired: 12/31/2001
Winter is the very best season
Yummy treats are just one reason
But gingerbread, cookies, and candy too
Can't beat cuddling up next to you!
UK exclusive.
7G - $15

Jinglepup™
#4394 · green hat with white tail

Birthday: 12/3/2000
Introduced: 10/1/2001
Retired: 12/31/2001
Winter is the very best season
Yummy treats are just one reason
But gingerbread, cookies, and candy too
Can't beat cuddling up next to you!
USA exclusive.
9G - $7

Jinglepup™
#4394 · white hat with green tail

Birthday: 12/3/2000
Introduced: 10/30/2001
Retired: 12/31/2001
Winter is the very best season
Yummy treats are just one reason
But gingerbread, cookies, and candy too
Can't beat cuddling up next to you!
Singapore exclusive.
9G - $10

Jinglepup™
#4394 · white hat with white tail

Birthday: 12/3/2000
Introduced: 10/25/2001
Retired: 12/31/2001
Winter is the very best season
Yummy treats are just one reason
But gingerbread, cookies, and candy too
Can't beat cuddling up next to you!
Canada exclusive.
9G - $10

Jinxy™
#44022

Birthday: 10/31/2004
Introduced: 9/27/2004
Retired: 11/1/2004
It would be bad luck, they say
If I happen to come your way
But that is not the truth, you see
Because good luck brought you to me!
Ty Store exclusive.
12G - $15

Joaquim™
#46004

Birthday: 1/28/2004
Introduced: 2/9/2004
Retired: 3/15/2006
Representing our national flower
A symbol of peace, love and power
United in brotherhood we stand
With our neighbors hand in hand!
Asian-Pacific exclusive.
12G - $15

John™
#40239

Birthday: 10/30/1735
Introduced: 4/29/2005
Retired: 8/26/2005
" . . . that among these are life, liberty, and
the pursuit of happiness."
13G/13EU - $10

Johnny™
#47044

Birthday: 6/24/2006
Introduced: 8/18/2006
Retired: 12/29/2006
Everyone across the land
Work together, hand in hand
Live well; love well; think things through
And you'll succeed in what you do!
4-H Club exclusive.
Also sold at John Deere retailers.
14G - $12

Jokester™
#44045

Birthday: 4/1/2005
Introduced: 3/8/2005
Retired: 5/6/2005
Jokes and tricks can be so much fun
My pranks will never be outdone
What can I say, I think it's cool
When I hear the words, "April Fool"!
Ty Store exclusive.
13G - $10

Jolly™
#4082

Birthday: 12/2/1996
Introduced: 5/11/1997
Retired: 5/1/1998
Jolly the walrus is not very serious
He laughs and laughs until he's delirious
He often reminds me of my dad
Always happy, never sad!
4G - $7 ♥ 5G - $7

Joy™
#40442

Birthday: 12/24/2005
Introduced: 9/29/2006
Retired: 12/21/2006
Fa, la, la and jingle bells
Cakes, cookies, delicious smells
Garland, wrappings, cards and bows
It's the holidays and it shows!
14G/14UK - $7

Joyful™
#40442

Birthday: 12/24/2005
Introduced: 9/29/2006
Retired: 12/21/2006
Trim the tree and deck the halls
Tinsel, lights, red and green balls
Garland, wrappings, cards and bows
It's the holidays and it shows!
14G/14UK - $7

Joyous™
#40442

Birthday: 12/24/2005
Introduced: 9/29/2006
Retired: 12/21/2006
Chestnuts roasting; silent night
Children beaming with delight
Garland, wrappings, cards and bows
It's the holidays and it shows!
14G/14UK - $7

Juggles™
#40277

Birthday: 10/9/2004
Introduced: 7/29/2005
Current
Who has a big, red, funny nose?
And floppy shoes upon his toes?
A squirting flower? A spinning tie?
It's a friendly clown, here to say, "HI"!
13G/13EU - Current Retail Value

July™
#4370

Birthday: None
Introduced: 7/3/2001
Retired: 8/30/2001
My nose is the color of my birthstone.
Ruby - It brings beauty, sincerity
and hope!
Birthday - $7

July 2003™
#4558

Birthday: None
Introduced: 5/29/2003
Retired: 11/25/2003
Sharing birthdays this month. . .
Nelson Mandela - July 18
Josh Hartnett - July 21
J.K. Rowling - July 31
Birthday - $7

Jumpshot™
#40073

Birthday: 8/14/2003
Introduced: 5/28/2004
Retired: 11/24/2004
I really have the best jump shot
It helps my team out quite a lot
If we're down a point or two
At the buzzer I'll come through!
12G - $7

Jumpshot™
#40073

Birthday: 8/14/2003
Introduced: 7/30/2005
Retired: 7/31/2005
I really have the best jump shot
It helps my team out quite a lot
If we're down a point or two
At the buzzer I'll come through!
Brookfield Zoo promotional item.
12G - $140

June™
#4393

Birthday: None
Introduced: 4/1/2002
Retired: 5/24/2002
My nose is the color of my birthstone.
Pearl - It brings purity, love
and humility!
Birthday - $10

June 2003™
#4557

Birthday: None
Introduced: 4/30/2003
Retired: 9/5/2003
Marilyn Monroe - June 1st
Venus Williams - June 17th
Prince William - June 21st
Birthday - $7

Juneau™
#40100

Birthday: 12/17/2003
Introduced: 6/30/2004
Current
Hurry, jump on, I'll pull the sled
Or we could play snow-tag instead
Either way we'll have such fun
What can I say? I love to run!
12G - Current Retail Value

Junglelove™
#40471

Birthday: 4/18/2006
Introduced: 11/30/2006
Retired: 1/24/2007
From vine to vine and tree to tree
I'm searching for the one for me
All through the jungle looking for
The only one that I adore!
Same style number as Lovesick.
14G/14UK - $7

Jurgen™
#46061

Birthday: 6/9/2006
Introduced: 4/28/2006
Retired: 5/26/2006
In the year of the World Cup I was born
Exclusive for Europe I was chosen
Football Bear is my name
A guest with friends in Germany
Europe exclusive.
14UK - $7

K™
#40511

Birthday: None
Introduced: 6/30/2005
Current
Alphabet Bears are issued without poems.
AB - Current Retail Value

Kaleidoscope™
#4348

Birthday: 6/24/2000
Introduced: 1/30/2001
Retired: 3/14/2001
I'm wild and crazy as you can see
Other cats want to be like me
Some may say I look like a clown
But I'm the coolest cat in town!
7G - $7 ♥ 8G - $7

Kanata™
#4621

Birthday: 10/14/2002
Introduced: 9/30/2002
Retired: 2/4/2003
13 different tags . Inside left side has
flag of each Territory/Province.
*Canada exclusive. See Kanata appendix
for poem and complete listing.*
10G - $10

126

Kansas™
#40130

Birthday: None
Introduced: 8/30/2004
Retired: 12/29/2005
STATE MOTTO: "Ad Astra Per Aspra"
(To The Stars Through Difficulty)
NICKNAME: Sunflower State
FACT: Dodge City, Kansas is the
windiest city in the U.S.!
Sold only in Kansas.
12G - $10

Kansas City™
#40118

Birthday: 6/3/2004
Introduced: 8/7/2004
Retired: 8/26/2004
You can listen to jazz or blues
Or try our famous barbeques
Hundreds of fountains you must see
When you visit Kansas City!
Trade Show exclusive.
12G - $25

Kansas Sunflower™
#40294

Birthday: None
Introduced: 8/6/2005
Retired: 12/29/2005
OFFICIAL FLOWER SINCE 1903
This simple, bright, and happy bloom
Is sure to take away the gloom
That's why in Kansas we all say
The sunflower is here to stay!
Trade Show exclusive.
13G - $10

Kernow™
#46057

Birthday: 3/5/2006
Introduced: 4/28/2006
Retired: 5/5/2006
St. Pirans Flag upon my chest
Cornwall really is the best
So full of sunshine, sea, and fun
There's lots to do for everyone!
UK exclusive.
14UK - $20

Kernow™ Key-clip
#46102

Birthday: None
Introduced: 5/29/2007
Retired: 6/6/2007
Onen Hag Oll
UK exclusive.
15UKsm - $

Khufu™
#4807

Birthday: 8/00/2003
Introduced: 7/31/2003
Retired: 9/1/2003
There's one thing that I know is true
Camels can have one hump or two
Either way, we love to play
Out in the desert sun all day!
August 2003 Beanie Baby of the Month.
BBOM - $7

Kia Ora™
#46095

Birthday: 3/29/2006
Introduced: 1/31/2007
Current
We live in the land of hte long white cloud
They call us Kiwis; we always stand proud
Our land is small, but there's so much to see
So won't you come and enjoy it with me?
New Zealand map. Asian-Pacific exclusive.
15G - $20

Kicks™
#4229

Birthday: 8/16/1998
Introduced: 1/1/1999
Retired: 12/23/1999
The world cup is his dream
Kicks the bear is the best on his team
He hopes that one day he'll be the pick
First he needs to improve his kick!
5G - $7

Killarney™
#40042

Birthday: 3/17/2003
Introduced: 12/30/2003
Retired: 4/16/2004
An old legend had been told
About a certain pot-o-gold
It can be found at rainbows end
Along with me, your Beanie friend!
12G - $7

Kippy™
#4902

Birthday: 9/00/2003
Introduced: 8/28/2003
Retired: 10/1/2003
Sometimes I bark, sometimes I howl
One thing's for sure, I'll never growl
I'm the nicest dog you'll ever see
I just want you to play with me!
*September 2003
Beanie Baby of the Month.*
BBOM - $9

Kirby™
#4396

Birthday: 5/5/2001
Introduced: 10/1/2001
Retired: 3/22/2002
Prancing on the icy snow
I put on quite a funny show
Slipping and sliding all around
I hope my paws stay on the ground!
7G - $7 ♥ 9G - $7

Kissable™
#40470

Birthday: 2/4/2006
Introduced: 11/30/2006
Retired: 1/24/2007
I wouldn't want to be remiss
So I'll give you a little kiss
No one's more kissable than you
So pucker up and kiss me too!
14G - $7

KISS-e™
#4419

Birthday: 2/14/2002
Introduced: 1/13/2003
Retired: 2/14/2003
This special little Valentine
Is here to ask if you'll be mine
A little smooch from me to you
KISS-e's the bear that's just for you!
Ty Store exclusive.
11G - $9

Kisses™
#47048

Birthday: 7/7/2007
Introduced: 12/21/2006
Current
To celebrate the hundredth year
Since Hershey's® Kisses® did appear
Wrapped up with a tell-tale bow
It's the cutest bear you'll ever know!
*In honor of the 100th anniversary of the
Hershey's Kiss. Sold only at Walgreens.*
14G - Current Retail Value

Kiss-kiss™
#40310

Birthday: 2/15/2005
Introduced: 11/30/2005
Retired: 1/27/2006
To me you're unlike any other
So here's a kiss and then another
Next I'll give you a hug or two
Just so you know that I love you!
13G/13UK - $7

Kissme™
#4504

Birthday: 2/7/2001
Introduced: 12/27/2001
Retired: 2/14/2002
I'm as sweet as I can be
Wearing hearts for you to see
My new outfit is quite dandy
It looks as if I'm wearing candy!
7G - $7 ♥ 9G - $7

Kissy™
#40037

Birthday: 2/7/2003
Introduced: 11/26/2003
Retired: 4/16/2004
Everybody will agree
That we were always meant to be
I just can't help myself; it's true
Kisses are best when shared with you!
11G - $7

Kiwi™
#4070

Birthday: 9/16/1995
Introduced: 6/3/1995
Retired: 1/1/1997
Kiwi waits for the April showers
Watching a garden bloom with flowers
There trees grow with fruit that's sweet
I'm sure you'll guess his favorite treat!
3G - $80 ♥ 4G - $40

Kiwiana™
#4627

Birthday: 5/1/2003
Introduced: 4/28/2003
Retired: 11/7/2003
We Kiwis love just having fun
We'll swim or hike 'til the day is done
A heritage that makes us proud
Our Maori past we shout out loud!
New Zealand exclusive.
11G - $20

KnOWLedge™
#47066

Birthday: 6/19/2006
Introduced: 6/7/2007
Current
Most every book that I embrace
Will take me to a special place
Tales of knights or ladies fair
Pick up a book and join me there!
Borders/Walden exclusive.
15G - $10

Knuckles™
#4247

Birthday: 3/25/1999
Introduced: 4/14/1999
Retired: 12/23/1999
In the kitchen working hard
Using ingredients from the yard
No one will eat it, can you guess why?
Her favorite recipe is for mud pie!
5G - $7

Kookie™
#40061

Birthday: 7/15/2003
Introduced: 2/26/2004
Retired: 7/28/2004
I'll run and jump and catch a ball
And come for you when you should call
After we play we'll snuggle, too
'cause I get sleepy just like you!
12G - $7

Kooky™
#4357

Birthday: 10/24/2000
Introduced: 5/1/2001
Retired: 7/12/2001
If you want to have some fun
Kooky will be number one
This cat loves to dance around
To his favorite groovy sounds!
7G - $9 ♥ 8G - $9

Koowee™
#46009

Birthday: 9/24/2003
Introduced: 7/28/2004
Current
Eating Gum leaves, sleeping in trees
Relaxing in the Aussie Breeze
Watching as the branches sway
That's how I like to spend my day!
Australia/New Zealand exclusive.
12G - $15

Korea™
#46027

Birthday: 10/3/2004
Introduced: 2/28/2005
Retired: 4/15/2006
Sandy beaches under summer sunlight
Snow mountains under winter breeze
Other things I love about Korea
Kimchi, Hanbok, K-pop and Korean drama!
Korea exclusive.
Also available in Asian-Pacific.
13G - $25

Korea™
#46043 · black nose

Birthday: 5/15/2005
Introduced: 9/12/2005
Retired: 6/15/2006
Do you want to visit to Korea?
Then, send me your wish list
Let me light on Lotus lanterns on Buddha's
birthday to make your dream come true!
Asian-Pacific exclusive.
13G - $25

Korea™
#46043 · flag nose

Birthday: 5/15/2005
Introduced: 10/15/2005
Retired: 6/15/2006
Do you want to visit to Korea?
Then, send me your wish list
Let me light on Lotus lanterns on Buddha's
birthday to make your dream come true!
Korea exclusive.
13G - $50

Kringle™
#40138

Birthday: 12/24/2004
Introduced: 9/30/2004
Retired: 12/29/2004
If you're a good little girl or boy
I'll bring you lots of holiday joy
But if you're naughty instead of nice
A lump of coal will have to suffice!
12G/12EU - $7

KuKu™
#4192

Birthday: 1/5/1997
Introduced: 5/30/1998
Retired: 12/23/1999
This fancy bird loves to converse
He talks in poems, rhythms and verse
So take him home and give him some time
You'll be surprised how he can rhyme!
5G - $7

L™
#40512

Birthday: None
Introduced: 6/30/2005
Current
Alphabet Bears are issued without poems.
AB - Current Retail Value

LA.™
#40117

Birthday: 4/4/2004
Introduced: 7/17/2004
Retired: 8/26/2004
City of life right by the sea
Los Angeles is the place to be
The perfect weather all year through
You can always enjoy a sunset view!
Trade Show exclusive.
12G - $7

L'amore™
#40008

Birthday: 11/16/2002
Introduced: 6/30/2003
Retired: 9/5/2003
All day long I bathe and primp
With the perfume I do not skimp
Take me home and you will see
Just how pretty I can be!
7G - $7 ♥ 11G - $7

Laguna™
#40646

Birthday: 6/26/2006
Introduced: 5/31/2007
Current
Flippers and fins and gills and tails
Plant life and coral, dolphins and whales
Such wondrous sights are deep in the sea
C,mon and take a marine tour with me!
15G - Current Retail Value

Lani™
#40141

Birthday: 3/26/2004
Introduced: 9/30/2004
Retired: 2/24/2005
To me, "aloha" means "hello"
It also means goodbye, you know
So many fun things we can do
Like swim and surf and hula, too!
12G/12EU - $7

Laptop™
#40150

Birthday: 8/9/2004
Introduced: 9/30/2004
Retired: 6/29/2005
Take that computer off your knee
That's the place that I should be
There couldn't be a better fit
Than a lap with a dog on it!
12G/12EU - $7

Las Vegas™
#40228

Birthday: 3/16/2005
Introduced: 4/5/2005
Current
The lights of Vegas shine so bright
A beacon glowing in the night
At any time throughout the year
Odds are that you'll love it here!
Las Vegas exclusive.
13G - Current Retail Value

Laughter™
#40384

Birthday: 2/12/2006
Introduced: 4/28/2006
Retired: 6/23/2006
20 years of love and great joy
For every adult and each girl and boy
20 years of good times and fun
And thanks to you we're second to none!
20th Anniversary Bear.
14G/14UK - $7

Laughter™ Key-clip (Smiley)
No Style

Birthday: None
Introduced: 8/6/2006
Retired: 1/24/2007
20 years of fun from our hearts to yours
NY Show 2/12/-2/15/06 and Dallas Show 6/23-6/26/06.
14sm - $25

Leaves™
#44092

Birthday: 9/23/2006
Introduced: 9/5/2006
Retired: 10/8/2006
The vivid colors of the fall
Are all so bright that they enthrall
With red and gold and orange, too
I simply love the fall; don't you?
Ty Store exclusive.
14G - $25

Leelo™
#40661

Birthday: 7/18/2006
Introduced: 6/29/2007
Current
With my teeth so sharp and white
You might worry that I'll bite
And that's just what I may do
If you have French fries with you!
15G - Current Retail Value

Lefty™
#4085

Birthday: 7/4/1996
Introduced: 6/15/1996
Retired: 1/1/1997
Donkeys to the left, elephants to the right
Often seems like a crazy sight
This whole game seems very funny
Until you realize they're spending
your money!
USA exclusive.
4G - $60

Lefty 2000™
#4290

Birthday: 7/4/2000
Introduced: 6/24/2000
Retired: 12/21/2000
This November make a note
The time has come for you to vote
Pick me when you have to choose
I'm a Beanie, you can't lose!
USA exclusive.
6G - $7

Lefty 2004™
#40045

Birthday: 6/25/2003
Introduced: 12/30/2003
Retired: 11/3/2004
When it's time for you to choose
There is a way that you can't lose
You'll never come in second place
When Beanie Babies win the race!
12G - $7

Legend™
#40076

Birthday: 12/9/2003
Introduced: 5/28/2004
Retired: 10/27/2004
Many tales have been told
Of ladies fair in days of old
Some say the knight would win the day
But this dragon says, "No way"!
12G - $12

Legs™
#4020

Birthday: 4/25/1993
Introduced: 1/8/1994
Retired: 10/1/1997
Legs lives in a hollow log
Legs likes to play leap frog
If you like to hang out at the lake
Legs will be the new friend you'll make!
1G - $1,400 ♥ 2G - $225 ♥
3G - $50 ♥ 4G - $7

Legs™
#49018

Birthday: 4/25/1993
Introduced: 10/3/2005
Retired: 3/9/2006
Legs lives in a hollow log
Legs likes to play leap frog
If you like to hang out at the lake
Legs will be the new friend you'll make!
*Available in BBOC Original 9
Assortments 1-5.
Beanie Baby Offcial Club exclusive.*
BBOC - $10

Lemonade Ice™
#40678

Birthday: 6/23/2007
Introduced: 6/29/2007
Current
Ready for a summer treat?
Something cool and oh-so sweet?
If the sun should get too hot
Lemonade Ice will hit the spot!
Trade Show exclusive.
15G - Current Retail Value

Leopold™
#47072

Birthday: 5/2/2007
Introduced: 6/29/2007
Current
The perfect place for a good time
For fun, laughter and food sublime
Rainforest Cafe is quite a treat
It's a wild place to shop and eat!
Rainforest Café exclusive.
15G - Current Retail Value

Lex™
#47001

Birthday: 9/10/2004
Introduced: 10/6/2004
Retired: 11/24/2004
Playtime can be so much fun
We'll play all day and when we're done
I hope we've learned a thing or two
'Cause learning is such fun for you!
Learning Express exclusive.
12G - $12

Li Mei™
#44200

Birthday: None
Introduced: 7/5/2004
Retired: 1/12/2005
BIRTHPLACE: Central China
TIDBIT: Although pandas are classified as
bears, they are unique in that they cannot
store enough body fat to hibernate.
Ty Store exclusive.
12G - $10

Libearty™
#4057

Birthday: Summer/1996
Introduced: 6/15/1996
Retired: 1/1/1997
I am called libearty
I wear the flag for all to see
Hope and freedom is my way
That's why I wear flag USA
USA exclusive.
4G - $90

LIBERT-e™
#44015

Birthday: 7/4/2004
Introduced: 6/8/2004
Retired: 8/4/2004
A famous statue shares my name
She stands for freedom, her claim to fame
And that's our nation's founding pride
One that cannot be denied!
Ty Store exclusive.
12G - $7

Liberty™
#4531 · blue face with
striped body

Birthday: 6/14/2001
Introduced: 4/30/2002
Retired: 7/17/2002
My colors are red, white and blue
It's not just me, they wear them, too
Line us up and you will see
How beautiful the flag can be!
USA exclusive.
10G - $7

Liberty™
#4531 · red face with
stars on body

Birthday: 6/14/2001
Introduced: 4/30/2002
Retired: 7/17/2002
My colors are red, white and blue
It's not just me, they wear them, too
Line us up and you will see
How beautiful the flag can be!
USA exclusive.
10G - $7

Liberty™
#4531 · white face with
striped body

Birthday: 6/14/2001
Introduced: 4/30/2002
Retired: 7/17/2002
My colors are red, white and blue
It's not just me, they wear them, too
Line us up and you will see
How beautiful the flag can be!
USA exclusive.
10G - $7

Lightning™
#4537

Birthday: 3/27/2002
Introduced: 5/31/2002
Retired: 8/8/2003
I love to run across the plains
So get a good grip on the reins
We'll go so fast, we'll almost fly
And watch the world go zooming by!
7G - $7 ♥ 10G - $7

Lime Ice™
#40678

Birthday: 6/23/2007
Introduced: 6/29/2007
Current
Ready for a summer treat?
Something cool and oh-so sweet?
When the days are hot and long
A Lime Ice is never wrong!
15G - Current Retail Value

Lips™
#4254

Birthday: 3/15/1999
Introduced: 7/14/1999
Retired: 12/23/1999
Did you ever see a fish like me?
I'm the most colorful in the sea
Traveling with friends in a school
Swimming all day is really cool!
5G - $7

Little Bear™
#40435

Birthday: 11/23/2006
Introduced: 9/29/2006
Retired: 12/21/2006
Let us give thanks for our good health
For the many different kinds of wealth
For the love of friends and family
Happy Thanksgiving to you from me!
14G/14UK - $7

Little Feather™
#40136

Birthday: 9/22/2003
Introduced: 9/1/2004
Retired: 10/14/2004
There's so much to be thankful for
Our health and families and much more
And as for me, I'd like to say
We should all give thanks everyday!
12G - $7

Little Kiss™
#47040

Birthday: 2/7/2006
Introduced: 11/30/2006
Retired: 12/21/2006
Here's a little kiss from me
Just to show my love, you see
I hope you feel the same way, too
Because I know our love is true!
Hallmark Gold Crown exclusive.
14G - $7

Little Squeeze™
#47040

Birthday: 2/7/2006
Introduced: 11/30/2006
Retired: 12/21/2006
Here's a little squeeze from me
Just to show my love, you see
I hope you feel the same way, too
Because I know our love is true!
Hallmark Gold Crown exclusive.
14G - $7

Little Star™
#47017

Birthday: 6/4/2005
Introduced: 8/31/2005
Retired: 6/23/2006
Children from both near and far
Remind me of a little star
Shining bright for all to see
A precious gift for you and me!
Benefits Little Star, Inc.
13G - $7

Lizzy™
#4033

Birthday: 5/11/1995
Introduced: 1/7/1996
Retired: 12/31/1997
Lizzy loves Legs the frog
She hides with him under logs
Both of them search for flies
Underneath the clear blue skies!
3G - $100 ♥ 4G - $7 ♥ 5G - $7

Lizzy™
#4033 · Ty Dye

Birthday: None
Introduced: 6/3/1995
Retired: 1/7/1996
Lizzy was issued without a poem.
3G - $400

Lollipup™
#40342

Birthday: 1/10/2005
Introduced: 1/31/2006
Current
"YIP," means I want to play with you
When I say, "YAP," I'm happy, too
"ARF," implies that this is fun
And "BARK" is "Join in everyone"!
14G/14UK - Current Retail Value

London™
#46015

Birthday: 7/19/2004
Introduced: 11/1/2004
Retired: 3/27/2006
In London there's so much to do
Art, theatre and culture, too
Great people, food and so much fun
And the shopping's second to none!
London exclusive.
12EU - $20

Loong™
#46045

Birthday: 9/9/2005
Introduced: 10/31/2005
Current
Look at the night sky and you'll see
Stars shining back at you and me
Each represents what used to be
Thousands of Dragons roaming free!
Asian-Pacific exclusive.
13G - $20

Loosy™
#4206

Birthday: 3/29/1998
Introduced: 9/30/1998
Retired: 9/1/1999
A tale has been told
Of a goose that laid gold
But try as she might
Loosy's eggs are just white!
5G - $7

Lot's O' Luck™
#48434

Birthday: 3/00/2007
Introduced: 3/1/2007
Retired: 4/1/2007
I will bring Lot's O'Luck, it's true
If you keep me right next to you
'Cause as we know, good luck is found
Wherever there are friends around!
March 2007 Beanie Baby of the Month.
BBOM - $7

Louisiana™
#40319

Birthday: None
Introduced: 9/9/2005
Retired: 5/24/2006
In memory of those who lost their homes,
their loved ones, or their lives, as a result of
Hurricane Katrina
We extend our deepest sympathies
Together we're a stronger nation
*$1 of sale donated to American Red
Cross Disaster Fund.*
13G/13UK - $7

Louisiana™
#44078

Birthday: None
Introduced: 9/6/2005
Retired: 5/24/2006
In memory of those who lost their homes,
their loved ones, or their lives, as a result of
Hurricane Katrina
We extend our deepest sympathies
Together we're a stronger nation
*$2 of sale donated to American Red
Cross Disaster Fund. Ty Store exclusive.*
13G - $7

Love and Kisses™
#40534

Birthday: None
Introduced: 4/28/2006
Current
Greetings Bears are issued without poems.
14G/14UK - Current Retail Value

Love Birds™
#47027

Birthday: None
Introduced: 6/30/2006
Current
Lovebirds was issued without a poem.
Hallmark Gold Crown exclusive.
14G - Current Retail Value

Love U Mom ™
#40348

Birthday: 5/14/2006
Introduced: 2/28/2006
Retired: 1/24/2007
My Mom is just the best there is
When it comes to caring she's a wiz
She's number one, the best, the bomb
And that's is why I love you mom!
USA/Canada exclusive.
14G - $7

Love U Mum™
#46056

Birthday: 3/26/2006
Introduced: 2/24/2006
Retired: 1/24/2007
My mum is just the best there is
When it comes to caring she's a wiz
She's top; She's better than the rest
I love you mum, you are the best!
UK/New Zealand/Australia exclusive.
14G/14UK - $7

Lovesick™
#40471

Birthday: 4/14/2006
Introduced: 11/30/2006
Retired: 1/24/2007
I know that I'm one lovesick pup
When I'm with you, my ears pink up
My knees get weak, my heart beats fast
My love for you is unsurpassed!
Same style # as Junglelove.
14G/14UK - $7

Lovesme™
#44082

Birthday: 2/14/2006
Introduced: 1/10/2006
Retired: 3/6/2006
Do you lovesme or lovesme not?
Well, I know I love you a lot
Lovesme not or lovesme do?
I just knew it! You love me, too!
Ty Store exclusive.
14G - $12

Lovey-Dovey™
#40159

Birthday: 6/25/2004
Introduced: 12/6/2004
Retired: 1/28/2005
A little pup so cute and sweet
Bringing you a special treat
Some love and cuddles just for you
Maybe even a kiss or two!
12G/12EU - $12

Luau™
#40069

Birthday: 8/21/2003
Introduced: 4/29/2004
Retired: 9/10/2004
I love my life; it's so much fun
Playing in the Hawaiian sun
And then I'll hula dance all night
It really is this pig's delight!
12G - $12

LUCK-e™
#4420

Birthday: 3/17/2003
Introduced: 2/17/2003
Retired: 3/17/2003
If your heart is pure and true
I will bring good luck to you
Let's celebrate St. Patrick's Day
'Cause it's my favorite holiday!
Ty Store exclusive.
11G - $7

Lucky™
#4040 • 7 glued felt spots

Birthday: None
Introduced: 6/25/1994
Retired: 2/27/1996
Lucky was issued without a poem.
1G - $2,000 ♥ 2G - $375 ♥ 3G - $150

Lucky™
#4040 • 11 printed spots

Birthday: 5/1/1995
Introduced: 2/27/1996
Retired: 5/1/1998
Lucky the lady bug loves the lotto
"Someone must win" that's her motto
But save your dimes and even a penny
Don't spend on the lotto and
you'll have many!
4G - $7 ♥ 5G - $7

Lucky™
#4040 • 21 printed spots

Birthday: 5/1/1995
Introduced: 2/27/1996
Retired: 10/1996
Lucky the lady bug loves the lotto
"Someone must win" that's her motto
But save your dimes and even a penny
Don't spend on the lotto and
you'll have many!
4G - $110

Lucky O'Day™
#40325

Birthday: 3/17/2006
Introduced: 12/30/2005
Retired: 3/27/2006
Good mornin'! I'm Lucky O'Day
I'm here to send fortune your way
Just remember when the long day ends
Fortune is yours, when you've got friends!
14G/14UK - $7

Luke™
#4214

Birthday: 6/15/1998
Introduced: 1/1/1999
Retired: 12/23/1999
After chewing on your favorite shoes
Luke gets tired, takes a snooze
Who wouldn't love a puppy like this?
Give him a hug, he'll give you a kiss!
5G - $7

Luke™ Key-clip
#40402

Birthday: None
Introduced: 6/30/2006
Current
Friends Fur-ever!
14G/14UKsm - Current Retail Value

Lullaby™
#4583

Birthday: 5/17/2002
Introduced: 1/30/2003
Retired: 5/25/2004
Please let me curl up on your lap
So I can take a little nap
If it's too hard to fall asleep
Then I'll just count my friends, the sheep!
7G - $7 ♥ 11G - $7

Lumberjack™
#40001

Birthday: 3/22/2003
Introduced: 5/29/2003
Retired: 6/24/2004
A carpenter is what I am
I'll build a lodge, I'll build a dam
A river and a couple trees
I really am easy to please!
7G - $7 ♥ 11G - $7

Lurkey™
#4309

Birthday: 6/13/2000
Introduced: 7/8/2000
Retired: 3/14/2001
Thanksgiving is my special day
But there's something I must say
When you sit down with your fork
Make sure your plate is full of pork!
6G - $7 ♥ 7G - $7

M™
#40513

Birthday: None
Introduced: 6/30/2005
Current
Alphabet Bears are issued without poems.
AB - Current Retail Value

M.C. Anniversary 1st Edition™
No Style

Birthday: 2/10/2002
Introduced: 12/11/2002
Retired: 8/6/2003
For having hit the mark and more
There's one more Beanie than before
Our way of showing we're sincere
And thanks for your support this year!
Ty MBNA exclusive.
11G - $90

M.C. Anniversary 2nd Edition™
#4982

Birthday: 8/10/2003
Introduced: 8/8/2003
Retired: 8/2/2004
To show our great appreciation
Come join in the celebration
We've created a special bear for you
M.C. Anniversary number 2!
Ty MBNA exclusive.
11G - $90

M.C. Anniversary 3rd Edition™
#49009

Birthday: 7/29/2004
Introduced: 8/2/2004
Retired: 8/1/2005
To mark your anniversary
A special gift . . . what could it be?
The newest bear for your collection
M.C. Anniversary 3rd Edition!
Ty MBNA exclusive.
12G - $90

M.C. Anniversary 4th Edition™
#49011

Birthday: 7/23/2005
Introduced: 8/2/2005
Retired: 8/26/2006
We'll shout out on the count of three
HAPPY ANNIVERSARY
And here's a bear you'll just adore
M.C. Anniversary number 4 !
Ty MBNA exclusive.
13G - $90

M.C. Anniversary 5th Edition™
#49032

Birthday: 10/24/2006
Introduced: 8/26/2006
Current
You have earned a special treat
It's one we think is really neat
Our newest bear to mark the year
The new Anniversary bear is here!
Ty MBNA exclusive.
14G - $90

M.C. Beanie™
#4997 · black nose

Birthday: None
Introduced: 8/14/2001
Retired: 8/15/2002
You shop and shop, so much to do
So little time, you're never through
Ty Mastercard will save the day
'Cause it's the easy way to pay!
Ty MBNA exclusive.
9G - $30

M.C. Beanie™
#4997 · brown nose

Birthday: None
Introduced: 8/14/2001
Retired: 8/15/2002
You shop and shop, so much to do
So little time, you're never through
Ty Mastercard will save the day
'Cause it's the easy way to pay!
Ty MBNA exclusive.
9G - $3,000

M.C. Beanie II™
#4987

Birthday: 1/11/2002
Introduced: 8/16/2002
Retired: 8/14/2003
For purchases both large and small
From on the Web or in the mall
Ty's Mastercard is the best way
To buy the things you want today!
Also available with Anniversary card.
Ty MBNA exclusive.
10G - $20

M.C. Beanie III™
#4981

Birthday: 7/13/2003
Introduced: 8/9/2003
Retired: 8/12/2004
A brand new card for you to use
To pay for gas, or food...or shoes
And with your MasterCard you get
The greatest little Beanie yet!
Ty MBNA exclusive.
11G - $20

M.C. Beanie IV™
#49006

Birthday: 8/16/2004
Introduced: 8/16/2004
Retired: 8/12/2005
If you like to shop on-line
Or go out someplace nice to dine
With a Ty MasterCard in hand
You can buy what you had planned!
Ty MBNA exclusive.
12G - $20

M.C. Beanie V™
#49010

Birthday: 8/5/2005
Introduced: 8/15/2005
Retired: 8/26/2006
For five long years our family's grown
And to celebrate this milestone
We've made this special bear for you
As M.C. V makes its debut!
Ty MBNA exclusive.
13G - $15

M.C. Beanie VI™
#49033

Birthday: 8/14/2006
Introduced: 8/26/2006
Current
Over the years our family's grown
And to celebrate this milestone
A new bear's here to get his kicks
Join us to welcome M.C. Six!
Ty MBNA exclusive.
14G - $15

M.C. Beanie™ Key-clip
#CC010

Birthday: None
Introduced: 8/26/2006
Current
Smart money's on me!
Ty MBNA exclusive.
14G - Current Retail Value

Mac™
#4225

Birthday: 6/10/1998
Introduced: 1/1/1999
Retired: 12/23/1999
Mac tries hard to prove he's the best
Swinging his bat harder than the rest
Breaking records, enjoying the game
Hitting home runs is his claim to fame!
5G - $7

Magic™
#4088 · pale pink thread

Birthday: 9/5/1995
Introduced: 6/3/1995
Retired: 12/31/1997
Magic the dragon lives in a dream
The most beautiful that you have ever seen
Through magic lands she likes to fly
Look up and watch her, way up high!
3G - $60

Magic™
#4088 · hot pink thread

Birthday: 9/5/1995
Introduced: 6/3/1996
Retired: 12/31/1996
Magic the dragon lives in a dream
The most beautiful that you have ever seen
Through magic lands she likes to fly
Look up and watch her, way up high!
4G - $60

Magic™
#4088 · medium pink thread

Birthday: 9/5/1995
Introduced: 6/3/1996
Retired: 12/31/1996
Magic the dragon lives in a dream
The most beautiful that you have ever seen
Through magic lands she likes to fly
Look up and watch her, way up high!
4G - $7

Majestic™
#46058

Birthday: 4/21/2006
Introduced: 4/21/2006
Retired: 5/12/2006
A wonderful day to celebrate
Right in front of the Palace gate
In honor of her 80 years
Filled with smiles and with cheers!
UK/Australia/New Zealand exclusive.
14UK - $15

Maju™
#46040 · black nose

Birthday: 8/9/2005
Introduced: 9/12/2005
Retired: 6/15/2006
Red above white, stars in a circle
A nation grows; an island miracle
A rising crescent, 40 years long
As Singapore keeps going strong!
Asian-Pacific exclusive.
13G - $20

Maju™
#46040 · flag nose

Birthday: 8/9/2005
Introduced: 10/15/2005
Retired: 6/15/2006
Red above white, stars in a circle
A nation grows; an island miracle
A rising crescent, 40 years long
As Singapore keeps going strong!
Singapore exclusive.
13G - $50

Malaysia™
#46024

Birthday: 2/5/2005
Introduced: 2/28/2005
Retired: 4/15/2006
Our country has beauty and color all over
Giving splendour to its land, East and West
Its beauty stretches as high as Mount Kinabalu
Your heart will remain here once you visit
Malaysia!
Malaysia exclusive.
13G - $20

Maliha and Jade™
#40600

Birthday: 8/2/2006
Introduced: 5/20/2007
Current
St. Louis Zoo exclusive.
Jade birthday is 2/25/2007.
15G - $15

Manchu™
#40456

Birthday: 8/26/2006
Introduced: 10/31/2006
Current
I think I'll munch on some bamboo
Because that's what we pandas do
Then next maybe I'll climb a tree
Ah . . . this is the life for me!
14G/14UK - Current Retail Value

Mandy™
#40020

Birthday: 7/18/2002
Introduced: 8/28/2003
Retired: 6/24/2004
I love to have fun and run around
Play hide and seek and not be found
Give great big hugs and kisses, too
Say good night and I love you!
7G - $7 ♥ 11G - $7

Manes™
#40352

Birthday: 10/6/2005
Introduced: 2/28/2006
Current
As the king of jungle lore
I'll let out a mighty ROAR
But now the best that I can do
Sounds much more like a playful MEW!
14G/14UK - Current Retail Value

Manny™
#4081

Birthday: 6/8/1995
Introduced: 1/7/1996
Retired: 5/11/1997
Manny is sometimes called a sea cow
She likes to twirl and likes to bow
Manny sure is glad you bought her
Because it's so lonely under water!
3G - $70 ♥ 4G - $45

Maple™
#4600 · "Maple" on tush tag

Birthday: 7/1/1996
Introduced: 1/1/1997
Retired: 7/30/1999
Maple the bear likes to ski
With his friends, he plays hockey.
He loves his pancakes
and eats every crumb
Can you guess which country he's from?
Canada exclusive.
4G - $25 ♥ 5G - $25

Maple™
#4600 · "Pride" on tush tag

Birthday: 7/1/1996
Introduced: 1/1/1997
Retired: 1/1997
Maple the bear likes to ski
With his friends, he plays hockey.
He loves his pancakes
and eats every crumb
Can you guess which country he's from?
Canada exclusive.
4G - $375

March™
#4390

Birthday: None
Introduced: 1/29/2002
Retired: 5/24/2002
My nose is the color of my birthstone.
Aquamarine - It brings determination
and self-confidence!
Birthday - $7

March 2003™
#4554

Birthday: None
Introduced: 1/30/2003
Retired: 5/29/2003
Dr. Seuss - Mar 2
Albert Einstein - Mar 14
Reese Witherspoon - Mar 22
Birthday - $7

Mardi Gras™
#40199

Birthday: 2/24/2004
Introduced: 1/31/2005
Retired: 3/24/2005
It's time for the parade to start
So grab a mask and play your part
We'll dance around and have great fun
Come on and join in everyone!
13G/13EU - $10

Marsh™
#48436

Birthday: 5/00/2007
Introduced: 5/1/2007
Retired: 6/1/2007
I find most people don't agree
But the marsh is the place to be
Our lily pads are just the best
The perfect place to sit and rest!
May 2007 Beanie Baby of the Month.
BBOM - $7

Marshall™
#40068

Birthday: 2/26/2004
Introduced: 4/29/2004
Retired: 10/27/2004
As the Marshall here in town
I'll never let the townsfolk down
I keep the peace and when I'm through
We'll horse around, just me and you!
12G - $7

Marshall™
#40068

Birthday: 2/26/2004
Introduced: 5/30/2005
Retired: 5/30/2005
As the Marshall here in town
I'll never let the townsfolk down
I keep the peace and when I'm through
We'll horse around, just me and you!
Arlington Park exclusive.
12G - $80

Marshall™
#40068

Birthday: 2/26/2004
Introduced: 7/3/2005
Retired: 7/3/2005
As the Marshall here in town
I'll never let the townsfolk down
I keep the peace and when I'm through
We'll horse around, just me and you!
Arlington Jr. Jockey Club exclusive.
12G - $150

Marshmallow™
#40182

Birthday: 5/3/2004
Introduced: 12/30/2004
Retired: 6/29/2005
Hopping through the flower bed
I think I see a friend ahead
Maybe I'll stop and chat awhile
'Cause meeting new friends makes me smile!
13G/13EU - $7

Mary™
#46079

Birthday: 9/1/2006
Introduced: 8/31/2006
Retired: 1/24/2007
Princess Mary from the hidden land
With my smile I make friends
But my heart belongs to another
Pirate Roger he is the one!
Vedes exclusive.
14UK - $35

Mascotte™
#46060

Birthday: 6/9/2006
Introduced: 4/28/2006
Retired: 5/26/2006
Little blue bear
Will win for certain
The heart of people
Who will love him tomorrow
Europe exclusive.
14UK - $20

Masque™
#44044

Birthday: 2/8/2005
Introduced: 1/6/2005
Retired: 4/5/2005
This very festive time of year
It's time for fun, let's laugh and cheer
Whether you're a dad or mom-ba
It's time to dance . . . let's do the samba!
Ty Store exclusive.
13G - $8

Massachusetts™
#40125

Birthday: None
Introduced: 8/30/2004
Retired: 12/29/2005
STATE MOTTO: "By the Sword We Seek
Peace, But Peace Only Under Liberty"
NICKNAME: Bay State
FACT: Boston Common became the first
public park in the U.S. in 1634!
Sold only in Massachusetts.
12G - $7

Massachusetts Mayflower™
#40299

Birthday: None
Introduced: 9/10/2005
Retired: 12/29/2005
OFFICIAL FLOWER SINCE 1918
I grow around the towering pines
Small flowers on long, trailing vines
Five simple petals, soft, and white
Are Massachusetts' spring delight!
Trade Show exclusive.
13G - $10

Matlock™
#40656

Birthday: 6/1/2007
Introduced: 6/29/2007
Current
Please let me out into the yard
I promise that I will stand guard
I'll take good care of you; you'll see
It's part of being a family!
15G - Current Retail Value

Mattie™
#4521

Birthday: 4/26/2001
Introduced: 4/1/2002
Retired: 9/25/2002
Rub my tummy and you will see
Just how playful I can be
I'm warm and kind and faithful too
I'd like to curl up next to you!
7G - $7 ♥ 10G - $7

Max & Ruby™
Max™
#40606

Birthday: None
Introduced: 2/28/2007
Current
I'm Max! I love trucks, mud, candy, and my
big sister, Ruby!
USA/Canada exclusive.
Also available at Ty Store.
15G - Current Retail Value

Max & Ruby™ Ruby™
#40607

Birthday: None
Introduced: 2/28/2007
Current
I'm Ruby! I love shopping, tea parties, and helping my little brother, Max!
USA/Canada exclusive.
Also available at Ty Store.
15G - Current Retail Value

May™
#4392

Birthday: None
Introduced: 4/1/2002
Retired: 7/25/2002
My nose is the color of my birthstone.
Emerald - It brings good fortune & lots of fun!
Birthday - $7

May 2003™
#4556

Birthday: None
Introduced: 3/31/2003
Retired: 7/29/2003
Willie Mays - May 6
Sir Laurence Olivier - May 22
Rudolph Giuliani - May 28
Birthday - $7

McWooly™
#40174

Birthday: 5/10/2004
Introduced: 12/30/2004
Retired: 6/29/2005
Do you see shamrocks over there?
Where I come from they're everywhere
I wear them proudly for all to see
Because they bring good luck to me!
13G/13EU - $7

Meekins™
#40329

Birthday: 5/16/2005
Introduced: 12/30/2005
Retired: 12/21/2006
Lambs are gentle and lambs are kind
The sweetest animals you will find
Lambs are meek and lambs are shy
But they still take time to say, "HI"!
14G/14UK - $7

Mel™
#4162

Birthday: 1/14/1996
Introduced: 1/1/1997
Retired: 3/31/1999
How do you name a Koala bear?
It's rather tough, I do declare!
It confuses me, I get into a funk
I'll name him Mel after my favorite hunk!
4G - $7 ♥ 5G - $7

Melbourne™
#46053

Birthday: None
Introduced: 1/24/2006
Current
MOTTO: We gather strength as we go
FACT: Melbourne was incorporated as a town on 12 August 1842!
Australia exclusive.
14G - $20

Mellow™
#4344

Birthday: 12/7/2000
Introduced: 3/1/2001
Retired: 5/21/2001
My all time favorite thing to do
Is snuggle up real close to you
Take me home and you will see
How much fun a hug can be!
7G - $7 ♥ 8G - $7

Merlion™
#46091

Birthday: 8/9/2006
Introduced: 1/31/2007
Current
In a tropical paradise by the sea
That's where the mythical Merlion might be
A creature part lion, the other part fish
An ocean full of life is his greatest wish!
Asian-Pacific exclusive.
15G - Current Retail Value

Merriment™
#48431

Birthday: 12/00/2006
Introduced: 12/1/2006
Retired: 1/1/2007
Let's all sing carols and decorate
'Cause it's the time to celebrate
So join the fun; you know the reason
Help spread good cheer this holiday season!
December 2006
Beanie Baby of the Month.
BBOM - $7

Merry Kiss-mas™
#40276

Birthday: 12/30/2004
Introduced: 9/30/2005
Retired: 12/29/2005
This holiday's special, you see
'Cause it's the first for you and me
No need for gifts, you know it's true
My gift is spending it with you!
13G/13UK - $7

Merrybelle™
#40283

Birthday: 9/24/2004
Introduced: 9/30/2005
Retired: 12/29/2005
Dashing through the cold, white snow
With my friends, away we go
There's nothing better, you'll agree
Than a sleigh ride with my friends and me!
13G/13UK - $7

Miami™
#40378

Birthday: 6/21/2006
Introduced: 5/31/2006
Retired: 9/25/2006
Summertime is here once more
And I can't wait to hit the shore
Let's catch some waves and have some fun
Good times have only just begun!
14G/14UK - $7

Midnight™
#4355

Birthday: 12/23/2000
Introduced: 5/1/2001
Retired: 1/18/2002
Walking silent through the night
Always keeping out of sight
Not a single noise or sound
This is how he moves around!
7G - $7 ♥ 8G - $7

Millenium™
#4226 · errored spelling

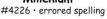

Birthday: 1/1/1999
Introduced: 1/1/1999
Retired: 1/1999
A brand new century has come to call
Health and happiness to one and all
Bring on the fireworks and all the fun
Let's keep the party going 'til 2001!
5G - $7

Millennium™
#4226 · correct spelling

Birthday: 1/1/1999
Introduced: 1/1/1999
Retired: 11/12/1999
A brand new century has come to call
Health and happiness to one and all
Bring on the fireworks and all the fun
Let's keep the party going 'til 2001!
5G - $7

Minksy™
#40185

Birthday: 6/4/2004
Introduced: 12/30/2004
Retired: 11/23/2005
Hopping down the bunny trail
With my little cotton tail
Winksy and Binksy by my side
Keep up with me! Don't break your stride!
13G/13EU - $7

Minneapolis™
#40132

Birthday: 3/1/2004
Introduced: 8/7/2004
Retired: 8/26/2004
Come to Minneapolis you'll want to stay
Such beautiful nature on display
Museums, theaters and music, too
The City of Lakes invites you!
Trade Show exclusive.
12G - $10

Minnesota™
#40119

Birthday: None
Introduced: 8/30/2004
Retired: 12/29/2005
STATE MOTTO: "Etoile du Nord"
(Star of the North)
NICKNAME: North Star State
FACT: Minnesota boasts over
90,000 miles of shoreline!
Sold only in Minnesota.
12G - $7

Minnesota Lady's-slipper™
#40295

Birthday: None
Introduced: 8/13/2005
Retired: 12/29/2005
OFFICIAL FLOWER SINCE 1902
In Minnesota you will see
Our state flower grows tall and free
Lady's-slipper of pink and white
Blooms brightly in the summer light!
Trade Show exclusive.
13G - $10

Mississippi™
#40320

Birthday: None
Introduced: 9/9/2005
Retired: 5/24/2006
In memory of those who lost their homes,
their loved ones, or their lives, as a result of
Hurricane Katrina
We extend our deepest sympathies
Together we're a stronger nation
*$1 of sale donated to American Red
Cross Disaster Fund.*
13G/13UK - $7

Mississippi™
#44079

Birthday: None
Introduced: 9/6/2005
Retired: 5/24/2006
In memory of those who lost their homes,
their loved ones, or their lives, as a result of
Hurricane Katrina
We extend our deepest sympathies
Together we're a stronger nation
*$2 of sale donated to American Red
Cross Disaster Fund. Ty Store exclusive.*
13G - $7

Mistletoe™
#4500

Birthday: 12/18/2000
Introduced: 10/1/2001
Retired: 12/31/2001
If you see some mistletoe
Take a chance and stand below
The custom is that if you do
You might just get a kiss or two!
7G - $7 ♥ 9G - $7

Mom™
#40216

Birthday: 5/9/2004
Introduced: 2/28/2005
Retired: 5/26/2005
Mom's kind, gentle and oh-so sweet
Mom's loving, caring and so neat
We all love Mom, so let her know
You are the best, I love you so!
13G/13EU - $7

Mom 2006™
#44086

Birthday: 5/14/2006
Introduced: 3/29/2006
Retired: 4/18/2006
They come in different shapes and sizes
Full of love, laughter, surprises
So special you just have to say,
"I love you; Happy Mother's Day!"
Ty Store exclusive.
14G - $7

Mom 2007™
#44103

Birthday: 5/13/2007
Introduced: 3/22/2007
Current
A mother's love is the best kind
It really isn't hard to find
Just look into a mother's eyes
You'll find it there, that's no surprise!
Ty Store exclusive.
15G - Current Retail Value

MOM-e™
#4411

Birthday: 5/12/2002
Introduced: 4/12/2002
Retired: 4/15/2002
Mother, you will always be
The one who loves me just for me
I want to show how much I care
By giving you this special bear!
Ty Store exclusive.
10G - $15

MOM-e 2003™
#4426

Birthday: 5/11/2002
Introduced: 4/14/2003
Retired: 4/17/2003
A gentle touch, a warm embrace
A loving smile upon her face
She loves you unlike any other
So take some time to honor mother!
Ty Store exclusive.
11G - $8

MOM-e 2004™
#4438

Birthday: 5/9/2004
Introduced: 4/14/2004
Retired: 5/7/2004
Mom, you're always there for me
With kisses when I scrape my knee
And smiles that say you are so proud
You're simply the best Mom around!
Ty Store exclusive.
12G - $7

MOM-e 2005™
#44048

Birthday: 5/8/2005
Introduced: 4/5/2005
Retired: 6/23/2005
Just what makes a great mom is this
She's always there with a hug and kiss
Caring and kind, with a gentle touch
That's why I love my mom so much!
Ty Store exclusive.
13G - $7

Monarch™
#47053

Birthday: None
Introduced: 5/9/2007
Current
Through the kindness of Mr. Hearst
The Monarch Grizzly was the first
And on our flag, so proud and true
First at the San Francisco Zoo!
San Francisco Zoo exclusive.
15G - Current Retail Value

Mooch™
#4224

Birthday: 8/1/1998
Introduced: 1/1/1999
Retired: 12/23/1999
Look in the treetops, up towards the sky
Swinging from branches way up high
Tempt him with a banana or fruit
When he's hungry, he acts so cute!
5G - $7

Moonlight™
#40263

Birthday: 5/13/2005
Introduced: 8/31/2005
Retired: 11/23/2005
Black cats are nothing to fear
Don't worry if you see me near
I don't mean to cause you a fright
There's no such thing as bad luck . . . right?
13G/13EU - $7

Mooosly™
#40377

Birthday: 1/4/2006
Introduced: 5/31/2006
Retired: 4/26/2007
Sometimes I find it hard to dine
With these extra long legs of mine
I can't reach the ground to graze
At this pace I won't eat for days!
14G/14UK - $7

Moosletoe™
#40137

Birthday: 12/23/2003
Introduced: 9/30/2004
Retired: 12/29/2004
Some hang out by the holiday tree
But that's not where you will find me
'Cause under the mistletoe is the place
To get a kiss and a warm embrace!
12G/12EU - $7

Morrie™
#4282

Birthday: 2/20/2000
Introduced: 3/1/2000
Retired: 12/15/2000
Over, under, upside and down
Morrie loves to swim all around
He looks like a snake - could be a fish
To be your best friend is his only wish!
6G/6EU - $7 ♥ 7G - $7

Mother™
#4588

Birthday: 5/16/2002
Introduced: 2/28/2003
Retired: 7/29/2003
Your mother can be so much fun
She'll treat you like you're number one
And cheer you up when you are blue
Your mother's love is always true!
7G - $7 ♥ 11G - $7

Mother 2004™
#40059

Birthday: 5/11/2003
Introduced: 2/26/2004
Retired: 5/24/2004
Because you show your love each day
With everything you do and say
For all the hugs and kisses, too
Three cheers for Mom, I love you!
12G - $7

Mr.™
#4363

Birthday: None
Introduced: 5/31/2001
Retired: 10/19/2001
All dressed up in black and white
Friends and family here tonight
Now our vows have all been said
With this ring, I thee wed!
7G - $7 ♥ 8G - $7

Mrs.™
#4364

Birthday: None
Introduced: 5/31/2001
Retired: 10/19/2001
All dressed up in satin and lace
A special day, a special place
Let's begin our brand new life
As we're pronounced man and wife!
7G - $7 ♥ 8G - $7

Muddy™
#40006

Birthday: 6/26/2002
Introduced: 5/29/2003
Retired: 2/26/2004
I just love swimming in the pool
And rolling in the dirt is real cool
Whether I'm a mess or squeaky clean
I'm the hippest dog you've ever seen!
11G - $7

Muff™
#40229

Birthday: 11/20/2004
Introduced: 5/31/2005
Retired: 6/29/2005
Get some string or a toy mouse
And we can play around the house
We can do tons of cool stuff
With my best friends, Pluff and Fluff!
13G/13EU - $7

Muffler™
#44062

Birthday: 12/31/2005
Introduced: 11/17/2005
Retired: 1/3/2006
I love to play out in the snow
But my little paws get cold, you know
I play for hours and hours, and then
My muffler gets them warm again!
Ty Store exclusive.
13G - $7

Mugungwha™
#4617

Birthday: 2/12/2002
Introduced: 1/29/2002
Retired: 7/31/2002
I am a white bear
Mugungwha blossomed in my heart
Living in a Mugungwha land of picturesque
rivers and mountains, throughout Korea
Born as your friend in memory of
(Lunar) New Year Day.
Korea exclusive.
10G - $20

Mukluk™
#40031 · blue right eye with green left eye

Birthday: 2/26/2003
Introduced: 10/30/2003
Retired: 7/16/2004
Just say "mush" and watch me run
I love the snow, it's so much fun
And when the day is finally through
I'd love to cuddle up with you!
7G - $8 ♥ 11G - $8

146

Mukluk™
#40031 · clear eyes

Birthday: 2/26/2003
Introduced: 10/30/2003
Retired: 7/16/2004
Just love "mush" and watch me run
I love the snow, it's so much fun
And when the day is finally through
I'd love to cuddle up with you!
7G - $8 ♥ 11G - $8

Mum™
#4517

Birthday: 5/13/2001
Introduced: 2/20/2002
Retired: 6/25/2002
She always looks at me with pride
When I'm in need, she's at my side
She cares for me, and she's my chum
And that is why I love my Mum!
7G - $8 ♥ 10G - $8

Mum™
#46028

Birthday: 3/6/2005
Introduced: 2/28/2005
Retired: 9/23/2005
Mum's kind, gentle and oh-so sweet
Mum's loving, caring and so neat
We all love Mum, so let her know
You are the best, I love you so!
*Ty Europe/Australia/New
Zealand exclusive.*
13G/13EU - $8

My Dad™
#40612

Birthday: 6/17/2006
Introduced: 3/30/2007
Current
My dad is brave and very strong
He helps to teach me right from wrong
The thing that sets my dad apart
Is the love for me that's in his heart!
15G - Current Retail Value

My Mom™
#40604

Birthday: 5/13/2007
Introduced: 2/28/2007
Current
My mom is always there for me
I know that's where she'll always be
Someone on whom you can depend
Not just a mom, but a best friend!
15G - Current Retail Value

My Mum™
#46097

Birthday: 3/18/2007
Introduced: 1/31/2007
Current
My mum is always there for me
I know that's where she'll always be
Someone on whom you can depend
Not just a mum, but a best friend!
UK/Australia exclusive.
15UK - Current Retail Value

Mystery™
#46030

Birthday: 6/22/2004
Introduced: 5/31/2005
Current
My size and shape a secret so old
Generations of tales greatly told
Any ripples or shadows you see
Just think aloud that it could be me!
UK exclusive.
13EU - $30

Mystic™
#4007 · tan horn with fine mane

Birthday: None
Introduced: 6/25/1994
Retired: 10/1995
Mystic was issued without a poem.
1G - $2,800 ♥ 2G - $400 ♥ 3G - $200

Mystic™
#4007 · tan horn with
coarse mane

Birthday: 5/21/1994
Introduced: Oct-95
Retired: 10/23/1997
Once upon a time so far away
A unicorn was born one day in May
Keep Mystic with you, she's a prize
You'll see the magic in her blue eyes!
3G - $150 ♥ 4G - $7

Mystic™
#4007 · iridescent horn with coarse mane

Birthday: 5/21/1994
Introduced: 10/23/1997
Retired: 12/31/1998
Once upon a time so far away
A unicorn was born one day in May
Keep Mystic with you, she's a prize
You'll see the magic in her blue eyes!
4G - $7 ♥ 5G - $7

Mystic™
#4007 · iridescent horn with rainbow mane

Birthday: 5/21/1994
Introduced: 1/1/1999
Retired: 5/18/1999
Once upon a time so far away
A unicorn was born one day in May
Keep Mystic with you, she's a prize
You'll see the magic in her blue eyes!
5G - $7

Mystique™
#40062

Birthday: 1/27/2004
Introduced: 2/26/2004
Retired: 7/28/2004
My favorite game is hide-and-seek
And when I'm "it" I never peek
But when I hide, although I try
I'm always found, I wonder why?!
12G - $7

N™
#40514

Birthday: None
Introduced: 6/30/2005
Current
Alphabet Bears are issued without poems.
AB - Current Retail Value

Nami™
#44201

Birthday: None
Introduced: 9/3/2004
Retired: 3/18/2005
BIRTHPLACE: South Central & Southern Africa
TIDBIT: Rhino horns are made of keratin, just like our fingernails, and they grow throughout the rhino's lifetime!
Ty Store/World Wildlife Fund exclusive.
12G - $7

Nana™
(later as "Bongo")
#4067

Birthday: None
Introduced: 6/3/1995
Retired: 1995
Nana was issued without a poem.
3G - $3,500

Nana™
#44090

Birthday: 9/10/2006
Introduced: 8/22/2006
Current
Her hugs make you feel safe and sound
Her advice is sometimes quite profound
Her loving nature comforts you
That's why you love grams like you do!
Ty Store exclusive.
14G - Current Retail Value

Nanook™
#4104

Birthday: 11/21/1996
Introduced: 5/11/1997
Retired: 3/31/1999
Nanook is a dog that loves cold weather
To him a sled is light as a feather
Over the snow and through the slush
He runs at hearing the cry of "mush!"
4G - $7 ♥ 5G - $7

Nara™
#46003

Birthday: 1/22/2004
Introduced: 2/9/2004
Retired: 3/15/2006
Mugungwha is our national flower
It is in beautiful bloom in our country
When we are in joy or in sorrow
It is always in bloom in our heart!
Korea exclusive.
12G - $15

148

NASCAR®
Carl Edwards #99™
#40645

Birthday: 8/15/1979
Introduced: 6/29/2007
Current
Roush Racing
CHECKERED FLAG: In Edwards' rookie season, he had three wins, 13 top-five finishes, 15 top-10 finishes and finished the season eighth in the point standings!
15G - Current Retail Value

NASCAR®
Casey Mears #25™
#40562

Birthday: 3/12/1978
Introduced: 6/29/2007
Current
Hendrick Motorsports
CHECKERED FLAG: Mears was the first ever full-time NASCAR driver to win the 24 Hours of Daytona in 2006!
15G - Current Retail Value

NASCAR®
Clint Bowyer™ No. 07™
#40644

Birthday: 5/30/1979
Introduced: 6/29/2007
Current
Richard Childress Racing Team
CHECKERED FLAG: Bowyer made his Busch Series debut in 2004 and in 17 races recorded four top-fives and seven top-10s!
15G - Current Retail Value

NASCAR®
Denny Hamlin #11™
#40641

Birthday: 11/18/1980
Introduced: 6/29/2007
Current
Joe Gibbs Racing
CHECKERED FLAG: Hamlin was the 2006 Rookie of the Year and became the first rookie to make the 10-race playoff, NASCAR's Chase format!
15G - Current Retail Value

NASCAR®
Elliott Sadler #19™
#40638

Birthday: 4/30/1975
Introduced: 6/29/2007
Current
Evernham Motorsports
CHECKERED FLAG: In 2004, Sadler was one of only four drivers to stay in the top 10 in points the entire year!
15G - Current Retail Value

NASCAR®
Greg Biffle #16™
#40567

Birthday: 12/23/1969
Introduced: 6/29/2007
Current
Roush Fenway Racing
CHECKERED FLAG: Biffle has 11 wins, 51 top-10's and 3 poles to his credit in NEXTEL Cup series racing!
15G - Current Retail Value

NASCAR®
J.J. Yeley #18™
#40642

Birthday: 10/5/1976
Introduced: 6/29/2007
Current
Joe Gibbs Racing
CHECKERED FLAG: One of Yeley's best NEXTEL Cup finishes of 2006 came at the California Speedway where he finished 8th!
15G - Current Retail Value

NASCAR®
Jeff Burton™ No. 31™
#40566

Birthday: 6/29/1967
Introduced: 6/29/2007
Current
Richard Childress Racing Team
CHECKERED FLAG: Burton is a 19-time NASCAR cup winner!
15G - Current Retail Value

NASCAR®
Jeff Gordon #24™
#40635

Birthday: 8/4/1971
Introduced: 6/29/2007
Current
Hendrick Motorsports
CHECKERED FLAG: Gordon is a four-time NASCAR Cup Series Champion!
15G - Current Retail Value

NASCAR®
Jimmie Johnson® #48™
#40636

Birthday: 9/17/1975
Introduced: 6/29/2007
Current
Hendrick Motorsports
CHECKERED FLAG: In 2006, Johnson won
the Daytona 500 and the Brickyard as well
as the NASCAR Nextel Cup Championship!
15G - Current Retail Value

NASCAR®
Kasey Kahne #9™
#40639

Birthday: 4/10/1980
Introduced: 6/29/2007
Current
Evernham Motorsports
CHECKERED FLAG: Kahne won the Rookie
of the Year Award in 2004!
15G - Current Retail Value

NASCAR®
Kevin Harvick® No. 29™
#40568

Birthday: 12/8/1975
Introduced: 6/29/2007
Current
Richard Childress Racing Team
CHECKERED FLAG: Harvick won his second
Busch Series Championship in 2006!
15G - Current Retail Value

NASCAR®
Kurt Busch #2™
#40564

Birthday: 8/4/1978
Introduced: 6/29/2007
Current
Penske Racing
CHECKERED FLAG: Kurt Busch, 2004
NEXTEL Cup Champion, has captured
five victories at Bristol!
15G - Current Retail Value

NASCAR®
Kyle Busch #5™
#40637

Birthday: 5/2/1985
Introduced: 6/29/2007
Current
Hendrick Motorsports
CHECKERED FLAG: Busch became the
youngest pole winner in NASCAR's premier
series (19 years, 9 months and 24 days)!
15G - Current Retail Value

NASCAR®
Mark Martin #01™
#40643

Birthday: 1/9/1959
Introduced: 6/29/2007
Current
GINN/Army Racing
CHECKERED FLAG: Martin has 12 top 5
finishes in points and has twice finished second!
15G - Current Retail Value

NASCAR®
Matt Kenseth #17™
#40561

Birthday: 3/10/1972
Introduced: 6/29/2007
Current
Roush Racing
CHECKERED FLAG: Kenseth was the 2000
Winston Cup Rookie of the Year and the
2003 Winston Cup Champion!
15G - Current Retail Value

NASCAR®
No. 3™
#40569

Birthday: None
Introduced: 6/29/2007
Current
Six NASCAR Championships
1986, 1987, 1990, 1991, 1993, 1994
The black No. 3 car continues to be one of
the most famous legends in racing. The No. 3
has been unofficially retired since 2001.
15G - Current Retail Value

NASCAR®
Racer™
#40563 · black

Birthday: 7/29/2007
Introduced: 6/29/2007
Current
Round and round the track we go
Just gotta win the race you know
I'll pass them all and I'll succeed
This sport's the best 'cause I love speed!
15G - Current Retail Value

NASCAR®
Racer™
#40563 · blue

Birthday: 5/27/2007
Introduced: 6/29/2007
Current
Round and round the track we go
Just gotta win the race you know
I know the cup will soon be mine
When I first cross the finish line!
15G - Current Retail Value

NASCAR®
Racer™
#40563 · red

Birthday: 2/18/2007
Introduced: 6/29/2007
Current
Round and round the track we go
Just gotta win the race you know
I don't mean to boast or brag
But I will take the checkered flag!
15G - Current Retail Value

NASCAR®
Ryan Newman #12™
#40565

Birthday: 12/8/1977
Introduced: 6/29/2007
Current
Penske Racing
CHECKERED FLAG: Ryan Newman's 37
Poles in 188 starts has earned him the
nickname - Rocket Man!
15G - Current Retail Value

NASCAR®
Tony Stewart #20™
#40640

Birthday: 5/20/1971
Introduced: 6/29/2007
Current
Joe Gibbs Racing
CHECKERED FLAG: Stewart has won
championships in sprint cars, Indy cars,
and stock cars!
15G - Current Retail Value

Nectar™
#4361

Birthday: 7/30/2000
Introduced: 5/1/2001
Retired: 5/21/2001
The smallest bird you'll ever see
Flies as swiftly as can be
You might miss her if you blink
She moves faster than you think!
7G - $35 ▼ 8G - $35

Negaraku™
#46040 · black nose

Birthday: 6/15/2005
Introduced: 9/12/2005
Retired: 6/15/2006
It's our pride to raise the flag
It has become a symbol for everyone
The flag is given the name for its
bright colours
Let's share our love for it!
Asian-Pacific exclusive.
13G - $25

Negaraku™
#46040 · flag nose

Birthday: 6/15/2005
Introduced: 10/15/2005
Retired: 6/15/2006
It's our pride to raise the flag
It has become a symbol for everyone
The flag is given the name for its
bright colours
Let's share our love for it!
Malaysia exclusive.
13G - $50

Neon™
#4239

Birthday: 4/1/1999
Introduced: 4/8/1999
Retired: 12/23/1999
Born in shallow water in a sea grass bay
Their eyes can swivel and look every way
Walk down the beach on a
bright sunny day
Jump into the sea and watch them play!
5G - $7

New Jersey™
#40227

Birthday: 12/18/1787
Introduced: 4/5/2005
Retired: 12/29/2005
STATE MOTTO: "Liberty and Prosperity"
NICKNAME: Garden State
FACT: Thomas Edison invented the light bulb
and phonograph his Menlo Park, NJ laborator
Sold only in New Jersey.
13G - $7

151

New Year™
#40309

Birthday: 12/31/2005
Introduced: 11/30/2005
Retired: 1/27/2006
Let's celebrate the New Year right
We'll laugh and dance into the night
And when the clock strikes 12 we'll cheer
"3...2...1...Happy New Year"!
13G/13UK - $7

New Year 2007™
#40457

Birthday: 1/1/2007
Introduced: 10/31/2006
Retired: 3/27/2007
Anticipation fills the air
2007 . . . we're almost there
The countdown begins for all to hear
And then we'll shout, "2007 Happy New Year"!
14G/14UK - $7

New York™
#40050 · I ♥ New York

Birthday: 7/26/2003
Introduced: 2/26/2004
Retired: 7/22/2004
You'll never bring New Yorkers down
That's why I love this special town
Like our friend Lady Liberty
We stand with pride and unity!
12G - $7

New York™
#40049 · I ♥ NY

Birthday: 7/26/2003
Introduced: 2/15/2004
Retired: 7/22/2004
You'll never bring New Yorkers down
That's why I love this special town
Like our friend Lady Liberty
We stand with pride and unity!
Trade Show exclusive.
12G - $90

New York Rose™
#40288

Birthday: None
Introduced: 8/14/2005
Retired: 12/29/2005
OFFICIAL FLOWER SINCE 1955
The sweetest scent, the softest touch
This flower that we love so much
We wrote this very special prose
In honor of the New York rose!
Trade Show exclusive.
13G - $10

New York State™
#40148

Birthday: None
Introduced: 8/30/2004
Retired: 11/24/2004
STATE MOTTO: "Excelsior" (Ever Upward)
NICKNAME: Empire State
FACT: The 1st railroad in the U.S. ran
form Albany to Schenectady, NY!
Sold only in New York.
12G - $10

New Zealand ™
#46026

Birthday: 1/16/2005
Introduced: 2/28/2005
Retired: 4/15/2006
Volcanic rock and lakes and streams
Such beauty as if in your dreams
Mountains that seem to touch the sky
I love New Zealand; you can see why!
New Zealand exclusive.
Also available in Asian-Pacific.
13G - $20

Nibble™
#40494

Birthday: 1/6/2007
Introduced: 1/31/2007
Retired: 5/25/2007
There's so much that I like to eat
I have no single favorite treat
A nibble of each thing is what I do
Some carrots, cabbage, adn parsley, too!
15G - $7

Nibbler™
#4216 · frowning

Birthday: 4/6/1998
Introduced: 1/1/1999
Retired: 7/9/1999
Twitching her nose, she looks so sweet
Small in size, she's very petite
Soft and furry, hopping with grace
She'll visit your garden, her favorite place!
5G - $7

Nibbler™
#4216 · smiling

Birthday: 4/6/1998
Introduced: 1/1/1999
Retired: 7/9/1999
Twitching her nose, she looks so sweet
Small in size, she's very petite
Soft and furry, hopping with grace
She'll visit your garden, her favorite place!
5G - $7

Nibblies™
#4584

Birthday: 3/26/2002
Introduced: 1/30/2003
Retired: 7/29/2003
There is a snack I love to munch
For breakfast, dinner, even lunch
That's why I carry it with me
Try a carrot and you'll agree!
7G - $7 ♥ 11G - $7

Nibbly™
#4217 · frowning

Birthday: 5/7/1998
Introduced: 1/1/1999
Retired: 7/20/1999
Wonderful ways to spend a day
Bright and sunny in the month of May
Hopping around as trees sway
Looking for friends, out to play!
5G - $7

Nibbly™
#4217 · smiling

Birthday: 5/7/1998
Introduced: 1/1/1999
Retired: 7/20/1999
Wonderful ways to spend a day
Bright and sunny in the month of May
Hopping around as trees sway
Looking for friends, out to play!
5G - $7

Nigel™
#46086

Birthday: 10/1/2006
Introduced: 9/22/2006
Retired: 12/21/2006
We're celebrating here at Beales
And we've got some special deals
125 years of great selection
So why not add Nigel to your collection!
Beales exclusive.
14UK - $15

Niklas™
#46105

Birthday: 11/5/2006
Introduced: 7/2/2007
Current
I love all varieties of plants
as I work in the garden.
I am known as Florian
the garden bear from Floralan!
German exclusive.
15UK - Current Retail Value

Niles™
#4284

Birthday: 2/1/2000
Introduced: 3/1/2000
Retired: 3/14/2001
The desert is a dry, hot land
Filled with lots and lots of sand
But I can still have so much fun
As long as we play in the sun!
6G - $7 ♥ 7G - $7

Nina™
#44021

Birthday: 10/12/2004
Introduced: 9/10/2004
Retired: 12/20/2004
In 1492, you see
Three ships sailed into history
New trade routes they hoped to gain
When the Nina sailed from Palos, Spain!
Ty Store exclusive.
12G - $7

Nip™
#4003 · white face

Birthday: None
Introduced: 1/7/1995
Retired: 1/7/1996
Nip was issued without a poem.
2G - $500 ♥ 3G - $240

Nip™
#4003 · all gold

Birthday: None
Introduced: 1/7/1996
Retired: 3/10/1996
Nip was issued without a poem.
3G - $375

Nip™
#4003 · white paws

Birthday: 3/6/1994
Introduced: 3/10/1996
Retired: 12/31/1997
His name is Nipper, but we call him Nip
His best friend is a black cat named Zip
Nip likes to run in races for fun
He runs so fast he's always number one!
3G - $150 ♥ 4G - $7 ♥ 5G - $7

Nipponia™
#4605

Birthday: 9/15/2000
Introduced: 9/9/2000
Retired: 3/21/2001
The new morning has come
Let's get out from the small Island
And shine on the world with everybody
Japan exclusive.
6G - $20 ♥ 7G - $15

Northland™
#46020

Birthday: 4/17/2005
Introduced: 9/30/2005
Current
It has been a long held belief
Our foremost symbol; the maple leaf
In '65 we did decree
It's on our flag for all to see!
Canada exclusive.
13G - Current Retail Value

November™
#4386

Birthday: None
Introduced: 10/1/2001
Retired: 12/31/2001
My nose is the color of my birthstone.
Topaz - It brings courage,
honor and optimism!
Birthday - $7

November 2002™
#4550

Birthday: None
Introduced: 9/30/2002
Retired: 12/27/2002
Whoopie Goldberg - November 13th
John F. Kennedy Jr. - November 25th
Mark Twain - November 30th
Birthday - $7

Nuts™
#4114

Birthday: 1/21/1996
Introduced: 1/1/1997
Retired: 12/31/1998
With his bushy tail, he'll scamper up a tree
The most cheerful critter you'll ever see,
He's nuts about nuts, and he loves to chat
Have you ever seen a squirrel like that?
4G - $7 ♥ 5G - $7

Nutty™
#4587

Birthday: 8/3/2002
Introduced: 2/28/2003
Retired: 10/8/2003
I spend my days running 'round
Both in the trees and on the ground
I chase my friends and they chase me
That is what makes us most happy!
7G - $7 ♥ 11G - $7

O™
#40515

Birthday: None
Introduced: 6/30/2005
Current
Alphabet Bears are issued without poems.
AB - Current Retail Value

O'Fortune™
#40481

Birthday: 3/17/2007
Introduced: 12/29/2006
Retired: 5/25/2007
Good fortune will be yours for sure
From this day forth 'til evermore
If by lucky chance you see
A certain Irish bear . . . that's me!
15G/15UK - $7

O'Lucky™
#44101

Birthday: 3/17/2007
Introduced: 1/31//2007
Retired: 6/9/07
Oh lucky me; I've finally found
The most charming bear around
I'm as fortunate as I can be
O'Lucky is the bear for me!
Ty Store exclusive.
15G - $8

Oats™
#4305

Birthday: 7/5/2000
Introduced: 7/8/2000
Retired: 6/18/2001
Hop on my back, we'll have a ball
Just hold on tight, so you won't fall
Over hills and trails we'll go
I won't stop 'till you say "whoa!"
6G - $7 ♥ 7G - $7

Ocker™
#46000

Birthday: 1/1/2004
Introduced: 2/9/2004
Retired: 3/15/2006
The Wattle blooms in gold & green
The prettiest thing I've ever seen
I'd like to share this one with you
What Ocker wouldn't love it too?
*Australian exclusive and
Asia Pacific exclusive.*
12G - $15

October™
#4380

Birthday: None
Introduced: 9/3/2001
Retired: 12/31/2001
My nose is the color of my birthstone.
Opal - It brings sensitivity,
Patience and innocence!
Birthday - $7

October 2002™
#4549

Birthday: None
Introduced: 8/29/2002
Retired: 12/27/2002
Gwen Stefani - Oct. 3rd
Dale Earnhardt Jr. - Oct. 10th
Martin Luther King Jr. - Oct. 23rd
Birthday - $7

Ohio™
#40122

Birthday: None
Introduced: 8/30/2004
Retired: 12/29/2005
STATE MOTTO: "With God,
All Things Are Possible"
NICKNAME: Buckeye State
FACT: The flag of Ohio is the only
state flag in a pennant design!
Sold only in Ohio.
12G - $7

Ohio Scarlet Carnation™
#40296

Birthday: None
Introduced: 8/20/2005
Retired: 12/29/2005
OFFICIAL FLOWER SINCE 1904
This fragrant flower's great to wear
As a corsage or boutonnière
The prettiest flower in creation
Ohio loves the scarlet carnation!
Trade Show exclusive.
13G - $10

Old Timer™
#47002

Birthday: 9/26/2004
Introduced: 9/27/2004
Retired: 12/29/2004
Old Timer is here to say
Rise and shine and greet the day
Stop in for breakfast, you'll agree
That Cracker Barrel's the place to be!
Cracker Barrel exclusive.
12G - $7

Olé™ (nobre)
#46006

Birthday: 1/8/2004
Introduced: 7/7/2004
Retired: 9/21/2006
Poem translation:
My name is OLE!
I am brave and strong
I have a heart of gold
Even thought I am just a little bull!
Spain exclusive. Also available in Europe.
12G - $24

Olé™ (nombre)
#46006

Birthday: 1/8/2004
Introduced: 7/7/2004
Retired: 9/21/2006
Poem translation:
My name is OLE!
I am brave and strong
I have a heart of gold
Even thought I am just a little bull!
Spain exclusive. Also available in Europe.
12G - $125

Ontario White Trillium™
#46037

Birthday: None
Introduced: 8/5/2005
Retired: 8/26/2005
OFFICIAL FLOWER SINCE 1937
I bloom when robins first arrive
It feels so good to be alive
My flower's white, but don't you blink
Because it may soon turn to pink!
Trade Show exclusive.
13G - $15

Ooh-La-La™
#40093

Birthday: 5/6/2004
Introduced: 6/30/2004
Retired: 12/29/2004
Can you guess my favorite hue
To me, it seems easy to do
Take a minute, stop and think
My most favorite color's pink!
12G - $7

Opie™
#40246

Birthday: 4/23/2005
Introduced: 4/29/2005
Retired: 3/27/2006
I live in the ocean blue
Have eight arms and a siphon, too
I squirt black ink and have two eyes
My body fits to any size!
13G/13EU - $7

Opie™
#47007

Birthday: 4/23/2005
Introduced: 4/23/2005
Retired: 4/25/2005
I live in the ocean blue
Have eight arms and a siphon, too
I squirt black ink and have two eyes
My body fits to any size!
Ty Warner Sea Center exclusive.
13G - $10

Orange Ice™
#40678

Birthday: 6/23/2007
Introduced: 6/29/2007
Current
Ready for a summer treat?
Something cool and oh-so sweet?
Here's just the thing; it's really nice
A smooth, refreshing Orange Ice!
Trade Show exclusive.
15G - Current Retail Value

Oriel™
#40249

Birthday: 9/28/2004
Introduced: 6/30/2005
Retired: 4/21/2006
The sweetest fishy in the sea
I guess that would be little me
Your guardian angel; I'll remain true
And keep a very close eye on you!
13G - $7

Orion™
#40019

Birthday: 7/21/2003
Introduced: 7/31/2003
Retired: 6/24/2004
Don't worry that I have this name
The truth is that I'm very tame
The only hunting I will do
Will be to find more friends like you!
7G - $7 ♥ 11G - $7

Osito™
#4244

Birthday: 2/5/1999
Introduced: 4/17/1999
Retired: 11/30/1999
Across the waters of the Rio Grande
Lies a beautiful and mystic land
A place we all should plan to go
Known by all as Mexico!
USA exclusive.
5G - $7

Outlaw™
#40389

Birthday: 1/9/2006
Introduced: 6/30/2006
Retired: 12/21/2006
I think that I got a bad rap
Just 'cause I took a tiny scrap
I'm sorry; it was a mistake
Who knew they'd miss that t-bone steak!
14G/14UK - $7

P™
#40516

Birthday: None
Introduced: 6/30/2005
Current
Alphabet Bears are issued without poems.
AB - Current Retail Value

P.F.C.™
#46018

Birthday: 9/3/2004
Introduced: 11/10/2004
Retired: 3/27/2006
We were down and then back up
And we went on to win the Cup
The Premiership is the final test
But Pompey will always be the best!
UK exclusive.
12EU - $15

P.F.C.™
#46018 · boxed with certificate

Birthday: 9/3/2004
Introduced: 11/10/2004
Retired: 3/27/2006
We were down and then back up
And we went on to win the Cup
The Premiership is the final test
But Pompey will always be the best!
UK exclusive.
12EU - $15

Packer™
#46073

Birthday: 4/22/2006
Introduced: 8/10/2006
Retired: 9/21/2006
Because I work hard all day long
To make sure all the goods are gone
I'm so tired when the day is done
But I still make some time for fun!
UK exclusive.
14UK - $15

Pads™
#46089

Birthday: 11/7/2007
Introduced: 2/16/2007
Current
For those in need who have a poorly pet
PDSA can supply a vet
But our support is what they really need
This charity that is a friend indeed!
UK exclusive.
15UK - Current Retail Value

Pal™
#44089

Birthday: 8/8/2006
Introduced: 7/6/2006
Current
Throughout all of the ups and downs
The laughter, tears, smiles, and frowns
Each day, beginning to the end
I know you are my true best friend!
Ty Store exclusive.
14G - Current Retail Value

Palace™
#48435

Birthday: 4/00/2007
Introduced: 4/1/2007
Retired: 5/1/2007
Life in a palace can be nice
But let me give you some advice
If you get up for a late snack
Take a map to find your way back!
April 2007 Beanie Baby of the Month
BBOM - $7

Palms™
#40554

Birthday: 5/22/2006
Introduced: 2/28/2007
Current
I'll hop out of my big blue pond
And fan myself with a palm frond
Here you just can't beat the weather
So why not play a game together!
15G - Current Retail Value

Panama™
#4520

Birthday: 8/25/2001
Introduced: 3/1/2002
Retired: 10/29/2002
Want to know what's really neat?
I have suction cups on my feet
They help me climb high up a tree
To see the jungle under me!
7G - $7 ♥ 10G - $7

Panmunjom™
#46094

Birthday: 6/24/2006
Introduced: 1/31/2007
Current
We have been apart for long
Parents, siblings and friends
No more war in Korea
And I hoe the north and south will be one!
Korean map. Asian-Pacific exclusive.
15G - $20

Pansy™
#47041

Birthday: 4/21/2006
Introduced: 1/31/2007
Current
Now that spring is finally here
Let's let out a great big cheer
Flowers in bloom, as you can see
So here's a Pansy to you from me!
Hallmark Gold Crown exclusive.
15G - Current Retail Value

Papa™
#44091

Birthday: 9/10/2006
Introduced: 8/22/2006
Current
The fun things grandpas like to do
Like going to the park or zoo
Are really great but better yet
The love and kindness that you get!
Ty Store exclusive.
14G - Current Retail Value

Pappa™
#4593

Birthday: 6/15/2002
Introduced: 3/31/2003
Retired: 7/29/2003
He is a very special man
That's why I'm his number one fan
This bear is just my special way
To say I love him every day!
7G - $7 ♥ 11G - $7

Pappa 2004™
#40065

Birthday: 6/19/2003
Introduced: 3/30/2004
Retired: 6/24/2004
You taught me how to throw a ball
And picked me up if I would fall
You made me feel so safe and sound
You're truly the best Dad around!
12G - $7

Parka™
#40411

Birthday: 1/6/2006
Introduced: 7/31/2006
Current
Now I'm not here to brag or gloat
But I've got the warmest furry coat
I wear it everywhere I go
To help keep out the cold and snow!
14G/14UK - Current Retail Value

Patriot™
#4360 · flag on left foot

Birthday: 5/29/2000
Introduced: 5/1/2001
Retired: 6/20/2001
I'm proud to wear flag USA
I wear it each and every day
I think we all should celebrate
Because our country is so great!
USA exclusive.
8G - $15

Patriot™
#4360 · flag on right foot

Birthday: 5/29/2000
Introduced: 5/1/2001
Retired: 6/20/2001
I'm proud to wear flag USA
I wear it each and every day
I think we all should celebrate
Because our country is so great!
USA exclusive.
8G - $10

Patti™
#4025 · deep fuchsia body

Birthday: None
Introduced: 1993
Retired: 1993
Patti was issued without a poem.
1G - $2,800

Patti™
#4025 · raspberry body

Birthday: None
Introduced: 1994
Retired: 1994
Patti was issued without a poem.
1G - $2,500 ♥ 2G - $750

Patti™
#4025 · magenta/maroon

Birthday: None
Introduced: 1995
Retired: 1995
Patti was issued without a poem.
3G - $475

Patti™
#4025 · fuchsia body

Birthday: 1/6/1993
Introduced: 1996
Retired: 5/1/1998
Ran into Patti one day while walking
Believe me she wouldn't stop talking
Listened and listened to her speak
That would explain her extra large beak!
3G - $125 ♥ 4G - $7 ♥ 5G - $7

Patti™
#49026 · fuchsia/light pink

Birthday: 1/6/1993
Introduced: 10/3/2005
Retired: 3/9/2006
Patti was issued without a poem.
*Available in BBOC Original 9
Assortment 2-4.
Beanie Baby Offcial Club exclusive.*
BBOC2 - $15

Patti™
#49027 · deep fuchsia

Birthday: None
Introduced: 10/7/2005
Retired: 3/9/2006
Patti was issued without a poem.
*Available in BBOC Original 9
Assortment 5.
Beanie Baby Offcial Club exclusive.*
BBOC2 - $10

Patti™
#49028 · raspberry/magenta

Birthday: None
Introduced: 10/5/2005
Retired: 3/9/2006
Patti was issued without a poem.
*Available in BBOC Original 9 Assortment
1. Beanie Baby Offcial Club exclusive.*
BBOC2 - $50

Patty O'Lucky™
#44081

Birthday: 3/17/2006
Introduced: 2/8/2006
Retired: 3/11/2006
Top o' the mornin' to you, friend
I've some good luck that I'll send
To you and all those you hold dear
Be glad Patty O'Lucky's here!
Ty Store exclusive.
14G - $7

Paul™
#4248

Birthday: 2/23/1999
Introduced: 4/12/1999
Retired: 12/23/1999
Traveling the ocean in a submarine
Singing and playing a tambourine
One day hoping to lead a band
First he needs to find dry land!
5G - $7

Peace™
#4053 · China

Birthday: 2/1/1996
Introduced: 6/1/1998
Retired: 9/1/1998
Many factors determine the price of Peace
bears. There are so many that it is
impossible to list them all.
The common version is valued at $6 while
the Neon version is valued at $55.
5G - $7 - $200

Peace™
#4053 · Indo

Birthday: 2/1/1996
Introduced: 5/11/1997
Retired: 7/14/1999
All races, all colors, under the sun
Join hands together and have some fun
Dance to the music, rock and roll is the sound
Symbols of peace and love abound!
5G - $25 - $200

Peace Symbol Bear™
#4599 · filled-in symbol

Birthday: 11/17/2002
Introduced: 3/19/2003
Retired: 9/10/2004
Let's say a prayer
That Peace will come
For you, for me
For everyone!
USA exclusive.
11G - $9

Peace Symbol Bear™
#4599 · hollow symbol

Birthday: 11/17/2002
Introduced: 3/19/2003
Retired: 9/10/2004
Let's say a prayer
That Peace will come
For you, for me
For everyone!
UK/Singapore exclusive.
11G - $9

Peanut™
#4062 · royal blue body

Birthday: 1/25/1995
Introduced: 6/3/1995
Retired: 10/2/1995
Peanut was issued without a poem.
3G - $1,800

Peanut™
#4062 · light blue body

Birthday: 1/25/1995
Introduced: 10/2/1995
Retired: 5/1/1998
Peanut the elephant walks on tip-toes
Quietly sneaking wherever she goes
She'll sneak up on you and a hug you will get
Peanut is a friend you won't soon forget!
3G - $175 ♥ 4G - $7 ♥ 5G - $7

Pecan™
#4251

Birthday: 4/15/1999
Introduced: 4/8/1999
Retired: 12/23/1999
In late fall, as wind gusts blow
Pecan hibernates before winter snow
In early spring, sweet scent of a flower
Wakes her up to take a shower!
5G - $7

Peekaboo™
#4303

Birthday: 4/11/2000
Introduced: 6/24/2000
Retired: 4/19/2001
Underneath my shell I hide
I try to keep my head inside
If you'll be my friend today
I'll come out so we can play!
6G - $7 ♥ 7G - $7

Peepers™
#4814

Birthday: 3/00/2004
Introduced: 3/1/2004
Retired: 4/1/2004
You might think that I'm asleep
'Cause I won't make a single peep
Until you take me home with you
And then we'll chat the whole night through!
March 2004 Beanie Baby of the Month.
BBOM - $7

Peeps™
#40168

Birthday: 4/28/2004
Introduced: 12/30/2004
Retired: 4/28/2005
A little ball of fuzz, that's me
I'm very cute, don't you agree?
Of all the chicks here in the coop
I'm the sweetest of the group !
13G/13EU - $7

Pegasus™
#4542

Birthday: 9/1/2001
Introduced: 7/30/2002
Retired: 4/28/2003
I dance with clouds and ride the wind
I'm Pegasus and I'm your friend
At home on Earth or in the sky
Why walk, I say, when I can fly!
7G - $8 ♥ 10G - $8

Peking™
#4013

Birthday: None
Introduced: 6/25/1994
Retired: 1/7/1996
Peking was issued without a poem.
1G - $2,500 ♥ 2G - $900 ♥ 3G - $750

Pellet™
#4313

Birthday: 7/29/2000
Introduced: 7/8/2000
Retired: 6/20/2001
I have many things to do
But it seems I'm never through
On my wheel I spin all day
This is how I love to play!
6G - $7 ♥ 7G - $7

Pennsylvania™
#40084

Birthday: None
Introduced: 8/30/2004
Retired: 12/29/2005
STATE MOTTO: "Virtue, Liberty
and Independence"
NICKNAME: Keystone State
FACT: The Declaration of Independence
was signed in Philadelphia, PA!
Sold only in Pennsylvania.
12G - $7

Pennsylvania Mountain Laurel™
#40290

Birthday: None
Introduced: 7/9/2005
Retired: 12/29/2005
OFFICIAL FLOWER SINCE 1933
The Pennsylvania mountain laurel
Our first choice for all things floral
Beautiful bloom so bright and pink
Simply the best, what do you think?
Trade Show exclusive.
13G - $10

Periwinkle™
#4400

Birthday: 2/8/2000
Introduced: 11/30/2000
Retired: 12/8/2000
Into cyberspace I go
Where I'll end up, I don't know
It's such a thrill, a wild ride
I'll keep Periwinkle by my side!
6G - $7

Petunia™
#47041

Birthday: 4/21/2006
Introduced: 1/31/2007
Current
Now that spring is finally here
Let's let out a great big cheer
Flowers in bloom, as you can see
So here's a Petunia to you from me!
Hallmark Gold Crown exclusive.
15G - Current Retail Value

Philadelphia™
#40126

Birthday: 3/11/2003
Introduced: 7/18/2004
Retired: 8/26/2004
Our founding fathers did agree
That Philly is the place to be
And so in this historic place
Our freedom they did embrace!
Trade Show exclusive.
12G - $7

Pierre™
#4607

Birthday: 5/4/2001
Introduced: 8/12/2001
Retired: 4/1/2002
I am Pierre the Canadian bear
My country's flag I proudly wear
My hope for all from sea to sea:
That Canadians live in harmony!
Canada exclusive.
9G - $15

Piñata™
#40051 · black nose

Birthday: 5/5/2003
Introduced: 3/30/2004
Retired: 7/16/2004
South of the border, we celebrate
The fifth of May - a special date
There's songs to sing and games to play
Everybody shout "OLE"!
12G - $7

Piñata™
#40051 · Mexican flag nose

Birthday: 5/5/2003
Introduced: 3/30/2004
Retired: 7/16/2004
South of the border, we celebrate
The fifth of May - a special date
There's songs to sing and games to play
Everybody shout "OLE"!
12G - $7

Pinchers™
#4026

Birthday: 6/19/1993
Introduced: 1/8/1994
Retired: 5/1/1998
This lobster loves to pinch
Eating his food inch by inch
Balancing carefully with his tail
Moving forward slow as a snail!
1G - $2,500 ♥ 2G - $325 ♥ 3G - $60 ♥
4G - $7 ♥ 5G - $7

Pinchers™
#49024

Birthday: 6/19/1993
Introduced: 10/3/2005
Retired: 3/9/2006
This lobster loves to pinch
Eating his food inch by inch
Balancing carefully with his tail
Moving forward slow as a snail!
*Available in BBOC Original 9
Assortment 1, 2, 3 and 5.
Beanie Baby Offcial Club exclusive.*
BBOC2 - $10

Pinkerton™
#40360

Birthday: 1/16/2006
Introduced: 3/31/2006
Current
Kittens bounding to and fro
This way that way, off they go
They're all fun, but the best I think
Is a kitten that is white and pink!
14G/14UK - Current Retail Value

Pinky™
#4072

Birthday: 2/13/1995
Introduced: 6/3/1995
Retired: 12/31/1998
Pinky loves the everglades
From the hottest pink she's made
With floppy legs and big orange beak
She's the Beanie that you seek!
3G - $50 ♥ 4G - $7 ♥ 5G - $7

Pinta™
#44021

Birthday: 10/12/2004
Introduced: 9/10/2004
Retired: 12/20/2004
In 1492, you see
Three ships sailed into history
The Pinta sailed with all her crew
'Til Watlings Island was in view!
Ty Store exclusive.
12G - $7

Pippo™
#46008

Birthday: 3/19/2004
Introduced: 9/1/2004
Retired: 9/21/2006
There's an exceptional place
In the form of a boot
Where everything's special and grand
Come join us and be,
By air and by sea,
In this wonderful, magnificent land!
Italy & Harrods exclusive.
12G - $10

Pique™
#40340

Birthday: 11/12/2005
Introduced: 1/31/2006
Retired: 9/25/2006
I love to dance ballet with grace
Wearing tulle and frilly lace
I'll spin and leap on tippy-toes
Ballet is fun; I think it shows!
14G/14UK - $7

Piran™
#46100 · black nose

Birthday: 3/5/2007
Introduced: 5/26/2007
Retired: 6/6/2007
My black and white flag upon my chest
Proud to be part of the rugged south west
"Onen Hag Oll" declares the Cornish motto
"One And All" to our beloved land, "Kernow"!
Cornish exclusive.
Approximately 6,000 produced.
15UK - $25

Piran™
#46100 · flag nose

Birthday: 3/5/2007
Introduced: 5/26/2007
Retired: 6/6/2007
My black and white flag upon my chest
Proud to be part of the rugged south west
"Onen Hag Oll" declares the Cornish motto
"One And All" to our beloved land, "Kernow"!
Cornish exclusive.
Approximately 1,100 produced.
15UK - $85

Piran™
#46101 · black nose, boxed

Birthday: 3/5/2007
Introduced: 5/26/2007
Retired: 6/6/2007
My black and white flag upon my chest
Proud to be part of the rugged south west
"Onen Hag Oll" declares the Cornish motto
"One And All" to our beloved land, "Kernow"!
Less than 950 produced. Abbey Bears
exclusive with certificate.
15UK - $130

Pirouette™
#40255

Birthday: 11/17/2004
Introduced: 7/29/2005
Retired: 9/25/2006
With grace and style you won't forget
I'll turn a perfect pirouette
Then I'll chasse across the floor
The crowd will cheer and ask for more!
Sold out May 10th.
13G/13EU - $7

Pittsburgh™
#40129

Birthday: 7/20/2004
Introduced: 8/1/2004
Retired: 8/26/2004
Our bridges take you everywhere
That's how we get from here to there
Three rivers slowly flow along
Symbols of Pittsburgh, proud and strong!
Trade Show exclusive.
12G - $20

Pluff™
#40235

Birthday: 11/20/2004
Introduced: 10/31/2005
Retired: 12/29/2005
Get some string or a toy mouse
And we can play around the house
We can do tons of cool stuff
With my best friends, Fluff & Muff!
13G/13EU - $7

Plymouth™
#40272

Birthday: 12/21/2004
Introduced: 9/30/2005
Retired: 12/29/2005
Years ago a boat did dock
At a place called Plymouth Rock
When we set foot upon the ground
We knew that "home" is what we found!
13G - $7

Pocus™
#48417

Birthday: 10/00/2005
Introduced: 10/1/2005
Retired: 11/1/2005
In my cauldron just for you
I've made a special witch's brew
A little tart, a dash of sweet
Ready when you say, "Trick or Treat"!
October 2005 Beanie Baby of the Month.
BBOM - $8

Poet™
#40160

Birthday: 10/16/2004
Introduced: 11/30/2004
Retired: 4/28/2005
Straight from a heart that's pure and true
This poem is my gift to you
To ask you if you would be mine
My one and only Valentine!
12G/12EU - $7

Pompey™
#4625

Birthday: 8/10/2002
Introduced: 10/22/2002
Retired: 8/9/2004
Play up Pompey
Pompey play up!
Portsmouth Football Club exclusive.
7G - $25

Pompoms™
#40386

Birthday: 2/27/2006
Introduced: 6/30/2006
Current
Get up and clap! HIP, HIP, HORRAY!
C'MON! LET'S GO TEAM! ALL THE WAY!
Wave your pompoms! Shout with glee!
Let's cheer our team to VICTORY!
14G/14UK - Current Retail Value

Ponder™
#40663

Birthday: 3/5/2007
Introduced: 6/29/2007
Current
On my pad, way over yonder
I like to take the time to ponder
About the things I've done and seen
I think so much it turned me green!
15G - Current Retail Value

Poochie Poo™ Key-clip
#40671

Birthday: None
Introduced: 6/29/2007
Current
I'm Just Poochie - Keen
15Gsm - Current Retail Value

Poofie™
#4505

Birthday: 7/17/2001
Introduced: 11/30/2001
Retired: 8/29/2002
My favorite thing to do inside
Is run across the floor and slide
It's very easy for me to do
With fur like mine, then you could too!
7G - $8 ♥ 9G - $8

Poofie™ Key-clip
#40400

Birthday: None
Introduced: 6/30/2006
Current
Pretty Puppy!
14G/14UKsm - Current Retail Value

Poolside™
#44110

Birthday: 6/21/2007
Introduced: 6/20/2007
Current
I don't take my vacation lightly
On days when the sun shines so brightly
Come sit with me next to the pool
With fruity drinks to keep us cool!
Ty Store exclusive.
15G - Current Retail Value

Poopsie™
#4381

Birthday: 3/31/2001
Introduced: 7/31/2001
Retired: 4/8/2002
I'm a bear who's sweet as honey
I'm also cute and very funny
Take me home, we'll laugh and play
'Cause by your side is where I'll stay!
7G - $7 ♥ 9G - $7

Popcorn™
#4809

Birthday: 10/00/2003
Introduced: 9/30/2003
Retired: 11/1/2003
I don't mean to toot my horn
But I can make the best popcorn
I'll add some salt and butter, too
I'll make enough to share with you!
October 2003 Beanie Baby of the Month.
BBOM - $7

Pops™
#4522 · American tie

Birthday: 6/16/2001
Introduced: 4/1/2002
Retired: 7/17/2002
My Dad has such a great big heart
He's kind and fun and really smart
He always finds the time to play
I want to be like him someday!
10G - $8

Pops™
#4522 · British tie

Birthday: 6/16/2001
Introduced: 4/1/2002
Retired: 7/17/2002
My Dad has such a great big heart
He's kind and fun and really smart
He always finds the time to play
I want to be like him someday!
UK exclusive.
7G - $15

Pops™
#4522 · Canadian tie

Birthday: 6/16/2001
Introduced: 4/1/2002
Retired: 7/17/2002
My Dad has such a great big heart
He's kind and fun and really smart
He always finds the time to play
I want to be like him someday!
Canada exclusive.
10G - $12

Poseidon™
#4356

Birthday: 9/14/2000
Introduced: 5/1/2001
Retired: 7/25/2001
He sports a rather silly grin
Wearing spots from head to fin
Look around and you'll agree
Nothing's bigger in the sea!
7G - $8 ♥ 8G - $7

Posy™
#47041

Birthday: 4/21/2006
Introduced: 1/31/2007
Current
Now that spring is finally here
Let's let out a great big cheer
Flowers in bloom, as you can see
So here's a Posy to you from me!
Hallmark Gold Crown exclusive.
15G - Current Retail Value

Pouch™
#4161

Birthday: 11/6/1996
Introduced: 1/1/1997
Retired: 3/31/1999
My little pouch is handy I've found
It helps me carry my baby around
I hop up and down without any fear
Knowing my baby is safe and near.
4G - $7 ♥ 5G - $7

Pounce™
#4122

Birthday: 8/28/1997
Introduced: 12/31/1997
Retired: 3/31/1999
Sneaking and slinking down the hall
To pounce upon a fluffy yarn ball
Under the tables, around the chairs
Through the rooms and down the stairs!
5G - $7

Pounds™
#4530

Birthday: 3/30/2002
Introduced: 4/30/2002
Retired: 9/25/2002
Marching across the dusty ground
You'll hear me from miles around
My trunk is swinging to and fro
Listen to my trumpet blow!
7G - $7 ♥ 10G - $7

Prance™
#4123

Birthday: 11/20/1997
Introduced: 12/31/1997
Retired: 3/31/1999
She darts around and swats the air
Then looks confused when nothing's there
Pick her up and pet her soft fur
Listen closely, and you'll hear her purr!
5G - $7

Premier™
#4635 · Portsmouth Football Club

Birthday: 8/18/2002
Introduced: 7/24/2003
Retired: 12/29/2004
The crowd sang songs of cheer
And Pompey played well all year
We are now where we want to be
Let's hear, "Play up Pompey"!
Portsmouth Football Club exclusive.
7G - $25

Pretzels™
#40192

Birthday: 10/19/2004
Introduced: 12/30/2004
Retired: 5/26/2005
I'm looking for my favorite treat
It's something that is not too sweet
A hint of salt and mustard, too
I love pretzels; how 'bout you?
13G/13EU - $9

Prickles™
#4220

Birthday: 2/19/1998
Introduced: 1/1/1999
Retired: 12/23/1999
Prickles the hedgehog loves to play
She rolls around the meadow all day
Tucking under her feet and head
Suddenly she looks like a ball instead!
5G - $7

Pride™
#46029

Birthday: 9/21/2004
Introduced: 5/31/2005
Retired: 9/23/2005
Across the land the English be
So proud to have so much to see
We'll show you all our history, too
For England is the place for you!
UK exclusive.
13EU - $7

Prima™
#40304

Birthday: 4/28/2005
Introduced: 10/31/2005
Retired: 12/21/2006
A demure smile upon my face
As I move with such style and grace
An arabesque, pique, and then
Glissade, sissone, and start again!
13G/13EU - $7

Prince™
#4312

Birthday: 7/3/2000
Introduced: 7/8/2000
Retired: 6/20/2001
Sitting on a lily pad
I'm all alone and feeling sad
So won't you be a friend to me
And let me jump upon your knee!
6G - $7 ♥ 7G - $7

Princess™
#4300 · Indo

Birthday: None
Introduced: 10/29/1997
Retired: 10/1997
Like an angel, she came from heaven above
She shared compassion, her pain, her love
She only stayed with us
long enough to teach
The world to share, to give, to reach.
5G - $45

166

Princess™
#4300 · PE pellets

Birthday: None
Introduced: 10/29/1997
Retired: 4/13/1999
Like an angel, she came from heaven above
She shared compassion, her pain, her love
She only stayed with us
long enough to teach
The world to share, to give, to reach.
Also PVC $12.
5G - $7

Prinz von Gold™
#4613

Birthday: 10/3/2001
Introduced: 5/15/2002
Retired: 10/7/2002
I'm the third of the group,
Prince von gold, on everyone's lips.
Gold being the most treasured item.
In a Kingdom where all people are equal.
German exclusive.
7G - $25

Promise™
#47014 · blue

Birthday: 7/23/2005
Introduced: 7/23/2005
Retired: 12/29/2005
I promise to protect those dear
And do what's right year after year
Mutual values, sure and true
Are what I pledge to bring to you!
Northwestern Mutual exclusive.
13G - $50

Promise™
#47013 · brown

Birthday: 7/23/2005
Introduced: 7/23/2005
Retired: 12/29/2005
I promise to protect those dear
And do what's right year after year
Mutual values, sure and true
Are what I pledge to bring to you!
Northwestern Mutual exclusive.
13G - $50

Propeller™
#4366

Birthday: 8/8/2000
Introduced: 5/31/2001
Retired: 7/12/2001
In the water and the air
He can go most anywhere
Propelling out into the sky
We can watch him sail on by!
7G - $7 ♥ 8G - $7

Prunella™
#47016

Birthday: 8/1/2005
Introduced: 9/13/2005
Retired: 12/29/2005
If you could use a spell or two
Prunella is the witch for you
Just ask the spider on her hat
It used to be a kitty cat!
Hallmark exclusive.
13G - $7

Pudding™
#40474

Birthday: 11/13/2006
Introduced: 11/30/2006
Current
Can I sit upon your lap?
Not to sleep or take a nap
I just like being close to you
Isn't that what puppies do?!
14G/14UK - Current Retail Value

Puffer™
#4181

Birthday: 11/3/1997
Introduced: 12/31/1997
Retired: 9/18/1998
What in the world does a puffin do?
We're sure that you would like to know too
We asked Puffer how she spends her days
Before she answered, she flew away!
5G - $7

Pugsly™
#4106

Birthday: 5/2/1996
Introduced: 5/11/1997
Retired: 3/31/1999
Pugsly is picky about what he will wear
Never a spot, a stain or a tear
Image is something of which he'll gloat
Until he noticed his wrinkled coat!
4G - $7 ♥ 5G - $7

Pumkin'™
#4205

Birthday: 10/31/1998
Introduced: 9/30/1998
Retired: 12/31/1998
Ghost and goblins are out tonight
Witches try hard to cause fright
This little pumpkin is very sweet
He only wants to trick or treat!
5G - $7

Punchers™
#4026

Birthday: None
Introduced: 1/6/1994
Retired: 1994
Punchers was issued without a poem.
1G - $2,800

Punchers™
#49025

Birthday: None
Introduced: 10/5/2005
Retired: 3/9/2006
Punchers was issued without a poem.
*Available in BBOC Original 9
Assortment 4.
Beanie Baby Offcial Club exclusive.*
BBOC2 - $75

Punchline™
#44084

Birthday: 4/1/2006
Introduced: 2/23/2006
Retired: 3/14/2006
I'm funnier than all the rest
I just love saying things in jest
What's my best joke? You will agree
I'm really a Great Dane, you see!
Ty Store exclusive.
14G - $7

Pungo™
#44202

Birthday: None
Introduced: 8/2/2005
Retired: 1/2/2007
FACT: Due to captive breeding programs, this
highly endangered animal is slowly increasing
its numbers and some have even been introduced into the wild!
Ty Store/World Wildlife Fund exclusive.
13G - $7

PUNXSUTAWN-e PHIL™
#4418

Birthday: 2/2/2002
Introduced: 1/6/2003
Retired: 2/11/2003
At Gobbler's Knob in Punxsutawney
Lives a groundhog who's big and brawny
Punxsutawney Phil's the name
Predicting spring is his game!
Ty Store exclusive.
11G - $12

Punxsutawney Phil™
#4418

Birthday: 2/2/2002
Introduced: 1/6/2003
Retired: 2/11/2003
At Gobbler's Knob in Punxsutawney
Lives a groundhog who's big and brawny
Punxsutawney Phil's the name
Predicting spring is his game!
*Punxsutawney Chamber of
Commerce exclusive.*
11G - $175

PUNXSUTAWN-e PHIL 2004™
#4434 · light fur

Birthday: 2/2/2004
Introduced: 1/5/2004
Retired: 2/27/2004
February 2nd has been decreed
A special day, special indeed
When I predict just once a year
If winter stays or spring is near!
Ty Store exclusive.
12G - $7

Punxsutawney Phil 2004™
#40034 · dark fur

Birthday: 2/2/2004
Introduced: 12/30/2003
Retired: 5/25/2004
February 2nd has been decreed
A special day, special indeed
When I predict just once a year
If winter stays or spring is near!
12G - $7

Punxsutawney Phil 2004™
#4705 · light fur

Birthday: 2/2/2004
Introduced: 12/30/2003
Retired: 1/26/2004
February 2nd has been decreed
A special day, special indeed
When I predict just once a year
If winter stays or spring is near!
*Punxsutawney Chamber of
Commerce exclusive.*
12G - $12

PUNXSUTAWN-e PHIL 2005™
#44039

Birthday: 2/2/2005
Introduced: 1/3/2005
Retired: 3/18/2005
In Punxsutawney at Gobbler's Knob
I have a most important job
Although I'm not quite sure the reasons
I've learned I can predict the seasons!
Ty Store exclusive.
13G - $9

Punxsutawney Phil 2005™
#40197

Birthday: 2/2/2005
Introduced: 12/30/2004
Retired: 2/24/2005
In Punxsutawney at Gobbler's Knob
I have a most important job
Although I'm not quite sure the reasons
I've learned I can predict the seasons!
13G/13EU - $9

Punxsutawney Phil 2005™
#47006

Birthday: 2/2/2005
Introduced: 1/12/2005
Retired: 2/24/2005
In Punxsutawney at Gobbler's Knob
I have a most important job
Although I'm not quite sure the reasons
I've learned I can predict the seasons!
*Punxsutawney Chamber of
Commerce exclusive.*
13G - $9

PUNXSUTAWN-e PHIL 2006™
#44080

Birthday: 2/2/2006
Introduced: 1/4/2006
Retired: 2/7/2006
I've an important job to do
Each year on February two
I'll pop out, look around, then say
If spring will come or winter stay!
Ty Store exclusive.
14G - $7

Punxsutawney Phil 2006™
#40326

Birthday: 2/2/2006
Introduced: 12/30/2005
Retired: 2/24/2006
I've an important job to do
Each year on February two
I'll pop out, look around, then say
If spring will come or winter stay!
14G/14UK - $7

Punxsutawney Phil 2006™
#47022

Birthday: 2/2/2006
Introduced: 1/11/2006
Retired: 2/24/2006
I've an important job to do
Each year on February two
I'll pop out, look around, then say
If spring will come or winter stay!
*Punxsutawney Chamber of
Commerce exclusive.*
14G - $7

PUNXSUTAWN-e PHIL 2007™
#44099

Birthday: 2/2/2007
Introduced: 1/2/2007
Retired: 1/19/2007
Gobbler's Knob is where I'll be
The second of February
And if my shadow I should see
6 weeks of winter I'll decree!
Ty Store exclusive.
15G - $7

Punxsutawney Phil 2007™
#40477

Birthday: 2/2/2007
Introduced: 12/29/2006
Retired: 2/27/2007
Gobbler's Knob is where I'll be
The second of February
And if my shadow I should see
6 weeks of winter I'll decree!
15G/15UK - $7

Punxsutawney Phil 2007™
#47059

Birthday: 2/2/2007
Introduced: 1/10/2007
Retired: 2/27/2007
Gobbler's Knob is where I'll be
The second of February
And if my shadow I should see
6 weeks of winter I'll decree!
*Punxsutawney Chamber of
Commerce exclusive.*
14G - $12

Pup-in-Love™
#40309

Birthday: 10/12/2005
Introduced: 11/30/2005
Retired: 4/21/2006
I got this very special treat
It's just for you 'cause you're so sweet
It tells you how I feel for you
I hope you feel the same way, too!
13G/13UK - $7

Purr™
#4346

Birthday: 3/18/2000
Introduced: 3/1/2001
Retired: 6/18/2001
Today feels like a lazy day
I don't even want to play
I won't try to catch a mouse
I'll just lay around the house!
7G - $7 ♥ 8G - $7

Q™
#40517

Birthday: None
Introduced: 6/30/2005
Current
Alphabet Bears are issued without poems.
AB - Current Retail Value

Quacker™
#4024 · no wings

Birthday: None
Introduced: 6/25/1994
Retired: 1/7/1995
Quacker was issued without a poem.
2G - $1,500 ♥ 3G - $1,500

Quacker™
#4024 · with wings

Birthday: None
Introduced: 6/25/1994
Retired: 1/7/1995
Quacker was issued without a poem.
2G - $600 ♥ 3G - $600

Quackers™
#4024 · no wings

Birthday: None
Introduced: 6/25/1994
Retired: 1/7/1995
Quackers was issued without a poem.
1G - $2,800

Quackers™
#4024 · with wings

Birthday: 4/19/1994
Introduced: 1/7/1995
Retired: 5/1/1998
There is a duck by the name of Quackers
Every night he eats animal crackers
He swims in a lake that's clear and blue
But he'll come to the shore to be with you!
3G - $70 ♥ 4G - $7 ♥ 5G - $7

Quebec Iris Versicolor™
#46036

Birthday: None
Introduced: 8/28/2005
Retired: 1/27/2006
OFFICIAL FLOWER SINCE 1999
My purple flowers have some flair
With streaks of yellow everywhere
Out in a marsh is where I'll be
If you should come and visit me!
Trade Show exclusive.
13G - $20

Quiet™
#47064

Birthday: 3/2/2007
Introduced: 1/30/2007
Current
One hundred fifty years ago
Our founders pledged to serve and grow
We quietly pause and send a cheer
To celebrate this milestone year!
Northwestern Mutual exclusive
15G - $30

Quivers™
#40018

Birthday: 10/22/2002
Introduced: 7/31/2003
Retired: 10/31/2003
Some people get the shakes and shivers
When they see a ghost names Quivers
But he's not here to scare anyone
He wants to have some Halloween fun!
7G - $7 ♥ 11G - $7

R™
#40518

Birthday: None
Introduced: 6/30/2005
Current
Alphabet Bears are issued without poems.
AB - Current Retail Value

Radar™
#4091

Birthday: 10/30/1995
Introduced: 9/1/1995
Retired: 5/11/1997
Radar the bat flies late at night
He can soar to an amazing height
If you see something as high as a star
Take a good look, it might be Radar!
3G - $80 ♥ 4G - $45

Rainbow™
#4037 · blue with no tongue

Birthday: 10/14/1997
Introduced: 12/31/1997
Retired: 6/1/1998
Red, green, blue and yellow
This chameleon is a colorful fellow.
A blend of colors, his own unique hue
Rainbow was made especially for you!
5G - $7

Rainbow™
#4037 · tie-dye rainbow
with tongue

Birthday: 10/14/1997
Introduced: 8/1/1998
Retired: 3/31/1999
Red, green, blue and yellow
This chameleon is a colorful fellow.
A blend of colors, his own unique hue
Rainbow was made especially for you!
5G - $7

Raine™
#44085

Birthday: 3/20/2006
Introduced: 3/2/2006
Retired: 3/15/2006
After the night becomes the dawn
And the spring rain has come and gone
It washed away all of the gloom
And little buds begin to bloom!
Ty Store exclusive.
14G - $35

Rally Monkey™
#47067

Birthday: 6/6/2000
Introduced: 5/8/2007
Retired: 5/9/2007
It's late in the game when I come in
To help the Angels get the win
Believe in the power, when I appear
2007 will be our year!
LA Angels exclusive.
All Fans vs. Cleveland Indians.
15G - $50

Ramble™
#48415

Birthday: 8/00/2005
Introduced: 8/1/2005
Retired: 9/1/2005
I'm such a loyal pup, you know
And where you lead I will follow
We'll laugh and play and smile and grin
Hand in paw, through thick and thin!
August 2005 Beanie Baby of the Month.
BBOM - $7

Ratzo™
#40099

Birthday: 4/1/2004
Introduced: 6/30/2004
Retired: 7/9/2004
Just what are you laughing at?
Do you think I'm a funny rat?
Of course I am, I know it's true
When I see myself I laugh too!
12G - $7

Ratzo™
#44059

Birthday: 10/31/2005
Introduced: 9/27/2005
Retired: 11/1/2005
Ever since the day I was born
I have just loved my candy corn
I take it with me everywhere
But don't you worry, I will share!
Ty Store exclusive.
13G - $7

Red™
#40000

Birthday: 1/23/2003
Introduced: 4/30/2003
Retired: 6/9/2003
A symbol of the U.S.A.
Americans proudly display
My color signifies the brave
For whom our flag will always wave!
USA exclusive.
11G - $9

Red, White & Blue™
#40000

Birthday: 7/4/2002
Introduced: 4/30/2003
Retired: 6/9/2003
A symbol of the U.S.A.
Americans proudly display
Let's all wave the Red, White and Blue
'Cause, America, we love you!
USA exclusive.
11G - $9

Redford™
#40157

Birthday: 8/18/2004
Introduced: 10/29/2004
Retired: 11/24/2004
See that red-bird in the tree
He sings a special tune for me
I'll even whistle right along
'Cause it's our own special song!
12G/12EU - $7

Reefs™
#40558

Birthday: 6/2/2006
Introduced: 3/30/2007
Current
Swimming through the ocean blue
So close I brush right next to you
You won't believe the sights you'll see
15G - Current Retail Value

Regal™
#4358

Birthday: 11/11/2000
Introduced: 5/1/2001
Retired: 10/8/2001
It's not easy being King
I just want to do my thing
I would rather jump and play
Than sit on my throne today!
7G - $7 ♥ 8G - $7

Rescue™
#4514 · flag on left or right leg

Birthday: None
Introduced: 10/12/2001
Retired: 7/25/2002
To honor our heroes
who lost their lives in the
national catastrophe that
took place on September 11, 2001.
We mourn for them and express our
deepest sympathy to their families.
God Bless America
*Available in Japan with Japanese
writing on hang tag.*
7G - $7 ♥ 9G - $7

Rescue™
#4514 · flag on right leg

Birthday: None
Introduced: 10/12/2001
Retired: 7/25/2002
To honor our heroes
who lost their lives in the
national catastrophe that
took place on September 11, 2001.
We mourn for them and express our
deepest sympathy to their families.
God Bless America
Ty Store exclusive.
9G - $7

Rex™
#4086

Birthday: 8/1/1994
Introduced: 6/3/1995
Retired: 6/15/1996
Rex was issued without a poem.
3G - $350

Rhapsody™
#40473

Birthday: 8/11/2006
Introduced: 11/30/2006
Current
I wrote this special rhapsody
With a sweet sounding melody
Just for you I'll sing this song
And if you like, just hum along!
14G/14UK - Current Retail Value

Righty™
#4086

Birthday: 7/4/1996
Introduced: 6/15/1996
Retired: 1/1/1997
Donkeys to the left, elephants to the right
Often seems like a crazy sight
This whole game seems very funny
Until you realize they're spending your money!
USA exclusive.
4G - $60

Righty 2000™
#4289

Birthday: 7/4/2000
Introduced: 6/24/2000
Retired: 12/21/2000
On and on the race will go
Who will win we just don't know
No matter how this all will end
You will always be my friend!
USA exclusive.
6G - $8

Righty 2004™
#40044

Birthday: 6/25/2003
Introduced: 12/30/2003
Retired: 11/24/2004
When it's time to cast your vote
Just jot this down or make a note
No matter who will win this race
The fun is in the Beanie chase!
12G - $7

Ringo™
#4014

Birthday: 7/14/1995
Introduced: 1/7/1996
Retired: 9/16/1998
Ringo hides behind his mask
He will come out, if you should ask
He loves to chitter. He loves to chatter
Just about anything, it doesn't matter!
3G - $50 ♥ 4G - $7 ♥ 5G - $7

Roam™
#4209

Birthday: 9/27/1998
Introduced: 9/30/1998
Retired: 12/23/1999
Once roaming wild on American land
Tall and strong, wooly and grand
So rare and special is this guy
Find him quickly, he's quite a buy!
5G - $7

Roary™
#4069

Birthday: 2/20/1996
Introduced: 5/11/1997
Retired: 12/31/1998
Deep in the jungle they crowned him king
But being brave is not his thing
A cowardly lion some may say
He hears his roar and runs away!
4G - $7 ♥ 5G - $7

Roary™
#4069

Birthday: None
Introduced: 4/22/1998
Retired: 4/22/1998
Ty appreciates your support and
participation, too. Teenie Beanie Babies®
are a roaring success, thanks to you!!
Given to top McDonald producers.
TBB - $1,800

Rocket™
#4202

Birthday: 3/12/1997
Introduced: 5/30/1998
Retired: 12/23/1999
Rocket is the fastest blue jay ever
He flies in all sorts of weather
Aerial tricks are his specialty
He's so entertaining for you and me!
5G - $7

Roger™
#46078

Birthday: 8/23/2006
Introduced: 8/31/2006
Retired: 1/24/2007
Gold and silver I like a lot
Sailing over the open waters
Roger the Pirate I am called
Travelling to the hidden land!
Vedes exclusive.
14UK - $35

Romance™
#4398

Birthday: 2/2/2001
Introduced: 12/27/2001
Retired: 2/14/2002
Valentine's Day is the perfect chance
To give some love and show romance
This little bear can hardly wait
She wants to help you celebrate!
7G - $7 ♥ 9G - $7

Romeo and Juliet™
#40306

Birthday: 2/9/2005
Introduced: 11/30/2005
Retired: 4/21/2006
Each time I feel your warm embrace
I know there's nothing I can't face
Wrapped in your arms and holding tight
When I'm with you things feel so right!
13G/13EU - $9

Ronald McDonald™
#47000

Birthday: 4/19/2004
Introduced: 4/19/2004
Retired: 5/3/2004
25 years of Happy Meal fun
All around the world we're second to none
And Ronald the bear knows it won't quit
Cause kids with Happy Meals
Shout, "I'm lovin' it"!
*Provided at McDonald's Worldwide
Convention to employees.*
12G - $175

Ronnie™
#40015

Birthday: 2/6/2003
Introduced: 7/7/2003
Retired: 8/11/2004
As you sail out on your way
In our hearts you'll always stay
And because you're brave and true
This special bear is just for you!
USA exclusive.
11G - $7

Rose™
#4622

Birthday: 4/23/2002
Introduced: 10/18/2002
Retired: 1/3/2003
Roses are found throughout the land
In gardens, where they're tall and grand
A symbol that fills us all with pride
From cities to the countryside!
UK exclusive.
7G - $30

Rover™
#4101

Birthday: 5/30/1996
Introduced: 6/15/1996
Retired: 5/1/1998
This dog is red and his name is Rover
If you call him he is sure to come over
He barks and plays with all his might
But worry not, he won't bite!
4G - $7 ♥ 5G - $7

Rowdy™
#40367

Birthday: 6/11/2005
Introduced: 4/28/2006
Retired: 12/21/2006
Some dogs like sleeping in the sun
But I don't think that's any fun
I'd rather romp and bark out loudly
C'mon people! Let's all get ROWDY!
14G/14UK - $7

174

Roxie™
#4334 · red nose

Birthday: 12/1/2000
Introduced: 9/28/2000
Retired: 12/12/2000
Once every year I pull a sleigh
Come with me on that special day
We will soar high in the sky
Because you know reindeer can fly!
6G - $7 ♥ 7G - $7

Roxie™
#4334 · black nose

Birthday: 12/1/2000
Introduced: 10/23/2000
Retired: 12/12/2000
Once every year I pull a sleigh
Come with me on that special day
We will soar high in the sky
Because you know reindeer can fly!
6G - $7 ♥ 7G - $7

Ruby™
#40365

Birthday: 7/2/2005
Introduced: 4/28/2006
Retired: 6/23/2006
The best things that are meant for me
A life full of vitality
The ultimate goal, it's no surprise
To laugh, have fun and socialize!
14G/14UK - $15

Rudy™
#40029

Birthday: 5/22/2003
Introduced: 9/30/2003
Retired: 12/26/2003
When the holidays come around
You know where I can be found
With my red nose I'll be the guide
For that special nighttime ride!
7G - $7 ♥ 11G - $7

Rufus™
#4280

Birthday: 2/28/2000
Introduced: 3/1/2000
Retired: 6/11/2001
Smart and friendly as can be
I'm really cute as you can see
Play with me, we'll have some fun
Throw a ball and watch me run!
6G - $7 ♥ 7G - $7

Rumba™
#40007

Birthday: 12/27/2002
Introduced: 6/30/2003
Retired: 6/24/2004
Let's toot the horns and beat the drum-ba
C'mon and play and don't be glum-ba
It doesn't matter where you're from-ba
We'll do the dance that's called the rum-ba!
7G - $7 ♥ 11G - $7

Runner™
#4304 · cobra poem

Birthday: 5/25/2000
Introduced: 6/24/2000
Retired: 4/11/2001
I'm not so mean, I'm really shy
But every cobra has to die
I grab them by their little head
And whack them till they're
stone cold dead!
6G - $45

Runner™
#4304 · ferret poem

Birthday: 5/25/2000
Introduced: 6/24/2000
Retired: 4/11/2001
A ferret, mongoose, weasel or mink
What am I...what do you think?
Find a book, look and see
I'm whatever you want me to be!
6G - $7 ♥ 7G - $7

Rusty™
#4563

Birthday: 2/18/2002
Introduced: 8/29/2002
Retired: 2/24/2003
Is every panda black and white?
If you said "no" then you were right
'Cause I'm a panda, through and through
I even love to eat bamboo!
7G - $7 ♥ 10G - $7

S™
#40519

Birthday: None
Introduced: 6/30/2005
Current
Alphabet Bears are issued without poems.
AB - Current Retail Value

Saffron™
#40360

Birthday: 1/16/2006
Introduced: 3/31/2006
Current
Kittens bounding to and fro
This way that way, off they go
They're all fun, but the cutest fellow
Is a kitten that is white and yellow!
14G/14UK - Current Retail Value

Sakura™
#4602

Birthday: 3/25/2000
Introduced: 3/17/2000
Retired: 5/24/2000
I'm the treasure of Japan
I will bring spring and love to you
A hug will warm my heart
As you watch my flower bloom
Japan exclusive.
6G - $75

Sakura II™
#4619

Birthday: 3/3/2002
Introduced: 1/29/2002
Retired: 3/31/2003
Dreams and hope are children's heart
Grown up can have one, too.
The bud will keep on blooming
Like your dreams and hope.
Japan exclusive.
10G - $20

Salute™
#40486 · flag on chest

Birthday: 11/11/2006
Introduced: 12/29/2006
Current
Answering our nation's call
I'll stand in line, so brave and tall
I serve for life and liberty
And the pride I have in my country !
15G - Current Retail Value

Salute™
#44104 · flag on sleeve

Birthday: 11/11/2006
Introduced: 4/10/2007
Current
I proudly stand for what is right
I won't back down, I'll stand and fight
It's my duty and I'll persevere
To protect all that we hold dear !
Ty Store exclusive.
15G - Current Retail Value

Sam™
#40075 · blue body

Birthday: 7/4/2003
Introduced: 4/29/2004
Retired: 6/15/2004
Celebrate the Fourth of July
Show your pride, now don't be shy
I want you . . . to join today
In honoring the U.S.A.!
12G - $7

Sam™
#40075 · red body

Birthday: 7/4/2003
Introduced: 4/29/2004
Retired: 6/15/2004
Celebrate the Fourth of July
Show your pride, now don't be shy
I want you . . . to join today
In honoring the U.S.A.!
12G - $7

Sam™
#40075 · white body

Birthday: 7/4/2003
Introduced: 4/29/2004
Retired: 6/15/2004
Celebrate the Fourth of July
Show your pride, now don't be shy
I want you . . . to join today
In honoring the U.S.A.!
12G - $7

Sammy™
#4215

Birthday: 6/23/1998
Introduced: 1/1/1999
Retired: 12/23/1999
As Sammy steps up to the plate
The crowd gets excited, can hardly wait
We know Sammy won't let us down
He makes us the happiest fans in town!
5G - $7

Sampson™
#4540

Birthday: 12/29/2001
Introduced: 6/28/2002
Retired: 9/5/2003
Lets take a walk around the park
I promise that I will not bark
The thing I really want to do
Is spend the afternoon with you!
7G - $7 ♥ 10G - $7

San Francisco™
#40146

Birthday: 4/15/2004
Introduced: 7/24/2004
Retired: 8/26/2004
I love the twists on Lombard Street
And cable car rides are a treat
Golden Gate Bridge over the Bay
San Fran is a great place to play!
Trade Show exclusive.
12G - $10

Sandals™
#40557

Birthday: 3/30/2006
Introduced: 3/30/2007
Current
I keep my sandals within reach
For when I go down to the beach
Sometimes I'll bring a big ball, too
To play sand volleyball with you!
15G - Current Retail Value

Santa™
#4203

Birthday: 12/6/1998
Introduced: 9/30/1998
Retired: 12/31/1998
Known by all in his suit of red
Piles of presents on his sled
Generous and giving, he brings us joy
Peace and love, plus this special toy!
5G - $7

Santa Maria™
#44021

Birthday: 10/12/2004
Introduced: 9/10/2004
Retired: 12/20/2004
In 1492, you see
Three ships sailed into history
The Santa Maria found new land
Under Columbus' command!
Ty Store exclusive.
12G - $7

Sapphire™
#48400

Birthday: 5/00/2004
Introduced: 5/1/2004
Retired: 6/1/2004
If it's love and faithfulness
That you feel, you should confess
Sapphire will show you are sincere
Perfect for those who are dear!.
May 2004 Beanie Baby of the Month.
BBOM - $7

Sarge™
#4277

Birthday: 2/14/2000
Introduced: 3/1/2000
Retired: 4/4/2001
I defend you, so count on me
To stay by your side, that's where I'll be
Protect and serve is what I do
For just a little hug from you!
6G - $7 ♥ 7G - $7

Scaly™
#4263

Birthday: 2/9/1999
Introduced: 8/31/1999
Retired: 12/23/1999
I love to lie, basking in the sun
Living in the desert sure is fun
Climbing up cactus, avoiding a spike
I'm the Beanie you're sure to like!
5G - $7

Scampy™
#40106

Birthday: 9/9/2003
Introduced: 6/30/2004
Retired: 10/27/2004
We can run and jump and play
Outside on a summer's day
We'll play all day and when we're through
I'll snuggle up and sleep with you!
12G - $7

Scared-e™
#4415

Birthday: 10/26/2001
Introduced: 10/2/2002
Retired: 10/31/2002
Halloween is very scary
My fur stands up so I look hairy
Ghosts, goblins and witches, too
Don't scare me when I'm with you!
Ty Store exclusive.
10G - $15

Scares™
#48429

Birthday: 10/00/2006
Introduced: 10/1/2006
Retired: 11/1/2006
Let's stay up late Halloween night
And tell stories to cause a fright
Don't get too scared, but if you do
I'll be right there to comfort you!
October 2006 Beanie Baby of the Month.
BBOM - $7

Scary™
#4378

Birthday: 10/25/2000
Introduced: 9/3/2001
Retired: 11/12/2001
Flying around on Halloween night
Trying so hard to give you a fright
She will not cast a spell on you
She'll just play a trick or two!
7G - $7 ♥ 9G - $7

Scat™
#4231 · frowning

Birthday: 5/27/1998
Introduced: 1/1/1999
Retired: 12/23/1999
Newborn kittens require lots of sleep
Shh...it's naptime, don't make a peep
Touch her fur, it feels like silk
Wake her up to drink mother's milk!
5G - $7

Scat™
#4231 · smiling

Birthday: 5/27/1998
Introduced: 1/1/1999
Retired: 12/23/1999
Newborn kittens require lots of sleep
Shh...it's naptime, don't make a peep
Touch her fur, it feels like silk
Wake her up to drink mother's milk!
5G - $7

Schnitzel™
#4578

Birthday: 10/15/2002
Introduced: 12/27/2002
Retired: 5/25/2004
I'll do a special doggie feat
For my favorite doggie treat
But I don't want a bone to chew
Only Wiener Schnitzel will do!
7G - $7 ♥ 11G - $7

Scholar™
#40619

Birthday: 3/11/2006
Introduced: 3/30/2007
Current
It's graduation day at last
All grades are in; each test you've passed
Your hard work has paid off, it's true
And so I'll say "congrats" to you!
15G - Current Retail Value

School Rocks™
#47025 · 2 cool 4 school

Birthday: 8/30/2006
Introduced: 6/30/2006
Current
You're smart and you know that it's cool
To study hard and stay in school
Just try your best and when the day's done
You're sure to see that learning is fun!
Hallmark Gold Crown exclusive.
14G - Current Retail Value

178

School Rocks™
#47025 · allstar kid

Birthday: 8/30/2006
Introduced: 6/30/2006
Current
You studied hard, got that gold star
Now keep it up and you'll go far
Just try your best and when the day's done
You're sure to see that learning is fun!
Hallmark Gold Crown exclusive.
14G - Current Retail Value

School Rocks™
#47025 · recess rulez

Birthday: 8/30/2006
Introduced: 6/30/2006
Current
You know that to be a huge success
There's more to school than just recess
Just try your best and when the day's done
You're sure to see that learning is fun!
Hallmark Gold Crown exclusive.
14G - Current Retail Value

Schweetheart™
#4252

Birthday: 1/23/1999
Introduced: 4/11/1999
Retired: 12/23/1999
Of all the jungles filled with vines
Traveling about, you came to mine
Because of all the things you said
I can't seem to get you outta my head!
5G - $7

Scoop™
#4107

Birthday: 7/1/1996
Introduced: 6/15/1996
Retired: 12/31/1998
All day long he scoops up fish
To fill his bill, is his wish
Diving fast and diving low
Hoping those fish are very slow!
4G - $7 ♥ 5G - $7

Scorch™
#4210

Birthday: 7/31/1998
Introduced: 9/30/1998
Retired: 12/23/1999
A magical mystery with glowing wings
Made by wizards and other things
Known to breathe fire with lots of smoke
Scorch is really a friendly ol' bloke!
5G - $7

Scotland™
#4609

Birthday: 11/1/2001
Introduced: 2/3/2002
Retired: 9/27/2002
With its mountains, lochs and glens
Scotland's the place to make new friends
From Edinburgh to Aberdeen
A bonnier country I've never seen!
Scotland exclusive.
7G - $30

Scotland™
#46013

Birthday: 6/22/2004
Introduced: 9/5/2004
Retired: 10/8/2004
Scotland smells of the purple heather
Especially when you get nice weather
With hills and glens for you to see
I'm sure you'll love it just like me!
UK exclusive.
12EU G - $25

Scottie™
#4102

Birthday: 6/3/1996
Introduced: 6/15/1996
Retired: 5/1/1998
Scottie is a friendly sort
Even though his legs are short
He is always happy as can be
His best friends are you and me!
Also has birthday of 6/15/1996.
4G - $7 ♥ 5G - $7

Scrappy™
#40102

Birthday: 11/11/2003
Introduced: 6/30/2004
Retired: 10/27/2004
I am such a playful pup
Most other dogs just can't keep up
From morning 'til the sun goes down
I'm the most lively dog in town!
12G - $7

Scrum™
#46055

Birthday: 11/22/2003
Introduced: 1/31/2006
Retired: 9/21/2006
With a rose upon our chest
We will surely beat the rest
Let Jerusalem sing out loud
We'll win the game and make you proud!
UK exclusive.
14UK - $15

Scurry™
#4281

Birthday: 1/18/2000
Introduced: 3/1/2000
Retired: 12/15/2000
I play in the cellar with all of my friends
We laugh, we sing, the fun never ends
I hurry and scurry and hide most of the day
But if you come down, I'll stay out and play!
6G/6EU - $7 ♥ 7G - $7

Seadog™
#4566

Birthday: 7/22/2001
Introduced: 9/30/2002
Retired: 2/26/2004
I love to feel the ocean breeze
When I sail on the open seas
A sailor's life is right for me
There's no place that I'd rather be!
7G - $7 ♥ 10G - $7

Seamore™
#4029

Birthday: 12/14/1996
Introduced: 6/25/1994
Retired: 10/1/1997
Seamore is a little white seal
Fish and clams are her favorite meal
Playing and laughing in the sand
She's the happiest seal in the land!
**1G - $2,500 ♥ 2G - $350 ♥
3G - $75 ♥ 4G - $40**

Season's Greetings™
#47010

Birthday: 12/26/2004
Introduced: 10/26/2005
Retired: 12/29/2005
You should take the time each year
To spread some joy and peace and cheer
So tell your friends, both old and new
"SEASONS GREETINGS from me to you"!
Hallmark Gold Crown exclusive.
13G - $7

Seattle™
#40121

Birthday: 12/2/2003
Introduced: 8/23/2004
Retired: 9/10/2004
The Space Needle to Puget Sound
Great food and shops, the best around
A landscape that is more than pretty
Earned us the name "Emerald City"!
Trade Show exclusive.
12G - $14

Seaweed™
#4080

Birthday: 3/19/1996
Introduced: 1/7/1996
Retired: 9/19/1998
Seaweed is what she likes to eat
It's supposed to be a delicious treat
Have you tried a treat from the water
If you haven't, maybe you "otter"!
3G - $40 ♥ 4G - $7 ♥ 5G - $9

Secret™
#40035

Birthday: 1/19/2003
Introduced: 11/26/2003
Retired: 12/29/2004
I have a secret I must tell
One that I haven't hidden well.
You must know you've won my heart
And we will never, ever part!
7G - $9 ♥ 11G - $9

Secretariat 1973™
#40478

Birthday: 3/30/2007
Introduced: 1/31/2007
Current
Birthdate: March 30, 1970
Winning time: 1:59 2/5
Owner: Penny Chenery
Secretariat was the only horse to make
the covers of Newsweek, Sports Illustrated,
and Time magazines.
*1973 Kentucky Derby Triple Crown
Winner. USA exclusive.*
15G - Current Retail Value

Secretariat 1973™
#40478

Birthday: 3/30/2007
Introduced: 2/5/2007
Current
Birthdate: March 30, 1970
Winning time: 1:59 2/5
Owner: Penny Chenery
Secretariat was the only horse to make
the covers of Newsweek, Sports Illustrated,
and Time magazines.
*1973 Kentucky Derby Triple Crown
Winner. Kentucky Derby exclusive.*
15G - $15

Senna-kun™
#46046 · brown paws

Birthday: 8/31/2004
Introduced: 11/14/2005
Retired: 9/25/2006
Hi! My name is Senna
I like the charming ladies
I am always waiting for you
To come to the Kitamura shop.
Motomachi Kitamura exclusive.
13G - $175

Senna-kun™
#46049 · pink paws

Birthday: 8/31/2004
Introduced: 11/14/2005
Retired: 9/25/2006
Hi! My name is Senna
I like the charming ladies
I am always waiting for you
To come to the Kitamura shop.
Motomachi Kitamura exclusive.
13G - $650

September™
#4372

Birthday: None
Introduced: 7/3/2001
Retired: 12/31/2001
My nose is the color of my birthstone.
Sapphire - It brings good luck
and lots of $$!
Birthday - $7

September 2002™
#4548

Birthday: None
Introduced: 7/30/2002
Retired: 11/26/2002
Pink - Sept. 8th
Prince Harry - Sept. 15th
Serena Williams - Sept. 26th
Birthday - $7

Sequoia™
#4516

Birthday: 7/17/2001
Introduced: 1/29/2002
Retired: 10/29/2002
In the mountains where I roam
You'll find a cave that I call home
All winter long that's where I stay
'Til spring when I come out to play!
7G - $7 ♥ 10G - $7

Serenade™
#48410

Birthday: 4/00/2005
Introduced: 4/1/2005
Retired: 5/2/2005
I hope the neighbors don't complain
When I'm outside your windowpane
I'll sing and play a song or two
A serenade that's just for you!
April 2005 Beanie Baby of the Month.
BBOM - $7

Serenity™
#4533

Birthday: 2/15/2002
Introduced: 5/31/2002
Retired: 6/11/2002
When the world is full of fear
Do not worry, for I am here
Bringing comfort, peace and joy
To every girl and every boy!
7G - $7 ♥ 10G - $7

Shamrock™
#4338

Birthday: 3/17/2000
Introduced: 1/1/2001
Retired: 3/6/2001
I wear a shamrock on my chest
With good luck I have been blessed
I will share my luck with you
So all your dreams will come true!
7G - $7 ♥ 8G - $7

ShaqBear™
#40372

Birthday: 3/6/2006
Introduced: 5/31/2006
Current
Shaquille Says
"Make working hard a habit. There are no shortcuts to success."
"Never feel like you have to be like everyone else. To be a leader, you must be different."
"Get the best grades that you can. Knowledge is the best gift."
3 variations of poem.
Also available at Ty Store.
14G/14UK - Current Retail Value

Shasta™
#40070

Birthday: 5/23/2003
Introduced: 3/30/2004
Retired: 7/28/2004
Flowers colored sunshine bright
Brings big smiles of delight
And cheers you up when you feel blue
The perfect gift to share with you!
12G - $7

Sheets™
#4260

Birthday: 10/31/1999
Introduced: 8/31/1999
Retired: 12/23/1999
Living alone in a haunted house
Friend to the spider, bat and mouse
Often heard, but never seen
Waiting to wish you "Happy Halloween!"
5G - $7

Sherbet™
#4560 · light green body

Birthday: 11/26/2001
Introduced: 7/30/2002
Retired: 9/10/2002
Sherbet is my favorite treat
Always light and fun to eat
Raspberry, lime and lemon, too
They're all my favorites, how about you?
7G - $7 ♥ 10G - $7

Sherbet™
#4560 · light pink body

Birthday: 11/26/2001
Introduced: 7/30/2002
Retired: 9/10/2002
Sherbet is my favorite treat
Always light and fun to eat
Raspberry, lime and lemon, too
They're all my favorites, how about you?
7G - $7 ♥ 10G - $7

Sherbet™
#4560 · light yellow body

Birthday: 11/26/2001
Introduced: 7/30/2002
Retired: 9/10/2002
Sherbet is my favorite treat
Always light and fun to eat
Raspberry, lime and lemon, too
They're all my favorites, how about you?
7G - $7 ♥ 10G - $7

Sherbet™
#40004 · blue body

Birthday: 8/2/2002
Introduced: 5/29/2003
Retired: 6/24/2004
One scoop of sherbet sure is nice
It's better than a lemon ice
Two scoops are good, but why stop there
With three scoops there's enough to share!
7G - $7 ♥ 11G - $7

Sherbet™
#40004 · hot pink body

Birthday: 8/2/2002
Introduced: 5/29/2003
Retired: 6/24/2004
One scoop of sherbet sure is nice
It's better than a lemon ice
Two scoops are good, but why stop there
With three scoops there's enough to share!
7G - $7 ♥ 11G - $10

Sherbet™
#40004 · lilac body

Birthday: 8/2/2002
Introduced: 5/29/2003
Retired: 6/24/2004
One scoop of sherbet sure is nice
It's better than a lemon ice
Two scoops are good, but why stop there
With three scoops there's enough to share!
7G - $7 ♥ 11G - $7

Sherwood™
#40023

Birthday: 9/8/2002
Introduced: 8/28/2003
Retired: 5/25/2004
In the woods that I call home
A band of merry men do roam
They help the poor; and when they're done
We sing songs and have great fun!
7G - $7 ♥ 11G - $7

Shiloh™
#44208

Birthday: None
Introduced: 1/19/2006
Retired: 3/10/2006
FACT: WWF is active in the Great Plains, home
to a variety of species like the black footed
ferret. WWF is working to restore the region
and bring the black footed ferret back from
the brink of extinction!
Ty Store/World Wildlife Fund exclusive.
14G - $20

Shivers™
#40115

Birthday: 10/30/2003
Introduced: 8/30/2004
Retired: 11/24/2004
I don't want to brag or boast
As you can see, I'm not like most
Ghosts are white, but that's not me
Orange just suits me perfectly!
12G - $7

Shocks™
#40600

Birthday: 5/24/2006
Introduced: 1/31/2007
Current
You won't need to wonder why
The ground will shake when I walk by
I'm not sure how I got so big
I eat grass and fruit, sometimes a twig!
15G - Current Retail Value

Shooting Star™
#46048 · gray

Birthday: 11/5/2005
Introduced: 11/4/2005
Retired: 11/23/2005
Of all the kingdoms in the land
We think that you'll find ours most grand
Let it be known from sea to sea
Harrods Toy Kingdom's the place to be!
Harrods UK exclusive.
13UK - $65

Shooting Star™
#46048 · gray, boxed

Birthday: 11/5/2005
Introduced: 11/4/2005
Retired: 11/23/2005
Of all the kingdoms in the land
We think that you'll find ours most grand
Let it be known from sea to sea
Harrods Toy Kingdom's the place to be!
Harrods UK exclusive.
13UK - $95

Shooting Star™
#46047 · white

Birthday: 11/5/2005
Introduced: 11/4/2005
Retired: 1/27/2006
Of all the kingdoms in the land
We think that you'll find ours most grand
Let it be known from sea to sea
Harrods Toy Kingdom's the place to be!
Harrods UK exclusive.
13UK - $45

Shooting Star™
#46047 · white, boxed

Birthday: 11/5/2005
Introduced: 11/4/2005
Retired: 1/27/2006
Of all the kingdoms in the land
We think that you'll find ours most grand
Let it be known from sea to sea
Harrods Toy Kingdom's the place to be!
If signed by TY - $700.
Harrods UK exclusive.
13UK - $65

Shortstop™
#40252

Birthday: 4/3/2005
Introduced: 6/30/2005
Current
Just put those runs up on the board
Cheers and high fives because you scored
And now the fans will shout, "Hey, hey!"
You've helped us win the game today!
13G/13EU - Current Retail Value

Shudders™
#40418

Birthday: 9/20/2005
Introduced: 8/31/2006
Retired: 10/25/2006
When the wind howls or the floorboards creak
I just can't help but shout out, "EEEK"!
Look in the mirror, what can I say
The ghost I see scares me away!
14G/14UK - $7

Siam™
#4369

Birthday: 10/19/2000
Introduced: 7/3/2001
Retired: 12/12/2001
She has a rather regal air
Other cats cannot compare
Standing straight and full of pride
You can't resist her deep blue eyes!
7G - $7 ♥ 9G - $7

Siberia™
#40662

Birthday: 1/31/2007
Introduced: 6/29/2007
Current
My winter coat is thick and plush
So I stay warm in snow and slush
But if the hot sun shines and glows
I'll put some sunscreen on my nose!
15G - Current Retail Value

Side-Kick™
#4532

Birthday: 1/30/2002
Introduced: 4/30/2002
Retired: 6/24/2004
I sniff and run and jump and play
I'm always busy every day
I'm loyal to the very end
That's why I'll always be your friend!
7G - $7 ♥ 10G - $7

Siesta™
#4439

Birthday: 7/31/2003
Introduced: 4/2/2004
Retired: 6/4/2004
After any good fiesta
You should take a short siesta
And now if I may suggest
Let's lay down and take a rest!
Ty Store exclusive.
12G - $8

Silver™
#4242

Birthday: 2/11/1999
Introduced: 4/21/1999
Retired: 12/23/1999
Curled up, sleeping in the sun
He's worn out from having fun
Chasing dust specks in the sunrays
This is how he spends his days!
5G - $7

Silver™
#46001

Birthday: 2/7/2004
Introduced: 2/9/2004
Retired: 3/15/2006
New Zealand is my home, you see
This beautiful land is the place for me
The Silver Fern fills us with pride
From the city to the countryside!
Asian-Pacific exclusive.
12G - $15

Singabear™
#4630

Birthday: 8/9/2002
Introduced: 4/28/2003
Retired: 11/7/2003
We're among the world's very best
A bustling city with no rest
But whether we're at work or play
We enjoy our lives every day!
Singapore exclusive.
11G - $15

Singapore™
#46023

Birthday: 2/9/2005
Introduced: 2/28/2005
Retired: 4/15/2006
Though this island may be small
This land stands so proud and tall
We all live here in harmony
Singapore, the jewel of the sea!
Singapore exclusive.
Also available in Asian-Pacific.
13G - $15

Sis™
#44017

Birthday: 8/5/2003
Introduced: 7/8/2004
Retired: 10/25/2004
You've helped me through
good times and bad
You've cheered me up when I've been sad
A better friend I never knew
Happy Sister's Day to you!
Ty Store exclusive.
12G - $7

Sizzle™
#4399

Birthday: 8/25/2001
Introduced: 11/30/2001
Retired: 3/18/2002
Look at me, I'm quite a bear
I love my soft and furry hair
Make me sizzle, is what I said
That's why I'm such a vibrant red!
7G - $7 ♥ 9G - $7

Skips™
#44083

Birthday: 4/16/2006
Introduced: 3/14/2006
Retired: 4/8/2006
On this magical spring night
I'll make a wish with all my might
That when I wake on Easter Day
The Easter Bunny and I can play!
Ty Store exclusive.
14G - $10

Skis™
#40438

Birthday: 2/13/2006
Introduced: 9/29/2006
Retired: 3/27/2007
It is one of my greatest hopes
That I will get to hit the slopes
Shushing down the cold white snow
I'll ski so fast; it's go, go, GO!
14G/14UK - $7

Slamdunk™
#40414

Birthday: 12/30/2005
Introduced: 8/31/2006
Current
Basketball's my favorite sport
I love to dribble down the court
The crowd will all let out a "WHOOP"
Because I dunked it through the hoop!
14G - Current Retail Value

Slapshot™
#40618

Birthday: 10/27/2006
Introduced: 3/30/2007
Current
Some penguins like to figure skate
To spin or make a figure eight
But if you would like my advice
Hockey's the thing when on the ice!
15G - Current Retail Value

Slayer™
#4307

Birthday: 9/26/2000
Introduced: 7/8/2000
Retired: 4/4/2001
If you want to have some fun
Try to make Slayer run
Tickle his tail, then you'll know
Just how fast he can go!
6G - $7 ♥ 7G - $7

Sledge™
#4538

Birthday: 4/26/2002
Introduced: 5/31/2002
Retired: 10/29/2002
Of all the sharks to swim the sea
The most unusual is me
My head is flat, my eyes are wide
But I am beautiful inside!
7G - $7 ♥ 10G - $7

Sleighbelle™
#40144 · green

Birthday: 6/5/2004
Introduced: 9/30/2004
Retired: 12/29/2004
When I hear the sleigh bells ring
It makes me think of just one thing
That special ride made once each year
That spreads joy and holiday cheer!
12G/12EU - $7

Sleighbelle™
#40144 · white

Birthday: 6/5/2004
Introduced: 9/30/2004
Retired: 12/29/2004
When I hear the sleigh bells ring
It makes me think of just one thing
That special ride made once each year
That spreads joy and holiday cheer!
12G/12EU - $7

Slick™
#40072

Birthday: 8/11/2003
Introduced: 3/30/2004
Retired: 7/28/2004
I like to read detective books
I love when the good guys catch the crooks
I enjoy word puzzles, too
Especially when I play with you!
12G - $7

Slippery™
#4222

Birthday: 1/17/1998
Introduced: 1/1/1999
Retired: 12/23/1999
In the ocean, near a breaking wave
Slippery the seal acts very brave
On his surfboard, he sees a swell
He's riding the wave Oooops . . . he fell!
5G - $7

Slither™
#4031

Birthday: None
Introduced: 6/25/1994
Retired: 6/15/1995
Slither was issued without a poem.
1G - $2,500 ♥ 2G - $1,000 ♥ 3G - $800

Slowpoke™
#4261

Birthday: 5/20/1999
Introduced: 8/31/1999
Retired: 12/23/1999
Look up in the sky to the top of the tree
What in the world is that you see?
A little sloth as sweet as can be
Munching on leaves very slowly!
5G - $7

Sly™
#4115 · brown belly

Birthday: 9/12/1996
Introduced: 6/15/1996
Retired: 8/6/1996
Sly is a fox and tricky is he
Please don't chase him, let him be
If you want him, just say when
He'll peek out from his den!
4G - $45

Sly™
#4115 · white belly

Birthday: 9/12/1996
Introduced: 8/6/1996
Retired: 9/22/1998
Sly is a fox and tricky is he
Please don't chase him, let him be
If you want him, just say when
He'll peek out from his den!
4G - $8 ♥ 5G - $7

Smart™
#4353

Birthday: 6/7/2000
Introduced: 4/1/2001
Retired: 5/30/2001
A special song they will play
On your graduation day
Relax and smile, you're finally done
Congratulations...class of 2001!
7G - $7 ♥ 8G - $7

Smarter™
#4526

Birthday: 6/12/2001
Introduced: 4/1/2002
Retired: 8/29/2002
It's so exciting, you can't wait
You finally get to graduate
We hope that all your dreams come true
Congratulations, class of 2002!
7G - $7 ♥ 10G - $7

186

Smartest™
#4591

Birthday: 6/9/2002
Introduced: 3/31/2003
Retired: 7/29/2003
Although school has been so much fun
We've made it! Now we're finally done
And for our Graduation Day
Join me and shout, "Hoot-hoot, hooray"!
7G - $7 ♥ 11G - $7

Smarty™
#40232

Birthday: 4/13/2004
Introduced: 3/31/2005
Retired: 11/23/2005
You made it to this day at last
With each and every test you passed
Today's the day you graduate
So toss your hat and celebrate!
13G/13EU - $7

Smarty™
#44050

Birthday: 4/29/2005
Introduced: 4/27/2005
Retired: 8/1/2005
The time has flown by very fast
It's graduation day at last
You've worked so hard the whole year through
Sincere congrats from me to you!
Ty Store exclusive.
13G - $7

Smash™
#40270 · gold logo

Birthday: 8/29/2005
Introduced: 7/29/2005
Retired: 10/21/2005
With a racket and a tennis ball
Game, set, match, I'll beat them all
Serve and volley across the court
I know that I won't come up short!
USA exclusive.
13G - $10

Smash™
#47011 · silver logo

Birthday: 8/29/2005
Introduced: 8/29/2005
Retired: 10/21/2005
With a racket and a tennis ball
Game, set, match, I'll beat them all
Serve and volley across the court
I know that I won't come up short!
US Open exclusive.
13G - $225

Smitten™
#4577 · black nose

Birthday: 2/16/2002
Introduced: 12/27/2002
Retired: 5/29/2003
I am the bear that can't be missed
The one that no one can resist
Just take me home and you will see
How smitten you become with me!
7G - $7 ♥ 11G - $7

Smitten™
#4577 · pink nose

Birthday: 2/16/2002
Introduced: 12/27/2002
Retired: 5/29/2003
I am the bear that can't be missed
The one that no one can resist
Just take me home and you will see
How smitten you become with me!
7G - $7 ♥ 11G - $7

Smooch™
#4335

Birthday: 2/14/2000
Introduced: 1/1/2001
Retired: 2/14/2001
Chocolate candy and flowers are fine
They help to say, "Will you be mine?"
But there's a better thing to do
Let me deliver kisses for you!
7G - $10 ♥ 8G - $10

SMOOCH-e™
#4435

Birthday: 2/14/2004
Introduced: 1/12/2004
Retired: 3/1/2004
On this romantic holiday
There is something I'd like to say
I want to know if you'll be mine
My one and only Valentine!
Ty Store exclusive.
12G - $9

Smoochy™
#4039 • double thread mouth

Birthday: 10/1/1997
Introduced: 12/31/1997
Retired: 3/31/1999
Is he a frog or maybe a prince?
This confusion makes him wince
Find the answer, help him with this
Be the one to give him a kiss!
5G - $7

Smoochy™
#4039 • felt mouth

Birthday: 10/1/1997
Introduced: 12/31/1997
Retired: 3/31/1999
Is he a frog or maybe a prince?
This confusion makes him wince
Find the answer, help him with this
Be the one to give him a kiss!
5G - $7

Smoochy™
#4039 • single thread mouth

Birthday: 10/1/1997
Introduced: 12/31/1997
Retired: 3/31/1999
Is he a frog or maybe a prince?
This confusion makes him wince
Find the answer, help him with this
Be the one to give him a kiss!
5G - $7

Smudges™
#40225

Birthday: 8/4/2004
Introduced: 5/31/2005
Retired: 7/25/2006
My furry coat is black as night
And boy, I'm glad it isn't white
I love to play in dirt and grime
It's how I like to spend my time!
13G/13EU - $7

Sneakers™
#40461

Birthday: 10/26/2006
Introduced: 10/31/2006
Current
When I look for something to chew
Watch out, 'cause I might get your shoe
A tasty treat that I can munch
Your sneakers might make a good lunch!
14G/14UK - Current Retail Value

Sneaky™
#4278

Birthday: 2/22/2000
Introduced: 3/1/2000
Retired: 4/4/2001
A shadow in the dark you'll see
Don't be afraid, it's only me
My spots will hide me 'til I see
That you are just the friend for me!
6G - $7 ♥ 7G - $7

Sniffer™
#4299

Birthday: 5/6/2000
Introduced: 6/24/2000
Retired: 4/24/2001
When I run fast, my ears will flap
When I get tired, I sit in your lap
All through the night, I'll tickle your toes
And say I love you by licking your nose!
6G - $7 ♥ 7G - $7

Snip™
#4120

Birthday: 10/22/1996
Introduced: 1/1/1997
Retired: 12/31/1998
Snip the cat is Siamese
She'll be your friend if you please
So toss her a toy or a piece of string
Playing with you is her favorite thing!
4G - $7 ♥ 5G - $7

Snips™
#49008

Birthday: 1/31/2004
Introduced: 12/1/2004
Retired: 4/6/2005
Nothing to do? Give Snips a call
Just for the shear fun of it all
This cut-up knows just what to do
Create a surprise just for you!
Beanie Baby Offcial Club exclusive.
12G/12EU - $12

Snips™
#49008 · with memory box

Birthday: 1/31/2004
Introduced: 12/1/2004
Retired: 4/6/2005
Nothing to do? Give Snips a call
Just for the shear fun of it all
This cut-up knows just what to do
Create a surprise just for you!
Beanie Baby Offcial Club exclusive.
12G/12EU - $25

Snocap™
#4573

Birthday: 11/8/2001
Introduced: 11/27/2002
Retired: 10/8/2003
On a snowy winter's day
A game of hide and seek we'll play
White like the snow, I'm very sly
Can you find me? I dare you to try!
7G - $8 ♥ 10G - $8

Snocap™
#4573

Birthday: 11/8/2001
Introduced: 7/26/2003
Retired: 7/27/2003
On a snowy winter's day
A game of hide and seek we'll play
White like the snow, I'm very sly
Can you find me? I dare you to try!
Brookfield Zoo promotional item.
7G - $75 ♥ 10G - $75

Snookums™
#40261

Birthday: 10/13/2004
Introduced: 7/29/2005
Retired: 2/24/2006
In my heart you'll always be
The only person meant for me
I'll shout it out and beat the drums
So all will know you're my Snookums!
13G/13EU - $7

Snoops™
#40244

Birthday: 10/20/2004
Introduced: 5/31/2005
Retired: 12/29/2005
Under the porch, behind a tree
I wonder what it is I'll see?
I love to search and to explore
A good friend's what I'm looking for!
13G/13EU - $7

Snoopy™
#47078

Birthday: 6/1/2007
Introduced: 6/29/2007
Current
Come join Snoopy and his friends
When you're here the fun never ends
At Camp Snoopy there's much to do
We just can't wait 'til we see YOU!
Camp Snoopy exclusive.
15G - Current Retail Value

Snoopy™
#47068

Birthday: 6/1/2007
Introduced: 6/29/2007
Current
Come join Snoopy and his friends
When you're here the fun never ends
At Camp Snoopy there's much to do
We just can't wait 'til we see YOU!
Knott's Berry Farm exclusive.
15G - Current Retail Value

Snort™
#4002

Birthday: 5/15/1995
Introduced: 1/1/1997
Retired: 9/15/1998
Although Snort is not so tall
He loves to play basketball
He is a star player in his dreams
Can you guess his favorite team?
4G - $7 ♥ 5G - $7

Snowball™
#4201

Birthday: 12/22/1996
Introduced: 10/1/1997
Retired: 12/31/1997
There is a snowman, I've been told
That plays with Beanies out in the cold
What is better in a winter wonderland
Than a Beanie snowman in your hand!
4G - $7

Snowbelles™
#47028 · red

Birthday: 12/1/2006
Introduced: 9/29/2006
Retired: 10/25/2006
It's time to spread both peace and love
To give to those you're thinking of
A time for kindness and for joy
For each man, woman, girl, and boy!
Hallmark exclusive.
14G - $12

Snowbelles™
#47028 · white

Birthday: 12/1/2006
Introduced: 9/29/2006
Retired: 10/25/2006
It's time to spread both peace and love
To give to those you're thinking of
A time for kindness and for joy
For each man, woman, girl, and boy!
Hallmark exclusive.
14G - $12

Snowdrift™
#40026

Birthday: 12/29/2002
Introduced: 9/30/2003
Retired: 12/26/2003
When the snow drifts up so high
You might think it will touch the sky
Then we can play a game or two
Something that's fun for me and you!
7G - $7 ♥ 11G - $7

Snowdrop™
#44095

Birthday: 12/22/2006
Introduced: 11/9/2006
Retired: 12/14/2006
The northern winds begin to blow
Noses and cheeks so red they glow
And then snowflakes start to appear
That means that winter's finally here!
Ty Store exclusive.
14G - $7

Snowgirl™
#4333

Birthday: 11/30/2000
Introduced: 9/28/2000
Retired: 12/12/2000
Look outside that's where I'm at
Wearing a warm scarf and hat
So even though the wind gusts blow
We can still play in the snow!
6G - $7 ♥ 7G - $7

Snuggins™
#48433

Birthday: 2/00/2007
Introduced: 2/1/2007
Retired: 3/1/2007
Come over here right next to me
About as close as you can be
I love it when we cuddle up
I can't help being a snuggly pup!
*February 2007
Beanie Baby of the Month.*
BBOM - $7

Soar™
#4410

Birthday: 7/4/2001
Introduced: 6/10/2002
Retired: 6/14/2002
The symbol of freedom soaring high
The eagle glides across the sky
He's proud to wear red, white and blue
He's patriotic through and through!
Ty Store exclusive.
10G - $8

Soar™ Key-clip
#40369

Birthday: None
Introduced: 4/28/2006
Current
Happy Independence Day!
14/14UKsm - Current Retail Value

SoftBank HAWKS™
#46098

Birthday: 1/28/2005
Introduced: 7/9/2007
Retired: 7/27/2007
SoftBank HAWKS was issued without a poem.
Club HAWKS exclusive.
15G - $2,800

190

Sonnet™
#40036

Birthday: 2/19/2003
Introduced: 11/26/2003
Retired: 4/16/2004
This poem is my special way
To express the joy I feel today
And so you know my love is true
I pledge my heart to only you!
7G - $7 ♥ 11G - $7

South Carolina™
#40301

Birthday: None
Introduced: 11/30/2005
Retired: 5/24/2006
STATE MOTTO: "Animis Opibusque Parati"
(Prepared in mind and resources)
NICKNAME: Palmetto State
FACT: The Upper Whitewater Falls is the highest cascade in eastern America, descending nearly 411 feet!
Sold only in South Carolina.
13G - $7

Soybean™
#40615

Birthday: 1/3/2007
Introduced: 3/30/2007
Current
It seems that whatever I do
This place is filthy; sad, but true
No matter how hard I might try
This place is simply a pig sty!
15G - Current Retail Value

Spangle™
#4245 · pink head

Birthday: 6/14/1999
Introduced: 4/24/1999
Retired: 12/23/1999
Stars and stripes he wear proudly
Everywhere he goes he says loudly
"Hip, hip hooray, for the land of the free
There's no place on earth I'd rather be!"
5G - $7

Spangle™
#4245 · white head

Birthday: 6/14/1999
Introduced: 8/16/1999
Retired: 12/23/1999
Stars and stripes he wears proudly
Everywhere he goes he says loudly
"Hip hip hooray, for the land of the free
There's no place on earth I'd rather be!"
5G - $7

Spangle™
#4245 · blue head

Birthday: 6/14/1999
Introduced: 10/21/1999
Retired: 12/23/1999
Stars and stripes he wears proudly
Everywhere he goes he says loudly
"Hip, hip hooray, for the land of the free
There's no place on earth I'd rather be!
5G - $7

Spangle™ Key-clip
#40370

Birthday: None
Introduced: 4/28/2006
Current
Land of the Free!
14/14UKsm - Current Retail Value

Sparklers™
#44107

Birthday: 7/4/2007
Introduced: 5/29/2007
Current
Each year on July the fourth
From west to east and south to north
We proudly wear red, white and blue
U.S. of A we all love you
Ty Store exclusive.
15G - Current Retail Value

Sparkles™
#4800

Birthday: 1/00/2003
Introduced: 11/8/2002
Retired: 1/30/2003
My name means glisten, shine or light
But this is only partly right
Please take me home and you will see
My sparkling personality!
January 2003
Beanie Baby of the Month.
BBOM - $7

Sparks™
#4633

Birthday: 11/5/2002
Introduced: 9/22/2003
Retired: 1/20/2004
Fireworks light up the night
Bonfires lit are burning bright
Never forget the reason why
It's just simply because of Guy!
UK exclusive.
7G - $15

Sparky™
#4100

Birthday: 2/27/1996
Introduced: 6/15/1996
Retired: 5/11/1997
Sparky rides proud on the fire truck
Ringing the bell and pushing his luck
He gets under foot when trying to help
He often gets stepped on and lets out a yelp!
3 variations of poem.
Also with Dotty tush tag - $55.
4G - $40

Speckles™
#4402

Birthday: 2/17/2000
Introduced: 6/29/2000
Retired: 1/2/2002
Surfing on the Internet
I think of friends I've never met
They're 'round the world both near and far
I hope they know how dear they are!
Ty Store exclusive.
6G - $7

Speedster™
#40183

Birthday: 11/16/2004
Introduced: 12/30/2004
Retired: 2/24/2005
When swimming through the deep blue sea
I like to view the scenery
I'll take it slow and make it last
There's just no need to go so fast!
13G/13EU - $12

Speedy™
#4030

Birthday: 8/14/1994
Introduced: 6/25/1994
Retired: 10/1/1997
Speedy ran marathons in the past
Such a shame, always last
Now Speedy is a big star
After he bought a racing car!
1G - $2,500 ♥ 2G - $300 ♥
3G - $60 ♥ 4G - $7

Spells™
#44094

Birthday: 10/31/2006
Introduced: 9/27/2006
Retired: 11/1/2006
When it gets dark on Halloween
That is when I'll hit the scene
I'll make a special witches' brew
There's just enough for me and you!
Ty Store exclusive.
14G - $7

Spike™
#4060

Birthday: 8/13/1996
Introduced: 6/15/1996
Retired: 12/31/1998
Spike the rhino likes to stampede
He's the bruiser that you need
Gentle to birds on his back and spike
You can be his friend if you like!
4G - $7 ♥ 5G - $7

Spinner™
#4036 · "Creepy" on tush tags

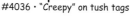

Birthday: 10/28/1996
Introduced: 10/1/1997
Retired: 9/19/1998
Does this spider make you scared?
Among many people that feeling is shared
Remember spiders have feelings too
In fact, this spider really likes you!
5G - $60

Spinner™
#4036 · "Spinner" on tush tag

Birthday: 10/28/1996
Introduced: 10/1/1997
Retired: 9/19/1998
Does this spider make you scared?
Among many people that feeling is shared
Remember spiders have feelings too
In fact, this spider really likes you!
4G - $7 ♥ 5G - $7

Splash™
#4022

Birthday: 7/8/1993
Introduced: 1/8/1994
Retired: 5/11/1997
Splash loves to jump and dive
He's the fastest whale alive
He always wins the 100 yard dash
With a victory jump he'll make a splash!
1G - $1,400 ♥ 2G - $250 ♥
3G - $75 ♥ 4G - $35

Splash™
#49020

Birthday: 7/8/1993
Introduced: 10/3/2005
Retired: 3/9/2006
Splash loves to jump and dive
He's the fastest whale alive
He always wins the 100 yard dash
With a victory jump he'll make a splash!
*Available in BBOC Original 9
Assortments 1-5.
Beanie Baby Offcial Club exclusive.*
BBOC2 - $10

SpongeBob™
(Stuck On You)
#40623

Birthday: None
Introduced: 7-May
Current
He's been known to hang around
Squidward's front yard...
Weenie Hut Jr.'s...
and now your place.
Oh buoy!
Also available at Ty Store.
15G - Current Retail Value

SpongeBob Best
Day Ever™
#40466

Birthday: None
Introduced: 11/30/2006
Current
SpongeBob once tried to give Squidward the
best day ever by taking him jellyfishing. They
did not have a good time.
Also available at Ty Store.
14G/14UK - $8

SpongeBob Best
Day Ever™
#47054

Birthday: None
Introduced: 11/30/2006
Retired: 2/27/2007
SpongeBob once tried to give Squidward the
best day ever by taking him jellyfishing. They
did not have a good time.
Best Buy exclusive.
14G - $12

SpongeBob
FrankenStein™
#40257

Birthday: None
Introduced: 8/31/2005
Retired: 11/23/2005
NAME GAME: SpongeBob's doodle drawing in
the episode Frankendoodle is referred to as
Spongedoodle, DoodleBob, and Doodle Boy!
SUPER ABSORBENT TRIVIA: The main
character in the episode, Frankendoodle, is a
parody of Frankenstein!
13G - $9

SpongeBob JollyElf™
#40281

Birthday: None
Introduced: 9/30/2005
Retired: 12/29/2005
WISH LIST: SpongeBob gives Squidward a
hand carved driftwood clarinet for Christmas!
SUPER ABSORBENT TRIVIA: In Christmas
Who?, we learn about the 1st Christmas
celebrated in Bikini Bottom!
13G - $8

SpongeBob Mermaidman™
#40432

Birthday: None
Introduced: 8/31/2006
Current
THE SUPERHEROES: Mermaidman and Barnacleboy often stop by The Krusty Krab
for a quick meal!
SUPER ABSORBENT TRIVIA: In Mermaidman
and Barnacleboy IV, Mermaidman accidentally
leaves his utility belt at The Krusty Krab
and SpongeBob finds it!
Also available at Ty Store.
14G/14UK - Current Retail Value

SpongeBob PinkPants™
#40416

Birthday: None
Introduced: 8/31/2006
Current
WATCHA WEARIN'?: SpongeBob typically
wears a white shirt, tie and brown trousers!
SUPER ABSORBENT TRIVIA: In "The Chaper-
one" SpongeBob dons a tuxedo when he escorts
Pearl to the prom!
UK/Canada exclusive.
14G/14UK - Current Retail Value

SpongeBob PinkPants™
#40416

Birthday: None
Introduced: 8/31/2006
Current
Every two minutes a woman is diagnosed with breast cancer.
Exercise and a healthy diet can help lower the risk of breast cancer.
When found early, the five-year breast cancer survival rate is about 96%.
3 variations of comment. USA exclusive.
Also available at Ty Store.
14G - Current Retail Value

SpongeBob PumpkinMask™
#40258

Birthday: None
Introduced: 8/31/2005
Retired: 11/23/2005
Current
DRESS UP TIME: SpongeBob dresses up as the legendary Flying Dutchman at Mr. Krabs' Halloween party!
SUPER ABSORBENT TRIVIA: In the episode, Scaredy Pants, the Flying Dutchman makes his first appearance!
13G - $9

SpongeBob QB™
#40462

Birthday: None
Introduced: 10/31/2006
Current
TOUCHDOWN! We don't know how good he is at football, but SpongeBob loves practicing karate, which he pronounces, Kah Rah Tay"!
SUPER ABSORBENT TRIVIA: In The Fry Cook Games, SpongeBob enters representing Mr. Krabs, while Patrick is representing Plankton!
Also available at Ty Store.
14G/14UK - Current Retail Value

SpongeBob SleighRide™
#40280

Birthday: None
Introduced: 9/30/2005
Retired: 12/29/2005
WISH LIST: For Christmas, Mr. Krabs asks Santa for a pony . . . with saddlebags full of money!
SUPER ABSORBENT TRIVIA: In Christmas Who?, SpongeBob learns all about Christmas from Sandy Cheeks!
13G - $8

SpongeBob SquarePants™
#40163

Birthday: None
Introduced: 10/29/2004
Retired: 2/24/2006
HOBBIES: Blowing bubbles and going jellyfishing
SUPER ABSORBENT TRIVIA: SpongeBob loves his driver's ed class with his favorite teacher, Mrs. Puff!
12G/14UK - $8

SpongeBob SquarePants™ Key-clip
#40406

Birthday: None
Introduced: 6/30/2006
Current
In school, SpongeBob made a spatula out of toothpicks in wood shop!
Also available at Ty Store.
14sm - Current Retail Value

SpongeBob Squarepants™ Football Star™
#40463

Birthday: None
Introduced: 10/31/2006
Current
TOUCHDOWN! We don't know how good he is at football, but Patrick has a talent for paddleball!
SUPER ABSORBENT TRIVIA: In the episode, The Fry Cook Games, the final event is "Bun Wrestling!"
Also available at Ty Store.
14G/14UK - Current Retail Value

SpongeBob Squarepants™ Gary the Snail™
#40469

Birthday: None
Introduced: 11/30/2006
Current
HOBBIES: Pretending to be Squidward, and eating Snail-Po Snail Food
SUPER ABSORBENT TRIVIA: In the episode, I Was a Teenage Gary, SpongeBob learns what it's like to be Gary!
Also available at Ty Store.
14G/14UK - Current Retail Value

SpongeBob Squarepants™ Gary the Snail™
#47057

Birthday: None
Introduced: 11/12/2006
Retired: 2/27/2007
HOBBIES: Pretending to be Squidward, and eating Snail-Po Snail Food
SUPER ABSORBENT TRIVIA: In the episode, I Was a Teenage Gary, SpongeBob learns what it's like to be Gary!
Best Buy exclusive.
14G - $12

SpongeBob Squarepants™
Mr. Krabs™
#40468

Birthday: None
Introduced: 11/30/2006
Current
HOBBIES: Counting money!
SUPER ABSORBENT TRIVIA: In the episode, Born Again Krabs, Mr. Krabs gave up SpongeBob to the Flying Dutchman for only sixty-two cents!
Also available at Ty Store.
14G/14UK - Current Retail Value

SpongeBob Squarepants™
Mr. Krabs™
#47056

Birthday: None
Introduced: 10/29/2006
Retired: 2/27/2007
HOBBIES: Counting money!
SUPER ABSORBENT TRIVIA: In the episode, Born Again Krabs, Mr. Krabs gave up SpongeBob to the Flying Dutchman for only sixty-two cents!
Best Buy exclusive.
14G - $12

SpongeBob Squarepants™
Muscle Man Star™
#40381

Birthday: None
Introduced: 6/30/2006
Current
MUSSEL BEACH: At Goo Lagoon, Patrick mistakenly believes the sign that reads, "No Swimming" actually says, "Ice Cream"!
SUPER ABSORBENT TRIVIA: In "Sponge-Guard On Duty" Patrick accidentally drowns when SpongeBob is mistaken for a lifeguard!
Also available at Ty Store.
14G/14UK - Current Retail Value

SpongeBob Squarepants™
MuscleBob BuffPants™
#40382

Birthday: None
Introduced: 6/30/2006
Current
MUSSEL BEACH: When SpongeBob finds out that he is extremely weak, he buys a set of "Anchor Arms"!
SUPER ABSORBENT TRIVIA: In "MuscleBob BuffPants" Sandy enrolls SpongeBob in an Anchor Toss Competition!
Also available at Ty Store.
14G/14UK - Current Retail Value

SpongeBob Squarepants™
Patrick Barnacleboy™
#40433

Birthday: None
Introduced: 8/31/2006
Current
THE SUPERHEROES: Some of Mermaidman's crimefighting tools include the Orb of Confusion, the Aqua Glove and the Tickle Belt!
SUPER ABSORBENT TRIVIA: In Mermaidman and Barnacleboy III, SpongeBob and Patrick look after the Mermalair while Mermaidman and Barnacleboy go on vacation!
Also available at Ty Store.
14G/14UK - Current Retail Value

SpongeBob Squarepants™
Patrick Claus™
#40282

Birthday: None
Introduced: 9/30/2005
Retired: 12/29/2005
WISH LIST: In Patrick's letter to Santa, he asks for a piece of paper!
SUPER ABSORBENT TRIVIA: In Christmas Who?, everyone in Bikini Bottom sends their wish list to Santa in a bottle!
13G - $8

SpongeBob Squarepants™
Patrick Star™
#40164

Birthday: None
Introduced: 10/29/2004
Retired: 3/27/2006
HOBBIES: Playing games with SpongeBob!
SUPER ABSORBENT TRIVIA: Patrick's big ambition in life can be summed up in four words: "uh . . . I . . . uh . . . forget"
12G/14UK - $9

SpongeBob Squarepants™
Patrick Star Best Day Ever™
#40467

Birthday: None
Introduced: 11/30/2006
Current
Patrick considers lying dormant for 24 hours to be a perfect day!
Also available at Ty Store.
14G/14UK - Current Retail Value

SpongeBob Squarepants™
Patrick Star Best Day Ever™
#47055

Birthday: None
Introduced: 11/19/2006
Retired: 2/27/2007
Patrick considers lying dormant for 24 hours to be a perfect day!
Best Buy exclusive.
14G - $12

SpongeBob Squarepants™ Patrick Star™ Key-clip
#40407

Birthday: None
Introduced: 6/30/2006
Current
Patrick was once vacuum packed inside a tuna can!!
Also available at Ty Store.
14sm - Current Retail Value

SpongeBob Squarepants™ Squidward Tentacles™
#40165

Birthday: None
Introduced: 10/29/2004
Retired: 9/25/2006
HOBBIES: Playing the clarinet and trying to avoid SpongeBob
SUPER ABSORBENT TRIVIA: Squidward lives in an Easter Island head between the homes of SpongeBob and Patrick!
12G/14UK - $9

SpongeBob ThumbsUp™
#40217

Birthday: None
Introduced: 2/28/2005
Current
HOBBIES: When SpongeBob takes an art class, Squidward tries to pass of SpongeBob's creation as his own!
SUPER ABSORBENT TRIVIA: The sculpture the SpongeBob created was actually Michelangelo's David!
Also available at Ty Store.
13G - Current Retail Value

SpongeBob TuxedoPants™
#40218

Birthday: None
Introduced: 2/28/2005
Current
DANCIN' MACHINE: SpongeBob agrees to take Mr. Krabs' daughter, Pearl, to her school prom after she gets dumped by her boyfriend!
SUPER ABSORBENT TRIVIA: In "SpongeBob's House Party" SpongeBob invites 177 of his closest frineds to his house party!
Also available at Ty Store.
13G - Current Retail Value

Spook™
#4090

Birthday: None
Introduced: 9/1/1995
Retired: 10/1995
Spook was issued without a poem.
3G - $425

Spooky™
#4090

Birthday: 10/31/1995
Introduced: 9/1/1995
Retired: 12/31/1997
Ghosts can be a scary sight
But don't let Spooky bring you any fright
Because when you're alone, you will see
The best friend that Spooky can be!
3G - $80 ♥ 4G - $10

Sport™
#4590

Birthday: 9/2/2002
Introduced: 3/31/2003
Retired: 5/25/2004
I bark and bark the whole day through
But not because I'm mad at you
It's really just the only way
To let you know I want to play!
7G - $7 ♥ 11G - $7

Spot™
#4000 • no spot

Birthday: None
Introduced: 1/8/1994
Retired: 4/13/1994
Spot was issued without a poem.
1G - $2,800 ♥ 2G - $1,600

Spot™
#4000 • with spot

Birthday: 1/3/1993
Introduced: 4/13/1994
Retired: 10/1/1997
See Spot sprint, see Spot run
You and Spot will have lots of fun
Watch out now, because he's not slow
Just stand back and watch him go!
2G - $1,000 ♥ 3G - $60 ♥ 4G - $7

Spot™
#49023 · no spot

Birthday: None
Introduced: 10/5/2005
Retired: 3/9/2006
Spot was issued without a poem.
Available in BBOC Original 9
Assortment 2.
Beanie Baby Offcial Club exclusive.
BBOC2 - $100

Spot™
#49022 · with spot

Birthday: 1/3/1993
Introduced: 10/3/2005
Retired: 3/9/2006
Spot was issued without a poem.
Available in BBOC Original 9
Assortment 1, 3, 4 and 5.
Beanie Baby Offcial Club exclusive.
BBOC2 - $10

Spotter™
#40354

Birthday: 12/7/2005
Introduced: 2/28/2006
Current
Sleek and stealthy, I'll prowl around
Skulking across the jungle ground
Then I'll pounce just when I see
Another friend to play with me!
14G/14UK - Current Retail Value

Spring™
#4513

Birthday: 3/7/2001
Introduced: 12/27/2001
Retired: 4/16/2002
Springtime is my favorite season
Maybe you can guess the reason
Pretty colored flowers bloom
And bring us out of winter's gloom!
7G - $7 ♥ 10G - $7

Springfield™
#40053

Birthday: 6/18/2003
Introduced: 1/30/2004
Retired: 6/24/2004
Hippity hopping down the lane
Over the hills, across the plain
What do I search for? You will see
A special friend to play with me!
12G - $7

Springston™
#40601

Birthday: 3/19/2006
Introduced: 1/31/2007
Retired: 5/25/2007
Just looking at the ears I wear
You'd guess that I'm a springtime bear
I help my pal with the cotton tail
Delivering goodies without fail!
15G - $7

Springy™
#4272

Birthday: 2/29/2000
Introduced: 3/1/2000
Retired: 7/14/2000
Hopping and jumping all around
I never stay long on the ground
I might be gone for just a while
But I'll be back and make you smile!
6G - $7 ♥ 7G - $7

Spuds™
#40191

Birthday: 7/6/2004
Introduced: 12/30/2004
Retired: 6/29/2005
Being a dog is great, you see
It really is the life for me
I get to eat and sleep and play
I do it almost every day!
13G/13EU - $8

Spunky™
#4184

Birthday: 1/14/1997
Introduced: 12/31/1997
Retired: 3/31/1999
Bouncing around without much grace
To jump on your lap and lick your face
But watch him closely he has no fears
He'll run so fast he'll trip over his ears
5G - $7

Squealer™
#4005

Birthday: 4/23/1993
Introduced: 1/8/1994
Retired: 5/1/1998
Squealer likes to joke around
He is known as class clown
Listen to his stories awhile
There is no doubt he'll make you smile!
1G - $2,500 ♥ 2G - $300 ♥ 3G - $50 ♥
4G - $7 ♥ 5G - $7

Squealer™
#49017

Birthday: 4/23/1993
Introduced: 10/3/2005
Retired: 3/9/2006
Squealer likes to joke around
He is known as class clown
Listen to his stories awhile
There is no doubt he'll make you smile!
*Available in BBOC Original 9
Assortment 1-5.
Beanie Baby Offcial Club exclusive.*
BBOC2 - $10

Squirmy™
#4302

Birthday: 4/13/2000
Introduced: 6/24/2000
Retired: 12/15/2000
I can't sit still, it's just too hard
I roll and wiggle in the yard
They try to tell me not to squirm
But I can't help it, I'm a worm!
6G - $7 ♥ 7G - $7

Star™
#40030 · gold star

Birthday: 11/19/2002
Introduced: 10/30/2003
Retired: 6/24/2004
Our angel watches over you
When you are sad or feeling blue
Our angel is your special friend
Whose love for you will never end!
7G - $8 ♥ 11G - $8

Star™
#40030 · gold star

Birthday: 11/19/2002
Introduced: 10/30/2003
Retired: 6/24/2004
Our angel watches over you
When you are sad or feeling blue
Our angel is your special friend
Whose love for you will never end!
Bon-Ton and Elder-Beerman exclusive.
11G - $50

Star™
#4703 · blue star

Birthday: 11/19/2002
Introduced: 10/30/2003
Retired: 1/7/2004
Our angel watches over you
When you are sad or feeling blue
Our angel is your special friend
Whose love for you will never end!
Ideation exclusive.
11G - $12

Starboard™
#40396

Birthday: 6/13/2006
Introduced: 6/30/2006
Current
I'd like to sail the ocean blue
With a special friend or two
And then I'll tour the seven seas
The aquatic life is such a breeze!
14G/14UK - Current Retail Value

Stargazer™
#40459

Birthday: 10/8/2006
Introduced: 10/31/2006
Current
Shining like the brightest star
I am the prettiest by far
And when you look at me you'll see
A unicorn of great beauty!
14G/14UK - Current Retail Value

Starlett™
#4382

Birthday: 1/9/2001
Introduced: 7/31/2001
Retired: 11/8/2002
Curled up snugly in your lap
Is where I'll take a little nap
And if you pet my long white fur
You'll be sure to hear me purr!
7G - $7 ♥ 9G - $7

Starlight™
#46010 · black

Birthday: 11/6/2003
Introduced: 11/6/2004
Retired: 3/27/2006
The Toy Kingdom at Harrods is really great
So go get your skates on and don't be late
It's a mystical, magical, wonderful sight
You'll have sweet dreams all through the night!
Harrods UK exclusive.
12EU - $25

Starlight™
#46010 · black, boxed

Birthday: 11/6/2003
Introduced: 11/6/2004
Retired: 3/27/2006
The Toy Kingdom at Harrods is really great
So go get your skates on and don't be late
It's a mystical, magical, wonderful sight
You'll have sweet dreams all through the night!
Limited to 1,000. Harrods UK exclusive.
12EU - $60

Starlight™
#46011 · white

Birthday: 11/6/2003
Introduced: 11/6/2004
Retired: 3/27/2006
The Toy Kingdom at Harrods is really great
So go get your skates on and don't be late
It's a mystical, magical, wonderful sight
You'll have sweet dreams all through the night!
Harrods UK exclusive.
12EU - $120

Starlight™
#46011 · white, boxed

Birthday: 11/6/2003
Introduced: 11/6/2004
Retired: 3/27/2006
The Toy Kingdom at Harrods is really great
So go get your skates on and don't be late
It's a mystical, magical, wonderful sight
You'll have sweet dreams all through the night!
Limited to 5000. Harrods UK exclusive.
12EU - $200

Starry™
#46042 · black nose

Birthday: 1/20/2005
Introduced: 9/12/2005
Retired: 6/15/2006
The Aussie flag's unique, you see
It tells you of our history
Under the Southern Cross stars at night
And the Commonwealth Star we did unite!
Asian-Pacific exclusive.
13G - $10

Starry™
#46042 · flag nose

Birthday: 1/20/2005
Introduced: 10/15/2005
Retired: 6/15/2006
The Aussie flag's unique, you see
It tells you of our history
Under the Southern Cross stars at night
And the Commonwealth Star we did unite!
Australia exclusive.
13G - $50

Steg™
#4087

Birthday: 11/1/1994
Introduced: 6/3/1995
Retired: 6/15/1996
Steg was issued without a poem.
3G - $400

Stilts™
#4221

Birthday: 6/16/1998
Introduced: 1/1/1999
Retired: 5/31/1999
Flying high over mountains and streams
Fulfilling wishes, hopes and dreams
The stork brings parents bundles of joy
The greatest gift, a girl or boy!
5G - $7

Sting™
#4077

Birthday: 8/27/1995
Introduced: 6/3/1995
Retired: 1/1/1997
I'm a manta ray and my name is Sting
I'm quite unusual and this is the thing
Under the water I glide like a bird
Have you ever seen something so absurd?
3G - $75 ♥ 4G - $40

Stinger™
#4193

Birthday: 9/29/1997
Introduced: 5/30/1998
Retired: 12/31/1998
Stinger the scorpion will run and dart
But this little fellow is really all heart
So if you see him don't run away
Say hello and ask him to play!
5G - $7

Stinky™
#4017

Birthday: 2/13/1995
Introduced: 6/3/1995
Retired: 9/28/1998
Deep in the woods he lived in a cave
Perfume and mints were the gifts he gave
He showered every night in the kitchen sink
Hoping one day he wouldn't stink!
3G - $50 ♥ 4G - $8 ♥ 5G - $7

Stockings™
#40140

Birthday: 11/26/2003
Introduced: 9/30/2004
Retired: 12/29/2004
Hanging right by the fireside
No ordinary treat inside
In your stocking what do you see?
A special little bear, that's me!
12G/12EU - $7

Stony™
#44204

Birthday: None
Introduced: 8/31/2005
Retired: 1/2/2007
FACT: Researchers have found that global
warming has contributed to diminishing pika
populations in certain areas of the northwestern United States!
Ty Store/World Wildlife Fund exclusive.
13G - $10

Stretch™
#4182

Birthday: 9/21/1997
Introduced: 12/31/1997
Retired: 3/31/1999
She thinks when her head is underground
The rest of her body can't be found
The Beanie Babies think it's absurd
To play hide and seek with this bird!
5G - $7

Stripers™
#40353

Birthday: 11/5/2005
Introduced: 2/28/2006
Current
Sneaking around; out on the prowl
You might hear a low, rumbling growl
Hunting's a tiger's favorite thing
Unless I see a ball of string!
14G/14UK - Current Retail Value

Stripes™
#4065 · orange stripes

Birthday: None
Introduced: 1/7/1996
Retired: 6/3/1996
Stripes was issued without a poem.
3G - $160

Stripes™
#4065 · orange stripes with
fuzzy belly

Birthday: None
Introduced: 1/7/1996
Retired: 6/3/1996
Stripes was issued without a poem.
3G - $400

Stripes™
#4065 · tan stripes

Birthday: 6/11/1995
Introduced: 6/3/1996
Retired: 5/1/1998
Stripes was never fierce nor strong
So with tigers, he didn't get along
Jungle life was hard to get by
So he came to his friends at Ty!
4G - $9 ♥ 5G - $7

Stripey™
#40256

Birthday: 1/8/2005
Introduced: 7/29/2005
Current
Some like plaid an awful lot
Others prefer the polka-dot
For me I'd rather just be bare
Than not have my great stripes to wear!
13G/13EU - Current Retail Value

Strut™
#4171

Birthday: 3/8/1996
Introduced: 7/12/1997
Retired: 3/31/1999
Listen closely to "cock-a-doodle-doo"
What's the rooster saying to you?
Hurry, wake up sleepy head
We have lots to do, get out of bed!
4G - $7 ♥ 5G - $7

Stubby™
#40180

Birthday: 1/20/2004
Introduced: 12/30/2004
Retired: 7/27/2005
Not every pig plays in the dirt
I'd rather eat a big dessert
Like strawberries or chocolate cake
I might just have to learn to bake!
13G/13EU - $7

Stuffed™
#48430

Birthday: 11/00/2006
Introduced: 11/1/2006
Retired: 12/1/2006
I'm not dinner, although I'm stuffed
Trust me, I'm really bland and tough
So won't you please give me a break
And this year eat a juicy steak!
November 2006
Beanie Baby of the Month.
BBOM - $9

Stuffings™
#48418

Birthday: 11/00/2005
Introduced: 11/1/2005
Retired: 12/1/2005
Let's go watch some football first
Then eat until our tummies burst
After a nap, what should we do?
Break out leftovers for round two!
November 2005
Beanie Baby of the Month.
BBOM - $8

Sugar-Pie™
#40159

Birthday: 6/25/2004
Introduced: 11/30/2004
Retired: 1/28/2005
A little pup so cute and sweet
Bringing you a special treat
Some love and cuddles just for you
Maybe even a kiss or two!
12G/12EU - $7

Sugarpup™
#40485

Birthday: 9/21/2006
Introduced: 12/29/2006
Current
When it's time for me to nap
I'll just let out a little yap
Then I'll lie down and curl up
Because I'm a good Sugarpup!
15G/15UK - Current Retail Value

Summerfest™
#47069

Birthday: 6/28/2007
Introduced: 5/21/2007
Current
Music, food and family fun
Summerfest has just begun
Come join in before its gone
And surely you will Smile On!
Greater Milwaukee Area exclusive.
15G - Current Retail Value

Summertime Fun™
#40428 · orange

Birthday: None
Introduced: 6/23/2006
Retired: 6/26/2006
20 years of summer fun
Good times have only just begun
I'll make a stop down in "Big D"
It's so much fun for you and me!
Dallas Show exclusive.
14G - $10

Summertime Fun™
#40427 · green

Birthday: None
Introduced: 7/14/2006
Retired: 7/18/2006
20 years of summer fun
Good times have only just begun
With parks and shops, Atlanta's king
C'mon; let's see what's happening!
Atlanta Show exclusive.
14G - $10

Summertime Fun™
#40426 · pink

Birthday: None
Introduced: 7/22/2006
Retired: 7/25/2006
20 years of summer fun
Good times have only just begun
In Chi-town I'll walk the Mag Mile
This toddlin' town sure makes me smile!
Chicago Show exclusive.
14G - $10

Summertime Fun™
#40430 · yellow

Birthday: None
Introduced: 7/28/2006
Retired: 7/31/2006
20 years of summer fun
Good times have only just begun
In L.A. where the stars all stay
It's a great place to laugh and play!
Los Angeles Show exclusive.
14G - $10

Summertime Fun™
#40431 · blue

Birthday: None
Introduced: 8/13/2006
Retired: 8/17/2006
20 years of summer fun
Good times have only just begun
In old New York, where to begin?
So much to see, it makes me grin!
New York Show exclusive.
14G - $10

Summertime Fun™
#40429 · purple

Birthday: None
Introduced: 8/13/2006
Retired: 8/17/2006
20 years of summer fun
Good times have only just begun
In Toronto we'll go play outisde
The beauty here can't be denied!
Toronto Show exclusive.
14G - $10

Sunbonnet™
#40324

Birthday: 4/24/2006
Introduced: 12/30/2005
Retired: 3/27/2006
I really love the sweet perfume
Of flowers when they are in bloom
I think I'll pick a few today
So I can make a nice bouquet!
14G/14UK - $7

Sunburst™
#40553

Birthday: 6/4/2006
Introduced: 2/28/2007
Current
Here in my island paradise
The weather's warm; the breeze so nice
I'll sun myself on the warm sand
Life on the beach is truly grand!
15G - Current Retail Value

Sundar™
#44203

Birthday: None
Introduced: 11/24/2004
Retired: 1/2/2007
FACT: WWF works with anti-poaching teams to
stop the illegal hunting of snow leopards & also
creates & maintains reserves to protect them!
Ty Store/World Wildlife Fund exclusive.
12G - $12

SUNGOLIATH™
#46070

Birthday: 8/29/2003
Introduced: 8/21/2006
Current
SUNGOLIATH was issued without a poem.
Suntory Sungoliath exclusive.
14G - $40

Sunnie™
#40555 · aqua

Birthday: 4/4/2006
Introduced: 2/28/2007
Current
Lazy days out in the sun
Playing in the sand's such fun
The creatures here are all so nice
I'm glad I came to paradise!
15G - Current Retail Value

Sunnie™
#40555 · purple

Birthday: 4/4/2006
Introduced: 2/28/2007
Current
I'll poke my head above the trees
To feel the warm tropical breeze
The creatures here are all so nice
I'm glad I came to paradise!
15G - Current Retail Value

Sunny™
#4401

Birthday: 2/13/2000
Introduced: 11/30/2000
Retired: 12/8/2000
There's some mail waiting for me
A real surprise - a mystery
It's a message just from you
Telling me secrets I never knew!
6G - $7

Sunray™
#4598

Birthday: 8/5/2002
Introduced: 4/30/2003
Retired: 5/25/2004
All of my friends call me Sunray
I swim the ocean everyday
Sometimes I'll jump into the sky
Having fun, wishing I could fly!
7G - $7 ▼ 11G - $7

Sunrise™
#40551

Birthday: 8/29/2006
Introduced: 2/28/2007
Current
Where I live there's no cause to worry
No need to stress or even hurry
That's why the island life's for me
My sandy home's the place to be!
15G - Current Retail Value

Sunrise™ Key-clip
#40560

Birthday: None
Introduced: 4/2/2007
Current
Rise and Shine!
15sm - Current Retail Value

Sunset™
#40556

Birthday: 7/18/2006
Introduced: 2/28/2007
Current
Wiggling my toes in the sand
With a nice cool drink in hand
Sun and sand and deep blue sea
Better than living in a tree!
15G - Current Retail Value

Superstition™
#40419

Birthday: 10/13/2006
Introduced: 8/31/2006
Retired: 10/25/2006
When I go out to trick or treat
I hope you'll give me something sweet
But if you give a healthy snack
I still won't let you take it back!
14G - $7

Surfin'™
#48437

Birthday: 6/00/2007
Introduced: 6/1/2007
Retired: 7/2/2007
The waves are just perfect you know
So grab your board it's time to go
We'll drop in and then hang ten
Back to the beach then start again!
June 2007 Beanie Baby of the Month.
BBOM - $7

Swampy™
#4273

Birthday: 1/24/2000
Introduced: 3/1/2000
Retired: 3/23/2001
Through the murky swamps I glide
My yellow eyes I try to hide
I drift as silent as a log
A friend to you and every frog!
6G - $7 ♥ 7G - $7

Sweeper™
#40254

Birthday: 10/23/2004
Introduced: 7/29/2005
Current
The sweeper's job can be intense
'Cause I'm the last line of defense
And you will have to get past me
If you want to score a goal, you see!
13G/13EU - Current Retail Value

Sweetiekins™
#47019

Birthday: 10/14/2005
Introduced: 1/5/2006
Retired: 3/27/2006
I waited for the perfect time
And I searched for the perfect rhyme
As each and every day begins
I hope you'll be my Sweetiekins!
Hallmark exclusive.
14G - $7

Sweetiepaws™
#44093

Birthday: 10/21/2006
Introduced: 9/18/2006
Retired: 2/16/2007
Can't catch my breath; my heart beats fast
Each time that I see you walk past
'Cause you're so sweet, I have to say,
I love you, Happy Sweetest Day!
Ty Store exclusive.
14G - $7

Swinger™
#40098

Birthday: 10/22/2003
Introduced: 6/30/2004
Current
In the jungle where I'm found
You'll see me monkeying around
My pals and I always hang out
We have great fun without a doubt!
12G - Current Retail Value

Swirly™
#4249

Birthday: 3/10/1999
Introduced: 4/14/1999
Retired: 12/23/1999
Carefully traveling, leaving a trail
I'm not very fast, for I am a snail
Although I go my own plodding pace
Slow and steady, wins the race!
5G - $7

Swoop™
#4268

Birthday: 2/24/2000
Introduced: 3/1/2000
Retired: 6/11/2001
Gliding through the summer sky
Looking low and looking high
Now I think my quest can end
I've found you, my special friend!
6G - $7 ♥ 7G - $7

T™
#40520

Birthday: None
Introduced: 6/30/2005
Current
Alphabet Bears are issued without poems.
AB - Current Retail Value

Tabasco™
#4002

Birthday: 5/15/1995
Introduced: 6/3/1995
Retired: 1/1/1997
Although Tabasco is not so tall
He loves to play basketball
He is a star player in his dream
Can you guess his favorite team?
3G - $80 ♥ 4G - $45

204

Tabbles™
#40605

Birthday: 7/5/2006
Introduced: 2/28/2007
Current
I like string and I like mice
Catnip is also really nice
But guess my favorite thing to do
Curl up and take a nap with you!
15G - Current Retail Value

Tabs™
#4571

Birthday: 9/17/2001
Introduced: 11/27/2002
Retired: 10/8/2003
I am a cat without a home
Around the town I always roam
I'll climb up trees and then get stuck
Until you call the fire truck!
7G - $7 ♥ 10G - $7

TANAHAIRKU™
#46092

Birthday: 10/31/2006
Introduced: 1/31/2007
Current
When you travel far & wide
Always keep me by your side
To remind you of a love so true
For Malaysia, our tanahairku
Asian-Pacific exclusive.
15G - $20

Tangles™
#4901

Birthday: 1/29/2003
Introduced: 8/28/2003
Retired: 7/16/2004
Give me a ball of string or twine
Either one would be just fine
Sometimes I'm having so much fun
I find I'm tangled when I'm done!
7G - $7 ♥ 11G - $7

Tank™
#4031 · 7 plates with no shell

Birthday: 2/22/1995
Introduced: 1/7/1996
Retired: 6/00/1996
This armadillo loves the south
Shoving Tex-Mex in his mouth
He sure loves it south of the border
Keeping his friends in good order!
3G - $150 ♥ 4G - $150

Tank™
#4031 · 9 plates with no shell

Birthday: 2/22/1995
Introduced: Jun-96
Retired: 12/00/1996
This armadillo loves the south
Shoving Tex-Mex in his mouth
He sure loves it south of the border
Keeping his friends in good order!
4G - $175

Tank™
#4031 · 9 plates with shell

Birthday: 2/22/1995
Introduced: Sep-96
Retired: 10/1/1997
This armadillo lives in the south
Shoving Tex-Mex in his mouth
He sure loves it south of the border
Keeping his friends in good order!
4G - $15

Tasty™
#40275

Birthday: 9/6/2005
Introduced: 9/30/2005
Retired: 12/29/2005
Cookies, cakes, and any sweets
These are my most favorite treats
In my stocking, hope I see
Some ginger bread that's just for me!
13G - $7

TED-e™
#4414

Birthday: 8/19/2002
Introduced: 8/7/2002
Retired: 8/12/2002
For TED-e's hundredth birthday bash
A dear old friend will make a splash
Old-faced bear is back anew
He wants to celebrate with you!
Ty Store exclusive.
10G - $7

Teddy™
#4050 · brown with old face

Birthday: None
Introduced: 6/25/1994
Retired: 1/7/1995
Teddy was issued without a poem.
1G - $1,500 ♥ 2G - $1,100

Teddy™
#4052 · cranberry with old face

Birthday: None
Introduced: 6/25/1994
Retired: 1/7/1995
Teddy was issued without a poem.
1G - $1,500 ♥ 2G - $1,100

Teddy™
#4057 · jade with old face

Birthday: None
Introduced: 6/25/1994
Retired: 1/7/1995
Teddy was issued without a poem.
1G - $1,500 ♥ 2G - $1,100

Teddy™
#4056 · magenta with old face

Birthday: None
Introduced: 6/25/1994
Retired: 1/7/1995
Teddy was issued without a poem.
1G - $1,500 ♥ 2G - $1,100

Teddy™
#4051 · teal with old face

Birthday: None
Introduced: 6/25/1994
Retired: 1/7/1995
Teddy was issued without a poem.
1G - $1,500 ♥ 2G - $1,100

Teddy™
#4055 · violet with old face

Birthday: None
Introduced: 6/25/1994
Retired: 1/7/1995
Teddy was issued without a poem.
1G - $1,500 ♥ 2G - $1,100

Teddy™
#4050 · brown with new face

Birthday: 11/28/1995
Introduced: 1/7/1995
Retired: 10/1/1997
Teddy wanted to go out today
All of his friends went out to play
But he'd rather help whatever you do
After all, his best friend is you!
2G - $800 ♥ 3G - $150 ♥ 4G - $25

Teddy™
#4052 · cranberry with new face

Birthday: None
Introduced: 1/7/1995
Retired: 1/7/1996
Teddy was issued without a poem.
2G - $850 ♥ 3G - $825

Teddy™
#4057 · jade with new face

Birthday: None
Introduced: 1/7/1995
Retired: 1/7/1996
Teddy was issued without a poem.
2G - $800 ♥ 3G - $825

Teddy™
#4056 · magenta with new face

Birthday: None
Introduced: 1/7/1995
Retired: 1/7/1996
Teddy was issued without a poem.
2G - $850 ♥ 3G - $825

Teddy™
#4051 · teal with new face

Birthday: None
Introduced: 1/7/1995
Retired: 1/7/1996
Teddy was issued without a poem.
2G - $850 ♥ 3G - $825

Teddy™
#4055 · violet with new face

Birthday: None
Introduced: 1/7/1995
Retired: 1/7/1996
Teddy was issued without a poem.
2G - $925 ♥ 3G - $900

Teddy™
#4347

Birthday: 1/20/2002
Introduced: 6/28/2002
Retired: 12/27/2002
I can't believe it's been so long
One hundred years have come and gone
But through it all I have stayed true
The cuddly bear you always knew!
100th Year Anniversary.
7G - $7 ♥ 10G - $7

Teegra™
#40659

Birthday: 12/27/2006
Introduced: 6/29/2007
Current
I'm the most fearsome cat you'll know
I'll growl and put on quite a show
Claws so lethal you can be sure
My gosh ! I need a pedicure!
15G - Current Retail Value

Tender™
#40167

Birthday: 2/10/2004
Introduced: 12/30/2004
Retired: 7/27/2005
Please be quiet, don't make a peep
This little lamb is trying to sleep
I need my rest just like you do
When I wake up I'll play with you!
13G/13EU - $7

Tennessee™
#40226

Birthday: 6/1/1796
Introduced: 4/5/2005
Retired: 12/29/2005
STATE MOTTO: "Agriculture and Commerce"
NICKNAME: Volunteer State
FACT: The nickname, "The Volunteer State,"
came as a result of the volunteer soldiers' valor
during the War of 1812!
Sold only in Tennessee.
13G - $7

Texas™
#40082

Birthday: 12/29/2003
Introduced: 6/25/2004
Retired: 9/23/2005
I hail from the Lone Star State
And here's why Texas is so great
Rich in culture and history
Texas is the place to be!
Trade Show exclusive.
12G - $7

Texas Bluebonnet™
#40289

Birthday: None
Introduced: 7/5/2005
Retired: 12/29/2005
OFFICIAL FLOWER SINCE 1901
Our State flower's named for its hue
It's really a beautiful shade of blue
It's one of our favorites, we must admit
That's why in Texas we love the bluebonnet!
Trade Show exclusive.
13G - $7

Thank You Bear™
#4330

Birthday: None
Introduced: 12/29/2000
Retired: 1/4/2001
Thanks for everything you've done
Because of you we're #1
We're a great team you and me
Thanks again for your loyalty!
With letter or card - $190.
Retailer exclusive.
6G - $100 ♥ 7G - $100

Thank You Bear™
#40040

Birthday: None
Introduced: 12/20/2003
Retired: 3/2/2004
Together we make quite a pair
So please accept this special bear
For your support and dedication
A token of my appreciation!
With letter or card - $100.
Retailer exclusive.
7G - $35 ♥ 8G - $35

Thank You Bear™
#4815

Birthday: 4/00/2004
Introduced: 4/1/2004
Retired: 5/1/2004
As a special way of thanking you
For supporting us the way you do
Our heartfelt thanks we do extend
And Thank You Bear is what we send!
April 2004 Beanie Baby of the Month.
BBOM - $7

Thankful™
#44098

Birthday: 11/23/2006
Introduced: 10/19/2006
Retired: 1/16/2007
Happiness, health and family
Kind hearts and generosity
Hope for what the future brings
We are thankful for all these things!
14G - $7

Thanks A Bunch™
#40531

Birthday: None
Introduced: 4/28/2006
Current
Greetings Bears are issued without poems.
14G - Current Retail Value

The Beginning™
#4267

Birthday: 1/1/2002
Introduced: 3/1/2000
Retired: 5/10/2000
Beanie Babies can never end
They'll always be our special friends
Start the fun because we're here
To bring you hope, love and cheer!
6G - $7

The End™
#4265

Birthday: None
Introduced: 8/31/1999
Retired: 12/23/1999
All good things come to an end
It's been fun for everyone
Peace and hope are never gone
Love you all and say, "So long!"
5G - $7

Thistle™
#4623

Birthday: 11/30/2001
Introduced: 10/18/2002
Retired: 1/3/2003
The color navy I'll proudly wear
There's no other shade that can compare
Upon my chest I wear a thistle
If you know where I'm from, just whistle!
UK exclusive.
7G - $30

Thomas™
#40239

Birthday: 4/13/1743
Introduced: 4/29/2005
Retired: 8/26/2005
"We hold these truths to be self-evident, that
all men are created equal . . . "
13G/13EU - $7

208

Thunderbolt™
#40408

Birthday: 2/16/2006
Introduced: 7/31/2006
Current
Running fast, wind in my mane
Don't stop me now; don't tug that rein
Galloping fast, just you and me
Don't you just love feeling so free?!
14G - Current Retail Value

Thunderbolt™ Key-clip
#40673

Birthday: None
Introduced: 6/29/2007
Current
Giddy Up!
15Gsm - Current Retail Value

Tibby™
#40253

Birthday: 12/14/2004
Introduced: 7/29/2005
Current
I love to comb and brush my hair
With my looks I take great care
With pretty bows and polish too
I think I look great, don't you?
13G/13EU - Current Retail Value

Ticklish™
#40497

Birthday: 12/16/2006
Introduced: 1/31/2007
Current
Tickle me under my chin
Your reward . . . a toothy grin
Keep it up; I'll start to wiggle
And then the grin becomes a giggle!
15G - Current Retail Value

Tidings™
#4431

Birthday: 12/22/2002
Introduced: 11/25/2003
Retired: 12/7/2003
Quiet as a mouse, they say
Well maybe not this holiday
Let's all gather 'round the tree
And celebrate with family!
Ty Store exclusive.
11G - $12

Tiggs™
#40658

Birthday: 5/26/2007
Introduced: 6/29/2007
Current
I'm crawling through the tall, tall grass
Quietly stalking you, I pass
When I catch you don't have a fit
I got you this time! Tag . . . you're it!
15G - Current Retail Value

Tiki™
#40631

Birthday: 4/17/2007
Introduced: 4/30/2007
Current
On a sunny beach is where I'll be
Lounging around so leisurely
First I need something cool to drink
A iced tea would be nice I think!
15G - Current Retail Value

Timbers™
#46103

Birthday: 7/1/2006
Introduced: 4/30/2007
Current
In the north woods where I roam
I built a lodge that I call home
I love it here, you understand
My peaceful part of this great land!
Canada exclusive.
15G - Current Retail Value

Tinsel™
#4811

Birthday: 12/00/2003
Introduced: 12/1/2003
Retired: 1/2/2004
I wear a hat to keep me warm
Especially during a winter storm
Take me home and we can play
Right by your side I'll always stay!
December 2003
Beanie Baby of the Month.
BBOM - $8

Tiny™
#4234

Birthday: 9/8/1998
Introduced: 1/1/1999
Retired: 12/23/1999
South of the Border, in the sun
Tiny the Chihuahua is having fun
Attending fiestas, breaking piñatas
Eating a taco, or some enchiladas!
5G - $7

Tiny Tim™
#44028

Birthday: 12/25/2004
Introduced: 11/26/2004
Retired: 12/30/2004
Creeping through your cozy house
As quiet as a little mouse
I bring a special gift to you
And hope your Christmas dreams come true!
With gift box. Ty Store exclusive.
12G - $7

Tipsy™
#40067

Birthday: 1/7/2004
Introduced: 4/29/2004
Retired: 10/27/2004
If you should hear a cow say, "MOO"
It means he really cares for you
You'll never hear him utter, "Neigh"
What silly cow has that to say?!
12G - $7

Tiptoe™
#4241

Birthday: 1/8/1999
Introduced: 4/16/1999
Retired: 10/21/2006
Creeping quietly along the wall
Little foot prints fast and small
Tiptoeing through the house with ease
Searching for a piece of cheese!
5G - $7

Titan™
#40251

Birthday: 8/17/2005
Introduced: 10/31/2005
Retired: 4/21/2006
Some say I'm the king of the hounds
Surpassing all by leaps and bounds
Majestic stature; regal air
The other dogs just can't compare!
13G/13UK - $7

Titan™
#40251

Birthday: 8/17/2005
Introduced: 6/10/2006
Retired: 6/11/2006
Some say I'm the king of the hounds
Surpassing all by leaps and bounds
Majestic stature; regal air
The other dogs just can't compare!
Knott's Berry Farm exclusive.
13G - $25

To Brighten Your Day™
#40533

Birthday: None
Introduced: 4/28/2006
Current
Greetings Bears are issued without poems.
14G/14UK - Current Retail Value

Toast™
#1984

Birthday: 2/16/2003
Introduced: 8/9/2003
Retired: 11/25/2003
The Beanie Babies celebrate
To mark this most auspicious date
Lift your glass and raise it high
10 years of Beanies...here's to Ty!
Trade Show exclusive.
11G - $7

Toboggan™
#40032

Birthday: 12/31/2002
Introduced: 10/30/2003
Retired: 11/25/2003
A snowy hill is where I'll go
To start my day out in the snow
Now climb aboard and hang on tight
A penguin sledding is a sight!
7G - $7 ♥ 11G - $7

TOM-e™
#4430

Birthday: 11/27/2003
Introduced: 11/4/2003
Retired: 11/12/2003
We celebrate Thanksgiving Day
By putting out a big buffet
So fill your plate and don't be shy
Just save some room for pumpkin pie!
Ty Store exclusive.
11G - $7

Tommy™
#40024

Birthday: 11/21/2002
Introduced: 8/28/2003
Retired: 12/26/2003
Make sure that you are at your place
When we say Thanksgiving grace
For friends and family we adore
There's so much to be thankful for!
7G - $7 ♥ 11G - $7

Tooter™
#4559

Birthday: 4/17/2002
Introduced: 7/30/2002
Retired: 2/24/2003
Since the day that I was born
I've had this crest that's like a horn
With it I play a happy tune
All morning and all afternoon!
7G - $7 ♥ 10G - $7

Toothy™
#4523

Birthday: 7/10/2001
Introduced: 4/1/2002
Retired: 9/25/2002
I brush my teeth each day and night
So they will stay both clean and white
With lots of teeth it takes a while
It's worth it for this dazzlin' smile!
7G - $8 ♥ 10G - $8

Tootoot™
#40441

Birthday: 3/10/2006
Introduced: 9/29/2006
Current
I think it would be really grand
If I could join a cool jazz band
We would surely draw a crowd
To hear me play my trumpet loud!
14G/14UK - Current Retail Value

Toronto™
#46016

Birthday: 5/25/2004
Introduced: 9/20/2004
Retired: 11/11/2004
Visit Toronto and you'll see
A city of diversity
So much variety to this place
A wonderful city I know you'll embrace!
Canada exclusive.
12G - $15

Tortuga™
#48426

Birthday: 7/00/2006
Introduced: 7/1/2006
Retired: 8/1/2006
I don't hear a single sound
So I'll take a look around
If I see something that I fear
I'll hide until the coast is clear!
July 2006 Beanie Baby of the Month.
BBOM - $8

TOUR Teddy™
#40347

Birthday: 2/1/2006
Introduced: 1/31/2006
Current
Being part of the TOUR is fun
We love to golf out in the sun
But the best thing, we all agree
Is the work we do for charity!
North America PGA exclusive. Also available at Ty Store with a barcode.
14G - Current Retail Value

Tracker™
#4198

Birthday: 6/5/1997
Introduced: 5/30/1998
Retired: 11/26/1999
Sniffing and tracking and following trails
Tracker the basset always wags his tail
It doesn't matter what you do
He's always happy when he's with you!
5G - $7

Tracks™
#4507

Birthday: 10/5/2001
Introduced: 1/29/2002
Retired: 6/25/2002
I like the game called hide and seek
I always win, I never peek
No matter if you're near or far
My nose can tell just where you are!
7G - $7 ♥ 10G - $7

Tradee™
#4403 · "check it out" poem

Birthday: 6/29/2000
Introduced: 6/26/2001
Retired: 5/21/2002
Now the trading has begun
Check it out, it's lots of fun
Come along and play with me
I have some things that you must see!
Ty Store exclusive.
9G - $7

Tradee™ 2000
#4403 · "buy and sell" poem

Birthday: 6/29/2000
Introduced: 6/26/2001
Retired: 7/2001
Now that the trading has begun
Let's buy and sell, it's lots of fun
So come along and play with me
I have some things that you must see!
Ty Store exclusive.
6G - $300

Trap™
#4042

Birthday: None
Introduced: 6/25/1994
Retired: 6/15/1995
Trap was issued without a poem.
1G - $2,500 ♥ 2G - $1,000 ♥ 3G - $800

Trick R. Treat™
#40420

Birthday: 10/31/2006
Introduced: 8/31/2006
Retired: 10/25/2006
At this spooky time of year
When ghosts and ghoulies might appear
You might see something really neat
A strange pumpkin named Trick R. Treat!
14G/14UK - $7

Tricks™
#4311

Birthday: 5/14/2000
Introduced: 7/8/2000
Retired: 6/18/2001
Some games that we always play
Are fetch and sit, give paw and stay
Teach me other tricks to do
And I'll have found a friend in you!
6G - $7 ♥ 7G - $7

Tricky™
#40017

Birthday: 11/15/2002
Introduced: 7/31/2003
Retired: 10/31/2003
When I come knocking on your door
I hope you've got goodies in store
But if you've got no treats for me
I'll play a prank 'cause I'm Tricky!
7G - $7 ♥ 11G - $7

Trident™
#48413

Birthday: 6/00/2005
Introduced: 6/1/2005
Retired: 7/1/2005
Looking across the ocean blue
To find a friend that's pure and true
Way deep beneath the briny sea
That's where you're sure to find me!
June 2005 Beanie Baby of the Month.
BBOM - $7

True™
#4636

Birthday: 7/1/2003
Introduced: 7/1/2003
Retired: 7/22/2004
This special Beanie we bring forth
For our good neighbors to the north
Since you were loyal and so true
This is our way of thanking you!
Canada exclusive.
11G - $15

True™ Key-clip
#46074

Birthday: None
Introduced: 7/31/2006
Current
Pride of the North!
Canada exclusive.
14sm - Current Retail Value

Truly™
#40162

Birthday: 11/3/2004
Introduced: 11/30/2004
Retired: 2/24/2005
If you just take a look at me
My feelings are easy to see
It is simple, plain and true
So obvious that I LOVE YOU!
12G/12EU - $7

Trumpet™
#4276

Birthday: 2/11/2000
Introduced: 3/1/2000
Retired: 4/19/2001
Trumpet uses his trunk to spray
Be careful you don't get in his way
He plays in mud - he never forgets
Give him some peanuts, he'll be your pet!
6G - $7 ♥ 7G - $7

Tubbo™
#4597

Birthday: 1/16/2003
Introduced: 4/30/2003
Retired: 5/25/2004
Of all the things I am most fond
It's lounging in my favorite pond
It keeps me from the mid-day heat
A hippo's life just can't be beat!
7G - $7 ♥ 11G - $7

Tuck™
#4076 · Tusk on tush tag

Birthday: 9/18/1995
Introduced: Jan-96
Retired: 1/1997
Tusk brushes his teeth everyday
To keep them shiny, it's the only way
Teeth are special, so you must try
And they will sparkle when you say "Hi!"
4G - $75

Tuffy™
#4108

Birthday: 10/12/1996
Introduced: 5/11/1997
Retired: 12/31/1998
Taking off with a thunderous blast
Tuffy rides his motorcycle fast
The Beanies roll with laughs and squeals
He never took off his training wheels!
4G - $7 ♥ 5G - $7

Tumba™
#40649

Birthday: 4/8/2007
Introduced: 5/31/2007
Current
Living on a mountainside
That misty place where I reside
And as far as the eye can see
My home, a land of such beauty!
15G - Current Retail Value

Tundra™
#40355

Birthday: 9/4/2005
Introduced: 2/28/2006
Current
So quiet you won't hear a sound
As I stalk and prowl around
Watch out or I'll give you a scare
When I jump out and say, "Hi there"!
14G/14UK - Current Retail Value

Tunnels™
#40233

Birthday: 7/28/2005
Introduced: 7/29/2005
Retired: 1/27/2006
I'll scout around the yard a bit
Until I find the perfect fit
Just the right spot to tunnel through
Where I can dig a hole or two!
13G/13EU - $7

TURK-e™
#4416

Birthday: 11/23/2001
Introduced: 11/4/2002
Retired: 11/29/2002
Although some people think I fear
Thanksgiving each and every year
I really love the holiday
If I'm not on the dinner tray!
Ty Store exclusive.
10G - $9

Tusk™
#4076

Birthday: 9/18/1995
Introduced: 1/7/1995
Retired: 1/1/1997
Tusk brushes his teeth everyday
To keep them shiny, it's the only way
Teeth are special, so you must try
And they will sparkle when you say "Hi!"
3G - $75 ♥ 4G - $40

Tux™
#40214

Birthday: 12/5/2004
Introduced: 6/30/2005
Retired: 7/27/2005
For a fun night on the town
I'll wear my tux you wear a gown
And to show off our fancy clothes
We'll dance around on twinkle toes!
13G/13EU - $7

Twigs™
#4068

Birthday: 5/19/1995
Introduced: 1/7/1996
Retired: 5/1/1998
Twigs has his head in the clouds
He stands tall, he stands proud
With legs so skinny they wobble and shake
What an unusual friend he will make!
3G - $60 ♥ 4G - $7 ♥ 5G - $7

Twilight™
#40105

Birthday: 8/3/2004
Introduced: 8/30/2004
Retired: 9/28/2004
Something's strange up in that tree
Two bright eyes looking back at me
Then you'll hear a playful, "WHOO"
As if to say, "Hey, I see you"!
12G - $7

Twirls™
#40169

Birthday: 1/5/2004
Introduced: 12/30/2004
Retired: 3/27/2007
A dash of color here and there
A splash of color everywhere
I'll twirl around so you can see
Just how colorful I can be!
13G/13EU - $7

Twitch™
#40108

Birthday: 8/2/2003
Introduced: 6/30/2004
Retired: 8/26/2004
As I scurry in my cage
The wheel I have is all the rage
Take me out so we can snuggle
I promise you that I won't struggle!
12G - $30

Twitterbug™
#4580

Birthday: 9/24/2002
Introduced: 12/27/2002
Retired: 3/27/2003
Once every dozen years or more
It's time for me to hit the door
I make a lot of noise because
That is what a cicada does!
7G - $7 ♥ 11G - $7

Ty 2K™
#4262

Birthday: 1/1/2000
Introduced: 8/31/1999
Retired: 12/23/1999
Red, yellow, green and blue
Let's have some fun me and you
So join the party, and let's all say
"Happy New Millennium" from Ty 2K!
5G - $7

214

U™
#40521

Birthday: None
Introduced: 6/30/2005
Current
Alphabet Bears are issued withou poems.
AB - Current Retail Value

U.S.A.™
#4287

Birthday: 7/4/2000
Introduced: 6/6/2000
Retired: 4/6/2001
From this land of liberty
Comes this bear for you and me
Proud to wear red, white and blue
He'll be a special friend to you!
USA exclusive.
6G - $7

Uncle Sam™
#40621 · blue nose

Birthday: 7/4/2007
Introduced: 4/30/2007
Current
Each year on the fourth of July
As fireworks light up the sky
To show our country's truly great
Just take my hand; let's celebrate!
15G - Current Retail Value

Uncle Sam™
#40621 · red nose

Birthday: 7/4/2007
Introduced: 4/30/2007
Current
Each year on the fourth of July
As fireworks light up the sky
With my hand on my heart I'll stand
I'm proud to live in this great land!
15G - Current Retail Value

Uncle Sam™
#40621 · white nose

Birthday: 7/4/2007
Introduced: 4/30/2007
Current
Each year on the fourth of July
As fireworks light up the sky
With all my friends and family
We'll celebrate that we are free!
15G - Current Retail Value

Union™
#40081 · black nose

Birthday: 8/1/2003
Introduced: 5/28/2004
Retired: 10/27/2004
We look to our flag with pride
All across the countryside
The Stars & Stripes will always be
A symbol of our liberty!
12G - $7

Union™
#40081 · flag nose

Birthday: 8/1/2003
Introduced: 5/28/2004
Retired: 10/27/2004
We look to our flag with pride
All across the countryside
The Stars & Stripes will always be
A symbol of our liberty!
USA exclusive.
12G - $7

Union™
#40081

Birthday: 8/1/2003
Introduced: 6/24/2006
Retired: 6/25/2006
We look to our flag with pride
All across the countryside
The Stars & Stripes will always be
A symbol of our liberty!
Knott's Berry Farm exclusive.
12G - $25

Unity™
#4606

Birthday: 9/28/2000
Introduced: 4/20/2001
Retired: 10/22/2001
The EU finally came to be
That's why I'm named Unity
Our countries now unite as one
A brand new era has begun!
Europe exclusive.
7G - $15 ♥ 8G - $15

USA™ Key-clip
#40371

Birthday: None
Introduced: 4/28/2006
Current
Sweet Land Of Liberty!
14/14UKsm - Current Retail Value

V™
#40522

Birthday: None
Introduced: 6/30/2005
Current
Alphabet Bears are issued without poems.
AB - Current Retail Value

Valentina™
#4233

Birthday: 2/14/1998
Introduced: 1/1/1999
Retired: 12/23/1999
Flowers, candy and hearts galore
Sweet words of love for those you adore
With this bear comes love that's true
On Valentine's Day and all year through!
5G - $7

Valentine™
#40038

Birthday: 2/14/2003
Introduced: 11/26/2003
Retired: 4/16/2004
Please let me be your Valentine
And say to me that you'll be mine
I will be forever true
Especially to a friend like you!
7G - $7 ♥ 11G - $7

Valentino™
#4058

Birthday: 2/14/1994
Introduced: 1/7/1995
Retired: 12/31/1998
His heart is red and full of love
He cares for you so give him a hug
Keep him close when feeling blue
Feel the love he has for you!
2G - $3,500 ♥ 3G - $140 ♥
4G - $7 ♥ 5G - $7

Valor™
#4433

Birthday: 9/11/2003
Introduced: 9/11/2003
Retired: 11/28/2003
To honor all of those who serve
Patriot Day we do observe
For the bravery you've displayed
Your memory will never fade!
Ty Store exclusive.
11G - $7

Vanda™
#4614

Birthday: 2/18/2002
Introduced: 1/29/2002
Retired: 8/31/2002
Like a flower I was born
Lilac is my shade in early morn
Mountains and fields through I may roam
Singapore is my native home!
Singapore exclusive.
10G - $15

Vegas™
#40063

Birthday: 12/10/2003
Introduced: 2/26/2004
Retired: 7/28/2004
Most other zebras are black and white
But that's not me, I'm quite a sight
With such bright colors I'm sure to be
The funkiest zebra you'll ever see!
12G - $7

Veggies™
#40322

Birthday: 3/20/2006
Introduced: 12/30/2005
Retired: 3/27/2006
In the garden's where I'll be
Searching for a treat for me
Maybe just a carrot or two
If there's more, I'll share with you!
14G/14UK - $7

216

Velvet™
#4064

Birthday: 12/16/1995
Introduced: 6/3/1995
Retired: 10/1/1997
Velvet loves to sleep in the trees
Lulled to dreams by the buzz of bees
She snoozes all day and plays all night
Running and jumping in the moonlight!
3G - $60 ♥ 4G - $9

Victory™
#44020

Birthday: 7/9/2004
Introduced: 8/13/2004
Retired: 9/8/2004
Always strive to do your best
And put your heart into the quest
With a drive you can't deny
You can reach the highest high!
Ty Store exclusive.
12G - $7

Villager™
#46032

Birthday: 7/1/2005
Introduced: 4/29/2005
Current
July 1st is a special day
Canadians join in and say
We're proud of our Confederation
And Happy Birthday to our nation!
Canada exclusive.
13G - Current Retail Value

Villager™ Key-clip
#46076

Birthday: None
Introduced: 7/31/2006
Current
One Dominion!
Canada exclusive.
14sm - Current Retail Value

Violetta™
#40360

Birthday: 1/16/2006
Introduced: 3/31/2006
Current
Kittens bounding to and fro
This way that way, off they go
They're all fun, but what's better yet
Is the kitten that's white and violet!
14G/14UK - Current Retail Value

Virunga™
#4805

Birthday: 6/00/2003
Introduced: 6/2/2003
Retired: 7/1/2003
Up in my mountain hideaway
We can laugh and have fun all day
I'll teach you how to climb a tree
What fun we'll have; just you and me!
June 2003 Beanie Baby of the Month.
BBOM - $7

W™
#40523

Birthday: None
Introduced: 6/30/2005
Current
Alphabet Bears are issued without poems.
AB - Current Retail Value

Waddle™
#4075

Birthday: 12/19/1995
Introduced: 6/3/1995
Retired: 5/1/1998
Waddle the Penguin likes to dress up
Every night he wears his tux
When Waddle walks, it never fails
He always trips over his tails!
3G - $60 ♥ 4G - $7 ♥ 5G - $7

Wailea™
#40379

Birthday: 6/21/2006
Introduced: 5/31/2006
Current
Summertime is here once more
And I can't wait to hit the shore
The beach is where I'll spend my days
Soaking up the summer rays!
14G/14UK - Current Retail Value

Wales™
#4610

Birthday: 9/23/2001
Introduced: 2/3/2002
Retired: 9/27/2002
Far away is the country of Wales
It has the most beautiful hills and vales
The men sing throughout the land
It's cheerful, warm and really grand!
Wales exclusive.
7G - $20

Wales™
#46012

Birthday: 10/27/2003
Introduced: 9/5/2004
Retired: 10/8/2004
I love Wales, a country of leisure
With lots of singing for everyone's pleasure.
Leeks, dragons and daffodils galore
Make all who visit come back for more!
UK exclusive.
12G - $30

Wallace™
#4264

Birthday: 1/25/1999
Introduced: 8/31/1999
Retired: 12/23/1999
Castles rise from misty glens
Shielding bands of warrior men
Wearing tartan of their clan
Red, green and a little tan!
5G - $7

Washington™
#40133

Birthday: None
Introduced: 8/30/2004
Retired: 12/29/2005
STATE MOTTO: "Alki" (BYE AND BYE)
NICKNAME: Evergreen State
FACT: Washington is the only state
named after a U.S. President!
Sold only in Washington.
12G - $7

Washington D.C.™
#40078

Birthday: 12/1/2003
Introduced: 7/25/2004
Retired: 12/29/2005
Capitol of the U.S.A.
Can't see it all in just one day
Museums, monuments galore
Memorials and so much more!
Trade Show exclusive.
12G - $7

Washington Rhododendron™
#40297

Birthday: None
Introduced: 8/27/2005
Retired: 12/29/2005
OFFICIAL FLOWER SINCE 1892
In eighteen hundred ninety-two
This flower made its grand debut
As symbol of Washington State
We think our "rhodie" is first rate!
Trade Show exclusive.
13G - $10

Wattlie™
#4616

Birthday: 1/26/2002
Introduced: 1/29/2002
Retired: 3/31/2003
I love to climb trees and play with you
My friends are Koala and Kangaroo
My name is Wattlie and that's who
Will you be my friend too?
Australia exclusive.
10G - $20

Waves™
#4084

Birthday: 12/8/1996
Introduced: 5/11/1997
Retired: 5/1/1998
Join him today on the Internet
Don't be afraid to get your feet wet
He taught all the Beanies how to surf
Our web page is his home turf!
4G - $7 ♥ 5G - $7

Waves™
#4084 · "Echo" tush tag

Birthday: 12/8/1996
Introduced: 5/11/1997
Retired: 5/1/1998
Join him today on the Internet
Don't be afraid to get your feet wet
He taught all the Beanies how to surf
Our web page is his home turf!
4G - $10 ♥ 5G - $10

We Do™
#40219

Birthday: None
Introduced: 3/31/2005
Current
On this very special day
We'll say the things we long to say
'Cause you love me and I love you
Today we will both say, "I do"!
13G/13EU - Current Retail Value

Weaver™
#40250

Birthday: 12/13/2004
Introduced: 6/30/2005
Retired: 12/29/2005
In the jungle above the ground
That's where I like to hang around
There's so much that I can see
From high up in my favorite tree!
13G/13EU - $7

Weaver™
#40250

Birthday: 12/13/2004
Introduced: 8/12/2006
Retired: 8/13/2006
In the jungle above the ground
That's where I like to hang around
There's so much that I can see
From high up in my favorite tree!
Brookfield Zoo promotional item.
13G - $50

Weaver™
#40250

Birthday: 12/13/2004
Introduced: 6/3/2006
Retired: 6/4/2006
In the jungle above the ground
That's where I like to hang around
There's so much that I can see
From high up in my favorite tree!
Knott's Berry Farm exclusive.
13G - $25

Web™
#4041

Birthday: None
Introduced: 6/25/1994
Retired: 1/7/1996
Web was issued without a poem
1G - $2,500 ♥ 2G - $1,000 ♥ 3G - $750

Webley™
#40484

Birthday: 8/27/2006
Introduced: 12/29/2006
Current
I live on a lily pad
With my froggie mom and dad
When I want to play with a friend
"Ribbit" is the message I'll send!
15G/15UK - Current Retail Value

Weenie™
#4013

Birthday: 7/20/1995
Introduced: 1/7/1996
Retired: 5/1/1998
Weenie the dog is quite a sight
Long of body and short of height
He perches himself high on a log
and considers himself to be top dog!
3G - $60 ♥ 4G - $8 ♥ 5G - $7

Whiskers™
#4317

Birthday: 8/6/2000
Introduced: 7/8/2000
Retired: 4/11/2001
Sometimes when we jump and play
I can't stop when you say "stay"
I'm very frisky, this is true
But I'll never run away from you!
6G - $7 ♥ 7G - $7

Whisper™
#4194

Birthday: 4/5/1997
Introduced: 5/30/1998
Retired: 12/23/1999
She's very shy as you can see
When she hides behind a tree
With big brown eyes and soft to touch
This little fawn will love you so much!
5G - $7

White™
#4423

Birthday: 4/13/2003
Introduced: 7/1/2003
Retired: 7/14/2003
A symbol of the U.S.A.
Americans proudly display
My color stands for all that's pure
The Stars and Stripes will long endure.
Ty Store exclusive.
11G - $7

Whittle™
#40096

Birthday: 11/19/2003
Introduced: 6/30/2004
Retired: 11/24/2004
A bear like me just loves to eat
And honey is my favorite treat
I'll find some in a hive, you see
Hope I don't meet a honeybee!
12G - $7

Wiggly™
#4275

Birthday: 1/25/2000
Introduced: 3/1/2000
Retired: 3/27/2001
Under the sea I travel with ease
I flip and flop - do whatever I please
Being a squid can be lots of fun
Because I swim faster than anyone!
6G - $7 ♥ 7G - $7

William™
#4632 · closed book

Birthday: 4/23/1564
Introduced: 7/16/2003
Retired: 3/27/2006
From Stratford came the tales he told
Of love and Kings and stories bold
Around the Globe can still be heard
Much rapt applause at every word!
UK exclusive.
7G - $25

William™
#4632 · open book

Birthday: 4/23. 1564
Introduced: 7/16/2003
Retired: 3/27/2006
From Stratford came the tales he told
Of love and Kings and stories bold
Around the Globe can still be heard
Much rapt applause at every word!
German exclusive.
7G - $25

William™
#46081

Birthday: 9/1/2006
Introduced: 9/16/2006
Retired: 10/25/2006
In 1760 the first Hamley's store
Was opened and filled up with toys galore
The best in the world he desired it to be
And achieve this he did, to all of our glee!
Hamley's exclusive.
14UK - $30

Willoughby™
#40188

Birthday: 7/25/2004
Introduced: 12/30/2004
Retired: 9/23/2005
If there's someplace I need to be
My baby rides along with me
He doesn't mind a bumpy ride
He's happy to be tucked inside!
13G/13EU - $7

Winksy™
#40195

Birthday: 6/4/2004
Introduced: 12/30/2004
Retired: 3/24/2005
Hopping down the bunny trail
With my little cotton tail
Binksy and Minksy by my side
Let's stop and play! You seek; I'll hide!
13G/13EU - $7

winstar™
#46071

Birthday: 10/8/1998
Introduced: 7/13/2006
Current
NICKNAME: Win
Do you remember on 1998?
May the star of victory at that
time twinkle again!
I always have the prayer in my heart.
Japan exclusive.
14G - $30

220

Wirabear™
#4631

Birthday: 8/31/2002
Introduced: 4/28/2003
Retired: 11/7/2003
Our vision is the hope of the country
May our nation be peaceful
Hang Tuah is our nation's hero
His name is as great as in person
Malaysia exclusive.
11G - $20

Wisconsin™
#40287

Birthday: None
Introduced: 11/30/2005
Retired: 7/25/2006
STATE MOTTO: "Forward"
NICKNAME: Badger State
FACT: Wisconsin produces more milk than
anywhere else in the United States!
Sold only in Wisconsin.
13G - $7

Wise™
#4187

Birthday: 5/31/1997
Introduced: 5/30/1998
Retired: 12/31/1998
Wise is at the head of the class
With A's and B's he'll always pass
He's got his diploma and feels really great
Meet the newest graduate: Class of '98!
5G - $7

Wiser™
#4238

Birthday: 6/4/1999
Introduced: 4/22/1999
Retired: 8/27/1999
Waking daily to the morning sun
Learning makes school so much fun
Looking great and feeling fine
The newest graduate, "Class of 99!"
5G - $7

Wisest™
#4286

Birthday: 6/6/2002
Introduced: 5/1/2000
Retired: 12/15/2000
I always try to do my best
And study hard for all my tests
Now it's time to celebrate
Because at last I graduate!
6G - $7 ♥ 7G - $7

Wish™
#4594

Birthday: 12/5/2002
Introduced: 3/31/2003
Retired: 2/26/2004
You made a wish the other day
For a good friend so you could play
Well, I'm that special friendly fish
So hold me close, you got your wish!
7G - $7 ♥ 11G - $7

Wonton™
#40657

Birthday: 3/21/2007
Introduced: 6/29/2007
Current
In the mountains; up so high
Where you feel you can touch the sky
In the shade of a bamboo tree
This is where I am meant to be!
15G - Current Retail Value

Woody™
#4539

Birthday: 1/28/2002
Introduced: 8/29/2002
Retired: 2/24/2003
The woods is where I love to be
Catching fish or up a tree
It's a lazy life, without a care
How wonderful to be a bear!
7G - $7 ♥ 10G - $7

Woolins™
#44047

Birthday: 3/17/2005
Introduced: 2/15/2005
Retired: 3/23/2005
If it's a cold and windy day
You'll want to keep the frost away
So when I find I get a chill
My wooly sweater fits the bill!
Ty Store exclusive.
13G - $7

Wrinkles™
#4103

Birthday: 5/1/1996
Introduced: 6/15/1996
Retired: 9/22/1998
This little dog is named Wrinkles
His nose is soft and often crinkles
Likes to climb up on your lap
He's a cheery sort of chap!
4G - $7 ♥ 5G - $7

X™
#40524

Birthday: None
Introduced: 6/30/2005
Current
Alphabet Bears are issued without poems.
AB - Current Retail Value

Y™
#40525

Birthday: None
Introduced: 6/30/2005
Current
Alphabet Bears are issued without poems.
AB - Current Retail Value

Y Ddraig Goch™
#46031

Birthday: 4/24/2004
Introduced: 5/31/2005
Current
With sheep on the hills, a beautiful view
Tales of red dragons, mythical or true
Sounds of the choir carry far and wide
I'd love to share it with you by my side!
UK exclusive.
13G/13EU/13UK - $25

Y Ddraig Goch™ Key-clip
#46104

Birthday: None
Introduced: 7/11/2007
Current
Cymru Am Byth!
UK exclusive.
15uksm - Current Retail Value

Yapper™
#40103

Birthday: 3/14/2004
Introduced: 6/30/2004
Retired: 12/29/2004
I love riding in the car
As long as we don't go too far
So take me on a little trip
And I'll let out a playful "YIP!"
12G - $7

Yikes™
#47026

Birthday: 10/31/2006
Introduced: 9/1/2006
Retired: 10/25/2006
I didn't mean to frighten you
'Cause spooky things will scare me, too
If I see ghosts and ghouls about
Then, "YIKES" is what I'm going to shout!
Hallmark Gold Crown exclusive.
14G - $7

Yokohama™
#46052

Birthday: None
Introduced: 1/24/2006
Current
FLOWER: Rose
NICKNAME: Hama (Bay)
FACT: When the port first opened it began an
influx of Western culture that influenced the
rest of the country!
Japan exclusive.
14G - Current Retail Value

You Did It™
#40535

Birthday: None
Introduced: 4/28/2006
Current
Greetings Bears are issued without poems.
14G - Current Retail Value

You're a Sweetie™
#40536

Birthday: None
Introduced: 8/31/2006
Retired: 2/27/2007
Greetings Bears are issued without poems.
14G - Current Retail Value

You're Special™
#44055

Birthday: 11/2/2004
Introduced: 6/28/2005
Retired: 11/10/2005
As I was sitting quietly
A special thought occurred to me
Here's a gift for all you do
Because the special thought was you!
Ty Store exclusive.
13G - $7

Yours Truly™
#4701

Birthday: 12/28/2002
Introduced: 3/28/2003
Retired: 4/9/2003
Because you want the very best
And I'm so different from the rest
Be happy that you found me
Forever I am . . . Yours Truly!
Hallmark Gold Crown exclusive.
11G - $7

Yummy™
#40275

Birthday: 9/6/2005
Introduced: 9/30/2005
Retired: 12/29/2005
Cookies, cakes, and any sweets
These are my most favorite treats
In my stocking, hope I see
Some peppermint that's just for me!
13G - $7

Z™
#40526

Birthday: None
Introduced: 6/30/2005
Current
Alphabet Bears are issued without poems.
AB - Current Retail Value

Zero™
#4207

Birthday: 1/2/1998
Introduced: 9/30/1998
Retired: 12/31/1998
Penguins love the ice and snow
Playing in weather twenty below
Antarctica is where I love to be
Splashing in the cold, cold sea!
5G - $7

Zeus™
#4589

Birthday: 10/23/2002
Introduced: 2/28/2003
Retired: 5/25/2004
With mighty antlers on my head
It's difficult to get in bed
But I sleep better, yes I do
When I am cuddled next to you!
7G - $7 ♥ 11G - $7

Ziggy™
#4063 · thin stripes

Birthday: 12/24/1995
Introduced: 6/3/1995
Retired: 5/1/1998
Ziggy likes soccer - he's a referee
That way he watches the games for free
The other Beanies don't think it's fair
But Ziggy the Zebra doesn't care!
3G - $60 ♥ 4G - $7

Ziggy™
#4063 · wide stripes

Birthday: 12/24/1995
Introduced: 6/3/1995
Retired: 5/1/1998
Ziggy likes soccer - he's a referee
That way he watches the games for free
The other Beanies don't think it's fair
But Ziggy the Zebra doesn't care!
4G - $7 ♥ 5G - $7

Zip™
#4004 · white face

Birthday: None
Introduced: 1/7/1995
Retired: 1/7/1996
Zip was issued without a poem.
2G — $525 ♥ 3G — $250

Zip™
#4004 · all black with pink ears

Birthday: None
Introduced: 1/7/1996
Retired: 3/10/1996
Zip was issued without a poem.
3G — $400

Zip™
#4004 · white paws

Birthday: 3/28/1994
Introduced: 3/10/1996
Retired: 5/1/1998
Keep Zip by your side all the day through
Zip is good luck, you'll see it's true
When you have something you need to do
Zip will always believe in you!
3G — $150 ♥ 4G — $9 ♥ 5G — $8

Zodiac DOG™
#4326

Birthday: None
Introduced: 8/19/2000
Retired: 6/8/2001
The Zodiac Series
1946, 1958, 1970, 1982, 1994, 2006
You work well with people
Often loyal and very honest
Can be stubborn and selfish
Marry a horse or tiger
Beware of dragons!
Hang tag on ear or leg.
6G — $9

Zodiac DRAGON™
#4322

Birthday: None
Introduced: 8/19/2000
Retired: 6/8/2001
The Zodiac Series
1940, 1952, 1964, 1976, 1988, 2000
You are eccentric and passionate
Have good health but complex life
Marry a monkey or rat late in life
Avoid the dog!
6G — $9

Zodiac GOAT™
#4329

Birthday: None
Introduced: 8/19/2000
Retired: 5/17/2001
The Zodiac Series
1943, 1955, 1967, 1979, 1991, 2003
You are timid and prefer anonymity
Often elegant and creative
Compatible with pigs and rabbits
Beware of the ox!
6G — $9

Zodiac HORSE™
#4324 · flat hooves with colored ears

Birthday: None
Introduced: 8/19/2000
Retired: 5/29/2001
The Zodiac Series
1942, 1954, 1966, 1978, 1990, 2002
Popular and very attractive to others
Often impatient and ostentatious
Marry a tiger early
The rat is your enemy!
6G — $9

Zodiac HORSE™
#4324 · flat hooves with pink ears

Birthday: None
Introduced: 8/19/2000
Retired: 5/29/2001
The Zodiac Series
1942, 1954, 1966, 1978, 1990, 2002
Popular and very attractive to others
Often impatient and ostentatious
Marry a tiger early
The rat is your enemy!
6G — $9

Zodiac HORSE™
#4324 · pointed hooves

Birthday: None
Introduced: 8/19/2000
Retired: 5/29/2001
The Zodiac Series
1942, 1954, 1966, 1978, 1990, 2002
Popular and very attractive to others
Often impatient and ostentatious
Marry a tiger early
The rat is your enemy!
6G — $9

Zodiac MONKEY™
#4328

Birthday: None
Introduced: 8/19/2000
Retired: 5/8/2001
The Zodiac Series
1944, 1956, 1968, 1980, 1992, 2004
Intelligent and enthusiastic achiever
Easily able to influence people
Seek a dragon or rat
Avoid tigers!
Hang tag on hand or ear.
6G — $7

Zodiac OX™
#4319

Birthday: None
Introduced: 8/19/2000
Retired: 5/8/2001
The Zodiac Series
1937, 1949, 1961, 1973, 1985, 1997
Bright, patient and inspiring to others
Often makes an outstanding parent
Snake and rooster suit your temperament
The goat will bring you trouble!
6G — $7

Zodiac PIG™
#4327

Birthday: None
Introduced: 8/19/2000
Retired: 5/11/2001
The Zodiac Series
1947, 1959, 1971, 1983, 1995, 2007
Often noble and chivalrous
Your friends will be life—long
Marry a rabbit or goat
The snake is your enemy!
Hang tag on leg or ear.
6G — $7

Zodiac RABBIT™
#4321

Birthday: None
Introduced: 8/19/2000
Retired: 5/24/2001
The Zodiac Series
1939, 1951, 1963, 1975, 1987, 1999
You are the luckiest of all signs
Talented, affectionate yet shy
Marry a goat or pig
The rooster is your enemy!
Hang tag on leg or ear.
6G — $7

Zodiac RAT™
#4318

Birthday: None
Introduced: 8/19/2000
Retired: 5/29/2001
The Zodiac Series
1936, 1948, 1960, 1972, 1984, 1996
Ambitious yet honest
Prone to spend freely
Seldom makes lasting friendships
Marry a dragon or monkey
Avoid horses!
Hang tag on ear or body.
6G — $7

Zodiac ROOSTER™
#4325

Birthday: None
Introduced: 8/19/2000
Retired: 5/11/2001
The Zodiac Series
1945, 1957, 1969, 1981, 1993, 2005
You are intelligent and devoted to work
Can be selfish and eccentric
Snakes and oxen are good for you
Rabbits are trouble!
6G — $9

Zodiac SNAKE™
#4323

Birthday: None
Introduced: 8/19/2000
Retired: 5/17/2001
The Zodiac Series
1941, 1953, 1965, 1977, 1989, 2001
Wise, intense and very attractive
Can be vain and high tempered
Rooster and ox are your best signs
The pig is your enemy!
6G — $7

Zodiac TIGER™
#4320 · less silver

Birthday: None
Introduced: 8/19/2000
Retired: 5/24/2001
The Zodiac Series
1938, 1950, 1962, 1974, 1986, 1998
You are aggressive and courageous
Often candid and sensitive
Look to the dog and horse for happiness
Beware of the monkey!
6G — $9

Zodiac TIGER™
#4320 · more silver

Birthday: None
Introduced: 8/19/2000
Retired: 5/24/2001
The Zodiac Series
1938, 1950, 1962, 1974, 1986, 1998
You are aggressive and courageous
Often candid and sensitive
Look to the dog and horse for happiness
Beware of the monkey!
6G — $9

Zoom™
#4545

Birthday: 9/19/2001
Introduced: 7/30/2002
Retired: 2/26/2004
Moving along at my own pace
I may not always win the race
But sometimes life can be more fun
When we don't try for number one!
7G — $7 ♥ 10G — $7

Zoomer™
#48421

Birthday: 2/00/2006
Introduced: 2/1/2006
Retired: 3/1/2006
I zoom through the air, to and fro
Swinging and swinging, just watch me go
I really love my life in the trees
You'll like it too, it's such a breeze !
February 2006
Beanie Baby of the Month.
BBOM — $8

Beanie Daffynitions
by Cliff Nebel

Arachnobeaned — although this is unlikely to occur to anyone reading this, it does happen. If a beanie is left unattended for many days by itself, it may become covered with spider webs.

Beanacho — a real manly beanie (e.g. Congo).

Beanchcomer — one who searches the sands for beanies.

Beandown — a state in which you can afford no more beanies.

Beandraggled — condition of a beanie after being caught in the rain.

Beaneferous — an evil beanie collector. Don't let this person near your collection.

Beanellet — a term used to describe a human whom you think is full of PE or PVC pellets.

Beanette — a female beanie (e.g. Ooh La La).

Beanfrenzied — state that occurs after the beantroduction, in anticipation of new retail arrivals.

Beanfuddled — this happens especially to new beanie collectors trying to figure out tag generations.

Beangagged — computer problems preventing you from posting on a beanie forum.

Beangenda — the list of beanies on one's want list.

Beanhoriffic — used to describe an exclusive missing a hang tag.

Beanicide — the ritual removal of pellets from a beanie. (Report all such Beanstances at once.)

Beanied — term used when you receive too many beanies at once. (Is that even possible?)

Beaninked — originally a pen marking on a hang tag. current usage is for any mark or stain anywhere on a beanie.

Beanieprimed — refers to a collector of 1st generation tags only. Also may refer to a person on the verge of starting a beanie collection.

Beanified — if you're reading this, you are.

Beanily — used for closing letters (e.g. beanily yours).

Beanifried — a point at which you must address you addiction.

Beanjoined — a term used when during production 2 beanies come attached to each other.

Beanlien — refers to a court order needed when someone else has actual control of a path to your beanies.

Beanmuda — a honeymoon island for just married beanies.

Beanongous — a description for any of the oversized buddies.

Beanplant — a surgical placement of a beanie to prevent withdrawal symtoms when you're away from your beantry too long.

Beansided — where all your values are skewed because of your love of beanies.

Beansigh — a sound made by a collector when the beanie desired is sold out before his/her arrival.

Beanspecs — what you use to protect your beanies eyes when you take them beancruizin'.

Beanstalk — something you do when the person before you bought the last of the beanies that you wanted. At this point you should realize that you are beanifried and seek help.

Beantiful — an adjective used to describe an especially nice looking beanie.

Beantroduction — the press release for the new beanies.

Beantry — a room or closet devoted solely for beanies.

Beanup — not the opposite of beandown. This is a command to Scottie (Mr. Scott) when you want your beanie to return to the Starship Enterprise.

Beanverted — happens when you first realize that beanies are an entity all to themselves.

Beanvestment (archaic) — the buying of beanies in the hopes of an increase in value.

Beanvitation — special request to attend an affair at which a beanie is given to guests, and not available to the general public.

Disbeaned — when you are persona non grata in the beanie world.

Discombobubeanied — so lost in the world of Ty that you don't know your beanies from your elbows.

Dypsobeanied — drunken with beanie power.

Eubeanie — a true Ty beanie (usually with a certificate of authenticity).

Excommunibeanied — when you are barred from a beanie forum, and have no one with whom to talk about beanies.

Fauxbeanie — a fake Ty beanie.

Proselybeaning — when you are out trying to beanievert others.

Quixotibeanie — the foolish pursuit of the unattainable beanies by mere mortals.

Taxobeanie — Beanie nomenclature (BBOC, BBOM, TY store, Exclusive, Common, etc.)

Unbeancided — when you can afford only one of the two beanies you would like.

Unbeaned — you don't even want to know!

Unibeanie — a beanie that some feel is female while others believe it to be male (e.g. Twitch).

The Pinkys line was first announced in February 2005, and soon after a comment was made by Ty on the "Ask Ty" page at Ty.com that Pinkys were created for a very special little girl who loves pink. The first releases included 9 Pinkys Beanie Babies, in addition to Pinkys in the Buddy/Classic size, and 2 little purses. Excitement was generated when one of the Beanies, Delights, first shipped with a regular Ty hang tag, and then quickly changed to a Pinkys hang tag.

Baubles™
#40205

Birthday: 6/6/2004
Introduced: 2/28/2005
Retired: 10/25/2006
Though I'm a girl who just loves pink
Some people never stop to think
That I like sports and big bugs, too
I like all different things, don't you?
1G - $6

Bonita™
#40375

Birthday: 3/12/2006
Introduced: 5/31/2006
Current
Pretty puppy that I see
Gazing lovingly at me
With soft and silky fur of pink
No dog's more beautiful, I think!
1G - Current Retail Value

Chenille™
#40210

Birthday: 11/4/2004
Introduced: 2/28/2005
Current
I'll do a dance on twinkle toes
I practice hard; I think it shows
Whether ballet, jazz or tap
I think dancing is a snap!
1G - Current Retail Value

Dazzler™
#40203

Birthday: 4/9/2004
Introduced: 2/28/2005
Current
Glitter adds some special style
Pizazz that simply makes you smile
Try it once and you will see
How fun it is to be sparkly!
1G - Current Retail Value

Dazzler™ Key-clip
#40269

Birthday: None
Introduced: 6/30/2005
Current
Super Pinkmendous!
1Gsm - Current Retail Value

Delights™
#44049

Birthday: 6/7/2004
Introduced: 5/5/2005
Retired: 8/25/2005
Ice cream, cookies, all kinds of sweets
These are my most favorite treats
But these delights cannot compare
To having friends with whom to share!
Ty Store exclusive.
1G - $10

Fanciful™
#40350

Birthday: 8/13/2005
Introduced: 2/28/2006
Retired: 6/23/2006
Fairy tales and frilly lace
Put a smile upon my face
Ponies, jewels and ribbons, too
These are things I love, don't you?
1G - $6

Frilly™
#40204

Birthday: 5/2/2004
Introduced: 3/31/2005
Current
Some people think I am quite vain
Because I love to brush my mane
But that's not true, I must object
It helps my hair look just perfect!
1G - Current Retail Value

Frilly™ Key-clip
#40399

Birthday: None
Introduced: 6/30/2006
Current
That's Pinktacular!
1Gsm - Current Retail Value

Gemma™
#40338

Birthday: 1/12/2005
Introduced: 1/31/2006
Current
Diamonds, rubies, sapphires, too
All valuable to me and you
But the most precious gem to me
Is having friends, don't you agree?
1G - Current Retail Value

Glitters™
#40207

Birthday: 10/15/2004
Introduced: 5/31/2005
Retired: 12/21/2006
I have a dream I must confess
I wish that I was a princess
I'd sit upon my royal throne
While servants bring my royal bone!
1G - $6

Glitters™ Key-clip
#40333

Birthday: None
Introduced: 12/30/2005
Retired: 12/21/2006
Perfectly Pinkriffic!
1Gsm - $5

Julep™
#40206

Birthday: 7/11/2004
Introduced: 2/28/2005
Current
My jungle party is sublime
And you will have a swingin' time
We'll talk and laugh and have some fun
Until we see the morning sun!
1G - Current Retail Value

Julep™ Key-clip
#40332

Birthday: None
Introduced: 12/30/2005
Current
Utterly Pinkmazing!
1Gsm - Current Retail Value

Minuet™
#40330

Birthday: 1/13/2005
Introduced: 12/30/2005
Current
I simply love to prance around
With grace I'll glide across the ground
And I believe the best dance yet
Is one that's called the minuet!
1G - Current Retail Value

Pinky Poo™
#40200

Birthday: 1/30/2005
Introduced: 2/28/2005
Current
A sparkle here, a twinkle there
I like to shine most everywhere
All the way from my hair bows
Right down to my polished toes!
1G - Current Retail Value

Pinky Poo™
No Style #

Birthday: None
Introduced: 2/20/2005
Retired: 2/27/05
A sparkle here, a twinkle there
I like to shine most everywhere
All the way from my hair bows
Right down to my polished toes!
New York Toy Fair exclusive.
1Gsm - $50

Pinky Poo™ Key-clip
#40267 · string legs

Birthday: None
Introduced: 6/30/2005
Current
Totally Pinkrageous!
1Gsm - Current Retail Value

Pinky Poo™ Key-clip
#44063

Birthday: None
Introduced: 8/26/2005
Current
Pinky Poo Key-clip was issued without a phrase.
Pinkys Pack exclusive.
1Gsm

Pupsicle™
#44108

Birthday: 1/15/2007
Introduced: 6/5/2007
Current
On days when you need a treat
Something cool and very sweet
I know the perfect thing, it's true
A little Pupsicle for you!
Ty Store exclusive.
1G - Current Retail Value

Radiance™
#40247

Birthday: 8/20/2004
Introduced: 6/30/2005
Current
A happy, curly bright pink bear
Will bring you joy without a care
I'll be the bright spot in your day
And help to take your cares away!
1G - Current Retail Value

Ratzo™
#40211

Birthday: 12/11/2004
Introduced: 5/31/2005
Retired: 12/21/2006
It's a glamorous life I lead
Full of charm and fun, indeed
I have a good time night and day
I wouldn't have it another way!
1G - $6

Ratzo™ Key-clip
#40268

Birthday: None
Introduced: 6/30/2005
Retired: 12/21/2006
Absolutely Pinkstraordinary!
1Gsm - $5

Rosa™
#40209

Birthday: 8/19/2004
Introduced: 2/28/2005
Current
I'll fluff my hair and powder my nose
And then I'll stop and strike a pose
I like to look my best each day
I think it worked; what do you say?
1G - Current Retail Value

Rosa™ Key-clip
#40331

Birthday: None
Introduced: 12/30/2005
Current
Positively Pinknificent!
1Gsm - Current Retail Value

Silky™
#40201

Birthday: 2/21/2004
Introduced: 2/28/2005
Retired: 12/21/2006
Manicure, pedicure and facial, too
The perfect treat for me and you
What a great way to unwind
From the normal daily grind!
1G - $6

Silky™ Key-clip
#40398

Birthday: None
Introduced: 6/30/2006
Retired 12/21/06
Totally Pinktastic!
1Gsm - $5

Sparkles™
#40208

Birthday: 9/26/2004
Introduced: 4/29/2005
Retired: 12/21/2006
Girlie things like ribbons and bows
You'll find on all my favorite clothes
It may not be so versatile
But it is my favorite style!
1G - $6

Taffeta™
#40202

Birthday: 3/14/2004
Introduced: 7/29/2005
Current
Please take me to a jewelry store
'Cause I like jewels and gems galore
I love how they sparkle and shine
Don't you think that they look divine?
1G - Current Retail Value

NOTES

Issy™ Beanies

Issy, named after Four Seasons Hotel & Resorts founder, Isadore Sharp, was created to raise money for pediatric cancer research. 62 were sold at retail outlets and 1 was sold exclusively to guests at the Four Seasons Hotel in New York.

IN MEMORY OF CHRISTOPHER SHARP 1960-1978
If you travel far and wide
Keep Issy always by your side
And when you must turn out the light

Issy (New York) - All proceeds go to Memorial Sloan-Kettering Cancer Center.
Issy (retail) - All proceeds go to the Terry Fox Foundation.

LOCATION	♥ 6G	♥ 7G	♥ 8G	♥ 9G
Alexandria		$50		$45
Amman		$7		$7
Atlanta		$7	$7	$7
Austin		$7	$7	$7
Bali		$7	$7	$7
Bangkok		$7	$7	$7
Beirut		$7		$7
Berlin		$7	$7	$7
Beverly Hills		$7	$7	$7
Boston		$7	$7	$7
Budapest		$25		$25
Cairo		$7	$7	$7
Caracas		$7	$7	$7
Chiang Mai		$7	$7	$7
Chicago		$7	$7	$7
Costa Rica		$75		$75
Dallas		$7	$7	$7
Doha		$7		$7
Dublin		$275	$250	$200
Exuma		$7		$7
Hong Kong		$7	$7	$7
Houston		$6	$6	$6
Hualalai		$7	$7	$7
Istanbul		$7	$7	$7
Jackson Hole		$7		$7
Jakarta		$7	$7	$7
Kuala Lumpur		$175	$175	$175
Las Vegas		$7	$7	$7
Lisbon		$7	$7	$7

LOCATION	♥ 6G	♥ 7G	♥ 8G	♥ 9G
London		$7	$7	$7
Los Angeles		$7	$7	$7
Maldives		$7	$7	$7
Maui		$7	$7	$7
Mexico City		$7	$7	$7
Miami		$50		$50
Milano		$7	$7	$7
Nevis		$7	$7	$7
New York Hotel	$225			
Newport Beach		$7	$7	$7
Palm Beach		$7	$7	$7
Paris		$7	$7	$7
Philadelphia		$7	$7	$7
Prague		$7	$7	$7
Puerto Rico		$7		$7
Punta Mita		$7	$7	$7
Riyadh		$7		$7
San Diego		$7	$7	$7
San Francisco		$7	$7	$7
Santa Barbara		$575	$575	
Sao Paulo		$7		$7
Scottsdale		$7	$7	$7
Seattle		$7	$7	$7
Shanghai		$7	$7	$7
Sharm El Sheikh		$7		$7
Singapore		$7	$7	$7
Sydney		$7	$7	$7
Taipei		$7	$7	$7
Terre Blanche		$7		$7
Tokyo		$7	$7	$7
Toronto		$7	$7	$7
Vancouver		$100	$100	$90
Washington D.C.		$7	$7	$7
Whistler		$7		$7

DATES FOR ISSYS

New York Hotel (1)   Introduced: Dec-30-2000 Retired: Feb-15-2004
Retail (47)   Introduced: Mar-01-2001 Retired: Dec-31-2001
Retail (15)   Introduced: Aug-04-2001 Retired: Dec-31-2001

Kanata™ Beanies

Cartier who ventured far and wide
Discovered a land too large to hide
"Kanata" was the native name
But soon "Canada" it became!
Birthday: 10/14/2002
Introduced: 9/30/2002 ♥ Retired: 2/4/2003

Alberta

10G - $15

British Columbia

10G - $15

Manitoba
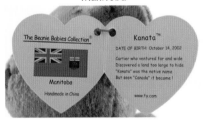

10G - $15

New Brunswick

10G - $15

Newfoundland

10G - $15

Northwest Territories

10G - $15

Nova Scotia

10G - $15

Nunavut

10G - $15

Ontario

10G - $15

Prince Edward's Island

10G - $15

Quebec

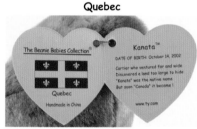

10G - $15

Saskatchewan

10G - $15

Yukon

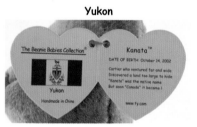

10G - $15

NOTES

BASKET BEANIES™

Like Jingle Beanies, these little guys have a loop for hanging anywhere they can brighten a room. Introduced in 2002, these small Beanies are a favorite for Easter decorating.

Baashful™
#35052

Introduced: 12/30/2004
Retired: 3/24/2005
1G - $3

Baskets™
#35053

Introduced: 12/30/2004
Retired: 3/24/2005
1G - $3

Billingsly™
#35072

Introduced: 12/30/2005
Retired: 4/21/2006
1G - $3

Bobsy™
#35087

Introduced: 1/31/2007
Retired: 3/27/2007
1G - $4

Candies™
#35051

Introduced: 12/30/2004
Retired: 3/24/2005
1G - $3

Carnation™
#3537

Introduced: 1/30/2004
Retired: 5/25/2004
1G - $3

Chickie™
#3526

Introduced: 1/30/2003
Retired: 7/29/2003
1G - $4

Duckling™
#35054

Introduced: 12/30/2004
Retired: 3/24/2005
1G - $3

Eggbert™
#3510

Introduced: 1/29/2002
Retired: 3/29/2002
1G - $3

Eggs™
#3509

Introduced: 1/29/2002
Retired: 3/29/2002
1G - $4

Eggs II™
#3524

Introduced: 1/30/2003
Retired: 7/29/2003
1G - $3

Eggs III™
#3525

Introduced: 1/30/2003
Retired: 7/29/2003
1G - $3

Ewey™
#3512

Introduced: 1/29/2002
Retired: 3/29/2002
1G - $3

Flipsy™
#35088

Introduced: 1/31/2007
Retired: 3/27/2007
1G - $4

Floppity™
#3511

Introduced: 1/29/2002
Retired: 3/29/2002
1G - $3

Grace™
#3513

Introduced: 1/29/2002
Retired: 3/29/2002
1G - $3

Hippie™
#3527

Introduced: 1/30/2003
Retired: 7/29/2003
1G - $3

Hippity™
#3514

Introduced: 1/29/2002
Retired: 3/29/2002
1G - $3

Hobsy™
#35087

Introduced: 1/31/2007
Retired: 3/27/2007
1G - $4

Lullaby™
#3540

Introduced: 1/30/2004
Retired: 5/25/2004
1G - $3

Marshmallow™
#35073

Introduced: 12/30/2005
Retired: 4/21/2006
1G - $3

Meekins™
#35075

Introduced: 12/30/2005
Retired: 4/21/2006
1G - $3

Mipsy™
#35088

Introduced: 1/31/2007
Retired: 3/27/2007
1G - $4

Nibbles™
#3539

Introduced: 1/30/2004
Retired: 5/25/2004
1G - $3

Petey™
#3538

Introduced: 1/30/2004
Retired: 5/25/2004
1G - $3

Pipsy™
#35088

Introduced: 1/31/2007
Retired: 3/27/2007
1G - $4

Sugartwist™
#35074

Introduced: 12/30/2005
Retired: 4/21/2006
1G - $3

Topsy™
#35087

Introduced: 1/31/2007
Retired: 3/27/2007
1G - $4

NOTES

NOTES

HALLOWEENIE BEANIES™

Halloweenie Beanies are counterparts to Jingle, Basket and Valenteenie Beanies. They make great seasonal gifts and are small enough to drop in children's trick-or-treat bags on Halloween. They are designed with loops for use as decorations. We hope Ty will keep these cuties coming.

BAT-e™
#35042

Introduced: 8/30/2004
Retired: 10/14/2004
1G - $4

Creeps™
#35080

Introduced: 8/31/2006
Retired: 10/25/2006
1G - $4

Fraidy™
#35043

Introduced: 8/30/2004
Retired: 10/14/2004
1G - $4

Ghosters™
#35058

Introduced: 8/31/2005
Retired: 11/23/2005
1G - $4

Ghoul™
#35077

Introduced: 8/31/2006
Retired: 10/25/2006
1G - $5

Ghoulianne™
#35076

Introduced: 8/31/2006
Retired: 10/25/2006
1G - $4

Hocus™
#35055

Introduced: 8/31/2005
Retired: 11/23/2005
1G - $4

Merlin™
#35057

Introduced: 8/31/2005
Retired: 11/23/2005
1G - $4

Pocus™
#35056

Introduced: 8/31/2005
Retired: 11/23/2005
1G - $5

Quivers™
#35041

Introduced: 8/30/2004
Retired: 10/14/2004
1G - $5

SCARED-e™
#35044

Introduced: 8/30/2004
Retired: 10/14/2004
1G - $5

Screams™
#35079

Introduced: 8/31/2006
Retired: 10/25/2006
1G - $4

Treats™
#35078

Introduced: 8/31/2006
Retired: 10/25/2006
1G - $4

Tricky™
#35045

Introduced: 8/30/2004
Retired: 10/14/2004
1G - $4

NOTES

JINGLE BEANIES™

Ty has created holiday ornaments by miniaturizing versions of consumers' favorite Beanies. Each has a loop or hook for use in decorating a tree or a package. Apart from the first released in 2001, a bell makes them "jingle". These little beanies are a big hit at holiday time.

1997 Holiday Teddy™
#3506 · button nose

Introduced: 9/17/2001
Retired: 1/1/2002
1G - $3

1997 Holiday Teddy™
#3506 · stitched nose

Introduced: 9/17/2001
Retired: 1/1/2002
1G - $3

1998 Holiday Teddy™
#3507 · button nose

Introduced: 9/17/2001
Retired: 1/1/2002
1G - $3

1998 Holiday Teddy™
#3507 · stitched nose

Introduced: 9/17/2001
Retired: 1/1/2002
1G - $3

1999 Holiday Teddy™
#3508 · button nose

Introduced: 9/17/2001
Retired: 1/1/2002
1G - $3

1999 Holiday Teddy™
#3508 · stitched nose

Introduced: 9/17/2001
Retired: 1/1/2002
1G - $3

2000 Holiday Teddy™
#3535

Introduced: 9/30/2003
Retired: 12/26/2003
1G - $3

2001 Holiday Teddy™
#3522

Introduced: 9/30/2002
Retired: 12/27/2002
1G - $3

2002 Holiday Teddy™
#3534 · green body

Introduced: 9/30/2003
Retired: 12/26/2003
1G - $3

2002 Holiday Teddy™
#3533 · red body

Introduced: 9/30/2003
Retired: 12/26/2003
1G - $3

2003 Holiday Teddy™
#35049

Introduced: 9/30/2004
Retired: 12/30/2004
1G - $3

Chillin'™
#3528

Introduced: 9/30/2003
Retired: 12/26/2003
1G - $3

Clubbies™
#3599 · Set of 4

Introduced: 9/24/2001
Retired: 1/23/2002
Beanie Baby Official Club exclusive.
1G - $10

Clubby I™
#3599 · button nose

Introduced: 9/24/2001
Retired: 1/23/2002
Beanie Baby Official Club exclusive.
1G - $4

Clubby I™
#3599 · stitched nose

Introduced: 9/24/2001
Retired: 1/23/2002
Beanie Baby Official Club exclusive.
1G - $3

Clubby II™
#3599 · button nose

Introduced: 9/24/2001
Retired: 1/23/2002
Beanie Baby Official Club exclusive.
1G - $4

Clubby II™
#3599 · stitched nose

Introduced: 9/24/2001
Retired: 1/23/2002
Beanie Baby Official Club exclusive.
1G - $3

Clubby III™
#3599 · button nose

Introduced: 9/24/2001
Retired: 1/23/2002
Beanie Baby Official Club exclusive.
1G - $3

Clubby III™
#3599 · stitched nose

Introduced: 9/24/2001
Retired: 1/23/2002
Beanie Baby Official Club exclusive.
1G - $4

Clubby IV™
#3599 · button nose

Introduced: 9/24/2001
Retired: 1/23/2002
Beanie Baby Official Club exclusive.
1G - $3

Clubby IV™
#3599 · stitched nose

Introduced: 9/24/2001
Retired: 1/23/2002
Beanie Baby Official Club exclusive.
1G - $4

Cornbread ™
#37002

Introduced: 11/10/2004
Retired: 12/30/2004
Cracker Barrel exclusive.
1G - $5

Decade™
#3536 · gold body

Introduced: 10/1/2003
Retired: 12/15/2003
Ty Store exclusive.
1G - $3

Decade™
#3536 · green body

Introduced: 10/1/2003
Retired: 12/15/2003
Ty Store exclusive.
1G - $3

Decade™
#3536 · red body

Introduced: 10/1/2003
Retired: 12/15/2003
Ty Store exclusive.
1G - $3

Decade™
#3536 · white body

Introduced: 10/1/2003
Retired: 12/15/2003
Ty Store exclusive.
1G - $3

Decades™
#3536 · Set of 4

Introduced: 10/1/2003
Retired: 12/15/2003
Ty Store exclusive.
1G - $10

Dizzy™
#3516

Introduced: 9/30/2002
Retired: 12/27/2002
1G - $3

Flakes™
#35082

Introduced: 9/29/2006
Retired: 11/22/2006
1G - $7

Flaky™
#3532

Introduced: 9/30/2003
Retired: 12/26/2003
1G - $3

Freezings™
#35086

Introduced: 9/29/2006
Retired: 11/22/2006
1G - $4

Gift™ (Joy)
#37005

Introduced: 10/26/2005
Retired: 12/29/2005
Hallmark Gold Crown exclusive.
1G - $4

Gift™ (Love)
#37004

Introduced: 10/26/2005
Retired: 12/29/2005
Hallmark Gold Crown exclusive.
1G - $4

Gift™ (Peace)
#37003

Introduced: 10/26/2005
Retired: 12/29/2005
Hallmark Gold Crown exclusive.
1G - $3

Gifts™
#35063

Introduced: 9/30/2005
Retired: 12/29/2005
1G - $4

Goody™
#35062 · center

Introduced: 9/30/2005
Retired: 12/29/2005
1G - $4

Goody™
#35062 · left

Introduced: 9/30/2005
Retired: 12/29/2005
1G - $3

Halo™
#3504 · button nose

Introduced: 9/17/2001
Retired: 1/1/2002
1G - $4

Halo™
#3504 · stitched nose

Introduced: 9/17/2001
Retired: 1/1/2002
1G - $4

Halo II™
#3517

Introduced: 9/30/2002
Retired: 12/27/2002
1G - $3

Herald™
#3529

Introduced: 9/30/2003
Retired: 12/26/2003
1G - $4

Herschel™
#37001

Introduced: 11/10/2004
Retired: 12/30/2004
Cracker Barrel exclusive.
1G - $5

Icecaps™
#35085

Introduced: 9/29/2006
Retired: 11/22/2006
1G - $4

Icicles™
#35081

Introduced: 9/29/2006
Retired: 11/22/2006
1G - $3

Jangle™
#3531

Introduced: 9/30/2003
Retired: 12/26/2003
1G - $3

Jinglepup™
#3518 · green hat with green tail

Introduced: 9/30/2002
Retired: 12/27/2002
UK exclusive.
1G - $3

Jinglepup™
#3518 · green hat with white tail

Introduced: 9/30/2002
Retired: 12/27/2002
USA exclusive.
1G - $3

Jinglepup™
#3518 · white hat with green tail

Introduced: 9/30/2002
Retired: 12/27/2002
Singapore exclusive.
1G - $5

Jinglepup™
#3518 · white hat with white tail

Introduced: 9/30/2002
Retired: 12/27/2002
Canada exclusive.
1G - $5

Kringles™
#35084

Introduced: 9/29/2006
Retired: 11/22/2006
1G - $3

Loosy™
#3501

Introduced: 9/17/2001
Retired: 1/1/2002
1G - $3

Melton™
#35050

Introduced: 9/30/2004
Retired: 12/30/2004
1G - $3

Mistletoe™
#3519

Introduced: 9/30/2002
Retired: 12/27/2002
1G - $3

Mr. Frost™
#35064

Introduced: 9/30/2005
Retired: 12/29/2005
1G - $4

Peace™
#3505 · button nose

Introduced: 9/17/2001
Retired: 1/1/2002
1G - $3

Peace™
#3505 · stitched nose

Introduced: 9/17/2001
Retired: 1/1/2002
1G - $3

Presents™
#35065

Introduced: 9/30/2005
Retired: 12/29/2005
1G - $4

246

Quackers™
#3500

Introduced: 9/17/2001
Retired: 1/1/2002
1G - $3

Rover™
#3503

Introduced: 9/17/2001
Retired: 1/1/2002
1G - $3

Roxie™
#3530

Introduced: 9/30/2003
Retired: 12/26/2003
1G - $3

Rudy™
#35046

Introduced: 9/30/2004
Retired: 12/30/2004
1G - $4

Santa™
#3520

Introduced: 9/30/2002
Retired: 12/27/2002
1G - $3

Slushes™
#35083

Introduced: 9/29/2006
Retired: 12/21/2006
1G - $3

Snowgirl™
#3521

Introduced: 9/30/2002
Retired: 12/27/2002
1G - $3

Star™
#35048

Introduced: 9/30/2004
Retired: 12/30/2004
1G - $3

The Beginning™
#3515

Introduced: 9/30/2002
Retired: 12/27/2002
1G - $3

Toboggan™
#35047

Introduced: 9/30/2004
Retired: 12/30/2004
1G - $4

Twigs™
#3502

Introduced: 9/17/2001
Retired: 1/1/2002
1G - $3

Twinkling™
#35066

Introduced: 9/30/2005
Retired: 12/29/2005
1G - $3

Yummy™
#35061

Introduced: 9/30/2005
Retired: 12/29/2005
1G - $3

Zero™
#3523

Introduced: 9/30/2002
Retired: 12/27/2002
1G - $3

Fun Facts

The First Jingle Beanies released in 2001 did not have a bell inside, so didn't 'jingle'. Subsequent releases did.

The first releases were:
1997 Holiday Teddy, 1998 Holiday Teddy, 1999 Holiday Teddy, Clubby I, Clubby II, Clubby III, Clubby IV, Halo (1st), Loosy, Peace, Quackers, Rover and Twigs.

The four Decade Jingle Beanies have their bells on the outside, instead of inside.

NOTES

teenie
BEANIE BABIES™

Ty and McDonald's ran successful Teenie Beanie Babies promotions from 1997 to 2000. New promotions were launched in 2004 in the United States and overseas in 2005 and 2006.

Antsy™ 5/1999 USA  3G - $1	**Big Red Shoe™** 7/2004 USA & Canada  6G - $1	**Birdie™** 7/2004 USA & Canada · 11/06 Malaysia 6G - $1 ♥ MAL - $8
Birthday™ 11/06 Malaysia  2006 - $15	**Blizz™** 6/2000 USA & Canada · 8/2001 Australia  *At The Zoo Collection.* 4G - $1 ♥ AUS - $1	**Blue™** 8/2006 Singapore  2006 - $7
Bones™ 5/1998 USA · 4/1999 UK & Germany  2G - $1 ♥ UK - $1 ♥ GER - $1	**Bongo™** 5/1998 USA · 4/1999 UK  2G - $1 ♥ UK - $1	**Britannia™** 6/1999 USA *International Bear Series.* 3G - $3
Bronty™ 6/2000 USA & Canada  *Dinosaur Trio Super Star.* 4G - $3	**Bumble™** 6/2000 USA & Canada · 10/2000 Japan  *Garden Bunch Collection.* 4G - $1 ♥ JPN - $2	**Burger™** 7/2004 USA & Canada  6G - $1

Bushy™
6/2000 USA & Canada ·
8/2001 Australia

Top Secret Collection.
4G - $1 ♥ AUS - $1

Chilly™
6/2000 USA & Canada

Legend Super Star.
4G - $3

Chip™
5/1999 USA & Canada

3G - $1

Chocolate™
4/1997 USA

1G - $3

Chops™
4/1997 USA

1G - $3

Claude™
5/1999 USA & Canada

3G - $1

Coral™
6/2000 USA & Canada

Under The Sea Collection.
4G - $1

Crew Glory™
5/1999 USA & Canada

Gift to McDonald's employees only.
3G - $10

Crew Millennium™
6/2000 USA & Canada

Gift to McDonald's employees only.
4G - $10

Doby™
5/1998 USA & Canada · 4/1999
UK & Germany

2G - $1 ♥ UK - $1 ♥ GER - $1

Dotty™
6/2000 USA & Canada ·
8/2001 Australia

Pet Pal Collection.
4G - $1 ♥ AUS - $1

Erin™
6/1999 USA · 10/2000 Japan

International Bear Series.
3G - $3 ♥ JPN - $4

Flip™
6/2000 USA & Canada ·
10/2000 Japan

Pet Pal Collection.
4G - $1 ♥ JPN - $2

Flitter™
6/2000 USA & Canada · 10/2000
Japan · 8/2001 Australia

Garden Bunch Collection.
4G - $1 ♥ JPN - $2 ♥ AUS - $1

Freckles™
5/1999 USA & Canada

3G - $1

Fries™
7/2004 USA & Canada ·
11/2006 Malaysia

6G - $1 ♥ MAL - $8

Germania™
6/2000 USA & Canada

International Bear Super Star.
4G - $3

Glory™
6/1999 USA

International Bear Series.
3G - $3

Golden Arches™
7/2004 USA & Canada ·
11/2006 Malaysia

6G - $1 ♥ MAL - $8

Goldie™
4/1997 USA

1G - $3

Goochy™
6/2000 USA & Canada ·
8/2001 Australia

Under The Sea Collection
4G - $1 ♥ AUS - $1

Grimace™
7/2004 USA & Canada ·
11/2006 Malaysia

6G - $1 ♥ MAL - $8

Hamburglar™
7/2004 USA & Canada ·
11/2006 Malaysia

6G - $1 ♥ MAL - $8

Happy Meal™
7/2004 USA & Canada ·
11/2006 Malaysia

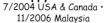

6G - $1 ♥ MAL - $8

Happy Meal 25th Bear™
7/2004 USA

6G - $2

Happy Meal 10th Bear™
7/2004 Canada

6G - $4

Happy™
5/1998 USA & Canada

2G - $1

Humphrey™
6/2000 USA & Canada

Legend Super Star.
4G - $3

Iggy™
5/1999 USA & Canada

3G - $1

Inch™
5/1998 USA & Canada ·
4/1999 UK & Germany

2G - $1 ♥ UK - $1 ♥ GER - $1

Lefty™
10/2000 USA & Canada

American Trio Super Star.
4G - $3

Leo™
9/2005 UK

2005 - $5

Libearty™
10/2000 USA & Canada

American Trio Super Star.
4G - $3

Lime Green™
8/2006 Singapore

2006 - $7

Lips™
6/2000 USA & Canada ·
10/2000 Japan

Pet Pal Collection.
4G - $1 ♥ JPN - $2

Lizz™
4/1997 USA

1G - $3

Lucky™
6/2000 USA & Canada ·
10/2000 Japan

Garden Bunch Collection.
4G - $1 ♥ JPN - $2

Magenta™
8/2006 Singapore

2006 - $7

Maple™
6/1999 USA

International Bear Series.
3G - $3

Maple™
6/1999 Canada

International Bear Series.
3G - $3

McNuggets™
7/2004 USA & Canada

6G - $1

Mel™
5/1998 USA & Canada ·
4/1999 UK & Germany

2G - $1 ♥ UK - $1 ♥ GER - $1

Millennium™
6/2000 USA & Canada

McHappy Day Super Star.
Sold first day only.
4G - $3

Mitch™
4/1999 Germany

Mitch is the German version of Bongo.
GER - $12

Molly™
9/2005 UK

2005 - $5

My MighTy Bear™
12/2006 Malaysia

2006 - $20

My SweeTy Bear™
12/2006 Malaysia

2006 - $20

My TrusTy Bear™
12/2006 Malaysia

2006 - $20

My UniTy Bear™
12/2006 Malaysia

2006 - $20

Navy™
8/2006 Singapore

2006 - $7

Neon™
6/2000 USA & Canada • 10/2000 Japan • 8/2001 Australia

Under The Sea Collection.
4G - $1 ♥ JPN - $2 ♥ AUS - $1

Nook™
5/1999 USA & Canada

3G - $1

Nuts™
5/1999 USA & Canada

3G - $1

Orange™
8/2006 Singapore

2006 - $7

Osito™
6/2000 USA & Canada

International Bear Super Star.
4G - $3

Patti™
4/1997 USA

1G - $3

Peanut Light Blue™
5/1998 USA & Canada • 4/1999 UK & Germany

2G - $1 ♥ UK - $1 ♥ GER - $1

Peanut Royal Blue™
6/2000 USA & Canada

Legend Super Star.
4G - $3

Penny™
9/2005 UK

2005 - $5

Percival™
4/1999 UK & Germany

Percival is the European version of Happy.
UK - $12 ♥ GER - $12

Pete™
9/2005 UK

2005 - $5

Pinchers™
5/1998 USA & Canada · 4/1999 UK & Germany

2G - $1 ♥ UK - $1 ♥ GER - $1

Pinky™
4/1997 USA

1G - $3

Purple™
8/2006 Singapore

2006 - $7

Quacks™
4/1997 USA

1G - $3

Rachel™
9/2005 UK

2005 - $5

Red™
8/2006 Singapore

2006 - $7

Rex™
6/2000 USA & Canada

Dinosaur Trio Super Star.
4G - $3

Righty™
10/2000 USA & Canada

American Trio Super Star.
4G - $3

Rocket™
5/1999 USA & Canada

3G - $1

Ronald McDonald™
7/2004 USA & Canada · 9/2005 UK · 11/2006 Malaysia

6G - $1 ♥ UK - $5 ♥ MAL - $8

Ronald McDonald™
8/2006 Singapore

2006 - $7

Ryan™
9/2005 UK

2005 - $5

Schweetheart™
6/2000 USA & Canada · 10/2000 Japan · 8/2001 Australia

At The Zoo Collection.
4G - $1 ♥ JPN - $2 ♥ AUS - $1

Scoop™
5/1998 USA & Canada · 4/1999 UK & Germany

2G - $1 ♥ UK - $1 ♥ GER - $1

Seamore™
4/1997 USA

1G - $3

Shake™
7/2004 USA & Canada

6G - $1

Slither™
6/2000 USA & Canada · 10/2000 Japan · 8/2001 Australia

Pet Pal Collection.
4G - $1 ♥ JPN - $2 ♥ AUS - $1

Smoochy™
5/1999 USA & Canada

3G - $1

Snort™
4/1997 USA

1G - $3

Spangle™
6/2000 USA & Canada

International Bear Super Star.
4G - $3

Speedy™
4/1997 USA

1G - $3

Spike™
6/2000 USA & Canada

At The Zoo Collection.
4G - $1

Spinner™
6/2000 USA & Canada

Garden Bunch Collection.
4G - $1

Springy™
6/2000 USA & Canada · 8/2001 Australia

Top Secret Collection.
4G - $1 ♥ AUS - $1

Spunky™
5/1999 USA & Canada

3G - $1

Steg™
6/2000 USA & Canada

Dinosaur Trio Super Star.
4G - $3

Sting™
6/2000 USA & Canada

Under The Sea Collection.
4G - $1

Stretchy™
5/1999 USA & Canada

3G - $1

Strut™
5/1999 USA & Canada

3G - $1

The End™
6/2000 USA & Canada

The End Bear Super Star.
Sold last day only.
4G - $3

Tusk™
6/2000 USA & Canada •
8/2001 Australia

At The Zoo Collection.
4G - $1 ♥ AUS - $1

Twigs™
5/1998 USA & Canada • 4/1999
UK & Germany

2G - $1 ♥ UK - $1 ♥ GER - $1

Waddle™
5/1998 USA & Canada • 4/1999
UK & Germany

2G - $1 ♥ UK - $1 ♥ GER - $1

Yazzie™
9/2005 UK

2005 - $5

Zip™
5/1998 USA & Canada • 4/1999
UK & Germany

2G - $1 ♥ UK - $1 ♥ GER - $1

NOTES

VALENTEENIES™

These little sweethearts make super Valentine gifts. Small enough to tuck in with a Valentine card or attach to the bow on a box of chocolates, they say "I love you." They are designed with loops for hanging in the home, or attaching to your valentine's rear view mirror.

Be Mine™ Key-clip
#35067

Introduced: 11/30/2005
Retired: 2/24/2006
1G - $5

Kiss Me™ Key-clip
#35068

Introduced: 11/30/2005
Retired: 2/24/2006
1G - $5

You're a Cutie™ Key-clip
#35069

Introduced: 11/30/2005
Retired: 2/24/2006
1G - $5

NOTES

NOTES

BEANIE BUDDIES®

Much larger than their Beanie Babies counterparts, Beanie Buddies are destined to be hugged. Ty Warner created them from an exquisitely soft, cool to the touch, high quality plush material named Tylon, which is designed specifically to hold vibrant colors. A few of Ty's favorites have been produced in large, extra large and jumbo sizes for those collectors who like to display them in "families."

#1 Bear™
#9474

Introduced: 12/27/2002
Retired: 12/29/2004
#1 Bear the Beanie Baby was designed exclusively for Ty sales representatives to mark sales over $1 billion in 1998!
4G - $11

1997 Holiday Teddy™
#9426

Introduced: 10/1/2001
Retired: 12/27/2001
This 1997 Beanie Baby was the first of the Holiday Teddy series!
4G - $11

1997 Holiday Teddy™ (large)
#9053

Introduced: 10/1/2001
Retired: 12/27/2001
This was the first Beanie Baby to wear a Santa hat!
4G - $11

1997 Holiday Teddy™ (extra-large)
#9054

Introduced: 10/1/2001
Retired: 12/27/2001
This Beanie Baby and one other were the first introduced to represent this holiday season!
4G - $11

1998 Holiday Teddy™
#9467

Introduced: 9/30/2002
Retired: 11/8/2002
1998 Holiday Teddy, the Beanie Baby, was also a Jingle Beanie, along with two other Beanie Baby bears. Can you name them?
4G - $11

1999 Holiday Teddy™
#9468

Introduced: 9/30/2002
Retired: 11/8/2002
The 1999 Holiday Teddy Beanie Baby was the first Holiday Teddy introduced without a hat!
4G - $11

2000 Signature Bear™
#9348

Introduced: 1/4/2000
Retired: 4/3/2000
2000 Ty Signature Bear Beanie Baby did not exist. This bear represents the future!
4G - $11

2001 Holiday Teddy™
#9427

Introduced: 10/1/2001
Retired: 12/19/2001
The 2001 Beanie and Buddy are the first Holiday Teddies to be introduced at the same time!
4G - $11

2002 Holiday Teddy™
#9701

Introduced: 9/30/2003
Retired: 12/26/2003
2002 Holiday Teddy the Beanie Baby had a holiday button on its chest!
4G - $11

2003 Holiday Teddy™
#90013

Introduced: 9/30/2004
Retired: 12/29/2004
2003 Holiday Teddy is the 2nd Holiday
Teddy to wear both a hat and a scarf!
4G - $11

2005 Holiday Teddy™
#90040

Introduced: 9/30/2005
Retired: 12/29/2005
U.S. Congress has named December 12th
as National Poinsettia Day!
4G - $11

2006 Holiday Teddy™
#90061

Introduced: 9/29/2006
Retired: 12/21/2006
Wreaths made of evergreen tree twigs,
sometimes with pine cones and bows, are
common Christmas decorations!
4G - $11

2006 Year of the Dog™
#96222

Introduced: 11/30/2005
Current
2006 Year of the Dog was issued
without a phrase.
Asian-Pacific exclusive.
4G - Current Retail Value

Aberdeen™
#90084

Introduced: 6/29/2007
Current
The Scottish terrier was originally bred
to chase and hunt small creatures including,
squirrels, mice and foxes!
4G - Current Retail Value

Addison™
#9454

Introduced: 5/31/2002
Retired: 9/9/2002
Addison Street, Waveland Ave., Sheffield
Ave. and Clark Street surround the oldest
ballpark in Major League Baseball.
Can you name the ballpark?
4G - $11

Admiral™
#90053

Introduced: 6/30/2006
Current
Penguins are one of very few birds that
are unable to fly; however they swim
faster than any other bird!
4G - Current Retail Value

Ai™
#9616

Introduced: 11/10/2003
Retired: 4/15/2004
Ai the BEANIE BABY's name means "love"
in Japanese! We love, Ai, don't you?
Asian-Pacific exclusive.
4G - $20

Almond™
#9425

Introduced: 7/31/2001
Retired: 10/16/2001
Almond the Beanie Baby was introduced
with a friend named "Pecan"!
4G - $11

Always™
#90043

Introduced: 11/30/2005
Retired: 5/25/2007
A rose just for you ...
4G - $11

Amber™
#9341

Introduced: 8/31/1999
Retired: 5/19/2000
Amber and Silver the Beanie Babies
were modeled after two orphaned
kittens found by Ty Warner!
3G - $11

America™
#9469 · blue body

Introduced: 8/29/2002
Retired: 10/8/2002
Thanks to you, the America trio of Beanie
Babies has raised over $2 million for the
American Red Cross Disaster Relief Fund!
4G - $11

America™
#9469 · red with blue right ear

Introduced: 8/29/2002
Retired: 10/8/2002
Thanks to you, the America trio of Beanie
Babies has raised over $2 million for the
American Red Cross Disaster Relief Fund!
4G - $11

America™
#9469 · red with reversed ears

Introduced: 8/29/2002
Retired: 10/8/2002
Thanks to you, the America trio of Beanie
Babies has raised over $2 million for the
American Red Cross Disaster Relief Fund!
4G - $11

America™
#9469 · white with reversed ears

Introduced: 8/29/2002
Retired: 10/8/2002
Thanks to you, the America trio of Beanie
Babies has raised over $2 million for the
American Red Cross Disaster Relief Fund!
4G - $11

America™
#9469 · white with right blue ear

Introduced: 8/29/2002
Retired: 10/8/2002
Thanks to you, the America trio of Beanie
Babies has raised over $2 million for the
American Red Cross Disaster Relief Fund!
4G - $11

Ariel™
#9409

Introduced: 4/1/2001
Retired: 4/16/2002
The flowers embroidered on the Ariel
Beanie Baby and Beanie Buddy were based
on a drawing by Ariel Glaser.
4G - $11

Aussiebear™
#9618

Introduced: 11/10/2003
Retired: 4/15/2004
Throughout the world, the people of
Australia are known as "Aussies"!
Asian-Pacific exclusive.
4G - $20

Avalon™
#90032

Introduced: 6/30/2005
Retired: 12/21/2006
According to legend, the mortally wounded
King Arthur was taken to the island of
Avalon, the land of immortal heroes!
4G - $11

B.B. Bear™
#9398

Introduced: 1/1/2001
Retired: 12/31/2001
B.B.Bear the Beanie Baby was the first
Beanie Baby created without a birthday.
4G - $11

Baby Boy™
#9479

Introduced: 12/27/2002
Retired: 4/28/2005
In Europe, a greater number of boy babies
are born in southern countries
than in the northern countries!
4G - $11

Baby Girl™
#9480

Introduced: 12/27/2002
Retired: 4/28/2005
In North America, more girl babies
are born in Mexico and the southern U.S. than
in the northern U.S. and Canada!
4G - $11

Baldy™
#9408

Introduced: 4/1/2001
Retired: 4/26/2001
Baldy the Beanie Baby
originally had a different name,
which was changed at the last minute.
4G - $11

Bananas™
#9402

Introduced: 1/1/2001
Retired: 6/14/2001
Bananas the Beanie Baby's beard was three
different colors before it was made yellow.
4G - $11

BAT-e™
#90009

Introduced: 8/30/2004
Retired: 9/28/2004
While most bats like to live in caves,
our friend BAT-e prefers to live with you!
4G - $11

Batty™
#9379 · black body

Introduced: 6/24/2000
Retired: 12/31/2001
Batty the Beanie Baby was the second bat
made by Ty. Batty came in two colors,
mocha rose and Ty-dyed!
4G - $115

Batty™
#9379 · brown body

Introduced: 6/24/2000
Retired: 12/31/2001
Batty the Beanie Baby was the second
bat made by Ty. Batty came in two colors,
mocha rose and Ty-dyed!
4G - $11

Beak™
#9301

Introduced: 9/30/1998
Retired: 3/31/1999
Beak the Beanie Baby and Beak the Beanie
Buddy are the first to be released as a set!
1G - $11 ♥ 2G - $11

Beani™
#9471

Introduced: 10/30/2002
Retired: 10/8/2003
Beani the cat was the first long-haired
cat Beanie Baby design!
4G - $11

Benjamin™
#90051

Introduced: 4/28/2006
Retired: 8/25/2006
Benjamin Franklin is credited with inventing
many things including the Franklin stove,
bifocals, and the lightning rod!
4G - $11

Billionaire™
#9470

Introduced: 9/30/2002
Retired: 2/26/2004
Billionaire the Beanie Baby was an exclusive
employee thank you gift for achieving sales
of over one billion dollars!
4G - $12

Blessed™
#90002

Introduced: 4/29/2004
Current
Blessed is the second praying bear
in the Beanie Baby collection!
4G - Current Retail Value

Bloom™
#9719

Introduced: 2/26/2004
Retired: 12/29/2005
The single most popular fresh cut
flower is the rose!
4G - $11

Blue™
#90001

Introduced: 4/29/2004
Retired: 11/24/2004
Betsy Ross, who stitched together the first
American Flag, was asked to do so
by George Washington!
4G - $11

Blue's Clues™ — Blue™
#90056

Introduced: 8/31/2006
Current
Do you know who loves to leave clues for you?
It's Blue!
Also available at Ty Store.
4G - Current Retail Value

Bo™
#9706

Introduced: 12/30/2003
Retired: 12/29/2005
When Dalmatian puppies are born,
they don't have any spots!
4G - $11

263

Bones™
#9377

Introduced: 6/24/2000
Retired: 4/16/2002
Bones the Beanie Baby was one of the longest
running and most popular Beanies ever made!
4G - $11

Bongo™
#9312

Introduced: 1/1/1999
Retired: 12/11/1999
Bongo the Beanie Baby was first named Nana.
Ty Warner liked the name Bongo better
because he plays the bongos!
2G - $11 ♥ 3G - $11

Bonnet™
#94003

Introduced: 2/22/2005
Retired: 4/5/2005
Bonnet is the first Beanie Baby bear to
dress up as a bunny!
Ty Store exclusive.
4G - $11

Bonnet™
#94003

Introduced: 2/22/2005
Retired: 4/5/2005
Bonnet is the first Beanie Baby bear to
dress up as a bunny!
Harrods UK exclusive.
4G - $18

Bonsai™
#9494

Introduced: 6/30/2003
Current
Bonsai the Beanie Baby is actually a
very unique chimpanzee because,
unlike actual chimps, he has a tail!
4G - Current Retail Value

Booties™
#90007

Introduced: 6/30/2004
Retired: 12/29/2005
Our friend Booties knows that cats
don't always land on their feet . . . So
she's extra careful when she jumps!
4G - $11

Bravo™
#9985

Introduced: 8/9/2003
Retired: 11/25/2003
The word "bravo" is generally used
to express appreciation for a job or
performance well done!
Trade Show exclusive.
4G - $12

Brigitte™
#9435

Introduced: 12/27/2001
Retired: 11/23/2005
The idea for Brigitte the Beanie Baby came
from the poodle skirts of the 1950's!
4G - $11

Britannia™
#9601

Introduced: 8/31/1999
Retired: 5/24/2000
Britannia the Beanie Baby was the first
international bear to have an embroidered
flag rather than a patch!
UK exclusive.
3G - $75

Bronty™
#9353

Introduced: 1/4/2000
Retired: 4/6/2002
Bronty the Beanie Baby was one of the
dinosaur trio. This trio
is highly prized by collectors!
4G - $13

Brutus™
#90082

Introduced: 6/29/2007
Current
The country of origin for the Rottweiler
breed is Germany!
4G - Current Retail Value

Bubbles™
#9323

Introduced: 1/1/1999
Retired: 11/29/1999
Bubbles the Beanie Baby
made in the swimming position was
quite a challenge to manufacture.
2G - $12 ♥ 3G - $11

Buckingham™
#9607

Introduced: 2/4/2001
Retired: 10/24/2001
Buckingham the Beanie Baby was one
of only a few bears to have two ribbons
Can you name the others?
UK exclusive.
4G - $45

Bunga Raya™
#9615

Introduced: 9/17/2002
Retired: 11/5/2003
Bunga Raya, the national flower of Malaysia,
means hibiscus in the Malay language!
Malaysia exclusive.
4G - $25

Bushy™
#9382

Introduced: 6/24/2000
Retired: 4/8/2002
Bushy the Beanie Baby's fabric has a
total of 4 colors: pink, orange, yellow,
and green. This fabric is very difficult
and expensive to produce!
4G - $11

Butch™
#9452

Introduced: 4/30/2002
Retired: 12/27/2002
One of the most famous fans of the Bull
Terrier was General George S. Patton,
who owned many dogs of this breed!
4G - $11

Carnation™
#90008

Introduced: 6/30/2004
Retired: 3/27/2006
Carnations, which were originally flesh
colored flowers, got their name from the
old Italian word meaning complexion!
4G - $11

Cashew™
#9437

Introduced: 1/29/2002
Retired: 9/25/2002
Cashew was one of several Beanie
Babies that shared their names with
nuts; can you name the rest?
4G - $11

Cashew™
#9437

Introduced: 1/29/2002
Retired: 9/25/2002
Cashew was one of several Beanie Babies
that shared their names with nuts;
can you name the rest?
American Red Cross exclusive.
4G - $11

Cassie™
#9405

Introduced: 4/1/2001
Retired: 7/17/2001
Cassie is the first Beanie Baby
dog designed with long fur.
4G - $11

Celebrate™
#9423

Introduced: 6/23/2001
Retired: 10/11/2001
Celebrate the Beanie Baby was the first bear
to commemorate our Company's birthday!
Issued for 15th Year Anniversary.
4G - $11

Centennial™
No Style #

Introduced: 9/14/2003
Retired: 9/14/2003
During 100 years of greatness, the New York
Yankees have won 26 World Championships!
Sold at New York Yankee games.
4G - $75

Champion™
#9501

Introduced: 4/4/2002
Retired: 5/24/2002
TY created Champion to celebrate the 2002
FIFA World Cup Tournament. Champion arrived
wearing 32 different flags representing each
country participating in the final phase of the
2002 FIFA World Cup Tournament.
*See Champion Buddies for a complete
listing of countries.*

Charmed™
#90067

Introduced: 12/29/2006
Current
Unicorns are said to be imaginary creatures.
We imagine you love Charmed!
4G - Current Retail Value

Charmer™
#9492

Introduced: 6/30/2003
Retired: 10/25/2006
Charmer the BEANIE BABY was the 2nd
unicorn created. Although with Mystic's 4
variations, some may consider it the 5th!
4G - $11

Charming™
#90046

Introduced: 1/31/2006
Current
Charming is waiting for her prince to come!
4G - Current Retail Value

Cheeks™
#9434

Introduced: 12/27/2001
Retired: 7/25/2002
Cheeks the Beanie Baby was named for ....
can you guess?
4G - $11

Cheery™
#9456

Introduced: 5/31/2002
Retired: 10/8/2003
Rainbows are seen in nature when two things
are present: rain and sunshine!
4G - $11

Chilly™
#9317

Introduced: 1/1/1999
Retired: 11/24/1999
Chilly the Beanie Baby
was introduced in June of 1994 and
retired in January of 1996 making
him one of the most sought after!
2G - $15 ♥ 3G - $15

Chinook™
#9605

Introduced: 7/30/2002
Retired: 1/10/2003
The warm, dry wind that blows down
the eastern slopes of the Rocky
Mountains is called a Chinook!
Canada exclusive.
4G - $18

Chip™
#9318

Introduced: 1/1/1999
Retired: 12/12/1999
Chip the Beanie Baby due to the variety
of colors and pattern shapes,
is one of the most difficult to produce.
It takes over 20 pieces to make Chip!
2G - $11 ♥ 3G - $11

Chocolate™
#9349

Introduced: 1/4/2000
Retired: 10/27/2000
Chocolate the Beanie Baby was the last of
the Original Nine to be retired!
4G - $11

Chops™
#9394

Introduced: 1/1/2001
Retired: 4/16/2001
Chops the Beanie Baby was the very first
Beanie Baby lamb created by Ty.
4G - $12

Cinders™
#9443

Introduced: 3/1/2002
Retired: 6/25/2002
Cinders the Beanie Baby was the
"polar opposite" of Aurora
the polar bear Beanie Baby!
4G - $11

Classy™
#9458

Introduced: 6/28/2002
Retired: 2/26/2004
Classy the Beanie Baby
was the sole survivor of an
elimination round and won the title
"The People's Beanie"!
4G - $11

Clover™
#9477

Introduced: 12/27/2002
Retired: 10/8/2003
Clover the Beanie Baby was the first Beanie
Baby bear commemorating St. Patrick's Day
that was not all green!
4G - $11

Clubby™
#9990

Introduced: 8/4/1999
Retired: 12/3/1999
Clubby the Beanie Baby
was not only the first BBOC Bear,
but also the first to wear a button!
3G - $11

Clubby II™
#9991

Introduced: 8/4/1999
Retired: 12/3/1999
Clubby II the Beanie Baby was the first to
be included in a BBOC Kit!
3G - $11

Clubby III™
#9993

Introduced: 9/18/2000
Retired: 12/10/2000
Clubby III the Beanie Baby is the first
BBOC Beanie Baby to be introduced
along with its Buddy counterpart!
4G - $11

Clubby IV™
#9994

Introduced: 9/24/2001
Retired: 1/23/2002
Clubby IV Beanie Baby was the first to
have several different
versions of the BBOC button!
4G - $11

Clubby V™
#9995

Introduced: 9/16/2002
Retired: 12/31/2002
The traditional gift for a fifth
anniversary is wood, but we prefer
the 5th Anniversary Edition of Clubby!
4G - $11

Clubby VI™
#99000

Introduced: 12/1/2004
Retired: 4/6/2005
Clubby VI the Beanie Buddy is a combination
of all 3 Clubby VI Beanie Babies!
Beanie Baby Official Club exclusive.
4G - $12

Colosso™
#9704

Introduced: 11/26/2003
Retired: 12/29/2005
We all loved Giganto so much that we
decided to create his pal, Colosso!
4G - $11

Congo™
#9361

Introduced: 1/4/2000
Retired: 11/10/2000
Congo the Beanie Baby was inspired by the
Ty plush gorilla George!
4G - $11

Coop™
#90072

Introduced: 1/31/2007
Retired: 2/27/2007
This chick was named after the place where
most farm chickens reside . . . a coop!
4G - $11

Coral™
#9381

Introduced: 6/24/2000
Retired: 12/31/2001
Coral the Beanie Baby shares its birthday
with Ty Warner's secretary!
4G - $11

Coreana™
#9617

Introduced: 11/10/2003
Retired: 4/15/2004
Coreana the BEANIE BABY's name
means "Korean"!
Asian-Pacific exclusive.
4G - $25

Corkie™
#90047

Introduced: 1/31/2006
Retired: 7/25/2006
Wire Fox Terriers are considered friendly,
alert, active, and lively, just like Corkie!
4G - $11

Courage™
#9503

Introduced: 5/24/2002
Retired: 7/25/2002
Courage and Rescue the Beanie Babies raised over $1 million for the New York Police & Fire Widows' & Children's Benefit Fund in the first six months!
Ty Store exclusive.
4G - $11

Cupid™
#9703

Introduced: 11/26/2003
Retired: 5/25/2004
Cupid was named for the ancient Roman god of love!
4G - $11

Curly™
#9463

Introduced: 7/30/2002
Retired: 4/28/2003
The brown bear, sometimes known as the grizzly bear, has a very thick fur coat that isn't curly at all!
4G - $11

Cutesy™
#90023

Introduced: 2/28/2005
Retired: 12/29/2005
Cutesy the Beanie Baby was named simply because it's the cutest dog ever!
4G - $11

DAD-e™
#9720

Introduced: 3/30/2004
Retired: 6/24/2004
In 1966 President Lyndon Johnson signed a presidential proclamation declaring the 3rd Sunday of June as Father's Day!
4G - $11

Darling™
#9464

Introduced: 7/30/2002
Retired: 12/29/2004
Darling is also the name of a beautiful town in South Africa!
4G - $11

Dearest™
#9448

Introduced: 3/1/2002
Retired: 9/25/2002
Dearest the Beanie Baby was created in honor of Mothers' Day.
4G - $11

Delilah™
#90026

Introduced: 3/31/2005
Retired: 12/21/2006
The ancient Egyptian word for cat is mau, which means "to see"!
4G - $11

Demure™
#90012

Introduced: 9/30/2004
Current
The name POODLE comes from the German word PUDELN, meaning "to splash in the water"!
4G - Current Retail Value

Diddley™
#9462

Introduced: 6/28/2002
Retired: 4/28/2003
The phrase "diddling around" with something, means you are toying or playing with it!
4G - $12

Digger™
#9351 · orange body

Introduced: 1/4/2000
Retired: 6/21/2000
Digger the Beanie Baby was originally made in orange and then changed to red!
4G - $12

Digger™
#9351 · tie-dye body

Introduced: 6/6/2000
Retired: 6/21/2000
Digger the Beanie Baby was originally made in orange and then changed to red!
4G - $12

268

Diggs™
#90015

Introduced: 12/30/2004
Current
Diggs was issued without a phrase.
4G - Current Retail Value

Diggs™ (large)
#90016

Introduced: 12/30/2004
Retired: 3/27/2006
The bigger the Diggs - the bigger the hugs!
4G - $25

Dippy™
#9716

Introduced: 1/30/2004
Retired: 3/15/2004
The Easter Bunny hopped into
existence during the 1700's!
4G - $11

Divalectable™
#90068

Introduced: 7/31/2006
Current
Divalectable's furry pink collar makes
her the envy of every dog!
4G - Current Retail Value

Dizzy™
#9450

Introduced: 4/1/2002
Retired: 1/9/2003
Dizzy the Beanie Baby got his name because
of the ever-changing color of his spots!
4G - $11

Docks™
#90076

Introduced: 2/28/2007
Current
Dolphins make sounds like clicking and
whistling that travel underwater to
communicate to other dolphins!
4G - Current Retail Value

Dora™
(Dora the Explorer™)
#90060

Introduced: 8/31/2006
Current
Dora loves to explore with her two best
friends - Boots . . . AND YOU!
Let's go!
¡Vamonos!
Also available at Ty Store.
4G - Current Retail Value

Dotty™
#9364

Introduced: 1/4/2000
Retired: 7/21/2000
Dotty the Beanie Baby was the second
Dalmatian produced by Ty and still
remains a favorite with collectors!
4G - $11

Dotty™ (large)
#9051

Introduced: 1/1/2001
Retired: 11/14/2001
There were two Dalmatian Beanie Babies
created:one with black ears
and one with spotted ears.
4G - $45

Dotty™ (extra-large)
#9052

Introduced: 1/1/2001
Retired: 9/5/2002
This Beanie Buddy is so big, you might
mistake him for a real dog!
4G - $75

Dragon™
#9365

Introduced: 1/4/2000
Retired: 6/13/2000
Scorch the Beanie Baby was one of the first
Beanies to feature the ty-dyed curly fabric!
4G - $11

Dublin™
#9711

Introduced: 12/30/2003
Retired: 5/25/2004
Four-leaf clovers are supposed to bring good
luck. It's lucky you've found Dublin!
4G - $15

Ears™
#9388

Introduced: 1/1/2001
Retired: 3/22/2002
Ears the Beanie Baby was the only Beanie Baby bunny ever created laying down.
4G - $12

Ears™ (large)
#9046

Introduced: 1/1/2001
Retired: 3/29/2001
Ears the Beanie Baby was never manufactured in a solid white color.
4G - $45

Ears™ (extra-large)
#9047

Introduced: 1/1/2001
Retired: 3/29/2001
Only time will tell if a new all white Ears Beanie Baby will appear!
4G - $75

Eggbert™
#9442

Introduced: 12/27/2001
Retired: 4/23/2002
Eggbert the Beanie Baby was "egg-ceptionally" difficult to make!
4G - $11

Eggs™
#9447

Introduced: 1/29/2002
Retired: 4/23/2002
There were many rumors that Eggs the Beanie Baby would be produced in different colors.
4G - $11

Employee Bear™
#9373

Introduced: 6/24/2000
Retired: 12/31/2001
The Employee Bear Beanie was the only Beanie produced without a hang tag!
4G - $12

Empress™
#9495

Introduced: 6/30/2003
Retired: 12/29/2005
In 1876, Queen Victoria of England was crowned Empress of India - a country she had never visited!
4G - $11

Erin™
#9309

Introduced: 1/1/1999
Retired: 11/19/1999
Erin the Beanie Baby is the first bear to represent a country but not wear the country's flag!
2G - $11 ♥ 3G - $11

Eucalyptus™
#9363

Introduced: 1/4/2000
Retired: 7/18/2000
Eucalyptus the Beanie Baby was the second koala to be made by Ty. He was made due to the popularity of Mel!
4G - $11

Fancy™
#9717

Introduced: 2/26/2004
Retired: 12/29/2005
Most cats have five toes on each front paw, but only four toes on each back paw!
4G - $11

Farley™
#90083

Introduced: 6/29/2007
Current
The West Highland White Terriers can easily be identified by their brilliant white coats!
4G - Current Retail Value

Ferny™
#9613

Introduced: 9/17/2002
Retired: 11/5/2003
Ferny is all black in colour with a silver fern on it's chest. The fern is a national symbol of New Zealand!
New Zealand exclusive.
4G - $35

Fetch™
#9338

Introduced: 8/31/1999
Retired: 3/10/2000
Fetch the Beanie Baby
was introduced in May of 1998 and
retired in December of 1998
when he was less than one year old!
3G - $30

Filly™
#9708

Introduced: 12/30/2003
Retired: 12/29/2005
When a horse is born it is called
a foal. Boy foals are known as
colts and girl foals are fillies!
4G - $11

First Dog™
#90078

Introduced: 4/30/2007
Current
Don't forget to vote for First Dog for the
cutest puppy in the USA!
4G - Current Retail Value

Fitz™
#90027

Introduced: 3/31/2005
Retired: 3/27/2007
The earliest ancestors of the Irish
Setter were not solid red in color but
instead red and white!
4G - $11

Fleece™
#9441

Introduced: 12/27/2001
Retired: 9/25/2002
Fleece the Beanie Baby was one of three
lambs; can you name the other two?
4G - $12

Flip™
#9359

Introduced: 1/4/2000
Retired: 1/12/2001
Flip the Beanie Baby was
reminiscent of the first item produced
by Ty. A white cat named Kashmir!
4G - $12

Flippity™
#9358

Introduced: 1/4/2000
Retired: 4/5/2000
Flippity the Beanie Baby was never made.
He is Floppity's missing twin!
4G - $11

Flitter™
#9384

Introduced: 6/24/2000
Retired: 3/22/2002
Flitter the Beanie Baby was a 1999 summer
show exclusive. This exclusivity makes
Flitter very collectible!
4G - $11

Floppity™
#9390

Introduced: 1/1/2001
Retired: 4/26/2001
Floppity the Beanie Baby was one of the "Bunny
Trio" that included Hippity and Hoppity.
4G - $12

Floxy™
#90071

Introduced: 1/31/2007
Retired: 3/27/2007
When Floxy and her friends gather
together, they're known a a flock!
4G - $11

Fraidy™
#9498

Introduced: 8/28/2003
Retired: 11/25/2003
Fraidy the Beanie Baby was the first to
have a trimmed design on its ribbon!
4G - $15

Frankenteddy™
#94006

Introduced: 9/27/2006
Retired: 11/1/2006
Frankenteddy may look scary, but he just
wants Halloween hugs from you!
Ty Store exclusive.
4G - $11

Frisbee™
#9455

Introduced: 5/31/2002
Retired: 12/27/2002
Weimaraners were originally
known as Weimer Pointers!
Also with Wham-o hang tag - $80.
4G - $19

Frisco™
#9705

Introduced: 11/26/2003
Retired: 12/29/2004
Today there are about 100 distinct
breeds of domestic cat!
4G - $12

Frolic™
#9484

Introduced: 2/28/2003
Retired: 5/25/2004
Frolic the Beanie Baby was created in
honor of a Ty employee's dog!
4G - $11

Fumbles™
#90021

Introduced: 2/28/2005
Current
Monkeys' hands and feet are highly
developed for grasping things, making
them less likely to FUMBLE!
4G - Current Retail Value

Fun™
#99001

Introduced: 10/2/2006
Retired: 1/26/2007
HAPPY ANNIVERSARY!
Did you know that the "Original 9"
Beanie Babies made their public debut
at a gift show in 1993?
In set with Laughter.
Beanie Baby Official Club exclusive.
4G - $11

Fuzz™
#9328

Introduced: 4/1/1999
Retired: 4/12/2000
Fuzz the Beanie Baby is made with Tylon that
is crimped under extremely high temperature.
3G - $11 ♥ 4G - $12

Fuzz™ (large)
#9040

Introduced: 1/4/2000
Retired: 7/26/2000
In order for Fuzz to maintain the
proper proportions, longer Tylon had to
be used. The longer the fur the more
difficult it is to distress!
4G - $45

Garfield™
#90020

Introduced: 1/31/2005
Current
Garfield the Beanie Baby was the first Beanie
to be modeled after a cartoon character!
Also available at Ty Store.
4G - Current Retail Value

Garfield™
#90074

Introduced: 3/30/2007
Current
Wake me when it's time to eat!
Also available at Ty Store.
4G - Current Retail Value

Garfield Season's Greetings™
#90063

Introduced: 9/29/2006
Retired: 12/21/2006
I've been nice . . . really!
4G - $11

Germania™
#9603

Introduced: 2/4/2000
Retired: 2/7/2001
Germania the Beanie Baby was the
first Beanie Baby to have its poem
in a language other than English!
German exclusive.
4G - $14

Ghoul™
#90058

Introduced: 8/31/2006
Retired: 10/25/2006
Trick or Treat!
4G - $11

272

Ghoulianne™
#90059

Introduced: 8/31/2006
Retired: 10/25/2006
Happy Halloween!
4G - $11

Gifts™
#90041

Introduced: 9/30/2005
Retired: 12/29/2005
You've made the "nice" list!
4G - $11

Gift-wrapped™
#90062

Introduced: 9/29/2006
Retired: 12/21/2006
A Holiday Surprise!
4G - $11

Giganto™
#9473

Introduced: 10/30/2002
Retired: 6/9/2003
Giganto the Beanie Baby was named so
because real wooly mammoths were gigantic,
weighing as much as eight tons!
4G - $20

GiGi™
#9700

Introduced: 9/30/2003
Retired: 12/29/2005
The poodle is believed to have originated
in Germany, despite being regarded as
the national dog of France!
4G - $11

Glory™
#9410

Introduced: 5/1/2001
Retired: 6/22/2001
The flag on Glory the Beanie Baby
has 12 stars and 13 stripes!
USA exclusive.
4G - $11

Gobbles™
#9333

Introduced: 8/31/1999
Retired: 12/12/1999
Gobbles the Beanie Baby
had several different types of waddles,
including single and double felt!
3G - $11

Goochy™
#9362

Introduced: 1/4/2000
Retired: 6/13/2000
Goochy the Beanie Baby's fabric was
one of the most expensive to produce.
The shine on the fabric makes the
ty-dying process more difficult!
4G - $11

Grace™
#9389

Introduced: 1/1/2001
Retired: 4/16/2001
Grace the Beanie Baby
was one of only two Beanies
to be featured in a prayerful position.
4G - $12

Groovy™
#9345

Introduced: 1/4/2000
Retired: 9/29/2000
Groovy the Beanie Baby was the first bear
to have a colored-flocked nose!
4G - $11

Gussy™
(Charlotte's Web™)
#90070

Introduced: 12/29/2006
Current
Gussy and her friend Wilbur reside
at Zuckerman's Farm!
Also available at Ty Store.
4G - Current Retail Value

Halo™
#9337

Introduced: 8/31/1999
Retired: 6/8/2000
Halo the Beanie Baby is made from a
special fabric that shimmers. This
fabric makes Halo even more heavenly!
3G - $12 ♥ 4G - $12

273

Halo II™
#9386

Introduced: 9/28/2000
Retired: 2/28/2001
Halo II the Beanie Baby's fabric is one
of the most expensive to make,
due to its special iridescent sparkle!
Variations: correct and misspelled tag.
4G - $12

Happy™
#9375

Introduced: 6/24/2000
Retired: 4/8/2002
Happy the Beanie Baby was originally
made in gray. The gray version is very
rare and is highly prized by collectors!
4G - $11

Happy Birthday™
#9491

Introduced: 6/30/2003
Retired: 9/25/2006
Happy Birthday was issued without a phrase.
4G - $11

Happy Birthday™
#90055 · blue

Introduced: 6/30/2006
Current
Happy Birthday was issued without a phrase.
4G - Current Retail Value

Happy Birthday™
#90055 · green

Introduced: 6/30/2006
Current
Happy Birthday was issued without a phrase.
4G - Current Retail Value

Haunt™
#9465

Introduced: 8/29/2002
Retired: 10/2/2002
The name jack-o'-lantern comes
from a character in British folktales!
4G - $11

Heartford™
#90014

Introduced: 11/30/2004
Retired: 1/28/2005
Heartford the Beanie Buddy sends "Lots of
Love" your way this Valentine's day!
4G - $11

Herald™
#9496

Introduced: 7/31/2003
Retired: 5/24/2006
A "herald" is an official messenger;
someone who proclaims or brings
word of happenings or events
usually to the king!
4G - $11

Herder™
#9487

Introduced: 4/30/2003
Retired: 12/29/2004
The Old English Sheepdog was originally
used for herding livestock down
the country road to the market!
4G - $11

Hero™
#9449

Introduced: 4/1/2002
Retired: 9/25/2002
Hero was the first Beanie Baby
design to wear a necktie!
4G - $11

Hero 2004™
#90004

Introduced: 5/28/2004
Retired: 7/2/2004
HERO the BEANIE BABY
salutes those men and women devoted to
establishing freedom for all!
4G - $11

Hippie™
#9357

Introduced: 1/4/2000
Retired: 4/4/2000
Hippie the Beanie Baby
was the first bunny to be ty-dyed!
4G - $11

274

Hippie™ (large)
#9039

Introduced: 1/4/2000
Retired: 4/24/2000
One large Hippie is the same size
as four Hippie Buddies!
4G - $45

Hippie™ (extra-large)
#9038

Introduced: 1/4/2000
Retired: 4/25/2000
The length of the ear on the extra large
Hippie is the same length as the Hippie Buddy!
4G - $75

Hippity™
#9324

Introduced: 1/1/1999
Retired: 12/11/1999
Hippity the Beanie Baby is a shade of
green called Spring Mint. This custom
color is very difficult to maintain
throughout production.
2G - $11 ♥ 3G - $11

Hocus™
#90038

Introduced: 8/31/2005
Retired: 11/23/2005
Hocus is the first Beanie Baby to have
a pet arachnid!
4G - $11

Hoofer™
#9472

Introduced: 10/30/2002
Retired: 9/16/2003
Clydesdale horses are known for the
large size of their hooves, which is how
Hoofer the Beanie Baby got its name!
4G - $14

Hope™
#9327

Introduced: 4/19/1999
Retired: 3/23/2000
Hope the Beanie Baby is the first Beanie Baby
to be modeled after one of Ty's plush bears!
3G - $11 ♥ 4G - $11

Hopper™
#9438

Introduced: 12/27/2001
Retired: 4/23/2002
The fabric on Hopper the Beanie Baby's
chest contains holographic fibers!
4G - $11

Hoppity™
#9439

Introduced: 12/27/2001
Retired: 4/23/2002
Hoppity was the last of the "Bunny Trio"
of Beanie Babies to be made into a Buddy;
the others were Hippity and Floppity!
4G - $13

Hornsly™
#9407

Introduced: 4/1/2001
Retired: 4/8/2002
Hornsly is the first Beanie Baby
dinosaur created with horns.
4G - $11

Hug-hug™
#94004

Introduced: 1/10/2006
Retired: 3/6/2006
Happy Valentine's Day!
Ty Store exclusive.
4G - $11

Huggy™
#9457

Introduced: 6/28/2002
Retired: 4/28/2003
When you give someone a "bear hug", you give
them a very strong and hearty embrace!
4G - $11

Humphrey™
#9307

Introduced: 9/30/1998
Retired: 12/11/1999
Humphrey the Beanie Baby was one of the
first to be retired. Very few were
produced, making him highly collectable!
1G - $12 ♥ 2G - $11 ♥ 3G - $11

Ice Skates™
#6228

Introduced: 4/30/2007
Current
On May 12, 1994, ice hockey was
officially declared to be the national
winter sport of Canada!
Canada exclusive.
4G - Current Retail Value

Inch™
#9331

Introduced: 6/26/1999
Retired: 1/1/2000
Inch the Beanie Baby was available with
both felt and yarn antennas!
3G - $11

Independence™
#90055 · blue

Introduced: 4/30/2007
Current
The Declaration of Independence measures
29-3/4 inches by 24-1/2 inches!
4G - Current Retail Value

Independence™
#90055 · red

Introduced: 4/30/2007
Current
On July 8, 1776, the first public reading
of the Declaration of Independence
took place in Philadelphia!
4G - Current Retail Value

Independence™
#90055 · white

Introduced: 4/30/2007
Current
Printed on the back of the Declaration of
Independence is, "Original Declaration of
Independence" and "4th July 1776"!
4G - Current Retail Value

India™
#9406

Introduced: 4/1/2001
Retired: 12/11/2001
India the Beanie Baby is one of only three
tiger styles ever created.
4G - $11

Inky™
#9404

Introduced: 4/1/2001
Retired: 4/26/2001
Inky the Beanie Baby was made in two
colors: can you name them?
4G - $11

Jabber™
#9326

Introduced: 4/16/1999
Retired: 12/12/1999
Jabber the Beanie Baby has 6 colors of fabric
and 17 pattern pieces which make him one of
the most difficult Beanies to produce!
3G - $11

Jake™
#9304

Introduced: 9/30/1998
Retired: 12/10/1999
Jake the Beanie Baby due to his numerous
colors was difficult to manufacture making
him one of the most sought after!
1G - $11 ♥ 2G - $11 ♥ 3G - $11

John™
#90052

Introduced: 4/28/2006
Retired: 8/25/2006
John Adams was the second President of
the United States of America!
4G - $11

Kicks™
#9343

Introduced: 1/4/2000
Retired: 6/15/2000
Kicks the Beanie Baby was the first
bear to represent a sport!
4G - $11

Kiki™
#90054

Introduced: 6/30/2006
Current
Unlike apes, most monkeys cannot swing arm-
over-arm, but move about in trees by running
along the branches on all fours!
4G - Current Retail Value

Kirby™
#9702

Introduced: 9/30/2003
Retired: 3/24/2005
The West Highland Terrier was bred in
Scotland as a hunter of foxes and badgers!
4G - $11

KISS-e™
#9507

Introduced: 1/13/2004
Retired: 3/1/2004
In medieval Italy, if a man and
a woman were seen kissing in public
they could be forced to marry!
Ty Store exclusive.
4G - $12

Kissme™
#9476

Introduced: 12/27/2002
Retired: 1/16/2004
Kissme the Beanie Baby was designed
with a very special nose...a heart!
4G - $12

Kiwiana™
#9619

Introduced: 11/10/2003
Retired: 4/15/2004
New Zealanders are known as
"kiwis" and this is how Kiwiana the
BEANIE BABY got its name!
Asian-Pacific exclusive.
4G - $25

Knuckles™
#9460

Introduced: 6/28/2002
Retired: 10/8/2003
Pigs are one of three animals
that can actually get sunburn!
4G - $14

Koowee™
#96229

Introduced: 7/6/2007
Current
Koalas sleep for 19 hours a day which only
leaves 5 hours for eating!
Australia/New Zealand exclusive.
4G - Current Retail Value

Laughter™
#99001

Introduced: 10/1/2006
Retired: 1/26/2007
HAPPY ANNIVERSARY!
Angel, Peaches, and Smokey were the very
first cats introduced by Ty in 1986!
In set with Fun.
Beanie Baby Official Club exclusive.
4G - $12

Lefty™
#9370

Introduced: 6/24/2000
Retired: 11/29/2000
Lefty and Righty the Beanie Babies were the
first two different Beanies to share a poem!
USA exclusive.
4G - $12

Legs™
#9445

Introduced: 3/1/2002
Retired: 12/27/2002
Legs the Beanie Baby was one
of the original nine Beanie Babies!
4G - $12

Li Mei™
#90033

Introduced: 5/31/2005
Current
Giant pandas weigh about 4 ounces at
birth, but when fully grown they can weigh
up to 300 pounds!
4G - Current Retail Value

Libearty™
#9371

Introduced: 6/24/2000
Retired: 1/12/2001
Libearty the Beanie Baby
was the first bear to wear a flag!
USA exclusive.
4G - $12

Libearty™ (large)
#9041

Introduced: 6/24/2000
Retired: 1/12/2001
Libearty the Beanie Baby
was the only Beanie to have
a few of his hang tags attached with
a white rather than a red tag pin!
USA exclusive.
4G - $45

Libearty™ (extra-large)
#9042

Introduced: 6/24/2000
Retired: 1/12/2001
This extra large Libearty
weighs as much as a dozen Beanie Babies!
USA exclusive.
4G - $75

Liberty™
#9488 · blue face

Introduced: 4/30/2003
Retired: 5/21/2003
Liberty, the beanie baby, was sold only in the
United States and came in three different
patriotic (red, white and blue) styles!
USA exclusive.
4G - $14

Liberty™
#9488 · red face

Introduced: 4/30/2003
Retired: 5/21/2003
Liberty, the beanie baby,was sold only in the
United States and came in three different
patriotic (red, white and blue) styles!
USA exclusive.
4G - $14

Liberty™
#9488 · white face

Introduced: 4/30/2003
Retired: 5/21/2003
Liberty, the beanie baby, was sold only in the
United States and came in three different
patriotic (red, white and blue) styles!
USA exclusive.
4G - $14

Lips™
#9355

Introduced: 1/4/2000
Retired: 9/21/2001
Lips the Beanie Baby was one of the first
summer show exclusives.This makes him
very rare and valuable!
4G - $11

Lizzy™
#9366

Introduced: 1/4/2000
Retired: 5/9/2000
Lizzy the Beanie Baby made with ty-dyed
fabric was only produced for six months,
making her one of the most valuable Beanies!
4G - $11

Loosy™
#9428

Introduced: 10/1/2001
Retired: 12/31/2001
Loosy the Beanie Baby was
created to represent the Canadian geese
that live in the United States!
4G - $11

Lucky™
#9354

Introduced: 1/4/2000
Retired: 6/13/2000
Lucky the Beanie Baby was produced
with three varieties of spots; 7 felt
spots, 11 printed spots and 21 printed
spots. Collectors are very lucky if
they have all three!
4G - $11

Luke™
#9412

Introduced: 7/3/2001
Retired: 12/11/2001
Luke the Beanie Baby was the first Beanie
Baby to have a checked ribbon!
4G - $15

Lullaby™
#9712

Introduced: 12/30/2003
Retired: 3/27/2006
A lullaby is a song that is used to relax a
child so they'll go to sleep!
4G - $11

M.C. Beanie™
#94005 · black nose

Introduced: 1/20/2006
Current
The first Beanie Baby ever to have the word
"Beanie" in its name was M.C. Beanie!
Ty MBNA exclusive.
4G - Current Retail Value

M.C. Beanie™
#94005 · brown nose

Introduced: 1/20/2006
Current
The first Beanie Baby ever to have the word
"Beanie" in its name was M.C. Beanie!
Ty MBNA exclusive.
4G - Current Retail Value

Magic™
#9466

Introduced: 8/29/2002
Retired: 2/26/2004
The Chinese people believe the dragon
is a sign of good will and prosperity!
4G - $11

Maple™
#9600

Introduced: 8/31/1999
Retired: 9/29/2000
Maple the Beanie Baby was the first
exclusive international bear!
Canada exclusive.
3G - $30 ♥ 4G - $30

Mattie™
#9481

Introduced: 12/27/2002
Retired: 10/8/2003
Mattie the Beanie Baby was named after a
pet cat owned by one of Ty's employees!
4G - $12

McWooly™
#90018

Introduced: 12/30/2004
Retired: 9/23/2005
McWooly stays nice and warm through the
winter thanks to his wool coat!
4G - $11

Meekins™
#90045

Introduced: 12/30/2005
Retired: 8/25/2006
Lambs' wool is known to be very soft . . .
just like Meekins!
4G - $11

Mellow™
#9411

Introduced: 7/3/2001
Retired: 5/24/2002
Do you know if Mellow the Beanie Baby was
produced both with and without eyebrows?
4G - $12

Millennium™
#9325

Introduced: 4/8/1999
Retired: 11/19/1999
Millennium the Beanie Baby commemorates
a once in a lifetime event, making it a once
in a lifetime Beanie Baby!
3G - $11

Mom™
#90025

Introduced: 3/31/2005
Retired: 12/29/2005
Happy Mother's Day!
4G - $11

Mooch™
#9416

Introduced: 7/31/2001
Retired: 9/13/2001
Mooch the Beanie Baby was created
in response to repeated requests
from fans for Spider Monkeys!
4G - $25

Mother™
#9718

Introduced: 2/26/2004
Retired: 6/24/2004
The earliest Mother's Day celebration
can be traced back to the spring
festival of ancient Greece!
4G - $11

Mr.™
#9714

Introduced: 1/30/2004
Retired: 12/29/2005
The groom's flower, worn on his lapel,
usually matches one of the flowers
in his bride's bouquet!
4G - $11

Mrs.™
#9715

Introduced: 1/30/2004
Retired: 12/29/2005
Traditionally, each flower in a wedding
bouquet has a special meaning!
4G - $11

Mugungwha™
#9611

Introduced: 9/17/2002
Retired: 11/5/2003
Mugungwha is the national flower of Korea. It is also known as the "Rose of Sharon"!
Korea exclusive.
4G - $25

Mum™
#9485

Introduced: 2/28/2003
Retired: 7/29/2003
Mum the Beanie Baby was the first Beanie created specifically to honor Mothers!
4G - $11

My Mom™
#90073

Introduced: 2/28/2007
Current
Love To Mom!
4G - Current Retail Value

Mystic™
#9396

Introduced: 1/1/2001
Retired: 12/11/2001
Mystic the Beanie Baby was produced with two different colored horns.
4G - $11

Nanook™
#9350

Introduced: 1/4/2000
Retired: 10/27/2000
Nanook the Beanie Baby was the first Beanie to feature blue eyes rather than black!
4G - $25

Neon™
#9417

Introduced: 7/31/2001
Retired: 9/20/2001
Neon the Beanie Baby was specifically designed to balance on his tail!
4G - $11

Nipponia™
#9606

Introduced: 5/1/2002
Retired: 12/27/2004
Nipponia the Beanie Baby's name comes from the word 'Nippon' which means 'Japan' in Japanese!
Japan exclusive.
4G - $30

Oats™
#9392

Introduced: 1/1/2001
Retired: 5/15/2001
Oats the Beanie Baby was the first horse made into a Beanie Buddy.
4G - $12

Osito™
#9344

Introduced: 1/4/2000
Retired: 10/25/2000
Osito the Beanie Baby was the first USA exclusive that did not have a US flag!
USA exclusive.
4G - $11

Parfum™
#9707

Introduced: 12/30/2003
Retired: 11/22/2006
France became most associated with perfumes around the time of the French Revolution!
4G - $12

Patti™
#9320

Introduced: 1/1/1999
Retired: 7/27/1999
Patti the Beanie Baby was one of the original nine. Patti was available in both maroon and magenta!
2G - $11 ♥ 3G - $11

Peace™
#9335 · dark original

Introduced: 8/31/1999
Retired: 6/23/2000
Peace the Beanie Baby was the first Beanie Baby with an embroidered emblem. This Ty-dye technique on a soft toy is the first in the World!
3G - $12

280

Peace™
#9335 · pastel body

Introduced: 8/31/1999
Retired: 6/23/2000
Peace the Beanie Baby was the first
Beanie Baby with an embroidered
emblem. This Ty-dye technique on
a soft toy is the first in the World!
4G - $12

Peace™ (large)
#9037

Introduced: 1/4/2000
Retired: 9/7/2000
The larger the Buddy, the longer
the fur and the more difficult
it is to ty-dye the fabric!
4G - $45

Peace™ (extra-large)
#9036

Introduced: 1/4/2000
Retired: 11/15/2001
The amount of pellets used to fill one extra
large Buddy can fill 75 Beanie Babies!
4G - $75

Peace™ (jumbo)
#9035

Introduced: 1/4/2000
Retired: 2/5/2002
It takes the same amount of fabric
to produce one jumbo Buddy as it
does to make 25 regular Buddies!
4G - $150

Peace Symbol™
#9709

Introduced: 12/30/2003
Retired: 11/24/2004
Peace Symbol Bear the BEANIE BABY's
birthday is on World Peace Day!
4G - $12

Peanut™
#9300 · light blue body

Introduced: 9/30/1998
Retired: 1/10/2000
Peanut the Beanie Baby made
in this royal blue color
is extremely rare and very valuable!
4G - $20

Peanut™
#9300 · royal blue body

Introduced: 9/30/1998
Retired: 1/10/2000
Peanut the Beanie Baby
made in this royal blue color
is extremely rare and very valuable!
1G - $20 ♥ 2G - $20 ♥ 3G - $20

Peking™
#9310

Introduced: 1/1/1999
Retired: 12/10/1999
Peking the Beanie Baby
was the first Panda made by Ty.
He was retired after only six months
making him highly collectible!
2G - $12 ♥ 3G - $12

Periwinkle™
#9415

Introduced: 7/3/2001
Retired: 4/23/2002
Collectors disagree as to whether Sunny and
Periwinkle the Beanie Babies were originally
planned to be sold via the Internet!
4G - $11

Pierre™
#9604

Introduced: 12/27/2001
Retired: 7/29/2002
Pierre the Beanie Baby was the second
bear to wear the flag of Canada!
Canada exclusive.
4G - $20

Pinchers™
#9424

Introduced: 7/31/2001
Retired: 9/20/2001
Pinchers the Beanie Baby was one of the
original nine to be introduced in 1993!
4G - $12

Pinky™
#9316

Introduced: 1/1/1999
Retired: 12/12/1999
Pinky the Beanie Baby was a manufacturing
challenge because of her long neck!
2G - $11 ♥ 3G - $11

Ponder™
#90085

Introduced: 6/29/2007
Current
Frogs belong to a group of animals called amphibians!
4G - Current Retail Value

Poofie™
#9461

Introduced: 6/28/2002
Retired: 11/24/2004
The title, "Best in Show", means you have won the Grand Prize in a dog show!
4G - $11

Pooky™
#90019

Introduced: 1/31/2005
Current
Garfield thinks that Pooky the Beanie Buddy is even more huggable than Pooky the Beanie Baby!
Also available at Ty Store.
4G - Current Retail Value

Pooky™
#90042 · with hat

Introduced: 9/30/2005
Retired: 12/29/2005
The holidays wouldn't be the same without Pooky wearing his festive hat!
4G - $11

Poopsie™
#9444

Introduced: 12/27/2001
Retired: 12/27/2002
Poopsie the Beanie Baby was one of the most controversial bears ever produced!
4G - $11

Poseidon™
#9490

Introduced: 4/30/2003
Retired: 2/26/2004
Poseidon, the beanie baby, was named after the mythological Greek god of the sea!
4G - $15

Pouch™
#9380

Introduced: 6/24/2000
Retired: 4/8/2002
Pouch the Beanie Baby's pattern was used to create this kangaroo's "joey"!
4G - $11

Pounce™
#9436

Introduced: 3/1/2002
Retired: 12/27/2002
Pounce was the first Beanie Baby cat that was made of Ty-dyed fabric!
4G - $11

Prince™
#9401

Introduced: 1/1/2001
Retired: 9/21/2001
Prince the Beanie Baby is twice as big as Legs.
4G - $11

Princess™
#9329

Introduced: 4/23/1999
Retired: 4/10/2000
Princess Approved for Charity on behalf of the Estate of DIANA, PRINCESS OF WALES.
3G - $12

Pugsly™
#9413

Introduced: 7/3/2001
Retired: 8/6/2001
Pugsly the Beanie Baby was difficult to produce because of the wrinkles in his face!
4G - $25

Pumkin'™
#9332

Introduced: 8/31/1999
Retired: 11/29/1999
Pumkin' the Beanie Baby was the first Beanie to represent a vegetable!
3G - $11

282

Purr™
#9451

Introduced: 5/1/2002
Retired: 4/30/2004
Cats are known to purr when they are happy,
but no-one knows exactly how they do it!
4G - $11

Quackers™
#9302 · no wings

Introduced: 9/30/1998
Retired: 7/21/1999
Quackers the Beanie Baby retired in May
1998, was once made without wings!
3G - $175

Quackers™
#9302 · with wings

Introduced: 9/30/1998
Retired: 7/21/1999
Quackers the Beanie Baby retired in May
1998, was once made without wings!
1G - $12 ♥ 2G - $12 ♥ 3G - $12

Quivers™
#94001

Introduced: 9/27/2004
Retired: 11/1/2004
Spooky the Beanie Baby was the first ghost
Beanie, but Quivers is the first ghost-bear!
Ty Store exclusive.
4G - $12

Radar™
#9422

Introduced: 9/3/2001
Retired: 11/28/2001
Radar is the first Beanie Baby
whose name is a palindrome!
4G - $12

Rainbow™
#9367

Introduced: 1/4/2000
Retired: 12/31/2001
Rainbow the Beanie Baby and his friend
Iggy loved to switch tags and colors, making
them the most confusing pair to date!
4G - $11

Ratzo™
#90039

Introduced: 8/31/2005
Retired: 11/23/2005
More than 35 million pounds of candy
corn is produced a year, clearly
that's plenty for Ratzo to share!
4G - $11

Red™
#90001

Introduced: 4/29/2004
Retired: 11/24/2004
Betsy Ross, who stitched together the first
American Flag, was asked to do so
by George Washington!
4G - $11

Regal™
#9433

Introduced: 12/27/2001
Retired: 12/27/2002
Regal the Beanie Baby escaped from the
factory before his red collar could be put on!
4G - $12

Rescue™
#9502

Introduced: 5/24/2002
Retired: 7/25/2002
Rescue and Courage the Beanie Babies
raised over $1 million for the New York
Police & Fire Widows' & Children's
Benefit Fund in the first six months!
Ty Store exclusive.
4G - $14

Rex™
#9368

Introduced: 5/1/2000
Retired: 6/21/2000
Rex the Beanie Baby was one of the
dinosaur trio. The poem and birthday for
this item have yet to be discovered!
4G - $12

Righty™
#9369

Introduced: 6/24/2000
Retired: 11/29/2000
Lefty and Righty the Beanie Babies were the
first two different Beanies to share a poem!
USA exclusive.
4G - $12

Roam™
#9378

Introduced: 6/24/2000
Retired: 12/31/2001
The only Beanie Buddy created in the
likeness of an original Beanie Baby -
but in a different color!
4G - $11

Romance™
#9475

Introduced: 12/27/2002
Retired: 2/24/2003
Romance the Beanie Baby was the
first Valentine bear designed
in the "pot belly" style!
4G - $11

Romeo & Juliet™
#90066

Introduced: 11/30/2006
Retired: 12/21/2006
These two loving monkeys were named
after the William Shakespeare classic
Romeo & Juliet!
4G - $12

Rover™
#9305

Introduced: 9/30/1998
Retired: 12/12/1999
Rover the Beanie Baby was the first non-breed
dog. Introduced in the summer of 1996
this red color set him apart!
1G - $12 ♥ 2G - $12 ♥ 3G - $12

Roxie™
#90011

Introduced: 9/30/2004
Retired: 10/27/2004
Both male and female reindeer have antlers !
4G - $12

Rufus™
#9393

Introduced: 1/1/2001
Retired: 9/13/2001
Rufus the Beanie Baby was inspired by a
puppy that Ty remembered as a child.
4G - $15

Sakura™
#9608

Introduced: 2/19/2001
Retired: 7/26/2001
Sakura, created as a Japanese exclusive,
was the first all pink Beanie Baby bear.
Japan exclusive.
4G - $22

Sakura II™
#9610

Introduced: 9/17/2002
Retired: 8/30/2004
Sakura, the flower, has been a favorite
theme for Japanese poets for centuries!
Japan exclusive.
4G - $22

Sam™
#90030 · blue

Introduced: 4/29/2005
Retired: 9/23/2005
In 1817, the Philadelphia Post published a
story claiming that Uncle Sam was simply a
play on the United States initials U.S.!
4G - $12

Sam™
#90030 · red

Introduced: 4/29/2005
Retired: 9/23/2005
A famous portrait of Uncle Sam was used
by the U.S. Army on a recruiting poster
during World War I!
4G - $12

Sam™
#90030 · white

Introduced: 4/29/2005
Retired: 9/23/2005
Some credit Samuel Wilson with creating
"Uncle Sam." He was an inspector of army
supplies and stamped all inspected goods
with the words "UNCLE SAM"!
4G - $12

Sampson™
#9710

Introduced: 12/30/2003
Retired: 6/23/2006
When a dog barks it's signaling
that you should be alert!
4G - $11

284

Santa™
#9385

Introduced: 9/28/2000
Retired: 11/17/2000
Santa the Beanie Baby has shed
his green mittens and changed
the color of the trim on his hat!
4G - $11

Scared-e™
#9497

Introduced: 8/28/2003
Retired: 10/31/2003
Scard-e was created with the exact opposite
coloring of Fraidy the Beanie Baby!
4G - $20

Schnitzel™
#9493

Introduced: 6/30/2003
Retired: 6/24/2004
Schnitzel the BEANIE BABY's favorite
treat is Wiener schnitzel, which is a breaded
veal cutlet that is seasoned or garnished!
4G - $11

Schweetheart™
#9330

Introduced: 6/26/1999
Retired: 1/1/2000
Schweetheart the Beanie Baby has fabric
that is tip dyed. It is made with a special
dying process where only the very tips
are dyed a separate color. It is a very
costly and difficult process!
3G - $15

Schweetheart™ (large)
#9043

Introduced: 6/24/2000
Retired: 1/24/2007
Schweetheart's hand-painted eyes are
very distinctive. The larger the eye,
the more skillful the painter must be!
4G - $45

Schweetheart™ (extra-large)
#9044

Introduced: 6/24/2000
Retired: 1/24/2007
This extra large Schweetheart is almost
the same size as a real orangutan!
4G - $75

Schweetheart™ (jumbo)
#9045

Introduced: 6/24/2000
Retired: 11/20/2001
Ty hadn't originally planned to make
Schweetheart this big, but his staff insisted
that he try it! What do you think?
4G - $175

Scoop™
#90003

Introduced: 4/29/2004
Retired: 3/24/2005
Scoop was issued without a phrase.
4G - $11

Seal™
#9419

Introduced: 7/3/2001
Retired: 3/22/2002
This Beanie Baby was the first and youngest
of two Beanie Baby seals made by Ty!
4G - $11

Secret™
#94002

Introduced: 1/12/2005
Retired: 3/18/2005
This Beanie Buddy isn't one for keeping a
Secret; he displays his feelings for all to see!
Ty Store exclusive.
4G - $12

Shamrock™
#9431

Introduced: 12/27/2001
Retired: 5/24/2002
Shamrock proudly wears a symbol of Irish
luck and good fortune on his chest!
4G - $11

Shamrock™ (large)
#9055

Introduced: 12/27/2001
Retired: 12/26/2003
Shamrock is an Irish word
that means "little clover"!
4G - $45

Shamrock™ (extra-large)
#9056

Introduced: 12/27/2001
Retired: 12/26/2003
Does an Extra Large Shamrock
bring extra good luck?
4G - $75

Sherbet™
#9482 · light green body

Introduced: 2/28/2003
Retired: 4/29/2004
Sherbet the Beanie Baby was
designed to be a 3-piece collection
resembling rainbow sherbet!
4G - $15

Sherbet™
#9482 · light yellow body

Introduced: 2/28/2003
Retired: 4/29/2004
Sherbet the Beanie Baby was
designed to be a 3-piece collection
resembling rainbow sherbet!
4G - $15

Sherbet™
#9486 · lilac body

Introduced: 5/29/2003
Retired: 12/29/2004
Sherbet the Beanie Baby was originally
designed to be a 3-piece collection
resembling rainbow sherbet!
4G - $15

Sherbet™
#9486 · pink body

Introduced: 5/29/2003
Retired: 12/29/2004
Sherbet the Beanie Baby was originally
designed to be a 3-piece collection
resembling rainbow sherbet!
4G - $15

Siam™
#9483

Introduced: 2/28/2003
Retired: 11/24/2004
The country of Thailand was
formerly known as Siam!
4G - $11

Silver™
#9340

Introduced: 8/31/1999
Retired: 5/19/2000
Silver and Amber the Beanie Babies
were modeled after two orphaned
kittens found by Ty Warner!
3G - $14

Singabear™
#9620

Introduced: 11/10/2003
Retired: 4/15/2004
In Malay "singa" means "lion"; the
symbol of Singapore!
Asian-Pacific exclusive.
4G - $25

Sizzle™
#9432

Introduced: 12/27/2001
Retired: 2/11/2002
Sizzle the Beanie Baby was named because
of his vibrant red fur... he's red hot!
4G - $11

Slither™
#9339

Introduced: 8/31/1999
Retired: 5/26/2000
Slither the Beanie Baby was the first snake
made by Ty. Since his retirement in 1995
he has learned how to coil!
3G - $12

Smooch™
#9430

Introduced: 12/27/2001
Retired: 2/11/2002
A Ty Employee actually made the kiss print
that is featured on Smooch's fabric!
4G - $12

Smoochy™
#9315

Introduced: 1/1/1999
Retired: 11/24/1999
Smoochy the Beanie Baby is the second
Beanie Baby frog made by Ty!
2G - $12 ♥ 3G - $12

Sneaky™
#9376

Introduced: 6/24/2000
Retired: 8/12/2004
Sneaky the Beanie Baby has very detailed paws. This attention to detail makes Sneaky very difficult to manufacture!
4G - $11

Snort™
#9311

Introduced: 1/1/1999
Retired: 12/12/1999
Snort the Beanie Baby is the second bull made by Ty. The first bull did not have hooves!
2G - $11 ♥ 3G - $11

Snowball™
#9429

Introduced: 10/1/2001
Retired: 12/31/2001
Snowball is one of the few Beanie Babies wearing a scarf instead of a ribbon. Do you know the others?
4G - $12

Snowboy™
#9342

Introduced: 8/31/1999
Retired: 12/12/1999
Snowboy the Beanie Baby was never made. This is the first and only time this pattern will be used!
3G - $12

Soar™
#9489

Introduced: 5/29/2003
Retired: 6/10/2003
The bald eagle has been the national symbol of the United States since June 20, 1782!
USA exclusive.
4G - $15

Spangle™
#9336

Introduced: 8/31/1999
Retired: 6/15/2000
Spangle the Beanie Baby is the first Beanie to feature two distinct patterned fabrics and three different head colors!
3G - $14 ♥ 4G - $14

Speckles™
#9500

Introduced: 1/10/2002
Retired: 4/5/2002
Speckles was the first Beanie Baby sold only on Ty's website!
Ty Store exclusive.
4G - $12

Speedy™
#9352

Introduced: 1/4/2000
Retired: 5/9/2000
Speedy the Beanie Baby was one of the first Beanie Babies to feature printed fabric!
4G - $12

Spinner™
#9334

Introduced: 8/31/1999
Retired: 12/12/1999
Spinner the Beanie Baby was the second spider to be made by Ty. The attention to detail includes a tiger striped body and red eyes!
3G - $11

SpongeBob Squarepants™
#90048

Introduced: 2/28/2006
Current
SpongeBob likes dancing to loading zone announcements!
Or
SpongeBob is ambidextrous!
2 different comments.
Also available at Ty Store.
4G - Current Retail Value

SpongeBob FrankenStein™
#90057

Introduced: 8/31/2006
Current
When SpongeBob's self-portrait comes to life in the episode entitled Frankendoodle, chaos ensues!
4G - Current Retail Value

SpongeBob Squarepants™ Patrick Star™
#90049

Introduced: 2/28/2006
Current
Patrick once entered a rock in a race!
Or
Patrick went to Community College!
2 different comments.
Also available at Ty Store.
4G - Current Retail Value

SpongeBob's Pineapple Home™
#90035

Introduced: 2/28/2005
Retired: 12/21/2006
HOMETOWN: Located in beautiful Bikini Bottom, this spacious two-story fruit bungalow is the perfect starter home for any sponge!
SUPER ABSORBENT TRIVIA: When SpongeBob's home was destroyed he decides he should move back in with his parents!
4G - $12

Spooky™
#9421

Introduced: 9/3/2001
Retired: 11/27/2001
Spooky the Beanie Baby was made in two versions: with and without his red felt mouth!
4G - $11

Sport™
#90031

Introduced: 6/30/2005
Retired: 12/21/2006
Our friend Sport just loves to play, and catch is his favorite game!
4G - $11

Spring™
#9478

Introduced: 12/27/2002
Retired: 4/29/2004
The original prototype of Spring the Beanie Baby was white instead of blue!
Which color do you prefer?
4G - $11

Spunky™
#9400

Introduced: 1/1/2001
Retired: 6/14/2001
Spunky the Beanie Baby got his name because of the "spunky" nature of Cocker Spaniels.
4G - $18

Squealer™
#9313

Introduced: 1/1/1999
Retired: 11/24/1999
Squealer the Beanie Baby was one of the original nine. Squealer was so popular that he didn't retire for over four years!
2G - $12 ♥ 3G - $12

Star™
#90036 · blue star

Introduced: 9/30/2005
Retired: 5/24/2006
Our friend Star is a special Beanie Buddy that will watch over you!
4G - $12

Star™
#90036 · gold star

Introduced: 9/30/2005
Retired: 5/24/2006
Our friend Star is a special Beanie Buddy that will watch over you!
4G - $12

Starlett™
#9459

Introduced: 6/28/2002
Retired: 7/29/2003
Cats are the most common house pets in America!
4G - $12

Steg™
#9383

Introduced: 6/24/2000
Retired: 8/30/2000
Steg the Beanie Baby was part of the dino trio. He is highly sought after and very collectible!
4G - $12

Stretch™
#9303

Introduced: 9/30/1998
Retired: 12/12/1999
Stretch the Beanie Baby is one of the most difficult to produce due to her long neck and numerous parts!
1G - $12 ♥ 2G - $12 ♥ 3G - $12

Sunburst™
#90077

Introduced: 2/28/2007
Current
Our pal Sunburst may be a crab, but he certainly has a sunny disposition!
due to her long neck and numerous parts!
4G - Current Retail Value

Sundar™
#90034

Introduced: 5/31/2005
Current
Snow leopards use their long tail for balance
and warmth in cold weather!
4G - Current Retail Value

Sunny™
#9414

Introduced: 7/3/2001
Retired: 4/23/2002
Sunny and Periwinkle the Beanie Babies
were introduced and then retired
only one week later!
4G - $12

Sweetest™
#94000

Introduced: 9/15/2004
Retired: 2/28/2005
The earliest known celebration of Sweetest
Day took place in Cleveland, Ohio in 1922!
Ty Store exclusive.
4G - $12

Swoop™
#9391

Introduced: 1/1/2001
Retired: 12/31/2001
Swoop the Beanie Baby was the fourth
dinosaur Beanie Baby made by Ty.
4G - $11

Tangerine™
#9418 · plush fabric

Introduced: 9/3/2001
Retired: 5/24/2002
Will there ever be a Tangerine
the Beanie Baby?
4G - $12

Tangerine™
#9418 · terry cloth

Introduced: 9/3/2001
Retired: 5/24/2002
Will there ever be a Tangerine
the Beanie Baby?
4G - $12

Teddy™
#9306 · cranberry body

Introduced: 9/30/1998
Retired: 11/17/1999
Teddy the Beanie Baby was made in six colors.
A very limited number were produced
in this special cranberry color!
1G - $11 ♥ 2G - $11 ♥ 3G - $11

Teddy™
#9372 · teal body

Introduced: 6/24/2000
Retired: 4/8/2002
The Teddy teal Beanie Baby was
produced with this style face.
Commonly referred to as an "old faced"
teddy, his value continues to grow!
4G - $11

The Beginning™
#9399

Introduced: 1/1/2001
Retired: 4/16/2001
The Beginning Bear Beanie Baby
marked the beginning of a new
millennium of Beanie Babies.
4G - $11

The Cardinal™
#9395

Introduced: 1/1/2001
Retired: 5/15/2001
The cardinal Beanie Baby's wings were
originally supposed to be black tipped.
4G - $11

Thomas™
#90050

Introduced: 4/28/2006
Retired: 8/25/2006
Thomas Jefferson authored the
Declaration of Independence!
4G - $11

Thunderbolt™
#90065

Introduced: 11/30/2006
Current
Horses are measured in "hands"; one hand
equals approximately 4 inches!
4G - Current Retail Value

Top Dog™
#90024

Introduced: 3/31/2005
Retired: 10/21/2005
Happy Father's Day!
4G - $12

Tracker™
#9319

Introduced: 1/1/1999
Retired: 11/29/1999
Tracker the Beanie Baby has the most
expressive eyes. Close attention to this
detail means limited production.
2G - $20 ♥ 3G - $20

Tradee™
#9504

Introduced: 4/30/2002
Retired: 5/21/2002
Tradee the Beanie Baby was designed as an
introduction to the Beanie Board of Trade!
Ty Store exclusive.
4G - $12

Tradition™
No Style #

Introduced: 9/25/2005
Retired: 9/25/2005
The interlocking NY symbol made its debut
on the Yankees uniforms in 1909!
Sold at New York Yankee games.
4G - $75

Trotter™
#9446

Introduced: 12/27/2001
Retired: 9/5/2002
Trotter is one of a few Beanie Buddies
introduced without a companion Beanie Baby.
Can you name the others?
4G - $30

True™
#96223

Introduced: 4/28/2006
Current
The maple leaf became the official
national symbol of Canada when the
current flag was introduced in 1965!
Canada exclusive.
4G - Current Retail Value

Trumpet™
#9403

Introduced: 4/1/2001
Retired: 8/6/2001
Trumpet the Beanie Baby was the first
elephant made in a sitting position.
4G - $15

Tumba™
#90080

Introduced: 5/31/2007
Current
Gorillas do not drink water; they receive
plenty of moisture from all the foliage
that they eat!
4G - Current Retail Value

Tumba™ (large)
#90081

Introduced: 5/31/2007
Current
At birth a gorilla normally weighs 4-5 pounds,
but as an adult can weigh in at 500 pounds!
4G - Current Retail Value

Twigs™
#9308

Introduced: 9/30/1998
Retired: 12/31/1998
Twigs the Beanie Baby was manufactured in
fabric created exclusively for Ty
and was retired in May 1998!
1G - $110 ♥ 2G - $110

Twitch™
#90028

Introduced: 4/29/2005
Retired: 8/26/2005
Baby guinea pigs are born with fur, teeth
and their eyes open!
4G - $20

Ty 2K™
#9346

Introduced: 1/4/2000
Retired: 3/8/2000
Ty 2K the Beanie Baby's name was the result
of a play on words with Y2K!
4G - $12

Unity™
#9609

Introduced: 10/1/2001
Current
The twelve stars on Unity's chest
represent the original twelve member
countries in the European Union!
Europe exclusive.
4G - $18

USA™
#9453

Introduced: 4/30/2002
Retired: 7/25/2002
The colors of the U.S. flag; red, white and blue,
stand for valor, purity and perseverance!
USA exclusive.
4G - $11

Valentina™
#9397

Introduced: 1/1/2001
Retired: 3/16/2001
Valentina the Beanie Baby
is the true love of Valentino.
4G - $11

Valentina™ (large)
#9048

Introduced: 1/1/2001
Retired: 3/16/2001
Valentina the Beanie Baby
was born on Valentine's Day.
4G - $45

Valentina™ (extra-large)
#9049

Introduced: 1/1/2001
Retired: 3/16/2001
Extra Large Valentina's heart
is twice as large as
Valentina the Beanie Baby's heart!
4G - $75

Valentina™ (jumbo)
#9050

Introduced: 1/1/2001
Retired: 3/16/2001
Jumbo Valentina is so large
that she is shipped in her own box!
4G - $175

Valentino™
#9347

Introduced: 1/4/2000
Retired: 6/8/2000
Valentino the Beanie Baby was the first
bear to feature embroidery!
4G - $11

Valor™
#90005

Introduced: 5/28/2004
Retired: 7/2/2004
President George W. Bush, along with
Congress declared September 11th
of each year as "Patriot Day"!
4G - $12

Vanda™
#9614

Introduced: 9/17/2002
Retired: 11/5/2003
Vanda Miss Joaquim is the full name of
Singapore's national flower. It is commonly
recognized as a unique variety of orchid!
Singapore exclusive.
4G - $25

Veggies™
#90044

Introduced: 12/30/2005
Retired: 5/24/2006
Veggies is always willing to share an
extra carrot with you!
4G - $11

Waddle™
#9314

Introduced: 1/1/1999
Retired: 12/12/1999
Waddle the Beanie Baby was the first of
two penguins to be made by Ty.
He was retired in April of 1998!
2G - $11 ♥ 3G - $11

Wallace™
#9387

Introduced: 9/28/2000
Retired: 1/12/2001
Wallace the Beanie Baby wore a tartan plaid
scarf. Can you guess which clan?
4G - $11

Wattlie™
#9612

Introduced: 9/17/2002
Retired: 11/5/2003
Wattlie named after the spring flowers
of the wattle bush and is regarded
as the national flower of Australia!
Australia exclusive.
4G - $25

Webley™
#90075

Introduced: 3/30/2007
Current
Frogs can live almost anywhere on Earth, but
our friend Webley prefers to live with you!
4G - Current Retail Value

Weenie™
#9356

Introduced: 1/4/2000
Retired: 5/26/2000
Weenie the Beanie Baby was the first
Beanie to stand on all four paws!
4G - $17

White™
#90001

Introduced: 4/29/2004
Retired: 11/24/2004
Betsy Ross, who stitched together the
first American Flag, was asked to do so
by George Washington!
4G - $11

White Tiger™
#9374

Introduced: 6/24/2000
Retired: 4/16/2002
The White tiger Beanie Baby's name was
inspired by the winter weather in Chicago!
4G - $17

Whittle™
#90022

Introduced: 2/28/2005
Retired: 12/21/2006
Bears are omnivores - meaning they'll eat
almost anything - but our friend Whittle's
favorite treat is honey!
4G - $11

Wilbur™
(Charlotte's Web™)
#90069

Introduced: 12/29/2006
Current
Wilbur, along with his friend Gussy, resides
at Zuckerman's Farm!
Also available at Ty Store.
4G - Current Retail Value

Wirabear™
#9621

Introduced: 11/10/2003
Retired: 4/15/2004
Wirabear the BEANIE BABY was dedicated
to Malaysian hero, Hang Tuah!
Asian-Pacific exclusive.
4G - $25

Woody™
#9499

Introduced: 8/28/2003
Retired: 5/25/2004
Woody the Beanie Baby was one of
the softest Beanie bears ever made!
4G - $12

World Class™
No Style #

Introduced: 8/8/2004
Retired: 8/8/2004
On March 30, 2004, the New York Yankees
opened their regular season in Tokyo, Japan!
Sold at New York Yankee games.
4G - $75

World Class 2nd™
No Style #

Introduced: 9/24/2004
Retired: 9/25/2005
The New York Yankees played their first game
at Yankee Stadium on April 18, 1923!
Sold at New York Yankee games.
4G - $75

Wrinkles™
#9440

Introduced: 3/1/2002
Retired: 12/27/2002
Wrinkles the Beanie Baby took a long time
to make, due to all the wrinkles in his face!
4G - $11

Y Ddraig Goch™
#96224

Introduced: 8/15/2006
Current
'Cymru Am Byth' means 'Wales Forever'!
UK exclusive.
4G - Current Retail Value

Yankees Pride™
No Style

Introduced: 10/1/2006
Retired: 10/1/2006
The Yankees' 26 World Championships and 39
American League Pennants are more than any
other team in Major League Baseball history!
Sold at New York Yankee games.
4G - $75

Yapper™
#90029

Introduced: 4/29/2005
Current
Yorkshire Terriers usually weigh between
4 ½ and 6 ½ pounds !
4G - Current Retail Value

Zeus™
#90006

Introduced: 6/30/2004
Retired: 3/24/2005
Moose may grow to be 7 feet tall and
1,500 pounds. Our Zeus has a lot of
growing up to do!
4G - $12

Zip™
#9360

Introduced: 1/4/2000
Retired: 2/27/2001
Zip the Beanie Baby was made in three styles;
all white, black and white and all black!
4G - $12

NOTES

Champion™ Buddies

Like the Beanie Babies, Champion Beanie Buddies wear the flag of one of the 2002 World Cup participating countries and have information about that country on their hang tag.
Introduced: 4/4/2002 ♥ Retired: 5/24/2002

Argentina
4G - $12

Belgium
4G - $12

Brazil
4G - $12

Cameroon
4G - $12

China PR
4G - $12

Costa Rica
4G - $11

Croatia
4G - $11

Denmark
4G - $11

Ecuador
4G - $11

England
4G - $11

France
4G - $11

Germany
4G - $11

Italy
4G - $11

Japan
4G - $11

Mexico
4G - $11

Nigeria	Paraguay	Poland

4G - $11	4G - $11	4G - $11

Portugal	Republic of Ireland	Republic of Korea
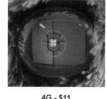		
4G - $11	4G - $11	4G - $11

Russia	Saudi Arabia	Senegal

4G - $11	4G - $11	4G - $11

Slovenia	South Africa	Spain

4G - $11	4G - $11	4G - $11

Sweden	Tunisia	Turkey
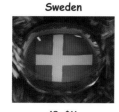		
4G - $11	4G - $11	4G - $11

Uruguay	USA	

4G - $11	4G - $11	

ANGELINE™

Angeline is in a category all by herself. She is a precious little angel doll with her very own sweet tale, "A Story of Love" to tell. What a beautiful bedtime story for parents to share with small children as they cuddle up to this cutie! Angeline comes in several sizes, including Ty Key-clips.

Angeline™
#63001

Introduced: 3/4/2005
Retired: 11/29/2005
1G - $7.00

Angeline™ Key-clip
#63008

Introduced: 3/4/2005
Retired: 11/29/2005
1Gsm - $4.00

Gift Bag™
#63010

Introduced: 3/4/2005
Retired
With tissue.
$3.00

Happy Birthday™
#63006

Introduced: 3/4/2005
Retired: 11/29/2005
1G - $8.00

Happy Holidays™
#63019

Introduced: 9/30/2005
Retired: 12/30/2005
2G - $8.00

Happy Valentine's Day™
#63028

Introduced: 12/30/2005
Retired: 3/27/2006
2G - $8.00

Holiday Angeline™
#63018

Introduced: 9/30/2005
Retired: 12/30/2005
2G - $8.00

Holiday Angeline™ (large)
#63012

Introduced: 9/30/2005
Retired: 12/30/2005
2G - $15.00

Holiday Angeline™ Key-clip
#63020

Introduced: 9/30/2005
Retired: 12/30/2005
2Gsm - $6.00

Holiday Gift Bag™
#63021

Introduced: 9/30/2005
Retired: 12/30/2005
With tissue.
$4.00

I Love You™
#63003

Introduced: 3/4/2005
Retired: 11/29/2005
1G - $8.00

Just for You™
#63005

Introduced: 3/4/2005
Retired: 11/29/2005
1G - $8.00

Spring Angeline™
#63035

Introduced: 4/28/2006
Retired: 7/25/2006
2G - $8.00

Spring Angeline™ (large)
#63036

Introduced: 4/28/2006
Retired: 7/25/2006
2G - $15.00

Spring Angeline (You're an Angel)™
#63037

Introduced: 3/4/2005
Retired: 7/25/2006
2G - $8.00

Story Book™
#66000

Introduced: 3/4/2005
Current
1G - Current Retail Value

To Cheer You™
#63002

Introduced: 3/4/2005
Retired: 11/29/2005
1G - $8.00

Valentine Angeline™
#63026

Introduced: 12/30/2005
Retired: 3/27/2006
2G - $8.00

Valentine Angeline™ (large)
#63030

Introduced: 12/30/2005
Retired: 3/27/2006
2G - $15.00

You are Special™
#63007

Introduced: 3/4/2005
Retired: 11/29/2005
1G - $8.00

You're an Angel™
#63004

Introduced: 3/4/2005
Retired: 11/29/2005
1G - $8.00

BEANiE KiDS™

Beanie kids, first available in early 2000, were Ty's first departure from plush animals into doll making. Children around the world can relate to Beanie Kids, with their dimples, lifelike skin in varying shades, detailed fingers and toes and even realistic belly buttons! Each comes with a name, a birthday and a poem all its own.

Angel™
#0001 · elastic fastener

Birthday: 3/29/1994
Introduced: 1/8/2000
Retired: 12/27/2002
Be my best friend and then you will see,
how very, very special you are to me!
2G - $8

Angel™
#0001 · velcro fastener

Birthday: 3/29/1994
Introduced: 1/8/2000
Retired: 12/27/2002
Be my best friend and then you will see,
how very, very special you are to me!
1G - $10

BABE-e™
#0024

Birthday: 1/1/2003
Introduced: 12/16/2002
Retired: 1/20/2003
My fondest wish for you and me;
a healthy, happy 2003!
Ty Store exclusive.
2G - $9

Baby 2002™
#0022

Birthday: 1/1/2002
Introduced: 11/30/2001
Retired: 1/1/2002
My fondest wish has just come true
To spend a brand new year with you!
2G - $10

Blondie™
#0017

Birthday: 1/2/1995
Introduced: 1/1/2001
Retired: 12/27/2002
Please dress me up and take me out,
making friends is what it's all about!
2G - $8

Boomer™
#0007

Birthday: 8/11/1994
Introduced: 1/8/2000
Retired: 1/25/2002
I like being noisy, it's lots of fun,
then I get attention from everyone!
1G - $8 ♥ 2G - $8

Buzz™
#0010

Birthday: 11/24/1997
Introduced: 6/24/2000
Retired: 12/27/2002
My hair is short, so is my name
Please take me home
and we'll play a game!
2G - $8

Calypso™
#0011

Birthday: 6/28/1997
Introduced: 6/24/2000
Retired: 12/27/2002
Please be my friend, give me a chance
We'll sing all day and then we'll dance!
2G - $8

Chipper™
#0008

Birthday: 7/20/1997
Introduced: 1/8/2000
Retired: 8/11/2000
Happy and cheerful, big hugs for all,
smiling and laughing - life is a ball!
1G - $8 ♥ 2G - $8

Cookie™
#0013

Birthday: 4/5/1995
Introduced: 6/24/2000
Retired: 12/27/2002
My name is Cookie and you'll agree
I'm as sweet as sweet can be!
2G - $8

Curly™
#0004 · elastic fastener

Birthday: 3/2/1997
Introduced: 1/8/2000
Retired: 8/10/2000
My curly hair is a sight to see,
a pretty bow makes me cute as can be!
2G - $8

Curly™
#0004 · velcro fastener

Birthday: 3/2/1997
Introduced: 1/8/2000
Retired: 8/10/2000
My curly hair is a sight to see,
a pretty bow makes me cute as can be!
1G - $10

Cutie™
#0005 · elastic fastener

Birthday: 12/26/1996
Introduced: 1/8/2000
Retired: 1/25/2002
I can't help but give you a hug,
in your arms is where I feel snug!
1G - $8

Cutie™
#0005 · velcro fastener

Birthday: 12/26/1996
Introduced: 1/8/2000
Retired: 1/25/2002
I can't help but give you a hug,
in your arms is where I feel snug!
2G - $10

Dumplin'™
#0023

Birthday: 4/2/1995
Introduced: 4/1/2002
Retired: 12/27/2002
Being outside is so much fun
Let's have a picnic in the sun!
2G - $9

Ginger™
#0003 · elastic fastener

Birthday: 6/12/1992
Introduced: 1/8/2000
Retired: 12/27/2002
Everyone says I'm all sugar and spice,
so when we play, I'll always be nice!
2G - $8

Ginger™
#0003 · velcro fastener

Birthday: 6/12/1992
Introduced: 1/8/2000
Retired: 12/27/2002
Everyone says I'm all sugar and spice,
so when we play, I'll always be nice!
1G - $10

Jammer™
#0016

Birthday: 7/9/1992
Introduced: 1/1/2001
Retired: 1/25/2002
Take me home and you'll agree
I'm as cool as I can be!
2G - $8

Luvie™
#0014

Birthday: 2/14/1994
Introduced: 1/1/2001
Retired: 12/27/2002
All my love I give to you
I hope you love me that much too!
2G - $9

Noelle™
#0020

Birthday: 12/10/1994
Introduced: 10/1/2001
Retired: 1/1/2002
Family, friends and lots of cheer
This is my favorite time of year!
2G - $12

Precious™
#0002 · elastic fastener

Birthday: 5/15/1993
Introduced: 1/8/2000
Retired: 6/25/2002
Hey, look at me and give me a smile,
take me home and we'll play awhile!
1G - $8

Precious™
#0002 · velcro fastener

Birthday: 5/15/1993
Introduced: 1/8/2000
Retired: 6/25/2002
Hey, look at me and give me a smile,
take me home and we'll play awhile!
2G - $18

Princess™
#0012

Birthday: 3/23/1996
Introduced: 6/24/2000
Retired: 12/27/2002
My hair is pretty, it's long and brown
Should we put it up or leave it down?
2G - $8

Rascal™
#0006

Birthday: 4/15/1995
Introduced: 1/8/2000
Retired: 12/27/2002
Hear me giggle and watch me dance,
I'll make you laugh, so give me a chance!
1G - $8 ♥ 2G - $8

Shenanigan™
#0015

Birthday: 3/17/1993
Introduced: 1/1/2001
Retired: 12/27/2002
I'll bring you luck the whole year through,
if you keep me close to you!
2G - $8

Specs™
#0018

Birthday: 9/25/1991
Introduced: 1/1/2001
Retired: 12/27/2002
Learning is so much fun to do.
May I go to school with you?
2G - $10

Sugar™
#0019

Birthday: 9/22/1996
Introduced: 11/30/2001
Retired: 2/8/2002
They say that I'm as sweet as pie
Once you see me you'll know why!
2G - $10

Sweetie™
#0021

Birthday: 9/23/1996
Introduced: 11/30/2001
Retired: 12/27/2002
Cute as a button, sweet as can be
That's how I got my name, you see!
2G - $10

Tumbles™
#0009

Birthday: 9/3/1996
Introduced: 1/8/2000
Retired: 12/27/2002
A little bit naughty I'm known to be,
make sure you don't take your eyes off me!
1G - $8 ♥ 2G - $8

Fun Facts

The four girls in the first shipment had Velcro fasteners on their underwear, then elastic.

ty GEAR™

Not long after the Beanie Kids were introduced in 2000, Ty added Ty Gear, a clothing line for the Kids, with an outfit for every child's fantasy.

Ballerina™
#508

Introduced: 9/22/2000
Retired: 12/27/2002
$5

Baseball™
#511

Introduced: 9/22/2000
Retired: 12/27/2002
$4

Beach Boy™
#515

Introduced: 7/31/2001
Retired: 9/13/2001
$4

Beach Girl™
#516

Introduced: 7/31/2001
Retired: 12/27/2002
$5

Bride™
#518

Introduced: 7/31/2001
Retired: 3/3/2002
$5

Bunny™
#512

Introduced: 1/1/2001
Retired: 9/13/2001
$9

Cheerleader™
#500

Introduced: 9/22/2000
Retired: 12/27/2002
$4

Doctor™
#509

Introduced: 9/22/2000
Retired: 12/27/2002
$4

Elf™
#525

Introduced: 11/1/2001
Retired: 12/27/2001
$4

Firefighter™
#506

Introduced: 9/22/2000
Retired: 12/27/2002
$4

Groom™
#519

Introduced: 7/3/2001
Retired: 9/13/2001
$6

In-Line Skater™
#517

Introduced: 7/3/2001
Retired: 12/27/2002
$4

Pajamas™
#503

Introduced: 9/22/2000
Retired: 12/27/2002
$8

Party Tyme™
#510

Introduced: 9/22/2000
Retired: 12/27/2002
$5

Princess™
#501

Introduced: 9/22/2000
Retired: 12/27/2002
$4

Purple Leopard Ty Tote™
#601

Introduced: 2/28/2003
Retired: 1/7/2004
$8

Santa™
#523

Introduced: 11/1/2001
Retired: 12/27/2001
$5

School Days™
#505

Introduced: 9/22/2000
Retired: 12/27/2002
$5

Skeleton™
#522

Introduced: 9/3/2001
Retired: 12/27/2002
$6

Snowboarder™
#514

Introduced: 1/1/2001
Retired: 9/13/2001
$8

Soccer™
#502

Introduced: 9/22/2000
Retired: 12/27/2002
$5

Stars and Stripes™
#527

Introduced: 5/31/2002
Retired: 12/27/2002
$5

Summer Fun™
#504

Introduced: 9/22/2000
Retired: 12/27/2002
$4

Sunday Best™
#513

Introduced: 1/1/2001
Retired: 12/27/2002
$6

The Count™
#521

Introduced: 9/3/2001
Retired: 12/27/2002
$4

Ty-Dye Ty Tote™
#602

Introduced: 2/28/2003
Retired: 1/7/2004
$10

Uncle Sam™
#526

Introduced: 5/31/2002
Retired: 12/27/2002
$4

Witch™
#507

Introduced: 9/22/2000
Retired: 12/27/2002
$4

Yellow Flower Ty Tote™
#600

Introduced: 2/28/2003
Retired: 1/7/2004
$10

NOTES

304

NOTES

BEANIE BOPPERS®

Boys and girls, teens and preteens were immediately drawn to Beanie Boppers, introduced in 2001. Some were clothed in replicas of actual sports team uniforms, including baseball, hockey, rugby and soccer. Others were dressed in hip fashions, reflecting the current trends of the school age set. The Ty site provides additional fun information, including a name, birthday, hometown, family and interests for each Bopper.

Adorable Annie™
#0221

Birthday: 12/20
Introduced: 2/28/2002
Retired: 12/27/2002
Hometown: Hoover, Alabama
Favorite Things: Amusement parks, cotton candy and making breakfast for my mom.
1G - $8

Boppin' Bobbi™
#0239

Birthday: 12/12
Introduced: 7/31/2003
Retired: 12/30/2004
Hometown: Baton Rouge, Louisiana
Favorite Things: Dancing, cool hats, and shopping for clothes.
1G - $7

Bronx Bomber™
#0100

Birthday: 8/5
Introduced: 8/5/2001
Retired: 8/7/2001
Hometown: Bronx, New York
Favorite Things: Playing baseball and cheering for the Yankees.
Promotion at New York Yankee games.
1G - $60

Bubbly Betty™
#0207

Birthday: 5/29
Introduced: 10/1/2001
Retired: 12/27/2002
Hometown: Golden, Colorado
Favorite Things: Snow boarding, pepperoni pizza, scary movies.
1G - $7

Christmas Carol™
#0232 · green pompom

Birthday: 12/24
Introduced: 9/30/2002
Retired: 12/27/2002
Hometown: Winter, Minnesota
Favorite Things: Candy canes, Christmas morning and making my own ornaments.
1G - $7

Christmas Carol™
#0232 · white pompom

Birthday: 12/24
Introduced: 9/30/2002
Retired: 12/27/2002
Hometown: Winter, Minnesota
Favorite Things: Candy canes, Christmas morning and making my own ornaments.
1G - $6

306

Cool Cassidy™
#0215

Birthday: 1/19
Introduced: 12/27/2001
Retired: 12/27/2002
Hometown: Henderson, Nevada
Favorite Things: Ballet, birthday parties
and puppies.
1G - $6

Cubbie Kerry™
#0106

Birthday: 6/1
Introduced: 6/1/2002
Retired: 6/1/2002
Hometown: Wrigleyville, Illinios
Favorite Things: Hot dogs, cotton candy
and watching games at Wrigley Field.
Promotion at Chicago Cubs games.
1G - $60

Cuddly Crystal™
#0109

Birthday: 5/29
Introduced: 9/24/2001
Retired: 1/23/2002
Hometown: St. Cloud, Minnesota
Favorite Things: Reading my BBOC newsletter,
joining clubs, collecting Beanie Babies.
Beanie Baby Official Club exclusive.
1G - $9

Cute Candy™
#0222

Birthday: 3/21
Introduced: 4/30/2002
Retired: 12/26/2003
Hometown: Myrtle Beach, South Carolina
Favorite Things: Collecting shells, nail designs
and charm bracelets.
1G - $8

Dainty Darla™
#0236

Birthday: 10/22
Introduced: 12/27/2002
Retired: 12/30/2004
Hometown: Sweet Home, Oregon
Favorite Things: Dressing up for parties,
school dances and shopping.
1G - $7

Darling Debbie™
#0219

Birthday: 6/20
Introduced: 2/28/2002
Retired: 12/27/2002
Hometown: New Hope, Pennsylvania
Favorite Things: Dancing until I'm dizzy,
chocolate covered raisins and sunny days.
1G - $7

Dazzlin' Destiny™
#0206

Birthday: 8/23
Introduced: 9/3/2001
Retired: 7/17/2002
Hometown: Redmond, Washington
Favorite Things: Chatting on-line, surfin'
the net, teen mags.
1G - $8

Elegant Ellie™
#0238

Birthday: 7/16
Introduced: 7/31/2003
Retired: 12/30/2004
Hometown: Savannah, Georgia
Favorite Things: Ballroom dancing, shoe
shopping, and vacations at the Hamptons.
1G - $9

Fastball Freddie™
#0107

Birthday: 9/7
Introduced: 9/7/2002
Retired: 9/7/2002
Hometown: Bronx, New York
Favorite Things: Popcorn, pitchers' duels and
watching the Yanks win another championship!
Promotion at New York Yankee games.
1G - $60

Festive Frannie™
#0240

Birthday: 11/3
Introduced: 9/30/2003
Retired: 12/26/2003
Hometown: Winterport, Maine
Favorite Things: Warm wool mittens, snow days, and homemade chicken soup.
1G - $7

Flirty Francie™
#0211

Birthday: 2/14
Introduced: 12/27/2001
Retired: 1/16/2004
Hometown: Brentwood, Tennessee
Favorite Things: Chocolate candy hearts, boy bands and getting Valentines.
1G - $8

Footie™
#0102

Birthday: 8/18
Introduced: 8/15/2001
Retired: 12/30/2004
Hometown: England
Favorite Things: A kick around the park, dreaming of winning the World Cup.
UK exclusive.
1G - $13

Fun Phoebe™
#0235

Birthday: 3/8
Introduced: 12/27/2002
Retired: 12/30/2004
Hometown: Hollywood, Arkansas
Favorite Things: Dancing with friends, soccer and decorating lockers in school.
1G - $7

Giggly Gracie™
#0220

Birthday: 4/17
Introduced: 2/28/2002
Retired: 12/30/2004
Hometown: Madison, Wisconsin
Favorite Things: Karaoke, cherry licorice and making scrapbooks.
1G - $8

Glitzy Gabby™
#0218

Birthday: 3/21
Introduced: 12/27/2001
Retired: 12/30/2004
Hometown: Pasadena, California
Favorite Things: Swimming in the ocean, horoscopes and hair accessories.
1G - $8

Happy Hanna™
#0227

Birthday: 1/31
Introduced: 6/28/2002
Retired: 12/26/2003
Hometown: Kings Mills, Ohio
Favorite Things: Slumber parties, doing makeovers and telling stories.
1G - $8

Hat Trick Hunter™
#0104 · 10 jersey

Birthday: 11/16
Introduced: 11/1/2001
Retired: 5/2/2002
Hometown: Aurora, Ontario, Canada
Favorite Things: Watching hockey on T.V., French fries and computer games.
Canada exclusive.
1G - $10

Hat Trick Hunter™
#0104 · 99 jersey

Birthday: 11/16
Introduced: 11/1/2001
Retired: 5/2/2002
Hometown: Aurora, Ontario, Canada
Favorite Things: Watching hockey on T.V., French fries and computer games.
Canada exclusive.
1G - $15

Heavenly Heather™
#0238

Birthday: 11/1
Introduced: 9/30/2003
Retired: 12/30/2004
Hometown: Santa Fe, New Mexico
Favorite Things: Choir practice, church bells,
and helping the elderly.
1G - $9

Holiday Heidi™
#0212

Birthday: 9/2
Introduced: 10/1/2001
Retired: 1/2/2002
Hometown: Ann Arbor, Michigan
Favorite Things: Holiday shopping, making
snowmen and wrapping presents.
1G - $10

Home Run Harry™
#0108

Birthday: 8/10
Introduced: 8/10/2002
Retired: 8/10/2002
Hometown: Houston, Texas
Favorite Things: Tacos, fireworks and
playing baseball with my friends!
Promotion at Houston Astros games.
1G - $60

Huggable Holly™
#0203

Birthday: 2/3
Introduced: 7/3/2001
Retired: 1/25/2002
Hometown: Overland Park, Kansas
Favorite Things: Soccer, body glitter,
and drawing.
1G - $8

Ivy Leaguer™
#0101

Birthday: 9/30
Introduced: 9/30/2001
Retired: 10/2/2001
Hometown: Chicago, Illinois
Favorite Things: Playing baseball and
cheering for the Cubs.
Promotion at Chicago Cubs games.
1G - $60

Jammin' Jenna™
#0224

Birthday: 8/26
Introduced: 4/30/2002
Retired: 12/26/2003
Hometown: Billings, Montana
Favorite Things: Painting, penguins and
playing chess.
1G - $8

Jazzy Jessie™
#0209

Birthday: 1/30
Introduced: 10/1/2001
Retired: 12/30/2004
Hometown: Queens, New York
Favorite Things: Jumping rope, visiting
my grandma and watching videos.
1G - $7

Jolly Janie™
#0210

Birthday: 3/30
Introduced: 10/1/2001
Retired: 1/2/2002
Hometown: Scottsdale, Arizona
Favorite Things: Baking holiday cookies,
caroling and trimming the tree.
1G - $10

Kooky Kandy™
#0202

Birthday: 5/20
Introduced: 7/3/2001
Retired: 1/2/2002
Hometown: Walnut Creek, California
Favorite Things: Boys, pink lip gloss,
talking on the phone.
1G - $6

Loveable Lulu™
#0204

Birthday: 7/17
Introduced: 7/3/2001
Retired: 1/25/2002
Hometown: Naperville, Illinois
Favorite Things: Popcorn, unicorns,
doing crafts.
1G - $5

Lovely Lily™
#0223

Birthday: 2/1
Introduced: 4/30/2002
Retired: 12/26/2003
Hometown: Sugarland, Texas
Favorite Things: Beaded necklaces, girl-boy
parties and grilled cheese sandwiches.
1G - $8

Lucky Lucy™
#0229

Birthday: 9/19
Introduced: 8/29/2002
Retired: 12/26/2003
Hometown: Newport Beach, California
Favorite Things: Dolphins, water skiing
and fish sticks.
1G - $8

Merry Margaret™
#0231

Birthday: 12/25
Introduced: 9/30/2002
Retired: 12/27/2002
Hometown: Santa, Idaho
Favorite Things: Sledding, stocking stuffers
and listening to holiday songs.
1G - $7

Naughty Natalie™
#0233

Birthday: 9/28
Introduced: 9/30/2002
Retired: 12/26/2003
Hometown: Autumn Acres, Ohio
Favorite Things: Teasing boys, playing tag
and telling jokes.
1G - $7

Paisley Payton™
#0241

Birthday: 6/1
Introduced: 7/31/2003
Retired: 12/30/2004
Hometown: Albuquerque, New Mexico
Favorite Things: Getting all dressed-up,
sewing class, and my hot pink lava lamp.
1G - $7

Pajama Pam™
#0234

Birthday: 1/4
Introduced: 12/27/2002
Retired: 12/30/2004
Hometown: Sleepy Eye, Minnesota
Favorite Things: Sleepovers at my friend's
house, popcorn and scary movies.
1G - $7

Paula Plappertasche™
#0103

Birthday: 4/1
Introduced: 1/15/2002
Retired: 12/30/2004
Hometown: Berlin
Favorite Things: To talk on the phone
for hours, to disguise myself, to stage
at school theater.
German exclusive.
1G - $20

Precious Pammy™
#0228

Birthday: 7/7
Introduced: 8/29/2002
Retired: 12/30/2004
Hometown: Brandon, Mississippi
Favorite Things: Board games, bunk beds
and soft ice cream with sprinkles.
1G - $9

Precious Penny™
#0226

Birthday: 9/7
Introduced: 6/28/2002
Retired: 12/30/2004
Hometown: Sandy, Utah
Favorite Things: Family picnics, picking
wildflowers and sweet smelling perfume!
1G - $8

Pretty Patti™
#0205

Birthday: 8/7
Introduced: 7/3/2001
Retired: 4/23/2002
Hometown: Tysons Corner, Virginia
Favorite Things: Roller coasters, green
nail polish, animals.
1G - $7

Pretty Penelope™
#0213

Birthday: 10/4
Introduced: 12/27/2001
Retired: 12/27/2002
Hometown: Quincy, Massachusetts
Favorite Things: Listening to CDs, rainbows
and sour gummy worms.
1G - $8

Punky Penny™
#0237

Birthday: 9/8
Introduced: 7/31/2003
Retired: 12/30/2004
Hometown: Fresno, California
Favorite Things: Rock music, skateboarding,
and music videos.
1G - $8

Rah-Rah Rachel™
#0245

Birthday: 2/19
Introduced: 12/30/2003
Retired: 12/30/2004
Hometown: Diamond City, Arkansas
Favorite Things: Dance lessons, Pep rallies,
and swimming at the buzzer.
1G - $9

Rockin' Rosie™
#0200

Birthday: 10/11
Introduced: 7/3/2001
Retired: 1/25/2002
Hometown: Plano, Texas
Favorite Things: Horseback riding,
sleep-overs, telling secrets.
1G - $5

Rugged Rusty™
#0214

Birthday: 11/3
Introduced: 12/27/2001
Retired: 12/26/2003
Hometown: St. Charles, Missouri
Favorite Things: Camping, tree houses
and playing basketball.
1G - $8

Sassy Sidney™
#0247

Birthday: 11/28
Introduced: 12/30/2003
Retired: 12/30/2004
Hometown: Morning Sun, Iowa
Favorite Things: Skate parks, scary movies,
and boys, boys, boys!
1G - $9

Sassy Star™
#0201

Birthday: 12/4
Introduced: 7/3/2001
Retired: 5/24/2002
Hometown: Sarasota, Florida
Favorite Things: Going to the mall, gel
pens, platform shoes.
1G - $9

Silly Sara™
#0225

Birthday: 11/10
Introduced: 6/28/2002
Retired: 10/8/2003
Hometown: Altamonte Springs, Florida
Favorite Things: Snow cones, the balance beam and going to the circus!
1G - $8

Snazzy Sabrina™
#0216

Birthday: 4/22
Introduced: 12/27/2001
Retired: 12/30/2004
Hometown: Metairie, Louisiana
Favorite Things: Saturdays, blueberry pancakes and making up dance routines.
1G - $8

Spunky Sammie™
#0217

Birthday: 6/8
Introduced: 12/27/2001
Retired: 12/27/2002
Hometown: Beaverton, Oregon
Favorite Things: Skiiing, getting e-mails and koala bears.
1G - $7

Star-Spangled Suzy™
#0242

Birthday: 9/14
Introduced: 7/31/2003
Retired: 12/30/2004
Hometown: Philadelphia, Pennsylvania
Favorite Things: The Pledge of Allegiance, fireworks, and apple pie.
USA exclusive.
1G - $8

Striker™
#0105 · gold boots

Birthday: 4/15
Introduced: 5/2/2002
Retired: 12/30/2004
Home Country: England
Favorite Things: Football, running, jet skiing and training.
UK exclusive.
1G - $25

Striker™
#0105 · white boots

Birthday: 4/15
Introduced: 5/2/2002
Retired: 12/30/2004
Home Country: England
Favorite Things: Football, running, jet skiing and training.
UK exclusive.
1G - $20

Sweet Sally™
#0208

Birthday: 7/26
Introduced: 10/1/2001
Retired: 12/27/2002
Hometown: Sandy Springs Georgia
Favorite Things: Gymnastics, babysitting and anything pink.
1G - $8

Totally Trish™
#0246

Birthday: 6/10
Introduced: 12/30/2003
Retired: 12/30/2004
Hometown: Boomer, Virginia
Favorite Things: Football players, Homecoming, and pom-poms.
1G - $8

NOTES

teeNie BeaNie BoPPeRs®

Smaller than the popular Beanie Bopper is the easily portable Teenie Beanie Bopper. Only 8" tall, each doll has a loop on its back which enables its owner to fasten it to a backpack, purse or zipper pull. Various professions, sports teams, ethnic characteristics and fashions trends are represented in these dolls, making them appropriate for children everywhere. Each Teenie Beanie Bopper has its own name, personality, wishes and dreams.

Ace Anthony™
#0328

Birthday: 9/17
Introduced: 6/30/2003
Retired: 12/30/2004
Hometown: Flushing, New York
Favorite Things: Tie-breakers, drop shots and new racquets.
1G - $4

American Millie™
#0308

Birthday: 7/4
Introduced: 6/28/2002
Retired: 11/22/2004
Hometown: Westchester, Pennsylvania
Favorite Things: Ferris wheels, fireworks and fireflies.
1G - $4

Bay Stars Bruth™
No Style #

Birthday: 10/5
Introduced: 3/10/2005
Retired: 3/15/2006
Favorite Things: Star gaze, my pet pig and crying out for love at the center of the world.
Yokohama BayStars exclusive.
1G - $175

Beautiful Belle™
#0313

Birthday: 2/21
Introduced: 9/30/2002
Retired: 12/30/2004
Hometown: Diamond, California
Favorite Things: Dressing up, fairy tales and frozen lemonade.
1G - $4

Blocka Bobby™
#0110

Birthday: 10/10
Introduced: 9/25/2003
Retired: 12/30/2004
Hometown: Sydney, Australia
Favorite things: Video games, bush walking and surfing.
Australia/New Zealand exclusive.
1G - $8

Brave Buddy™
#0320

Birthday: 1/9
Introduced: 9/30/2002
Retired: 12/30/2004
Hometown: Rochester, New York
Favorite Things: Fire engines, ladders and Dalmatians.
1G - $5

Captain™
#0114

Birthday: 8/31
Introduced: 1/10/2003
Retired: 12/30/2004
Hometown: Portsmouth, Hants, England
Favorite Things: Being the playmaker
and fast cars.
UK exclusive.
1G - $12

Captain Colin™
#0130

Birthday: 6/3
Introduced: 9/25/2003
Retired: 12/30/2004
Hometown: Cambridge, New Zealand
Favorite Things: Rugby, motor cross and
remote controlled cars.
Australia/New Zealand exclusive.
1G - $14

Caring Carla™
#0326

Birthday: 10/10
Introduced: 1/30/2003
Retired: 12/30/2004
Hometown: Caldwell, Idaho
Favorite Things: Pillow fights, puppet
shows and cookie dough.
1G - $5

Change-Up Charlie™
No Style

Birthday: 7/4
Introduced: 7/1/2003
Retired: 12/30/2004
Hometown: Cleveland, Ohio
Favorite Things: Striking out the side, the
Stars and Stripes, and the Cleveland Indians.
Ty MBNA exclusive.
1G - $60

Chillin' Charlie™
#0324

Birthday: 3/18
Introduced: 1/30/2003
Retired: 12/30/2004
Hometown: Sacramento, California
Favorite Things: Skateboarding, stunt
bikes and walkie-talkies.
1G - $4

Classy Cassie™
#0325

Birthday: 6/26
Introduced: 1/30/2003
Retired: 12/30/2004
Hometown: Norfolk, Virginia
Favorite Things: Rhinestones, playing jacks
and picking honeysuckle.
1G - $5

Clean Up Clark™
No Style

Birthday: 8/30
Introduced: 8/30/2003
Retired: 12/30/2004
Hometown: Chicago, Illinois
Favorite Things: Sitting in the bleachers,
the ivy wall, and the Chicago Cubs.
Ty MBNA exclusive.
1G - $60

Cool Cassidy™
#0304

Birthday: 1/19
Introduced: 6/28/2002
Retired: 12/26/2003
Hometown: Henderson, Nevada
Favorite Things: Ballet, birthday parties
and puppies.
1G - $5

Crosscourt Cathy™
#0327

Birthday: 3/7
Introduced: 6/30/2003
Retired: 12/30/2004
Hometown: Saginaw, Michigan
Favorite Things: Trophies, playing doubles
with my Mom and autographs.
1G - $5

Cubby Casey™
#0106

Birthday: 6/1
Introduced: 8/30/2003
Retired: 8/30/2003
Hometown: Chicago, Illinois
Favorite Things:Fastball pitchers, double headers and the Chicago Cubs.
Promotion at Wrigley Field.
1G - $50

Curve Ball Curt™
No Style #

Birthday: 8/1
Introduced: 8/1/2003
Retired: 12/30/2004
Hometown: Chicago, Illinois
Favorite Things: Hot dogs, the National Anthem, and the Chicago White Sox.
Ty MBNA exclusive.
1G - $60

Darling Daisy™
#0318

Birthday: 11/14
Introduced: 9/30/2002
Retired: 12/30/2004
Hometown: Goldsboro, North Carolina
Favorites: Flying kites, poetry and playing the flute.
1G - $5

Dear Debbie™
#0312

Birthday: 6/17
Introduced: 9/30/2002
Retired: 12/30/2004
Hometown: Oakland, California
Favorite Things: Cheerleading, Chihuahuas and anything chocolate.
1G - $5

Disco Diva™
#0336

Birthday: 5/1
Introduced: 4/29/2004
Retired: 12/30/2004
Hometown: Roxbury, Vermont
Favorite Things: Anything glittery, lava lamps and roller skating.
1G - $5

Footie™
#0112

Birthday: 8/18
Introduced: 6/28/2002
Retired: 11/22/2004
Hometown: England
Favorite Things: A kick around the park, dreaming of winning the World Cup.
1G - $6

Glitzy Gabby™
#0306

Birthday: 3/21
Introduced: 6/28/2002
Retired: 11/22/2004
Hometown: Pasadena, California
Favorite Things: Swimming in the ocean, horoscopes and hair accessories.
1G - $5

Hat-Trick Hunter™
#0111

Birthday: 11/16
Introduced: 6/28/2002
Retired: 12/26/2003
Hometown: Aurora, Ontario, Canada
Favorite Things: Watching hockey on T.V., French fries and computer games.
1G - $5

Home Run Hank™
#0319

Birthday: 5/21
Introduced: 9/30/2002
Retired: 12/30/2004
Hometown: Owings Mills, Maryland
Favorite Things: Home runs, stealing bases and the 7th Inning Stretch.
1G - $5

Hotshot™
#0115

Birthday: 9/17
Introduced: 1/10/2003
Retired: 12/30/2004
Hometown: Gosport, Hampshire, England
Favorite Things: Scoring goals and pizza.
UK exclusive.
1G - $10

Jazzy Jessie™
#0302

Birthday: 1/30
Introduced: 6/28/2002
Retired: 12/26/2003
Hometown: Queens, New York
Favorite Things: Jumping rope, visiting my
grandma and watching videos.
1G - $4

Kool Katy™
#0317

Birthday: 12/25
Introduced: 9/30/2002
Retired: 12/30/2004
Hometown: Dover, Oklahoma
Favorite Things: Colorful sneakers,
strawberries and collecting stickers.
1G - $5

Lead-Off Larry™
No Style #

Birthday: 8/5
Introduced: 7/31/2003
Retired: 12/30/2004
Hometown: Milwaukee, Wisconsin
Favorite Things: Stealing bases, sliding into
home, and the Milwaukee Brewers.
Ty MBNA exclusive.
1G - $60

Lucky Linda™
#0309

Birthday: 10/22
Introduced: 9/30/2002
Retired: 12/26/2003
Hometown: New York, New York
Favorite Things: Piano lessons, lip gloss
and dressing up.
1G - $5

Magic Molly™
#0333

Birthday: 9/25
Introduced: 9/30/2003
Retired: 12/30/2004
Hometown: Southampton, England
Favorite Things: Singing, drama and dancing.
1G - $6

Midfield Mandy™
#0323

Birthday: 5/12
Introduced: 1/30/2003
Retired: 12/30/2004
Hometown: Berryton, Kansas
Favorite Things: Scoring goals, getting A's
and grape soda pop.
1G - $4

Paula Plappertasche™
#0113

Birthday: 4/1
Introduced: 6/28/2002
Retired: 12/26/2003
Hometown: Berlin
Favorite Things: To talk on the phone
for hours, to disguise myself, to stage
at school theater.
1G - $6

Playful Peggy™
#0321

Birthday: 9/13
Introduced: 1/30/2003
Retired: 12/30/2004
Hometown: Alpharetta, Georgia
Favorite Things: Piggyback rides, butterflies
and running through sprinklers.
1G - $5

Pretty Penelope™
#0303

Birthday: 10/4
Introduced: 6/28/2002
Retired: 12/26/2003
Hometown: Quincy, Massachusetts
Favorite Things: Listening to CDs, rainbows
and sour gummy worms.
1G - $5

Pretty Penny™
#0311

Birthday: 5/10
Introduced: 9/30/2002
Retired: 12/30/2004
Hometown: Valparaiso, Indiana
Favorite Things: Brain teasers,
trampolines and teddy bears.
1G - $5

Private Pete™
#0330

Birthday: 11/11
Introduced: 5/29/2003
Retired: 8/8/2003
Hometown: Service, Mississippi
Favorite Things: Toy soldiers, my tree
house and marching bands.
1G - $6

Rockin Ruby™
#0310

Birthday: 8/30
Introduced: 9/30/2002
Retired: 12/26/2003
Hometown: Fashion Heights, Ohio
Favorite Things: Music videos, rock concerts
and rappin' with friends.
1G - $5

Rugged Rusty™
#0300

Birthday: 11/3
Introduced: 6/28/2002
Retired: 12/26/2003
Hometown: St. Charles, Missouri
Favorite Things: Camping, tree houses
and playing basketball.
1G - $5

Sailor Sam™
#0331

Birthday: 10/10
Introduced: 5/29/2003
Retired: 10/7/2003
Hometown: Annapolis, Maryland
Favorite Things: Swimming, surfing and
beach volleyball.
1G - $6

Sassy Star™
#0307

Birthday: 12/4
Introduced: 6/28/2002
Retired: 11/22/2004
Hometown: Sarasota, Florida
Favorite Things: Going to the mall, gel pens,
platform shoes.
1G - $6

Shy Shannon™
#0316

Birthday: 10/20
Introduced: 9/30/2002
Retired: 2/26/2004
Hometown: Rising Sun, Delaware
Favorite Things: Tap/ballet, DVDs
and doodling.
1G - $6

Sluggin' Steve™
No Style #

Birthday: 7/31
Introduced: 8/30/2003
Retired: 12/30/2004
Hometown: Seattle, Washington
Favorite Things: Grand slams, a .300 batting
average, and the Seattle Mariners.
Ty MBNA exclusive.
1G - $40

Smashing Cherise™
#0335

Birthday: 6/14
Introduced: 4/29/2004
Retired: 12/30/2004
Hometown: Rosebud, South Dakota
Favorite Things: Hard court - I don't play well on clay - and summertime.
1G - $4

Snappy Cindy™
#0315

Birthday: 1/14
Introduced: 9/30/2002
Retired: 12/26/2003
Hometown: Columbia, Maryland
Favorite Things: Caterpillars, campfires and trail mix.
1G - $6

Snazzy Sabrina™
#0305

Birthday: 4/22
Introduced: 6/28/2002
Retired: 11/22/2004
Hometown: Metairie, Louisiana
Favorite Things: Saturdays, blueberry pancakes and making up dance routines.
1G - $6

Sunny Sue™
#0314

Birthday: 12/2
Introduced: 9/30/2002
Retired: 12/30/2004
Hometown: Youngstown, Ohio
Favorite Things: Denim, lip-synching and fish sticks.
1G - $5

Suntory Sungoliath™
#0132

Birthday: 4/4
Introduced: 10/15/2004
Retired: 12/30/2004
Favorite Things: Playing rugby, seeing a rugby match in a stadium, and going to the zoo (gorillas are the best).
Japan exclusive.
1G - $10

Super Shuto™
#0131

Birthday: 7/4
Introduced: 10/30/2003
Retired: 11/15/2003
Hometown: Shizuoka, City, Japan
Favorite Things: Soccer games, skateboarding and Mountain Bikes.
Japan exclusive.
1G - $150

Sweet Sally™
#0301

Birthday: 7/26
Introduced: 6/28/2002
Retired: 12/26/2003
Hometown: Sandy Springs Georgia
Favorite Things: Gymnastics, babysitting and anything pink.
1G - $6

Terrific Tessa™
#0334

Birthday: 2/1
Introduced: 9/30/2003
Retired: 12/30/2004
Hometown: Fargo, North Dakota
Favorite Things: Cross country skiing, my furry coat & hat and toasting marshmallows.
1G - $5

Trendy Tracy™
#0322

Birthday: 4/2
Introduced: 1/30/2003
Retired: 12/30/2004
Hometown: Teaneck, New Jersey
Favorite Things: Ladybugs, ankle bracelets and brownies.
1G - $6

Wahoo Wally™
No Style #

Birthday: 8/30
Introduced: 8/30/2003
Retired: 8/30/2003
Hometown: Cleveland, Ohio
Favorite Things:My baseball mitt, my baseball
card collection and the Cleveland Indians.
Promotion at Jacob's Field.
1G - $60

Wishful Whitney™
#0332

Birthday: 12/24
Introduced: 9/30/2003
Retired: 12/26/2003
Hometown: Wiseman, Alaska
Favorite Things: Ice skating, hot cocoa and
my Christmas stocking.
1G - $6

Witty Wendy™
#0329

Birthday: 4/1
Introduced: 6/30/2003
Retired: 12/30/2004
Hometown: Largo, Florida
Favorite Things: Practical jokes, stand-up
comedians and squirt guns.
1G - $5

Fun Facts

All original 12 Teenie Beanie Boppers
have thread eyes: American Millie,
Cool Cassidy, Footie, Glitzy Gabby,
Hat Trick Hunter, Jazzy Jessie, Paula
Plappertasche, Pretty Penelope, Rug-
ged Rusty, Sassy Star, Snazzy Sabrina
and Sweet Sally.
Releases after those have plastic eyes.

NOTES

Teenie Beanie Boppers®

With their very own website, the Ty Girlz are ready to have fun. Released in the latest high end fashions, the Girlz are very popular with tweens and teens. Ty Girlz are all plush but have marvelous rooted hair that can be combed and styled again and again. Hair color ranges from traditional blond, brunette and black to many shades in between. A secret code is fastened in each hangtag, allowing members to register for safe, secure and entertaining visits online. Once the secret code is entered on the Ty Girlz site and registration is complete, members can decorate their virtual houses, chat on a secure moderated web page, play games, earn Ty$, go to the bank, shop at the mall, get make-overs, and try on clothes. Move over, all other teen-age dolls. This is the one!

Classy Carla™
#2210

Introduced: To Be Announced
Current
1G - Current Retail Value

Cute Candy™
#2208

Introduced: To Be Announced
Current
1G - Current Retail Value

Dazzlin Destiny™
#2205

Introduced: 3/23/2007
Current
1G - Current Retail Value

Jammin Jenna™
#2209

Introduced: To Be Announced
Current
1G - Current Retail Value

Lovely Lola™
#2204

Introduced: 3/23/2007
Current
1G - Current Retail Value

Pretty Patti™
#2207

Introduced: To Be Announced
Current
1G - Current Retail Value

Punky Penny™
#2202

Introduced: 3/23/2007
Current
1G - Current Retail Value

Rockin Ruby™
#2206 • blonde

Introduced: 2007
Current
1G - Current Retail Value

Rockin Ruby™
#2206 • brunette

Introduced: 3/23/2007
Current
1G - Current Retail Value

Sassy Star™
#2203 • blue lips

Introduced: 3/23/2007
Retired: 6/13/2007
1G - $15

Sassy Star™
#2203 • pink lips

Introduced: 3/23/2007
Retired: 6/13/2007
1G - $18

Sizzlin Sue™
#2201

Introduced: 3/23/2007
Current
1G - Current Retail Value

NOTES

Attic Treasures™

In 1993 TY introduced the first 12 of what soon became a very popular series known as "The Attic Treasures Collection". The designs for the original 12 were attributed to Linda Harris, Ruth Fraser, and Ty Warner. Starting in 1994, Nola Hart's designs began appearing. Each is handmade, has fully jointed arms and legs, and is poseable. They vary in size from the 6 inch Woolie Gold to the 20 inch Heather and are known for their high quality. Attic Treasures are made of textured fur and sport accessories that range from a single ribbon to a bow, hat, dress, vest, sweater, jumper, overalls, or combination of more than one. The clothing is often detailed with buttons, appliqués, or other accents, though later these were removed for child safety reasons.

Abby™
#6027 · with overalls · 8"

Introduced: 1995
Retired: 5/1/1998
Abby was issued
without a phrase.
Also with ribbon 2G - $90.
2G - $65 ♥ 3G - $30 ♥ 4G - $10 ♥
5G - $8 ♥ 6G - $10

Abby™
#6027 · with ribbon · 8"

Introduced: 1995
Retired: 5/1/1998
Abby was issued
without a phrase.
2G - $50 ♥ 3G - $20 ♥ 4G - $15

Adelaide™
#6262 · 10"

Introduced: 1/1/2001
Retired: 7/25/2002
Cat Got Your Tongue?
7G - $5

Alfalfa™
#6241 · 8"

Introduced: 8/27/2000
Retired: 1/1/2002
Let Them Eat Crow!
7G - $5

Allura™
#6058 · 8"

Introduced: 4/14/1999
Retired: 3/15/2000
Sunny Days Are Here Again!
7G - $5

Amethyst™
#6131 · 13"

Introduced: 1/1/1998
Retired: 7/31/1998
You're the sweetest
of them all!
6G - $10

Amoré™
#6206 · 8"

Introduced: 7/4/2000
Retired: 3/15/2000
With All My Heart!
7G - $5

April™
#6268 · 8"

Introduced: 1/1/2001
Retired: 4/23/2002
April Showers...
7G - $5

Arlen™
#6260 · 10"

Introduced: 1/1/2001
Retired: 12/27/2002
Let The Cat Out Of The Bag!
7G - $5

Armstrong™
#6226 · 8"

Introduced: 6/24/2000
Retired: 10/20/2000
And A Tuppence In My Shoe!
7G - $5

Azalea™
#6093 · 8"

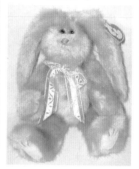

Introduced: 1/1/1999
Retired: 4/28/2000
Hare Today - Gone Tomorrow
Also with Piccadilly hang tag - $7.
7G - $5

Azure™
#6055 · 8"

Introduced: 4/20/1999
Retired: 5/22/2000
I'm Blue Without You
7G - $5

Babette™
#6263 · 8"

Introduced: 4/26/2001
Retired: 1/1/2002
Savoir - Faire!
7G - $5

Baron™
#6225 · 8"

Introduced: 6/24/2000
Retired: 4/23/2002
Fly High!
7G - $5

Barry™
#6073 · 12"

Introduced: 1997
Retired: 1997
Barry was issued
without a phrase.
5G - $30

Barrymore™
#6288 · 8"

Introduced: 12/27/2001
Retired: 2/12/2002
You Take My Breath Away!
7G - $5

Basil™
#6248 · 9"

Introduced: 8/27/2000
Retired: 1/1/2002
Imagine The Pawsibilities!
7G - $7

Beargundy™
#6205 · 8"

Introduced: 8/31/1999
Retired: 5/22/2000
Bear With Me!
7G - $5

Bearington™
#6102 · 14"

Introduced: 1/1/1998
Retired: 9/20/1998
Be My Bow
6G - $6

Bearkhardt™
#6204 · 8"

Introduced: 8/31/1999
Retired: 5/22/2000
You Make Things Bearable!
7G - $5

Beezee™
#6088 · 8"

Introduced: 1/1/1999
Retired: 12/12/1999
You BEE-long To Me
7G - $5

Benjamin™
#6023 · with ribbon · 9"

Introduced: 1995
Retired: 1997
Benjamin was issued
without a phrase.
2G - $30

Benjamin™
#6023 · with sweater · 9"

Introduced: 1995
Retired: 1997
Benjamin was issued
without a phrase.
Also with ribbon 2G - $40.
2G - $25 ♥ 5G - $15

Berkley™
#6218 · 8"

Introduced: 1/4/2000
Retired: 8/23/2000
Love Is The Answer!
7G - $5

326

Beverly™
#6210 · 8"

Introduced: 1/4/2000
Retired: 10/24/2000
You Have Me In A Whirlwind!
7G - $5

Birch™
#6232 · 8"

Introduced: 7/16/2000
Retired: 6/15/2001
Growing Old Gracefully!
7G - $5

Blarney™
#6215 · 8"

Introduced: 1/4/2000
Retired: 3/15/2002
Kiss Me, I'm Irish!
7G - $5

Bloom™
#6122 · 16"

Introduced: 1/1/1998
Retired: 5/1/1998
Bloom was issued without
a phrase.
6G - $10

Bluebeary™
#6080 · 8"

Introduced: 1/1/1998
Retired: 5/11/1999
Something Old,
Something New?
6G - $5 ♥ 7G - $5

Blush™
#6208 · 8"

Introduced: 1/4/2000
Retired: 1/25/2001
You Make Me Blush!
7G - $5

Bonnie™
#6075 · 9"

Introduced: 1/1/1998
Retired: 4/28/2000
Birds Of A Feather
Flock Together
6G - $5 ♥ 7G - $5

Boris™
#6041 · no clothes · 12"

Introduced: 1996
Retired: 1997
Boris was issued
without a phrase.
5G - $20

Boris™
#6041 · with sweater · 12"

Introduced: 1996
Retired: 1997
Boris was issued
without a phrase.
5G - $20

Breezy™
#6057 · 8"

Introduced: 4/21/1999
Retired: 5/22/2000
Ahoy Mate!
7G - $5

Brewster™
#6034 · with overalls · 9"

Introduced: 1995
Retired: 1997
Brewster was issued
without a phrase.
Also with no clothes
2G - $12, 3G - $10, 4G - $8
2G - $12 ♥ 3G - $10 ♥ 4G - $8 ♥ 5G - $5

Brisbane™
#6052 · 8"

Introduced: 4/20/1999
Retired: 5/22/2000
G-day Mate!
7G - $5

Buck™
#6281 · 8"

Introduced: 9/3/2001
Retired: 10/17/2001
Bright Eyed And Bushy Tailed!
7G - $5

Bugsy™
#6089 · 8"

Introduced: 1/1/1999
Retired: 7/29/1999
Always A Lady
7G - $5

Burrows™
#6291 · 8"

Introduced: 12/27/2001
Retired: 4/23/2002
Doing The Bunny Hop!
7G - $5

Caboose™
#6267 · 8"

Introduced: 6/23/2001
Retired: 4/23/2002
On The Right Track!
7G - $5

Calliope™
#6230 · 8"

Introduced: 6/24/2000
Retired: 6/15/2001
Surely You Jest!
7G - $5

Camelia™
#6094 · 8"

Introduced: 1/1/1999
Retired: 5/24/1999
Always In Bloom
7G - $5

Carey™
#6264 · 8"

Introduced: 1/1/2001
Retired: 1/1/2002
My Bark Is Worse
Than My Bite!
7G - $5

Carlisle™
#6279 · 8"

Introduced: 9/3/2001
Retired: 4/23/2002
Bear Hugs From Me To You!
7G - $5

Carlton™
#6064 · with overalls · 16"

Introduced: 1996
Retired: 1997
Carlton was issued
without a phrase.
5G - $30

Carlton™
#6064 · with ribbon · 16"

Introduced: 1996
Retired: 1997
Carlton was issued
without a phrase.
5G - $45

Carmella™
#6280 · 8"

Introduced: 6/23/2001
Retired: 9/11/2001
Color Me Happy!
7G - $5

Carmichael™
#6282 · 8"

Introduced: 6/23/2001
Retired: 10/17/2001
Over The Rainbow!
7G - $5

Carson™
#6216 · 8"

Introduced: 1/4/2000
Retired: 7/6/2000
You're As Sweet As Honey!
7G - $5

Carver™
#6271 · 8"

Introduced: 9/3/2001
Retired: 1/1/2002
Carve A Place In Your
Heart For Me!
7G - $5

Casanova™
#6073 · 8"

Introduced: 1/1/1998
Retired: 3/31/1999
You Hold The Key To
My Heart
6G - $6 ♥ 7G - $5

Cassandra™
#6249 · 8"

Introduced: 1/1/2001
Retired: 1/1/2002
I Feel Pretty!
7G - $5

Cassia™
#6306 · 8"

Introduced: 6/22/2002
Retired: 12/27/2002
Wish Upon A Star!
7G - $5

Cassie™
#6028 · with jumper · 12"

Introduced: 1995
Retired: 1997
Cassie was issued
without a phrase.
Also with ribbon 4G - $55.
2G - $55 ♥ 3G - $35 ♥
4G - $18 ♥ 5G - $7

Cassie™
#6028 · with ribbon · 12"

Introduced: 1995
Retired: 1997
Cassie was issued
without a phrase.
2G - $60 ♥ 3G - $45 ♥ 4G - $30

Cawley™
#6090 · 10"

Introduced: 1/1/1999
Retired: 5/22/2000
How Does Your Garden Grow?
7G - $5

Charles™
#6039 · no clothes · 12"

Introduced: 1996
Retired: 1997
Charles was issued
without a phrase.
5G - $25

Charles™
#6039 · with overalls · 12"

Introduced: 1996
Retired: 1997
Charles was issued
without a phrase.
5G - $25

Checkers™
#6031 · no clothes · 8"

Introduced: 1995
Retired: 5/30/2000
King Me
2G - $35 ♥ 3G - $25 ♥ 4G - $14 ♥
5G - $14 ♥ 6G - $5 ♥ 7G - $5

Checkers™
#6031 · with sweater · 8"

Introduced: 1995
Retired: 5/30/2000
King Me
2G - $40 ♥ 3G - $45 ♥ 5G - $7

Chelsea™
#6070 · 8"

Introduced: 1996
Retired: 9/20/1998
Bear Hugs Are Best
5G - $5 ♥ 6G - $5

Cheri™
#6200 · 8"

Introduced: 8/31/1999
Retired: 5/22/2000
Ooh La La!
7G - $5

Chillings™
#6286 · 8"

Introduced: 10/1/2001
Retired: 12/21/2001
Snow News Is Good News!
7G - $5

Christopher™
#6071 · 8"

Introduced: 1996
Retired: 7/31/1998
Christopher was issued
without a phrase.
5G - $6 ♥ 6G - $5

Clay™
#6233 · 8"

Introduced: 6/24/2000
Retired: 11/8/2000
Leave It To Me!
7G - $5

Clifford™
#6003 · humpback · 12"

Introduced: 1993
Retired: 1995
Clifford was issued
without a phrase.
1G - $200

Clifford™
#6003 · straightback · 12"

Introduced: 1993
Retired: 1995
Clifford was issued
without a phrase.
1G - $90

Clyde™
#6040 · no clothes · 12"

Introduced: 1996
Retired: 1997
Clyde was issued
without a phrase.
5G - $20

Clyde™
#6040 · with sweater · 12"

Introduced: 1996
Retired: 1997
Clyde was issued
without a phrase.
5G - $20

Cody™
#6030 · 8"

Introduced: 1995
Retired: 5/22/2000
You're As Sweet As Honey
2G - $40 ♥ 3G - $30 ♥ 4G - $10 ♥
5G - $5 ♥ 6G - $5 ♥ 7G - $5

Colby™
#6043 · no clothes · 11"

Introduced: 1996
Retired: 1997
Colby was issued
without a phrase.
5G - $16

Colby™
#6043 · with jumper · 11"

Introduced: 1996
Retired: 1997
Colby was issued
without a phrase.
5G - $13

Cooper™
#6251 · 8"

Introduced: 1/1/2001
Retired: 12/27/2002
Take Me Out To The Ballgame!
7G - $5

Copperfield™
#6060 · with sweater · 16"

Introduced: 1996
Retired: 1997
Copperfield was issued
without a phrase.
Also with no clothes and ribbon
5G - $110.
5G - $20

Cromwell™
#6221 · 8"

Introduced: 1/4/2000
Retired: 12/19/2000
The Mice Will Play!
7G - $5

Dad™
#6297 · 8"

Introduced: 3/29/2002
Retired: 6/25/2002
Father Knows Best!
7G - $5

Darlene™
#6213 · 8"

Introduced: 1/4/2000
Retired: 1/1/2002
Your Heart Be Glad Forever!
7G - $5

Demetria™
#6307 · 8"

Introduced: 6/22/2002
Retired: 12/27/2002
Dreams Come True!
7G - $5

Devlin™
#6277 · 8"

Introduced: 9/3/2001
Retired: 10/17/2001
Some Like It Hot!
7G - $5

Dexter™
#6009 · with overalls · 9"

Introduced: 1993
Retired: 1997
Dexter was issued
without a phrase.
4G - $20 ♥ 5G - $13

Dexter™
#6009 · with ribbon · 9"

Introduced: 1993
Retired: 1997
Dexter was issued
without a phrase.
Also with Hong Kong hang tag.
1G - $50 ♥ 2G - $65 ♥
4G - $20 ♥ 5G - $25

Dexter™
#6009 · with ribbon and
overalls · 9"

Introduced: 1993
Retired: 1997
Dexter was issued
without a phrase.
4G - $15 ♥ 5G - $7

Dickens™
#6038 · no clothes · 8"

Introduced: 1995
Retired: 7/31/1998
You're Beary Special To Me
4G - $12 ♥ 5G - $6 ♥ 6G - $5

Dickens™
#6038 · with overalls · 8"

Introduced: 1995
Retired: 7/31/1998
You're Beary Special To Me
4G - $25 ♥ 5G - $6 ♥ 6G - $5

Digby™
#6013 · with ribbon and
humpback · 12"

Introduced: 1994
Retired: 1997
Digby was issued
without a phrase.
1G - $210

Digby™
#6013 · with ribbon and
straightback · 12"

Introduced: 1994
Retired: 1997
Digby was issued
without a phrase.
1G - $90 ♥ 4G - $65 ♥ 5G - $90

Digby™
#6013 · with sweater · 12"

Introduced: 1994
Retired: 1997
Digby was issued
without a phrase.
Also with ribbon 1G - $110.
4G - 50 ♥ 5G - $22

Domino™
#6042 · no clothes · 12"

Introduced: 1996
Retired: 1997
Domino was issued
without a phrase.
5G - $25

Domino™
#6042 · with overalls · 12"

Introduced: 1996
Retired: 1997
Domino was issued
without a phrase.
5G - $25

Easton™
#6217 · 8"

Introduced: 6/24/2000
Retired: 6/15/2001
Good Fortune To You!
7G - $5

Ebony™
#6130 · with jumper · 13"

Introduced: 1/1/1998
Retired: 7/31/1998
Ebony was issued
without a phrase.
6G - $11

Ebony™
#6063 · with jumper · 15"

Introduced: 1996
Retired: 1997
Ebony was issued
without a phrase.
Also with no clothes and ribbon 5G
- $125.
5G - $15

Elizabeth™
#6261 · 8"

Introduced: 6/23/2001
Retired: 9/11/2001
Easy On The Eyes!
7G - $5

Emily™
#6016 · with bow on head and
large feet · 12"

Introduced: 1994
Retired: 1997
Emily was issued
without a phrase.
1G - $120

Emily™
#6016 · with bow on head and
small feet · 12"

Introduced: 1994
Retired: 1997
Emily was issued
without a phrase.
1G - $90 ♥ 3G - $60 ♥
4G - $40 ♥ 5G - $70

Emily™
#6016 · with hat and dress · 12"

Introduced: 1994
Retired: 1997
Emily was issued
without a phrase.
Also with bow 4G - $100.
1G - $175 ♥ 3G - $90 ♥
4G - $75 ♥ 5G - $35

334

Emma™
#6299 • 8"

Introduced: 4/30/2002
Retired: 12/27/2002
Hats Off To You!
7G - $5

Emmet™
#6253 • 7"

Introduced: 1/1/2001
Retired: 1/1/2002
All The World Loves A Clown!
7G - $5

Esmerelda™
#6086 • 8"

Introduced: 9/30/1998
Retired: 12/31/1998
That Old Black Magic!
6G - $6 ♥ 7G - $5

Eva™
#6276 • 8"

Introduced: 6/23/2001
Retired: 9/11/2001
Let's Dance The Night Away!
7G - $5

Eve™
#6106 • 12"

Introduced: 5/30/1998
Retired: 5/22/2000
You're The Apple Of My Eye
6G - $6 ♥ 7G - $5

Fairbanks™
#6059 • 8"

Introduced: 4/21/1999
Retired: 5/22/2000
Land Of The Midnight Sun
7G - $5

Fairchild™
#6220 • 8"

Introduced: 1/4/2000
Retired: 12/19/2000
While The Cat's Away?
7G - $5

Fern™
#6235 • 8"

Introduced: 6/24/2000
Retired: 11/8/2000
Give Peas A Chance!
7G - $5

Fields™
#6292 • 8"

Introduced: 12/27/2001
Retired: 4/23/2002
Hopping Down The Bunny Trail!
7G - $5

Flannigan™
#6296 · 8"

Introduced: 12/27/2001
Retired: 12/27/2002
The Luck Of The Irish!
7G - $5

Fleecia™
#6293 · 8"

Introduced: 12/27/2001
Retired: 4/23/2002
As Gentle As A Lamb!
7G - $5

Flynn™
#6287 · 8"

Introduced: 12/27/2001
Retired: 2/12/2002
You Are My Heart's Delight!
7G - $5

Franny™
#6229 · 8"

Introduced: 6/24/2000
Retired: 9/10/2002
Hip Hip Hurray For The USA!
7G - $5

Fraser™
#6010 · with ribbon · 8"

Introduced: 1993
Retired: 7/31/1998
Fraser was issued
without a phrase.
Also with Hong Kong hang tag.
1G - $60 ♥ 2G - $40 ♥
4G - $16 ♥ 5G - $18

Fraser™
#6010 · with ribbon and artist
tush tag · 8"

Introduced: 1993
Retired: 7/31/1998
Fraser was issued
without a phrase.
1G - $95

Fraser™
#6010 · with sweater · 8"

Introduced: 1993
Retired: 7/31/1998
Come Sail Away With Me
5G - $6 ♥ 6G - $5

Frederick™
#6072 · 8"

Introduced: 1996
Retired: 1997
Frederick was issued
without a phrase.
5G - $18

Gem™
#6107 · 13"

Introduced: 9/30/1998
Retired: 12/31/1998
Let It Snow!
7G - $6

Genevieve™
#6274 · 8"

Introduced: 4/26/2001
Retired: 9/11/2001
Feline Great!
7G - $8

Georgette™
#6091 · 9"

Introduced: 1/1/1999
Retired: 5/22/2000
And They Lived Happily
Ever After!
7G - $5

Georgia™
#6095 · 8"

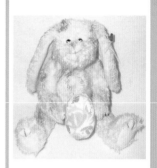

Introduced: 1/1/1999
Retired: 5/22/2000
Follow Your Rainbow
7G - $5

Gilbert Gold™
#6006 · with overalls · 8"

Introduced: 1993
Retired: 1997
Gilbert Gold was issued
without a phrase.
1G - $70 ♥ 5G - $5

Gilbert Gold™
#6006 · with ribbon · 8"

Introduced: 1993
Retired: 1997
Gilbert Gold was issued
without a phrase.
Also with Hong Kong hang tag.
1G - $80

Gilbert White™
#6015 · 8"

Introduced: 1993
Retired: 1993
Gilbert White was issued
without a phrase.
1G - $200

Gloria™
#6123 · 12"

Introduced: 5/30/1998
Retired: 7/31/1998
Gloria was issued
without a phrase.
6G - $11

Gordon™
#6110 · 13"

Introduced: 1/1/1999
Retired: 10/21/1999
Into Each Life A Little Rain
Must Fall
7G - $6

Grace™
#6142 · 12"

Introduced: 1/1/1998
Retired: 9/20/1998
Grace was issued
without a phrase.
6G - $5

Grady™ aka Grover™
#6051 · with sweater and Grady hang tag · 16"

Introduced: 1995
Retired: 1997
Grady was issued
without a phrase.
5G - $40

Grant™
#6101 · 13"

Introduced: 1/1/1998
Retired: 8/30/1999
Let Freedom Ring
6G - $7 ♥ 7G - $6

Greyson™
#6234 · long fur · 8"

Introduced: 7/16/2000
Retired: 6/15/2001
Behind Every Cloud Is A
Silver Lining!
7G - $5

Greyson™
#6234 · short fur · 8"

Introduced: 7/16/2000
Retired: 6/15/2001
Behind Every Cloud Is A
Silver Lining!
7G - $5

Grover™
#6050 · brown with overalls · 16"

Introduced: 1995
Retired: 1997
Grover was issued
without a phrase.
Also with ribbon 2G $45 ♥ 3G $30
5G - $12

Grover™
#6100 · brown with overalls · 13"

Introduced: 1/1/1998
Retired: 5/1/1998
You Make Things Bearable
6G - $10

Grover™
#6050 · brown with ribbon · 16"

Introduced: 1995
Retired: 1997
Grover was issued
without a phrase.
2G - $25 ♥ 3G - $18 ♥ 4G - $18

Grover Gold™
#6051 · with sweater · 16"

Introduced: 1995
Retired: 1997
Grover Gold was issued
without a phrase.
Also with no clothes and ribbon
4G - $20, 5G - $25.
5G - $19

Gwyndolyn™
#6209 · 8"

Introduced: 8/31/1999
Retired: 5/22/2000
All That Glitters!
7G - $5

Hagatha™
#6273 · 8"

Introduced: 9/3/2001
Retired: 10/17/2001
I'll Conjure Up Some Fun!
7G - $5

Harper™
#6214 · 8"

Introduced: 1/4/2000
Retired: 7/6/2000
Cream Of The Crop!
7G - $5

Hayes™
#6212 · 8"

Introduced: 1/4/2000
Retired: 7/6/2000
You're Peachy!
7G - $5

Heartley™
#6111 · 12"

Introduced: 1/1/1999
Retired: 5/22/2000
Love Conquers All
7G - $5

Heather™
#6061 · with overalls · 20"

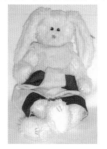

Introduced: 1996
Retired: 1997
Heather was issued
without a phrase.
Also with ribbon 5G - $95 and with no clothes and ribbon 5G - $55.
5G - $24

Henry Brown™
#6005 · with overalls · 8"

Introduced: 1994
Retired: 1997
Henry Brown was issued
without a phrase.
Also with ribbon 1G - $110.
1G - $80 ♥ 5G - $12

Henry Brown™
#6005 · with ribbon · 8"

Introduced: 1994
Retired: 1997
Henry Brown was issued
without a phrase.
Also with Hong Kong hang tag.
1G - $50

Henry Gold™
#6005 · 8"

Introduced: 1993
Retired: 1993
Henry Gold was issued
without a phrase.
1G - $320

Hogan™
#6245 · 7"

Introduced: 1/1/2001
Retired: 1/1/2002
No Worries!
7G - $5

Hutchins™
#6290 · 8"

Introduced: 12/27/2001
Retired: 4/23/2002
A Hop, Skip And A Jump!
7G - $5

Iris™
#6077 · 10"

Introduced: 1/1/1998
Retired: 12/31/1998
My Heart Belongs To You
6G - $5 ♥ 7G - $5

Isabella™
#6109 · 13"

Introduced: 9/30/1998
Retired: 5/22/2000
Puttin' On The Ritz
7G - $6

Ivan™
#6029 · 8"

Introduced: 1995
Retired: 7/13/1999
Grin And Bear It
2G - $70 ♥ 3G - $55 ♥ 4G - $18 ♥
5G - $6 ♥ 6G - $5 ♥ 7G - $5

Ivory™
#6062 · with overalls · 15"

Introduced: 1996
Retired: 1997
Ivory was issued
without a phrase.
Also with no clothes and ribbon - $120.
5G - $17

Ivy™
#6076 · 10"

Introduced: 1/1/1998
Retired: 12/31/1998
Hoppy Spring
6G - $5 ♥ 7G - $5

Jack™
#6989 · 13"

Introduced: 1998
Retired: 5/21/2000
Jack was issued
without a phrase.
UK Exclusive.
6G - $9 ♥ 7G - $8

Jangle™
#6082 · 8"

Introduced: 9/30/1998
Retired: 12/31/1998
Jingle All The Way
7G - $5

Jeremy™
#6008 · with overalls · 12"

Introduced: 1993
Retired: 1997
Jeremy was issued
without a phrase.
Also with no clothes and ribbon 1G -
$75, 2G - $35, 4G - $28, 5G - $35.
5G - $15

340

Jeremy™
#6008 · with sweater · 12"

Introduced: 1993
Retired: 1997
Jeremy was issued
without a phrase.
Also with ribbon
2G - $70, 4G - $50, 5G - $65.
4G - $45 ♥ 5G - $20

Justin™
#6044 · with sweater · 14"

Introduced: 1996
Retired: 1997
Justin was issued
without a phrase.
Also with no clothes 5G - $55.
5G - $65

Kaiser™
#6265 · 8"

Introduced: 4/26/2001
Retired: 1/1/2002
I'm On A Roll!
7G - $5

Karena™
#6301 · 8"

Introduced: 4/30/2002
Retired: 12/27/2002
A Rose Is A Rose!
7G - $5

Katrina™
#6054 · 8"

Introduced: 4/22/1999
Retired: 5/22/2000
Feline Fine!
7G - $5

King™
#6140 · 11"

Introduced: 1/1/1998
Retired: 5/1/1998
King was issued
without a phrase.
6G - $18

King™
#6049 · no clothes · 9"

Introduced: 1996
Retired: 1997
King was issued
without a phrase.
5G - $20

King™
#6049 · with cape · 9"

Introduced: 1996
Retired: 1997
King was issued
without a phrase.
5G - $20

Kingston™
#6236 · 7"

Introduced: 6/24/2000
Retired: 3/28/2001
King Of Hearts!
7G - $5

Klause™
#6239 · 8"

Introduced: 8/27/2000
Retired: 11/17/2000
Sleigh What?
7G - $5

Kyoto™
#6603 · 8"

Introduced: 10/18/2001
Retired: 12/20/2001
Stand On Ceremony!
Japan exclusive.
7G - $8

Lancaster™
#6289 · 8"

Introduced: 12/27/2001
Retired: 2/12/2002
You're Always On My Mind!
7G - $5

Laurel™
#6081 · 8"

Introduced: 9/30/1998
Retired: 12/31/1998
Happy Holly-days
Also known as Holly.
7G - $5

Lawrence™
#6053 · light print blanket · 9"

Introduced: 4/20/1999
Retired: 5/30/2000
I Won't Leave You High
And Dry!
7G - $5

Lawrence™
#6053 · dark print blanket · 9"

Introduced: 4/20/1999
Retired: 5/30/2000
I Won't Leave You High
And Dry!
7G - $5

Lilly™
#6037 · with jumper · 9"

Introduced: 1995
Retired: 5/1/1998
Love Ewe
Also with ribbon 2
G - $100, 3G - $85, 4G - $55.
2G - $80 ♥ 3G - $65 ♥ 4G - $40 ♥
5G - $7 ♥ 6G - $5

Lilly™
#6037 · with ribbon · 9"

Introduced: 1995
Retired: 5/1/1998
Lilly was issued
without a phrase.
2G - $65 ♥ 3G - $45 ♥ 4G - $40

Logan™
#6602 · 8"

Introduced: 10/1/2001
Retired: 9/30/2002
Out And About...Eh!
Canada exclusive.
7G - $8

Mackenzie™
#6999 · 13"

Introduced: 1998
Retired: 5/27/2000
Strong And Free - Patriot
of the North
*Canada exclusive. Also with Patriot
misspelt as Oatriot 7G - $35.*
6G - $28 ♥ 7G - $22

Madison™
#6035 · with overalls · 10"

Introduced: 1995
Retired: 5/1/1998
Madison was issued
without a phrase.
*Also with ribbon 4G - $35
and no clothes with ribbon
2G - $25, 3G - $25, 4G - $25.*
2G - $55 ♥ 3G - $45 ♥ 5G - $7 ♥ 6G - $5

Majesty™
#6259 · 8"

Introduced: 6/23/2001
Retired: 9/11/2001
Mane Attraction!
7G - $6

Malcolm™
#6112 · 13"

Introduced: 4/20/1999
Retired: 5/22/2000
March To A Different Drum
7G - $6

Malcolm™
#6026 · with sweater · 12"

Introduced: 1995
Retired: 1997
Malcolm was issued
without a phrase.
*Also with ribbon 4G - $45
and no clothes with ribbon
2G - $50, 3G - $40, 4G - $30.*
2G - $60 ♥ 3G - $55 ♥ 4G - $25 ♥
5G - $20

Marigold™
#6228 · 8"

Introduced: 6/24/2000
Retired: 10/20/2000
Happiness Is In Bloom!
7G - $5

Martina™
#6303 · 8"

Introduced: 4/30/2002
Retired: 12/27/2002
Roses Are Red!
7G - $5

Mason™
#6020 · with ribbon · 8"

Introduced: 1995
Retired: 5/1/1998
Mason was issued
without a phrase.
2G - $40 ♥ 4G - $25 ♥ 5G - $22

Mason™
#6020 · with sweater · 8"

Introduced: 1995
Retired: 5/1/1998
Mason was issued
without a phrase.
Also with ribbon 4G - $45.
4G - $35 ♥ 5G - $6 ♥ 6G - $5

Max™
#6246 · 9"

Introduced: 8/27/2000
Retired: 2/7/2001
Paws For Thought!
7G - $6

May™
#6256 · 8"

Introduced: 1/1/2001
Retired: 4/23/2002
Bring May Flowers!
7G - $5

McKinley™
#6604 · 8"

Introduced: 1/27/2002
Retired: 5/24/2002
Born In The USA!
USA exclusive.
7G - $5

Mei Li™
#6272 · 8"

Introduced: 6/23/2001
Retired: 4/23/2002
True Beauty Goes Beyond
The Physical!
7G - $5

Merwyn™
#6243 · 9"

Introduced: 8/27/2000
Retired: 11/14/2000
One Newt or Two?
7G - $5

Minerva™
#6247 · 7"

Introduced: 1/1/2001
Retired: 1/1/2002
Mind Your Manners!
7G - $5

Mom™
#6270 · 7"

Introduced: 3/3/2001
Retired: 7/16/2001
A Mother's Love Is The
Greatest Gift!
7G - $7

Mommy™
#6298 · 8"

Introduced: 3/29/2002
Retired: 5/24/2002
All You Need Is Love!
7G - $5

Montgomery™
#6143 · 15"

Introduced: 1/1/1998
Retired: 9/20/1998
Happy Trails To You
6G - $7

Morgan™
#6018 · with ribbon · 7"

Introduced: 1994
Retired: 7/31/1998
Morgan was issued
without a phrase.
1G - $52

Morgan™
#6018 · with vest · 8"

Introduced: 1994
Retired: 7/31/1998
"Monkey See, Monkey Do!"
5G - $6 ♥ 6G - $5

Mrs. Santabear™
#6285 · 8"

Introduced: 10/1/2001
Retired: 12/21/2001
Under The Mistletoe!
7G - $5

Mulligan™
#6231 · 8"

Introduced: 6/24/2000
Retired: 4/23/2002
Here Birdie Birdie Birdie...!
7G - $5

Murphy™
#6033 · no clothes · 9"

Introduced: 1995
Retired: 1997
Murphy was issued
without a phrase.
2G - $18 ♥ 3G - $18 ♥ 4G - $18

Murphy™
#6033 · with overalls · 9"

Introduced: 1995
Retired: 1997
Murphy was issued
without a phrase.
2G - $17 ♥ 3G - $17 ♥ 4G - $17 ♥ 5G - $6

Nicholas™
#6015 · with ribbon · 8"

Introduced: 1994
Retired: 7/31/1998
Nicholas was issued
without a phrase.
1G - $120 ♥ 4G - $140

Nicholas™
#6015 · with sweater · 8"

Introduced: 1994
Retired: 7/31/1998
Hearts Off To You
5G - $6 ♥ 6G - $5 ♥ 7G - $20

Nola™
#6014 · with hat and dress · 12"

Introduced: 1994
Retired: 1997
Nola was issued
without a phrase.
1G - $155 ♥ 5G - $45

Nola™
#6014 · with ribbon · 12"

Introduced: 1994
Retired: 1997
Nola was issued
without a phrase.
Also with no clothes and bow on head
1G - $130, 2G - $110, 3G - $90,
4G - $70, 5G - $80.
1G - $110

North™
#6244 · 8"

Introduced: 8/27/2000
Retired: 12/19/2000
Let It Snow!
7G - $5

Olivia™
#6258 · 8"

Introduced: 1/1/2001
Retired: 1/1/2002
Not Just Another Pretty Face!
7G - $5

Olympia™
#6308 · 8"

Introduced: 6/22/2002
Retired: 12/27/2002
Do You Believe In Magic?
7G - $5

Orion™
#6207 · 8"

Introduced: 9/31/1999
Retired: 5/22/2000
You're My Universe!
7G - $5

Oscar™
#6025 · with overalls · 8"

Introduced: 1995
Retired: 5/1/1998
Oscar was issued
without a phrase.
2G - $35 ♥ 3G - $22 ♥ 4G - $16 ♥
5G - $7 ♥ 6G - $6

Oscar™
#6025 · with ribbon · 8"

Introduced: 1995
Retired: 5/1/1998
Oscar was issued
without a phrase.
2G - $28 ♥ 3G - $20 ♥ 4G - $20

Penelope™
#6036 · no clothes · 9"

Introduced: 1995
Retired: 1997
Penelope was issued
without a phrase.
2G - $28 ♥ 3G - $22 ♥ 4G - $20

Penelope™
#6036 · with overalls · 9"

Introduced: 1995
Retired: 1997
Penelope was issued
without a phrase.
4G - $34 ♥ 5G - $12

Peppermint™
#6084 · 8"

Introduced: 1/1/1998
Retired: 7/13/1999
Love Me True
6G - $6 ♥ 7G - $5

Peter™
#6084 · 8"

Introduced: 9/30/1998
Retired: 12/31/1998
Trick Or Treat
7G - $5

Peter™ aka Pumpkin™
#6084 · with Pumpkin
hang tag · 8"

Introduced: 9/30/1998
Retired: 12/31/1998
Peter aka Pumpkin was i
ssued without a phrase.
6G - $7

Piccadilly™
#6069 · blue and green
outfit · 9"

Introduced: 5/30/1998
Retired: 5/22/2000
Laughter Is The Best Medicine
*Sometimes there is no phrase
in the hang tag.*
6G - $6 ♥ 7G - $5

Piccadilly™
#6069 · multicolored outfit · 9"

Introduced: 5/30/1998
Retired: 5/22/2000
Laughter Is The Best Medicine
7G - $5

Piccadilly™ aka
Small Bear™
#6069 · Small Bear hang tag · 9"

Introduced: 5/30/1998
Retired: 5/22/2000
Piccadilly aka Small Bear was
issued without a phrase.
6G - $7

Piccadilly™
#6069 · Azalea hang tag · 9"

Introduced: 5/30/1998
Retired: 5/22/2000
Piccadilly was issued
without a phrase.
7G - $8

Pouncer™
#6011 · with jumper · 8"

Introduced: 1994
Retired: 5/22/2000
Smiles Are Contagious
*Sometimes there is no phrase
in the hang tag.*
6G - $5 ♥ 7G - $5

Pouncer™
#6011 · with ribbon and
different colored ears · 8"

Introduced: 1994
Retired: 5/22/2000
Pouncer was issued
without a phrase.
1G - $170 ♥ 3G - $60

Pouncer™
#6011 · with ribbon and same colored ears · 8"

Introduced: 1994
Retired: 5/22/2000
Pouncer was issued
without a phrase.
1G - $60

Pouncer™
#6011 · with sweater · 8"

Introduced: 1994
Retired: 5/22/2000
Pouncer was issued
without a phrase.
5G - $6

Precious™
#6104 · 12"

Introduced: 1/1/1998
Retired: 9/20/1998
Early To Bed, Early To Rise
6G - $6

Prince™
#6048 · 7"

Introduced: 1996
Retired: 9/20/1998
Prince was issued
without a phrase.
6G - $7 ♥ 7G - $6

Priscilla™
#6045 · with overalls · 12"

Introduced: 1996
Retired: 1997
Priscilla was issued
without a phrase.
Also with no clothes 5G - $20.
5G - $15

Purrcy™
#6022 · with jumper · 8"

Introduced: 1995
Retired: 5/22/2000
You're The Cat's Meow
*Sometimes there is no phrase
in the hang tag.*
6G - $5 ♥ 7G - $5

Purrcy™
#6022 · with overalls · 8"

Introduced: 1995
Retired: 5/22/2000
Purrcy was issued
without a phrase.
5G - $5

Purrcy™
#6022 · with ribbon · 8"

Introduced: 1995
Retired: 5/22/2000
Purrcy was issued
without a phrase.
2G - $65 ♥ 3G - $60 ♥ 4G - $40 ♥
5G - $30

Radcliffe™
#6087 · 9"

Introduced: 1/1/1999
Retired: 5/22/2000
Thief Of Hearts
7G - $5

Rafaella™
#6066 · 8"

Introduced: 4/9/1999
Retired: 5/22/2000
All A Flutter Over You
7G - $5

Ramsey™
#6092 · 9"

Introduced: 1/1/1999
Retired: 5/22/2000
Little Lamsadivy
7G - $5

Rebecca™
#6019 · with overalls and red gingham bow on head · 12"

Introduced: 1995
Retired: 1997
Rebecca was issued
without a phrase.
Also with blue floral bow
2G - $75, 4G - $55, 5G - $75.
2G - $175 ♥ 4G - $90 ♥ 5G - $35

Reggie™
#6004 · with Hong Kong hang tag · 8"

Introduced: 1993
Retired: 1995
Reggie was issued
without a phrase.
1G - $110

Reggie™
#6004 · with Korea hang tag · 8"

Introduced: 1993
Retired: 1995
Reggie was issued
without a phrase.
1G - $95

Revere™
#6305 · 8"

Introduced: 4/30/2002
Retired: 12/27/2002
Stars and Stripes Forever!
7G - $5

Rhine™
#6601 · 8"

Introduced: 8/25/2001
Retired: 12/27/2002
Unite!
7G - $7

River™
#6237 · 8"

Introduced: 6/24/2000
Retired: 11/8/2000
Go With The Flow!
7G - $5

Rosalie™
#6068 · 9"

Introduced: 4/22/1999
Retired: 5/22/2000
A Rose By Any Other Name?
7G - $5

Rosalyne™
#6211 · 8"

Introduced: 1/4/2000
Retired: 3/22/2002
Everything Is Coming Up Roses!
7G - $5

Rose™
#6078 · 10"

Introduced: 1/1/1998
Retired: 12/31/1998
Take Time to Smell the Roses!
*Sometimes there is no phrase
in the hang tag.*
6G - $5 ♥ 7G - $5

Salty™
#6056 · 8"

Introduced: 4/22/1999
Retired: 5/22/2000
Anchors Away!
7G - $5

Samuel™
#6105 · 13"

Introduced: 5/30/1998
Retired: 5/22/2000
I WANT YOU
6G - $6 ♥ 7G - $5

Samuel™ aka Large Bear™
#6105 · Large Bear hang tag · 13"

Introduced: 5/30/1998
Retired: 5/22/2000
Samuel aka Large Bear was
issued without a phrase.
6G - $6

Santabear™
#6284 · 8"

Introduced: 10/1/2001
Retired: 12/21/2001
He Sees You When
You're Sleeping!
7G - $5

Sara™
#6120 · 15"

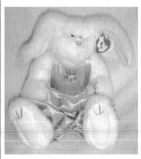

Introduced: 1/1/1998
Retired: 5/11/1999
Spring Is In The Air
*Sometimes there is no phrase
in the hang tag.*
6G - $7 ♥ 7G - $6

Sara™
#6007 · with jumper · 12"

Introduced: 1993
Retired: 1997
Sara was issued
without a phrase.
Also with ribbon 4G - $45, 5G - $55.
5G - $12

Sara™
#6007 · with ribbon · 12"

Introduced: 1993
Retired: 1997
Sara was issued
without a phrase.
Also with artist tush tag 1G - $215.
1G - $80 ♥ 2G - $70 ♥ 3G - $45 ♥
4G - $30 ♥ 5G - $40

Scarlet™
#6224 · 8"

Introduced: 6/24/2000
Retired: 10/20/2000
You're Mauve-alous!
7G - $5

Scooter™
#6032 · no clothes · 9"

Introduced: 1995
Retired: 1997
Scooter was issued
without a phrase.
2G - $20

Scooter™
#6032 · with sweater · 9"

Introduced: 1995
Retired: 1997
Scooter was issued
without a phrase.
2G - $20 ♥ 5G - $20

Scotch™
#6103 · 14"

Introduced: 1/1/1998
Retired: 7/31/1998
I'd Be Lost Without You!
*Sometimes there is no phrase
in the hang tag.*
6G - $10 ♥ 7G - $22

Scruffy™
#6085 · coarse, tacked ears · 9"

Introduced: 1/1/1998
Retired: 5/11/1999
Every Dog Has Its Day
6G - $5

Scruffy™
#6085 · medium plush, floppy
ears · 9"

Introduced: 1/1/1998
Retired: 5/11/1999
Every Dog Has Its Day
6G - $5

Scruffy™
#6085 · soft plush, floppy
ears · 9"

Introduced: 1/1/1998
Retired: 5/11/1999
Every Dog Has Its Day
7G - $5

Shelby™
#6024 · with dress · 9"

Introduced: 1995
Retired: 5/11/1999
Some-Bunny Loves You
*Sometimes there is no phrase
in the hang tag.*
2G - $40 ♥ 5G - $7 ♥ 6G - $6

Shelby™
#6024 · with ribbon · 9"

Introduced: 1995
Retired: 5/11/1999
Shelby was issued
without a phrase.
2G - $30

Sidney™
#6121 · 15"

Introduced: 1/1/1998
Retired: 7/31/1998
Sugar And Spice And
Everything Nice
6G - $8

Sire™
#6141 · 13"

Introduced: 1/1/1998
Retired: 9/20/1998
It's Good To Be King
6G - $6

Skylar™
#6096 · black nose · 9"

Introduced: 1/1/1999
Retired: 3/31/1999
The Sky Is The Limit
7G - $5

Skylar™
#6096 · rust colored nose · 9"

Introduced: 1/1/1999
Retired: 3/31/1999
The Sky Is The Limit
7G - $6

Socrates™
#6269 · 7"

Introduced: 3/30/2001
Retired: 7/16/2001
Wisdom Comes With Age!
7G - $6

Sophia™
#6278 · 8"

Introduced: 4/26/2001
Retired: 1/1/2002
Pretty As A Picture!
7G - $6

Spencer™
#6046 · no clothes · 15"

Introduced: 1996
Retired: 1997
Spencer was issued
without a phrase.
5G - $16

Spencer™
#6046 · with sweater · 15"

Introduced: 1996
Retired: 1997
Spencer was issued
without a phrase.
5G - $14

Spruce™
#6203 · 8"

Introduced: 8/31/1999
Retired: 12/10/1999
I'm Pining For You!
7G - $10

Squeaky™
#6017 · 8"

Introduced: 1994
Retired: 9/20/1998
Say Cheese!
*Sometimes there is no phrase
in the hang tag.*
1G - $70 ♥ 5G - $6 ♥ 6G - $5

Squeaky™
#6017 · black whiskers all
grey · 8"

Introduced: 1994
Retired: 9/20/1998
Squeaky was issued
without a phrase.
1G - $55

Squeaky™
#6017 · clear whiskers all
grey · 8"

Introduced: 1994
Retired: 9/20/1998
Squeaky was issued
without a phrase.
1G - $60

Sterling™
#6083 · 6" wings · 8"

Introduced: 9/30/1998
Retired: 5/24/1999
Make A Wish
7G - $5

Sterling™
#6083 · 7" wings · 8"

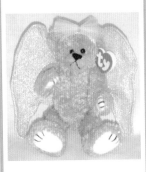

Introduced: 9/30/1998
Retired: 5/24/1999
Make A Wish
7G - $6

Strawbunny™
#6079 · 10"

Introduced: 1/1/1998
Retired: 5/11/1999
You Tickle Me Pink
6G - $5 ♥ 7G - $5

Suki™
#6266 · 8"

Introduced: 1/1/2001
Retired: 4/23/2002
The Heart That Loves Is
Always Young!
7G - $5

Surprise™
#6311 · 8"

Introduced: 6/22/2002
Retired: 11/26/2002
May Your Birthday Wish
Come True!
7G - $5

Susannah™
#6067 · 9"

Introduced: 4/17/1999
Retired: 5/22/2000
You Are My Sunshine
7G - $5

Tiny Tim™
#6001 · with overalls · 8"

Introduced: 1993
Retired: 1997
Tiny Tim was issued
without a phrase.
Also with ribbon
2G - $55, 4G - $30, 5G - $55.
2G - $50 ▼ 4G - $35 ▼ 5G - $8

Tiny Tim™
#6001 · with ribbon · 8"

Introduced: 1993
Retired: 1997
Tiny Tim was issued
without a phrase.
Also with Hong Kong hang tag.
1G - $65 ▼ 2G - $45 ▼ 4G - $20 ▼
5G - $35

Tracey™
#6047 · no clothes · 15"

Introduced: 1996
Retired: 1997
Tracey was issued
without a phrase.
5G - $18

Tracey™
#6047 · with overalls · 15"

Introduced: 1996
Retired: 1997
Tracey was issued
without a phrase.
5G - $16

Tudor™
#6600 · 8"

Introduced: 9/2/2001
Retired: 12/27/2002
Cheers!
UK exclusive.
7G - $9

Tyler™
#6002 · with humpback and
ribbon · 12"

Introduced: 1993
Retired: 1997
Tyler was issued
without a phrase.
First releases had darker nose.
Also with straightback 1G - $85,
2G - $40, 4G - $40, 5G - $30.
1G - $140

Tyler™
#6002 · with sweater · 12"

Introduced: 1993
Retired: 1997
Tyler was issued
without a phrase.
Also with ribbon
1G - $100, 2G - $80, 4G - $50.
2G - $65 ▼ 4G - $30 ▼ 5G - $18

Tyra™
#6201 · 8"

Introduced: 8/31/1999
Retired: 10/19/1999
High Spirits!
7G - $165

Tyra™
#6201 · with pompoms · 8"

Introduced: 8/31/1999
Retired: 10/19/1999
High Spirits!
7G - $500

354

Tyrone™
#6108 · 13"

Introduced: 9/30/1998
Retired: 5/22/2000
You're One Class Act
7G - $5

Uncle Sam™
#6257 · 8"

Introduced: 4/26/2001
Retired: 7/11/2001
As American As Apple Pie!
7G - $6

Vlad™
#6275 · 8"

Introduced: 9/3/2001
Retired: 10/17/2001
Good Night, Sleep Tight!
7G - $5

Waddlesworth™
#6202 · 8"

Introduced: 8/31/1999
Retired: 5/22/2000
I'm On Top Of The World!
7G - $5

Washington™
#6255 · 8"

Introduced: 4/26/2001
Retired: 7/11/2001
Land Of The Free!
7G - $5

Watson™
#6065 · with overalls · 14"

Introduced: 1996
Retired: 1997
Also with no clothes and ribbon - $75.
5G - $25

Weatherby™
#6283 · 8"

Introduced: 10/1/2001
Retired: 1/1/2002
Cold Hands, Warm Heart!
7G - $5

Wee Willie
#6021 · with overalls · 8"

Introduced: 1995
Retired: 1997
Wee Willie was issued
without a phrase.
*Also with ribbon 2G - $65, 4G - $75
and no clothes with ribbon
2G - $30, 5G - $50.*
4G - $70 ♥ 5G - $5

Wee Willie
#6021 · with overalls and Wee
Wiljje hang tag · 8"

Introduced: 1995
Retired: 1997
Wee Willie was issued
without a phrase.
Also no clothes & ribbon 2G $50
2G - $65

Whiskers™
#6012 · with jumper · 8"

Introduced: 1994
Retired: 8/2/1999
"You're Purr-fect!"
6G - $5 ♥ 7G - $5

Whiskers™
#6012 · with overalls · 8"

Introduced: 1994
Retired: 8/2/1999
Whiskers was issued
without a phrase.
5G - $6

Whiskers™
#6012 · with ribbon · 8"

Introduced: 1994
Retired: 8/2/1999
Whiskers was issued
without a phrase.
Also with different colored ears - $150.
1G - $85

William™
#6113 · 12"

Introduced: 4/12/1999
Retired: 5/22/2000
Dressed For Success
7G - $6

Winifred™
#6302 · 8"

Introduced: 4/30/2002
Retired: 12/27/2002
Ring Around The Rosie!
7G - $5

Winona
#6300 · 8"

Introduced: 4/30/2002
Retired: 12/27/2002
I Tip My Hat To You!
7G - $5

Woolie Brown™
#6012 · 6"

Introduced: 1993
Retired: 1993
Woolie Brown was issued
without a phrase.
*Extremely rare and value is
undetermined.*
1G - N/E

Woolie Gold™
#6011 · 6"

Introduced: 1993
Retired: 1993
Woolie Gold was issued
without a phrase.
1G - $470

NOTES

First came Pillow Pals and then came Baby Ty. In his search for the safest, softest cuddle toy for babies, Ty has made several transitions. Dogbaby, one of the first Baby Ty animals came with hang tags that read "The Pillow Pals Collection". Whether soft and smooth or silky and furry, all Baby Ty fabric offers gentle snuggles. The PJ bears in their pretty pastels, ready for beddie-bye and the Snoozies with their blankies make wonderful baby shower gifts.

Baby Blooms™
#34602

Introduced: 12/30/2004
Retired: 3/27/2006
1G - $10

Baby Blossoms™
#34600

Introduced: 12/30/2004
Retired: 3/27/2006
1G - $9

Baby Blue™
#31015

Introduced: 10/31/2006
Current
2G - Current Retail Value

Baby Dangles™
#31024 · blue

Introduced: 10/31/2006
Current
2G - Current Retail Value

Baby Dangles™
#31023 · pink

Introduced: 10/31/2006
Current
2G - Current Retail Value

Baby Growlers™
#31032 · blue

Introduced: 12/29/2006
Current
2G - Current Retail Value

Baby Growlers™
#31031 · pink

Introduced: 12/29/2006
Current
2G - Current Retail Value

Baby Petals™
#34601

Introduced: 12/30/2004
Retired: 3/27/2006
1G - $15

Baby Pink™
#31014

Introduced: 10/31/2006
Current
2G - Current Retail Value

Baby Pups™
#31034 · blue

Introduced: 2/28/2007
Current
2G - Current Retail Value

Baby Pups™
#31033 · pink

Introduced: 2/28/2007
Current
2G - Current Retail Value

Baby Tiptop™
#31030 · blue

Introduced: 12/29/2006
Current
2G - Current Retail Value

Baby Tiptop™
#31029 · pink

Introduced: 12/29/2006
Current
2G - Current Retail Value

Baby Whiffer™
#31026 · blue

Introduced: 10/31/2006
Current
2G - Current Retail Value

Baby Whiffer™
#31025 · pink

Introduced: 10/31/2006
Current
2G - Current Retail Value

Baby Winks™
#31028 · blue

Introduced: 10/31/2006
Current
2G - Current Retail Value

Baby Winks™
#31027 · pink

Introduced: 10/31/2006
Current
2G - Current Retail Value

Bearbaby™
#3209 · blue

Introduced: 1/1/2000
Retired: 11/8/2001
1G - $15

Bearbaby™
#3210 · pink

Introduced: 1/1/2000
Retired: 11/8/2001
1G - $15

Bearbaby™
#3200 · ty dye

Introduced: 1/1/2001
Retired: 11/8/2001
1G - $20

Blessings to Baby™
(Baby Blessings™)
#34508 · blue

Introduced: 1/31/2005
Retired: 6/29/2005
2G - $12

Blessings to Baby™ (Baby Blessings™)
#34510 · green

Introduced: 1/31/2005
Retired: 12/29/2005
2G - $12

Blessings to Baby™ (Baby Blessings™)
#34511 · pink

Introduced: 1/31/2005
Retired: 12/29/2005
2G - $12

Blessings to Baby™ (Baby Blessings™)
#34507 · white

Introduced: 1/31/2005
Retired: 12/29/2005
2G - $12

Blessings to Baby™ (Baby Blessings™)
#34509 · yellow

Introduced: 1/31/2005
Retired: 12/29/2005
2G - $12

Bunny Hop™
#34513 · blue

Introduced: 1/1/2006
Retired: 2/27/2007
2G - $8

Bunny Hop™
#34512 · pink

Introduced: 1/1/2006
Retired: 2/27/2007
2G - $9

Bunnybaby™
#3204

Introduced: 1/2000
Retired: 1/21/2001
1G - $18

Cubby Cuddles™
#31010

Introduced: 7/29/2005
Current
2G - Current Retail Value

Cuddle Bunny™
#34501 · blue

Introduced: 12/30/2004
Retired: 4/28/2005
1G - $16

Cuddle Bunny™
#34502 · pink

Introduced: 12/30/2004
Retired: 4/28/2005
1G - $16

Cuddlecub™
#3301 · blue

Introduced: 11/1/2001
Retired: 12/27/2002
1G - $18

Cuddlecub™
#3300 · pink

Introduced: 11/1/2001
Retired: 12/27/2002
1G - $18

Cuddlekitty™
#32005

Introduced: 10/20/2004
Retired: 12/21/2006
1G - $22

Cuddlepup™
#3303 · green

Introduced: 11/1/2001
Retired: 12/27/2002
1G - $45

Cuddlepup™
#34001 · yellow blanket

Introduced: 6/30/2004
Retired: 12/29/2005
1G - $22

Cuddleteddy™
#34100

Introduced: 6/30/2004
Retired: 6/29/2005 6/29/2005
1G - $20

Cutsiemoosie™
#3307

Introduced: 3/3/2002
Retired: 12/27/2002
1G - $60

Dogbaby™
#3205

Introduced: 1/2000
Retired: 11/08/2001
1G - $14

Elephantbaby™
#3207

Introduced: 7/2000
Retired: 11/08/2001
1G - $15

Elephanthugs™
#3310

Introduced: 4/30/2002
Retired: 12/27/2002
1G - $60

Frogbaby™
#3201

Introduced: 1/2000
Retired: 2/27/2001
1G - $40

Funky Monkey™
#31006

Introduced: 6/30/2005
Retired: 6/23/2006
2G - $12

Gwowls™
#31019

Introduced: 6/30/2006
Current
2G - Current Retail Value

Hippobaby™
#3206

Introduced: 7/2000
Retired: 2/27/2000
1G - $50

Honeybunnybaby™
#3212

Introduced: 1/1/2001
Retired: 11/8/2001
1G - $12

Huggybunny™
#3305 · blue

Introduced: 12/28/2001
Retired: 12/27/2002
1G - $30

Huggybunny™
#3304 · lilac/pink

Introduced: 12/28/2001
Retired: 12/27/2002
1G - $20

Huggyducky™
#3309

Introduced: 3/3/2002
Retired: 12/27/2002
1G - $60

Huggypup™
#31008

Introduced: 10/29/2004
Retired: 4/26/2007
1G - $8

Kitty Cat™
#31004

Introduced: 6/30/2005
Retired: 6/23/2006
2G - $10

Kittybaby™
#3211

Introduced: 1/1/2001
Retired: 11/08/2001
1G - $13

Kittyhugs™
#31009

Introduced: 10/29/2004
Retired: 4/26/2007
1G - $7

Kuddlekitty™
#3302

Introduced: 11/1/2001
Retired: 12/27/2002
1G - $25

Kutie Kat™
#31012

Introduced: 7/29/2005
Retired: 4/26/2007
2G - $7

Lamybaby™
#3202

Introduced: 1/1/2000
Retired: 1/21/2001
1G - $30

Little Piggy™
#31007

Introduced: 6/30/2005
Retired: 6/23/2006
2G - $10

362

Monkeybaby™
#3203

Introduced: 1/2000
Retired: 6/25/2000
1G - $35

Moocowbaby™
#3208

Introduced: 7/2000
Retired: 1/2/2000
1G - $10

My Baby Bear™
#34515 · blue

Introduced: 1/1/2006
Current
2G - Current Retail Value

My Baby Bear™
#34503 · brown

Introduced: 1/31/2005
Current
2G - Current Retail Value

My Baby Bear™
#34514 · pink

Introduced: 1/1/2006
Current
2G - Current Retail Value

My Baby Bear Baby's First Christmas™
#31021

Introduced: 9/29/2006
Retired: 10/25/2006
2G - $13

My Baby Bunny™
#34505

Introduced: 1/31/2005
Current
2G - Current Retail Value

My Baby Horsey Blue™
#31036

Introduced: 6/29/2007
Current
2G - Current Retail Value

My Baby Horsey Pink™
#31035

Introduced: 6/29/2007
Current
2G - Current Retail Value

Peekiepoo™
#3311

Introduced: 4/30/2002
Retired: 11/5/2002
1G - $26

PJ Bear™ (large)
#Unknown · blue

Introduced: 6/30/2004
Retired: 2/27/2005
1G - $22

PJ Bear™ (large)
#31202 · green

Introduced: 6/30/2004
Retired: 12/29/2005
1G - $15

PJ Bear™ (large)
#Unknown · pink

Introduced: 6/30/2004
Retired: 2/27/2005
1G - $22

PJ Bear™ (large)
#31201 · yellow

Introduced: 6/30/2004
Retired: 12/29/2005
1G - $15

PJ Bear™ (medium)
#31101 · blue

Introduced: 6/30/2004
Current
1G - Current Retail Value

PJ Bear™ (medium)
#31103 · green

Introduced: 6/30/2004
Retired: 12/29/2005
1G - $18

PJ Bear™ (medium)
#31104 · pink

Introduced: 6/30/2004
Current
1G - Current Retail Value

PJ Bear™ (medium)
#31102 · yellow

Introduced: 6/30/2004
Retired: 12/29/2005
1G - $18

PJ Bear™ (small)
#31000 · blue

Introduced: 6/30/2004
Current
1G - Current Retail Value

PJ Bear™ (small)
#31002 · green

Introduced: 6/30/2004
Retired: 12/29/2005
1G - $12

PJ Bear™ (small)
#31003 · pink

Introduced: 6/30/2004
Current
1G - Current Retail Value

PJ Bear™ (small)
#31001 · yellow

Introduced: 6/30/2004
Retired: 12/29/2005
1G - $12

P'nut™
#31017

Introduced: 6/30/2006
Current
2G - Current Retail Value

Pretty Pony™
#34517 · blue

Introduced: 1/31/2006
Current
2G - Current Retail Value

Pretty Pony™
#34516 · pink

Introduced: 1/31/2006
Current
2G - Current Retail Value

Pretty Pony™
#31022 · white

Introduced: 9/29/2006
Retired: 12/21/2006
2G - $8

Pretty Puppy™
#31005

Introduced: 6/30/2005
Retired: 6/23/2006
2G - $12

Snooziepup™
#34002

Introduced: 6/30/2004
Retired: 12/29/2005
1G - $20

Snoozieteddy™
#34103

Introduced: 6/30/2004
Retired: 5/26/2005
1G - $14

Snugger Pup™
#31011

Introduced: 7/29/2005
Current
2G - Current Retail Value

Snugglefrog™
#3306

Introduced: 12/28/2001
Retired: 10/25/2002
1G - $22

Snugglepup™
#32004

Introduced: 10/29/2004
Retired: 11/22/2006
1G - $22

Twacks™
#31020

Introduced: 6/30/2006
Current
2G - Current Retail Value

Tygerhugs™
#3308

Introduced: 3/3/2002
Retired: 12/27/2002
1G - $55

Collectors will no longer have to say, "My dog ate my Beanie Baby!" Thanks to Ty, the dogs have their OWN Beanies and they are so much more fun to chew on! Bow Wow Beanies are plump, hardy and ultimately chewable. They crinkle and squeak! But watch out! I think I just heard a border collie complaining that "The cat stole my Bow Wow!"

Bones™
#43007

Introduced: 3/31/2006
Current
1G - Current Retail Value

Camouflage™
#43300

Introduced: 3/31/2006
Current
1G - Current Retail Value

Camouflage™ (small)
#43301

Introduced: 3/31/2006
Retired: 12/21/2006
1G - $5

Chillin'™
#43016

Introduced: 9/29/2006
Retired: 12/21/2006
1G - $5

Chocolate™
#43017

Introduced: 9/29/2006
Retired: 12/21/2006
1G - $5

Cow Print™
#43314

Introduced: 12/29/2006
Current
1G - Current Retail Value

Garfield™ — Bite Me!™
#43019

Introduced: 2/28/2007
Current
1G - Current Retail Value

Garfield™ — Cats Rule!™
#43020

Introduced: 2/28/2007
Current
1G - Current Retail Value

Garfield™ — Play Nice!™
#43021

Introduced: 2/28/2007
Current
1G - Current Retail Value

Green Snowflake™
#43310

Introduced: 9/29/2006
Retired: 12/21/2006
1G - $5

Halloween™
#43308

Introduced: 8/31/2006
Retired: 12/21/2006
1G - $5

Hearts™
#43307

Introduced: 3/31/2006
Current
1G - Current Retail Value

Inky™
#43004

Introduced: 3/31/2006
Current
1G - Current Retail Value

Legs™
#43000

Introduced: 3/31/2006
Current
1G - Current Retail Value

Leopard Print™
#43313

Introduced: 12/29/206
Current
1G - Current Retail Value

Lil' Bones™
#43008

Introduced: 3/31/2006
Retired: 12/21/2006
1G - $5

Lil' Legs™
#43001

Introduced: 3/31/2006
Retired: 12/21/2006
1G - $5

Lizzy™
#43003

Introduced: 3/31/2006
Current
1G - Current Retail Value

Nuts™
#43005

Introduced: 3/31/2006
Current
1G - Current Retail Value

Palm Trees™
#43305

Introduced: 3/31/2006
Current
1G - Current Retail Value

Patti™
#43006

Introduced: 3/31/2006
Current
1G - Current Retail Value

Paw Prints™
#43304

Introduced: 3/31/2006
Current
1G - Current Retail Value

Pink 60's Print™
#43312

Introduced: 12/29/2006
Current
1G - Current Retail Value

Pink Stripe™
#43302

Introduced: 3/31/2006
Current
1G - Current Retail Value

Pink Stripe™ (small)
#43303

Introduced: 3/31/2006
Retired: 12/21/2006
1G - $5

Prickles™
#43011

Introduced: 3/31/2006
Current
1G - Current Retail Value

Pumpkin™
#43014

Introduced: 8/31/2006
Retired: 1/24/2007
1G - $5

Quackers™
#43010

Introduced: 3/31/2006
Current
1G - Current Retail Value

Red Snowflake™
#43309

Introduced: 9/29/2006
Retired: 12/21/2006
1G - $5

Red, White And Blue Stars™
#43306

Introduced: 3/31/2006
Current
1G - Current Retail Value

Snort™
#43012

Introduced: 3/31/2006
Current
1G - Current Retail Value

Springtime Bear™
#43018

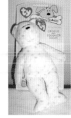

Introduced: 1/31/2007
Current
1G - Current Retail Value

Stinky™
#43013

Introduced: 3/31/2006
Current
1G - Current Retail Value

Stripe™
#43011

Introduced: 9/29/2006
Retired: 12/21/2006
1G - $5

Trap™
#43002

Introduced: 3/31/2006
Current
1G - Current Retail Value

Weenie™
#43009

Introduced: 3/31/2006
Current
1G - Current Retail Value

Zero™
#43015

Introduced: 9/29/2006
Retired: 12/21/2006
1G - $5

NOTES

Ty Classic®

Ty Classics led the way for all of the wonderful Ty plush lines. Since 1986 this impressive zoo of hundreds of animals has gradually become expanded and diversified from Ty's original small litter of beautifully designed cats and dogs. Originally called Ty Plush, they have been renamed Ty Classics. With a variety of different species, colors, fur fabrics, styles and positions, the scope of this menagerie seems endless. Some sit, some stand, others are flat or floppy and still others are crouching or curled.

1991 Ty Collectable Bear™
#5500 · 21"

Introduced: 1991
Retired: 1991
2G - $400

1992 Collectable Bear™ (Cederic)
#5500 · 21"

Introduced: 1992
Retired: 1992
2G - $350

1997 Holiday Bear™
#5700 · 14"

Introduced: 1997
Retired: 1997
3G - $20

Ace™
#2027 · 12"

Introduced: 1998
Retired: 1998
3G - $40

Al E Kat™
#1111 · gold striped, in curled position · 20"

Introduced: 1992
Retired: 1995
2G - $150

Al E Kat™
#1111 · gold striped, in curled position · 22"

Introduced: 1996
Retired: 3/24/2000
3G - $30

Al E Kat™
#1111 · gold striped, lays flat · 23"

Introduced: 1988
Retired: 1988
1G - $400

Al E Kat™
#1111 · gold striped, lays flat · 20"

Introduced: 1989
Retired: 1991
1G - $300

Al E Kat™
#1112 · grey striped, in curled position · 22"

Introduced: 1996
Retired: 1998
3G - $35

Al E Kat™
#1112 · grey striped, in curled position · 20"

Introduced: 1992
Retired: 1995
2G - $150

Al E Kat™
#1112 · grey striped, lays flat · 20"

Introduced: 1989
Retired: 1991
1G - $300

Alacazam™
#80110 · 11"

Introduced: 8/31/2005
Retired: 12/29/2005
4G - $11

Alfalfa™
#8103 · 12"

Introduced: 12/30/2003
Retired: 2/24/2006
4G - $13

Allioop™
#1132 · 18"

Introduced: 2001
Retired:12/27/2001
4G - $20

Alpine™
#50004 · 17"

Introduced: 10/29/2004
Retired: 12/30/2004
4G - $20

Angel™
#1001 · white, lays flat, Persian · 20"

Introduced: 1988
Retired: 1995
1G - $300 ♥ 2G - $100 ♥ 3G - $30

Angel™
#10015 · white with dark accents, Himalayan · 17"

Introduced: 4/28/2006
Current
4G - Current Retail Value

Angel™
#1001H · white with black accents, lays flat, Himalayan · 10"

Introduced: 1985
Retired: 1987
1G - $500 ♥ 2G - $250

Angel™
#1001H · white with black accents, lays flat, Himalayan · 12"

Introduced: 1985
Retired: 1987
1G - $600 ♥ 2G - $300

Angel™
#1001H · white with black accents, Himalayan · 20"

Introduced: 1985
Retired: 1990
1G - $700 ♥ 2G - $350

Angel™
#1122 · white, lays flat, Persian · 17"

Introduced: 1998
Retired: 1998
3G - $30

Angelina™
#5051 · 12"

Introduced: 9/30/2002
Retired: 7/25/2006
4G - $15

Angora™
#1001 · cat, lays flat

IMAGE UNAVAILABLE

Introduced: 1986
Retired: 1986
1G - $1,500

Angora™
#8004 · rabbit, sitting · 14"

Introduced: 1995
Retired: 1995
2G - $20 ♥ 3G - $35

Angora™
#8005 · rabbit, lays flat · 20"

Introduced: 1991
Retired: 1992
1G - $100 ♥ 2G - $100

Apricot™
#10002 · 13"

Introduced: 6/30/2004
Retired: 4/21/2006
4G - $13

Arctic™
#7419 · 12"

Introduced: 1995
Retired: 1998
3G - $20

Arnold™
#6002 · 20"

Introduced: 1990
Retired: 1990
1988 white #6001: 1G - $300
1G - $125

Ashes™
#2018 · 8"

Introduced: 1992
Retired: 1998
3G - $15

Aubrey™
#50026 · 14"

Introduced: 12/29/2006
Current
4G - Current Retail Value

Auburn™
#5119 · 18"

Introduced: 7/3/2001
Retired: 2002
4G - $20

Aurora™
#5103 · 13"

Introduced: 1996
Retired: 1998
3G - $25

Baby Angora™
#1002 · 10"

IMAGE UNAVAILABLE

Introduced: 1986
Retired: 1986
1G - $1,500

Baby Auburn™
#5118 · 13"

Introduced: 7/3/2001
Retired: 2002
4G - $13

Baby Bijan™
#1006 · 10"

Introduced: 1986
Retired: 1986
1G - $2,500

Baby Buddy™
#5011 · 20"

Introduced: 1992
Retired: 1992
2G - $200

Baby Butterball™
#2006 · 10"

IMAGE UNAVAILABLE

Introduced: 1986
Retired: 1986
1G - $1,500

Baby Camper™
#5123 · 15"

Introduced: 12/27/2002
Retired: 3/2/2005
4G - $16

Baby Cinnamon™
#5105 · 13"

Introduced: 1996
Retired: 1996
3G - $25

Baby Clover™
#8023 · 12"

Introduced: 1993
Retired: 1994
2G - $100

Baby Curly™
#5017 · darker fur · 12"

Introduced: 1993
Retired: 1997
2G - $65 ♥ 3G - $20

Baby Curly™
#5018 · 12"

Introduced: Unknown
RetiredRetired
LIMITED Stores exclusive.
No Ty Tag - $20

Baby Curly™
#5018 · blue plaid bow · 12"

Introduced: 1993
Retired: 1998
3G - $15

Baby Curly™
#5018 · green alphabet
sweater · 12"

Introduced: 2000
Retired: 11/15/2001
4G - $15

Baby Curly™
#5018 · leaf sweater · 12"

Introduced: 2000
Retired: 11/15/2001
4G - $15

Baby Curly™
#5018 · sunshine and flower sweater · 12"

Introduced: 2001
Retired: 11/15/2001
4G - $15

Baby Curly™
#5018 · USA sweater · 12"

Introduced: Fall 1998
Retired: 1999
3G - $15

Baby Curly™
#8024 · rabbit, white · 12"

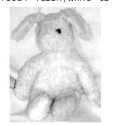

Introduced: 1993
Retired: 1997
2G - $50 ♥ 3G - $20

Baby Curly™
#8025 · rabbit, tan · 12"

Introduced: 1993
Retired: 1997
2G - $50 ♥ 3G - $20

Baby George™
#70010 · long fur, medium brown face · 12"

Introduced: 1/31/2006
Current
4G - Current Retail Value

Baby George™
#7300 · short fur, dark brown face · 12"

Introduced: 1996
Retired: 1998
3G - $20

Baby Ginger™
#5108 · 14"

Introduced: 1997
Retired: 1998
3G - $22

Baby Goldilocks™
#5057 · 13"

Introduced: 12/30/2003
Retired: 4/28/2005
4G - $12

Baby Iceberg™
#5040 · white, flag sweater · 13"

Introduced: 2003
Retired: 2003
4G - $13

Baby Iceberg™
#5040 · white, grey paw pads · 13"

Introduced: 2001
Retired: 2004
4G - $11

Baby Iceberg™
#5055 · ivory, beige paw pads · 13"

Introduced: 2004
Retired: 12/29/2005
4G - $11

Baby Jasmine™
#1004 · 10"

IMAGE UNAVAILABLE

Introduced: 1986
Retired: 1986
1G - $2,000

Baby Kasha™
#1008 · 10"

Introduced: 1986
Retired: 1986
1G - $2,000

Baby Kimchi™
#2004 · 10"

Introduced: 1986
Retired: 1986
1G - $2,000

Baby Li-Li™
#5115 · 13"

Introduced: 7/3/2001
Retired: 2/19/2004
4G - $14

Baby Lovie™
#8019 · lays flat · 20"

Introduced: 1992
Retired: 1992
2G - $90

Baby Lovie™
#8020 · sit up style · 12"

Introduced: 1993
Retired: 1994
2G - $70

Baby Oscar™
#2008 · 11"

IMAGE UNAVAILABLE

Introduced: 1986
Retired: 1986
1G - $1,500

Baby Patches™
#2030 · 12"

Introduced: 1999
Retired: 7/24/2000
3G - $40

Baby Paws™
#5004 · maple · 12"

Introduced: 6/30/2003
Retired: 12/29/2005
4G - $12

Baby Paws™
#5110 · sable · 12"

Introduced: 1997
Retired: 3/14/2000
3G - $22

Baby Paws™
#5111 · black · 12"

Introduced: 1997
Retired: 3/14/2000
3G - $22

Baby Paws™
#5112 · white · 12"

Introduced: 1998
Retired: 1998
3G - $25

Baby Petunia™
#8021 · blue ribbon · 12"

Introduced: 1993
Retired: 1993
Also red ribbon 1994 2G - $75
2G - $75

Baby Petunia™
#8021 · red checkered bow · 12"

Introduced: 1994
Retired: 1996
3G - $25

Baby PJ™
#5016 · brown · 12"

Introduced: 1993
Retired: 1998
2G - $30 ♥ 3G - $20

Baby PJ™
#5100 · white · 12"

Introduced: 1994
Retired: 1994
2G - $125

Baby Pokey™
#8022 · 13"

Introduced: 1996
Retired: 1997
3G - $25

Baby Powder™
#5109 · 14"

Introduced: 1997
Retired: 1998
3G - $24

Baby Rumbles™
#7411 · 13"

Introduced: 12/27/2002
Retired: 11/22/2006
4G - $20

Baby Schnapps™
#3001 · white dog · 10"

IMAGE UNAVAILABLE

Introduced: 1986
Retired: 1986
1G - $2,000

Baby Smokey™
#8023 · 13"

IMAGE UNAVAILABLE

Introduced: 1996
Retired: 1997
3G - $20

Baby Snowball™
#2002 · 14"

IMAGE UNAVAILABLE

Introduced: 1986
Retired: 1986
1G - $1,000

Baby Sparky™
#2012 · lays flat, no tongue · 20"

Introduced: 1992
Retired: 1993
2G - $70

Baby Sparky™
#2012 · with tongue · 20"

Introduced: 1994
Retired: 1994
3G - $40

Baby Spice™
#5104 · 13"

Introduced: 1996
Retired: 1997
3G - $20

Baby Xio Lin™
#5135 · 13"

Introduced: 2/26/2004
Current
4G - Current Retail Value

Bag O' Treats™
#80123 · 12"

Introduced: 8/31/2006
Retired: 10/25/2006
4G - $11

Bag O' Tricks™
#80123 · 12"

Introduced: 8/31/2006
Retired: 10/25/2006
4G - $11

Bailey™
#5502 · 19"

Introduced: 1997
Retired: 1997
3G - $30

Bamboo™
#5033 · 17"

Introduced: 2000
Retired: 12/27/2001
4G - $25

Bamboo™
#5106 · 13"

Introduced: 1996
Retired: 1997
3G - $25

Bamboo™
#5113 · 12"

Introduced: 1998
Retired: 1998
3G - $21

Bandit™
#1119 · grey · 20"

Introduced: 1990
Retired: 1990
1G - $200

Bandit™
#8009 · brown · 20"

Introduced: 1992
Retired: 1996
Also grey: 1991-1992 2G - $125.
2G - $75 ♥ 3G - $25

Bangles™
#10003 · 16"

Introduced: 11/30/2004
Retired: 6/23/2006
4G - $18

Barney™
#2003 · 20"

Introduced: 1990
Retired: 1992
1G - $175 ♥ 2G - $50

Baron™
#5200 · 18"

Introduced: 1995
Retired: 1996
2G - $30 ♥ 3G - $25

Bashful™
#20004 · 20"

Introduced: 1/3/2005
Retired: 12/29/2005
4G - $20

Bayou™
#7445 · 15"

Introduced: 12/31/2003
Current
4G - Current Retail Value

Beanie Bear™
#5000 · yellow/gold · 12"

Introduced: 1988
Retired: 1990
1G - $300 ▼ 2G - $150

Beanie Bear™
#5100 · 12"

Introduced: 1991
Retired: 1992
Aslo #5101 dark brown and #5102 white.
2G - $300

Beanie Bunny™
#8000 · tan · 12"

Introduced: 1989
Retired: 1992
1G - $250 ▼ 2G - $175

Beanie Bunny™
#8001 · white · 12"

Introduced: 1991
Retired: 1992
2G - $175

Beans™
#80121 · 14"

Introduced: 5/30/2006
Current
4G - Current Retail Value

Bearnaise™
#50033 · 14"

Introduced: 6/29/2007
Current
4G - Current Retail Value

Bearnard™
#53000 · 16"

Introduced: 6/30/2004
Retired: 12/29/2005
4G - $15

Beasley™
#2050 · 13"

Introduced: 6/28/2002
Retired: 12/29/2005
4G - $12

Beaut™
#7443 · 14"

Introduced: 6/30/2005
Current
4G - Current Retail Value

Belvedere™
#5031 · 17"

Introduced: 2000
Retired: 3/20/2001
4G - $18

Bengal™
#7423 · floppy · 12"

Introduced: 1998
Retired: 9/15/2000
3G - $20

Bengal™
#7423 · white chest · 12"

Introduced: 1995
Retired: 1997
2G - $30

Bengal™
#7423 · white facial fur · 8"

Introduced: 1998
Retired: 9/15/2000
3G - $15

Big Beanie Bear™
#5011 · gold · 15"

Introduced: 1990
Retired: 1990
Also # 5200 light gold, #5202 brown and
#5201 dark brown 1991-1991 2G - $350.
1G - $350

Big Beanie Bunny™
#8011 · brown, gold ribbon · 15"

Introduced: 1991
Retired: 1992
2G - $200

Big Beanie Bunny™
#8011 · brown, pink ribbon · 15"

Introduced: 1990
Retired: 1990
1G - $300

Big Beanie Bunny™
#8012 · white · 15"

Introduced: 1991
Retired: 1992
2G - $200

Big George™
#7302 · 27"

Introduced: 1990
Current
1G - $200 ♥ 2G - $75 ♥ 3G - $60 ♥
4G - Current Retail Value

Big Jake™
#7002C · chocolate · 16"

Introduced: 1989
Retired: 1989
1G - $200

Big Jake™
#7200 · white · 16"

Introduced: 1990
Retired: 1990
Also #7002 1989-1989.
1G - $200

Big Jake™
#7201 · auburn · 16"

Introduced: 1990
Retired: 1990
Also #7002A 1989-1989.
1G - $200

Big Jake™
#7202 · dark brown · 16"

Introduced: 1990
Retired: 1990
1G - $200

Big Pudgy™
#9006 · 28"

Introduced: 1994
Retired: 1996
2G - $70 ♥ 3G - $50

Big Shaggy™
#9015 · 26"

Introduced: 1992
Retired: 1992
2G - $125

Bijan™
#1005

IMAGE UNAVAILABLE

Introduced: 1986
Retired: 1986
1G - $1,500

Billings™
#80124 · 9"

Introduced: 1/31/2007
Retired: 6/25/2007
4G - $10

Billingsly™
#80115 · 9"

Introduced: 1/1/2006
Retired: 6/23/2006
4G - $12

Binks™
#5127 · 13"

Introduced: 12/27/2002
Retired: 12/29/2005
4G - $12

Biscuit™
#2026 · 17"

Introduced: 1997
Retired: 1997
3G - $30

Bixie™
#20047 · 11"

Introduced: 4/30/2007
Current
4G - Current Retail Value

Blackie™
#5003 · 13"

Introduced: 1988
Retired: 1990
1G - $200

Blossom™
#1134 · cat · 17"

Introduced: 8/31/2000
Retired: 12/27/2001
4G - $20

Blossom™
#8013 · rabbit · 18"

Introduced: 1996
Retired: 1997
Designed by Sally Winey.
3G - $30

Bluebeary™
#5312 · 14"

Introduced: 1999
Retired: 4/4/2001
4G - $13

Bluesy™
#75003 · 10"

Introduced: 6/30/2005
Retired: 3/7/2006
4G - $10

Blushed™
#70017 · 15"

Introduced: 11/30/2006
Retired: 2/27/2007
4G - $14

Blushing™
#5132 · 13"

Introduced: 11/26/2003
Retired: 12/30/2004
4G - $16

Bo™
#2009 · 20"

Introduced: 1994
Retired: 1995
2G - $100 ♥ 3G - $40

Boggs™
#20022 · 13"

Introduced: 1/1/2006
Current
4G - Current Retail Value

Bojangles™
#5126 · 13"

Introduced: 12/27/2002
Retired: 12/29/2005
4G - $14

Boone™
#20031 · 15"

Introduced: 6/30/2006
Current
4G - Current Retail Value

Boots™
#1132 · 16"

Introduced: 1998
Retired: 3/14/2000
3G - $28

Boudreaux™
#50012 · 12"

Introduced: 1/1/2006
Current
4G - Current Retail Value

Bows™
#8030 · 11"

Introduced: 1998
Retired: 1999
3G - $20

Bramble™
#80118 · 13"

Introduced: 1/1/2006
Retired: 3/27/2007
4G - $13

Brinksie™
#20024 · 13"

Introduced: 1/1/2006
Current
4G - Current Retail Value

Bristol™
#50002 · 14"

Introduced: 6/30/2005
Retired: 12/21/2006
4G - $14

Broderick™
#5032 · 17"

Introduced: 2000
Retired: 6/20/2001
4G - $16

Brodie™
#20023 · 13"

Introduced: 1/1/2006
Current
4G - Current Retail Value

Brooke™
#70009 · 12"

Introduced: 5/31/2005
Retired: 5/24/2006
4G - $15

Brownie™
#5100 · 13"

Introduced: 1996
Retired: 1998
2G - $35 ♥ 3G - $20

Buckshot™
#2009 · dog · 20"

Introduced: 1992
Retired: 1993
2G - $180

Buckshot™
#70005 · horse · 12"

Introduced: 2/28/2005
Retired: 12/29/2005
4G - $14

Buddy™
#5007 · standing on all fours · 20"

Introduced: 1990
Retired: 1992
1G - $300 ♥ 2G - $125

Buddy™
#5019 · crouching pose · 20"

Introduced: 1993
Retired: 1996
2G - $60 ♥ 3G - $30

Buster™
#2005 · 20"

Introduced: 1990
Retired: 1991
1G - $350 ♥ 2G - $100

Butterball™
#2005 · 12"

IMAGE UNAVAILABLE

Introduced: 1986
Retired: 1986
1G - $1,500

Butterbeary™
#5311 · 14"

Introduced: 1999
Retired: 12/27/2001
3G - $30

382

Buttercup™
#8012 · 18"

Introduced: 1996
Retired: 1997
3G - $35

Buttermilk™
#80122 · 8"

Introduced: 5/30/2006
Current
4G - Current Retail Value

Buttons™
#8031 · 11"

Introduced: 1998
Retired: 1999
3G - $18

Caboodle™
#10014 · 17"

Introduced: 10/31/2005
Retired: 12/21/2006
4G - $16

Caesar™
#7440 · 14"

Introduced: 6/30/2005
Retired: 8/25/2006
4G - $12

Calhoun™
#2063 · 13"

Introduced: 6/30/2005
Retired: 8/25/2006
4G - $16

Cameo™
#1144 · 12"

Introduced: 12/27/2002
Retired: 9/23/2005
4G - $11

Camper™
#5122 · 20"

Introduced: 12/27/2002
Retired: 3/2/2005
4G - $20

Candy™
#8011 · 17"

Introduced: 1996
Retired: 1996
3G - $40

Caressa™
#50009 · 11"

Introduced: 11/30/2005
Retired: 3/7/2006
4G - $18

Carley™
#1135 · 16"

Introduced: 1/1/2001
Retired: 5/2003
4G - $20

Carroty™
#50029 · 13"

Introduced: 1/31/2007
Retired: 4/26/2007
4G - $12

Cartwheels™
#70006 · 15"

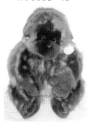

Introduced: 2/28/2005
Retired: 12/21/2006
4G - $16

Carver™
#50020 · 10"

Introduced: 8/31/2006
Retired: 11/22/2006
4G - $10

Carvington™
#80106 · 8"

Introduced: 8/31/2005
Retired: 12/29/2005
4G - $10

Cashmere™
#8032 · 15"

Introduced: 1/1/2001
Retired: 2001
4G - $13

Cashmere™
#8032 · blue or lilac · 13"

Introduced: 12/28/2001
Retired: 12/29/2005
4G - $12

Cassidy™
#10010 · 10"

Introduced: 6/30/2005
Current
4G - Current Retail Value

Catalina™
#10018 · 15"

Introduced: 6/30/2006
Current
4G - Current Retail Value

Catskills™
#10023 · 15"

Introduced: 12/29/2006
Current
4G - Current Retail Value

Caviar™
#10001 · 18"

Introduced: 6/30/2004
Retired: 7/25/2006
4G - $20

Celeste™
#50028 · 14"

Introduced: 12/29/2006
Current
4G - Current Retail Value

Cha Cha™
#7005 · 12"

Introduced: 1998
Retired: 9/15/2000
3G - $24

Champagne™
#10004 · 26"

Introduced: 2/28/2005
Retired: 12/29/2005
4G - $30

Charisse™
#50017 · 14"

Introduced: 6/30/2006
Current
4G - Current Retail Value

Charlie™
#2001 · no tongue · 20"

Introduced: 1988
Retired: 1989
1G - $225

Charlie™
#2001 · with tongue · 20"

Introduced: 1990
Retired: 1990
1G - $225

Charlie™
#2005 · lays flat · 20"

Introduced: 1996
Retired: 1998
3G - $35

Charlie™
#2005 · sitting · 20"

Introduced: 1994
Retired: 1995
2G - $75 ♥ 3G - $40

Chestnut™
#8022 · 12"

IMAGE UNAVAILABLE

Introduced: 1993
Retired: 1993
2G - $125

Chestnuts™
#70015 · 14"

Introduced: 9/29/2006
Retired: 12/21/2006
4G - $13

Chewey™
#2067 · 16"

Introduced: 12/31/2003
Retired: 12/29/2005
4G - $15

Chica™
#1147 · 10"

Introduced: 6/30/2005
Retired: 9/23/2005
4G - $12

Chi-Chi™
#1114 · with ribbon · 20"

Introduced: 1989
Retired: 1989
1G - $275

Chi-Chi™
#1114 · without ribbon · 20"

Introduced: 1990
Retired: 1990
2G - $100

Chi-Chi™
#7414 · 20"

Introduced: 1991
Retired: 1992
2G - $75

Chips™
#20006 · chocolate,
curled position · 14"

Introduced: 1/31/2005
Retired: 6/23/2006
4G - $13

Chips™
#2025 · light brown · 12"

Introduced: 1997
Retired: 1999
3G - $25

Chuckles™
#7303 · 15"

Introduced: 1997
Retired: 1997
3G - $30

Churchill™
#2017 · 12"

Introduced: 1996
Retired: 1999
3G - $25

Cinders™
#2008 · black and brown · 20"

Introduced: 1995
Retired: 1997
3G - $35

Cinders™
#2008 · floppy, all black · 20"

Introduced: 1994
Retired: 1994
2G - $60

Cinnamon™
#5004 · 13"

Introduced: 1989
Retired: 1990
1G - $200

Cinnamon™
#5021 · 18"

Introduced: 1996
Retired: 1996
3G - $35

Clover™
#8007 · no ribbon · 20"

Introduced: 1994
Retired: 1995
2G - $70

Clover™
#8007 · ribbon, felt nose · 20"

Introduced: 1991
Retired: 1992
2G - $175

Clover™
#8007 · vinyl nose, ribbon · 20"

Introduced: 1991
Retired: 1993
2G - $125 ♥ 3G in 1996-1996 - $40

Coal™
#1119 · 16"

Introduced: 1997
Retired: 1997
3G - $32

Cobble™
#10029 · 12"

Introduced: 4/30/2007
Current
4G - Current Retail Value

Cobbler™
#10031 · 16"

Introduced: 6/29/2007
Current
4G - Current Retail Value

Cocoa™
#5107 · floppy style · 12"

Introduced: 1997
Retired: 1998
3G - $22

Cocoa™
#57003 · blue ribbon · 12"

Introduced: Ghirardelli Exclusive
Current
Ghirardelli exclusive.
4G - Current Retail Value

Cocoa™
#57003 · red ribbon · 12"

Introduced: Ghirardelli Exclusive
Current
Ghirardelli exclusive.
4G - Current Retail Value

Cody™
#2051 · 14"

Introduced: 6/28/2002
Retired: 12/29/2005
4G - $20

Colonel™
#20027 · 10"

Introduced: 6/30/2006
Current
4G - Current Retail Value

Cooper™
#80109 · 9"

Introduced: 12/30/2004
Retired: 2/24/2005
4G - $10

Corky™
#2023 · 12"

Introduced: 1996
Retired: 5/24/2000
3G - $20

Cotton™
#8003 · 14"

Introduced: 1996
Retired: 1997
3G - $30

Cradles™
#53006 · 16"

Introduced: 2/28/2006
Current
4G - Current Retail Value

Crockett™
#5129 · 13"

Introduced: 6/30/2003
Retired: 11/23/2005
4G - $12

Crush™
#20020 · 10"

Introduced: 11/30/2005
Retired: 2/27/2007
4G - $11

Crystal™
#1120 · 16"

Introduced: 1997
Retired: 1999
3G - $35

Curly™
#5302 · bear, umbrella sweater · 18"

Introduced: 2000
Retired: 11/15/2001
4G - $20

Curly™
#5300 · tan chenille · 18"

Introduced: 1991
Retired:1992
Also 22" 1993 to 1998.
2G - $50 ♥ 3G - $35
2G - $100

Curly™
#5301 · dark brown bear, check-ered ribbon with red edge · 22"

IMAGE UNAVAILABLE

Introduced: 1991
Retired: 1991
2G - $125

Curly™
#5302 · bear, red with math equations sweater · 18"

Introduced: 2000
Retired: 11/15/2001
4G - $20

Curly™
#5302 · bear, gold chenille · 18"

Introduced: 1993
Retired: 1998
Also 22" 1991 to 1992. 2G - $100
2G - $50

Curly™
#5302 · bear, flag sweater · 18"

Introduced: Fall 1998
Retired: 1999
Also LIMITED Stores exclusive - $30.
3G - $30

Curly™
#5302 · bear, red flower and cloud sweater · 18"

Introduced: 2001
Retired: 2002
4G - $20

Curly Bunny™
#8017 · rabbit, tan with kite sweater · 22"

Introduced: 2001
Retired: 11/15/2001
4G - $25

Curly Bunny™
#8017 · white with balloon sweater · 22"

Introduced: 2001
Retired: 2001
4G - $25

Curly Bunny™
#8017 · tan, no clothes · 22"

Introduced: 1992
Retired: 1998
2G - $75 ♥ 3G - $35

Curly Bunny™
#8017 · tan, with carrot sweater · 22"

Introduced: 1998
Retired: 2002
2G - $50 ♥ 3G - $35

Curly Bunny™
#8018 · rabbit, white, no clothes · 22"

Introduced: 1992
Retired: 1998
2G - $75 ♥ 3G - $20

Curly Bunny™
#8018 · rabbit, white, with strawberry sweater · 22"

Introduced: 1998
Retired: 2002
2G - $50 ♥ 3G - $20

Cuzzy™
#5203 · 13"

Introduced: 1996
Retired: 1997
Designed by Sally Winey.
3G - $40

Cyrano™
#27003 · 11"

Introduced: 1/4/2007
Retired: 2/27/2007
American Greetings (USA) exclusive.
4G - $11

Cyrano™
#27003 · 11"

Introduced: 1/4/2007
Retired: 2/27/2007
Carlton Cards (Canada) exclusive.
4G - $11

Dakota™
#7418 · floppy · 12"

Introduced: 1998
Retired: 3/14/2000
3G - $20

Dakota™
#7418 · sitting · 12"

Introduced: 1995
Retired: 1997
Also 8": 2G - $25 ♥ 3G - $18
3G - $25

Dancer™
#20002 · 12"

Introduced: 9/30/2004
Retired: 5/24/2006
4G - $15

Dash™
#7432 · 14"

Introduced: 2000
Retired: 6/20/2001
4G - $16

Destiny™
#10009 · 11"

Introduced: 6/30/2005
Current
4G - Current Retail Value

Dewdrops™
#50034 · 13"

Introduced: 6/29/2007
Current
4G - Current Retail Value

Diesel™
#70025 · 21"

Introduced: 6/29/2007
Current
4G - Current Retail Value

Digby™
#56008 · 12"

Introduced: 11/4/2006
Current
UK Harrods exclusive.
4G - $30

Digits™
#7444 · 18"

Introduced: 12/31/2003
Current
4G - Current Retail Value

Dinger™
#20048 · 11"

Introduced: 5/31/2007
Current
4G - Current Retail Value

Diploma™
#20029

Introduced: 3/31/2006
Retired: 5/24/2006
4G - $12

Dipper™
#70022 · 14"

Introduced: 1/31/2007
Current
4G - Current Retail Value

Disco™
#2059 · 12"

Introduced: 5/29/2003
Retired: 12/30/2004
4G - $16

Divine™
#5045 · 13"

Introduced: 7/3/2001
Retired: 2002
4G - $14

Dodges™
#20017 · 15"

Introduced: 6/30/2005
Retired: 12/29/2005
4G - $16

Domino™
#8006 · 20"

Introduced: 1991
Retired: 1992
2G - $50

Dopey™
#2022 · 17"

Introduced: 1996
Retired: 1997
3G - $30

Dot™
#7433 · 14"

Introduced: 2000
Retired: 6/20/2001
4G - $15

Dreamland™
#80129 · 16"

Introduced: 6/29/2007
Current
4G - Current Retail Value

Droopy™
#2009 · 15"

Introduced: 1996
Retired: 1997
3G - $35

Duff™
#20049 · 11"

Introduced: 6/29/2007
Current
4G - Current Retail Value

Dumpling™
#5022 · brown · 12"

Introduced: 1996
Retired: 1996
3G - $35

Dumpling™
#5023 · white · 12"

Introduced: 1996
Retired: 1996
3G - $35

Duster™
#2031 · 17"

Introduced: 2000
Retired: 12/2002
3G - $30

Dustin™
#20003 · 13"

Introduced: 6/30/2004
Retired: 9/23/2005
4G - $20

Eggsworth™
#80117 · 11"

Introduced: 1/1/2006
Retired: 6/23/2006
4G - $15

Eleanor™
#5500 · 19"

Introduced: 1996
Retired: 1997
3G - $35

Elmer™
#1116 · with ribbon · 20"

Introduced: 1989
Retired: 1989
1G - $200

Elmer™
#1116 · without ribbon · 20"

Introduced: 1990
Retired: 1990
1G - $200

Elmer™
#7416 · grey ears, long trunk · 20"

Introduced: 1994
Retired: 1996
2G - $70 ♥ 3G - $30

Elmer™
#7416 · white ears, short trunk · 20"

Introduced: 1991
Retired: 1993
2G - $100

Elvis™
#2010 · 20"

Introduced: 1995
Retired: 1998
2G - $50 ♥ 3G - $25

Eureka™
#50027 · 14"

Introduced: 12/29/2006
Current
4G - Current Retail Value

Faith™
#5600 · 10"

Introduced: 1996
Retired: 1999
3G - $22

Faithful™
#50018 · 12"

Introduced: 6/30/2006
Current
4G - Current Retail Value

Fargo™
#50021 · 16"

Introduced: 9/29/2006
Retired: 12/21/2006
4G - $15

Fenwick Holiday Teddy™
#56003 · 15"

Introduced: 10/18/2005
Current
UK Fenwick exclusive.
4G - Current Retail Value

Fiddle™
#20025 · 14"

Introduced: 1/31/2006
Current
Squeaker inside nose.
4G - Current Retail Value

Fiddles™
#10028 · 11"

Introduced: 3/30/2007
Current
4G - Current Retail Value

Fido™
#2019 · 8"

Introduced: 1996
Retired: 1996
3G - $25

Flags™
#50015 · 14"

Introduced: 4/28/2006
Current
4G - Current Retail Value

Flecks™
#5036 · 13"

Introduced: 8/31/2000
Retired: 1/30/2002
4G - $11

Fletcher™
#50005 · 17"

Introduced: 5/31/2005
Retired: 7/27/2007
4G - $18

Flippers™
#7403 · 16"

Introduced: 12/27/2002
Current
4G - Current Retail Value

Flopper
#2037 · 16"

Introduced: 8/31/2000
Retired: 12/2002
4G - $25

Flopster™
#8035 · 22"

Introduced: 12/28/2001
Retired: 12/30/2004
4G - $16

Fluff™
#2053 · USA on back of
sweater · 14"

Introduced: summer 2003
Retired: 2003
4G - $15

Fluff™
#2053 · with collar only · 14"

Introduced: 8/29/2002
Retired: 8/4/2004
4G - $13

Fluff™
#2053 · with holiday sweater · 14"

Introduced: holiday season 2003
Retired: 2003
4G - $15

Fluff™
#2053 · with valentine
sweater · 14"

Introduced: valentine season 2004
Retired: 2004
4G - $15

Fluffy™
#1002 · 15"

Introduced: 1996
Retired: 1997
3G - $35

Foofie™
#20010 · 13"

Introduced: 12/30/2004
Current
4G - Current Retail Value

Forest™
#5048 · black · 10"

Introduced: 6/28/2002
Retired: 12/29/2005
4G - $11

Forest™
#5114 · brown · 12"

Introduced: 1998
Retired: 1998
3G - $25

Freddie™
#1117 · 10"

Introduced: 1989
Retired: 1989
1G - $200

Freddie™
#1117 · feet back · 12"

Introduced: 1990
Retired: 1990
1G - $200

Freddie™
#8010 · 12"

Introduced: 1991
Retired: 1991
2G - $75

Freddie™
#8010 · 16"

Introduced: 1992
Retired: 1998
2G - $50 ♥ 3G - $25

Fresco™
#53001 · blue ribbon · 13"

Introduced: 12/30/2004
Retired: 12/29/2005
4G - $15

Fresco™
#53001 · pink ribbon · 13"

Introduced: 12/30/2004
Retired: 12/29/2005
4G - $15

Frisky™
#1007 · 17"

Introduced: 1996
Retired: 1997
3G - $70

Fritz™
#2002 · no tongue · 20"

Introduced: 1988
Retired: 1989
1G - $200

Fritz™
#2002 · with tongue · 20"

Introduced: 1990
Retired: 1990
1G - $200

Fullhouse™
#57004 · 12"

Introduced: Jun-07
Current
Las Vegas exclusive.
4G - Current Retail Value

Fuzzy™
#5204 · 13"

Introduced: 1996
Retired: 1997
3G - $40

Galaxy™
#8102 · 15"

Introduced: 12/31/2003
Retired: 12/29/2005
4G - $15

Garfield & Pooky™
#10030 · 16"

Introduced: 5/31/2007
Current
Also available at Ty Store.
4G - Current Retail Value

Garland™
#5053 · 13"

Introduced: 9/30/2003
Retired: 1/8/2004
4G - $13

George™
#7301 · 20"

Introduced: 1990
Retired: 1999
1G - $150 ♥ 2G - $50 ♥ 3G - $35

Ginger™
#1007 · long haired, lays flat · 20"

Introduced: 1988
Retired: 1990
1G - $200

Ginger™
#1007H · lays flat, Himalayan w/dark accents · 10" or 12"

IMAGE UNAVAILABLE

Introduced: 1985
Retired: 1987
1G - $2,000 ♥ 2G - $1,000

Ginger™
#1007H · long haired, lays flat, Himalayan w/dark accents · 20"

Introduced: 1985
Retired: 1988
1G - $1,000

Ginger™
#5306 · sit up style · 18"

Introduced: 1997
Retired: 1997
3G - $70

Glamour™
#1145 · 10"

Introduced: 5/29/2003
Retired: 12/29/2005
4G - $10

Glitz™
#1146 · 19"

Introduced: 5/29/2003
Retired: 12/20/2004
4G - $18

Gloria™
#5052 · 12"

Introduced: 9/30/2003
Retired: 6/23/2006
4G - $15

Godzilla™
#5614 · black eyed · 11"

Introduced: 11/1/2001
Retired: 8/5/2005
Japan and NY Toy Fair 2003 exclusive.
4G - $20

Godzilla™
#5614 · white eyed · 11"

Introduced: 11/1/2001
Retired: 8/5/2005
Japan and NY Toy Fair 2003 exclusive.
4G - $30

Goldilocks™
#5308 · 16"

Introduced: 12/31/2003
Retired: 12/29/2005
4G - $20

Goldwyn™
#20042 · 11"

Introduced: 12/29/2006
Current
4G - Current Retail Value

Gourdin™
#80104 · 9"

Introduced: 8/30/2004
Retired: 9/30/2004
4G - $10

Grad™
#20046 · 13"

Introduced: 3/30/2007
Current
4G - Current Retail Value

Granola™
#5131 · 13"

Introduced: 6/30/2005
Retired: 11/22/2006
4G - $14

Griddles™
#5133 · 13"

Introduced: 12/31/2003
Current
4G - Current Retail Value

Grizzles™
#50013 · 10"

Introduced: 1/31/2006
Current
4G - Current Retail Value

Growl™
#7435 · 17"

Introduced: 12/28/2001
Retired: 5/2003
4G - $18

Gumdrop™
#5043 · 14"

Introduced: 1/1/2001
Retired: 2002
4G - $17

Hareston™
#80111 · 12"

Introduced: 12/30/2004
Retired: 4/5/2005
4G - $10

Harewood™
#80126 · 17"

Introduced: 1/31/2007
Retired: 2/27/2007
4G - $18

Harris™
#1115 · gold mane · 20"

Introduced: 1989
Retired: 1989
1G - $400

Harris™
#1115 · standing, gold and tan mane · 20"

Introduced: 1990
Retired: 1990
1G - $400

Harris™
#7415 · stands on all fours · 20"

Introduced: 1991
Retired: 1996
2G - $60 ♥ 3G - $40

Hatcher™
#80116 · 15"

Introduced: 1/1/2006
Retired: 6/23/2006
4G - $20

Hickory™
#50030 · 14"

Introduced: 5/31/2007
Current
4G - Current Retail Value

Hightops™
#7442 · sitting · 15"

Introduced: 6/30/2005
Current
4G - Current Retail Value

Hightops™ (large)
#70016 · large · 17"

Introduced: 10/31/2006
Current
4G - $35

Honey™
#2001 · dog · 20"

Introduced: 1995
Retired: 1998
3G - $35

Honey™
#5004 · bear, ribbon · 14"

Introduced: 1991
Retired: 1994
With blue or red ribbon.
2G - $80

Hooters™
#8016 · 9"

Introduced: 1992
Retired: 1994
2G - $125

Hope™
#5601 · 10"

Introduced: 1996
Retired: 1998
3G - $21

Hudson™
#50023 · 14"

Introduced: 10/31/2006
Retired: 4/26/2007
4G - $13

Hugston™
#27002

Introduced: 1/26/2006
Retired: 2/24/2006
Carlton Cards exclusive.
4G - $13

Hutch™
#20005 · 13"

Introduced: 6/30/2004
Current
4G - Current Retail Value

Iceberg™
#5041 · white, grey paw pads · 18"

Introduced: 1/1/2001
Retired: 2004
4G - $16

Iceberg™
#5041 · white, with stars and stripes sweater · 17"

Introduced: 2003
Retired 2003
4G - $18

Iceberg™
#5056 · ivory, beige paw pads · 17"

Introduced: 9/30/2003
Retired: 12/29/2005
4G - $16

Icicle™
#50008 · 14"

Introduced: 9/30/2005
Current
4G - Current Retail Value

Isis™
#1143 · 10"

Introduced: 12/27/2002
Retired: 11/22/2006
4G - $10

Jake™
#7001A · auburn · 12"

Introduced: 1989
Retired: 1989
1G - $250

Jake™
#7100 · white · 22" or 24"

Introduced: 1992
Retired: 1994
2G - $75

Jake™
#7100 · white · 16"

Introduced: 1990
Retired: 1990
Also #7001 12": 2G - $250
1G - $250

Jake™
#7101 · auburn · 22" or 24"

Introduced: 1992
Retired: 1993
2G - $75

Jake™
#7101 · auburn · 12"

Introduced: 1990
Retired: 1990
1G - $250

Jake™
#7102 · chocolate · 12"

Introduced: 1990
Retired: 1990
Also #7001C 1989.
1G - $250

Jake™
#7434 · dark brown · 18"

Introduced: 2000
Retired: 12/30/2004
4G - $18

Jasmine™
#1003

IMAGE UNAVAILABLE

Introduced: 1986
Retired: 1986
1G - $2,500

Java™
#5049 · 14"

Introduced: 6/28/2002
Retired: 12/30/2004
4G - $14

Jax™
#20041 · 11"

Introduced: 11/30/2006
Current
4G - Current Retail Value

Jazzy™
#75001 · 11"

Introduced: 6/30/2005
Retired: 3/7/2006
4G - $11

Jeeves™
#5038 · 13"

Introduced: 8/31/2000
Retired: 6/20/2001
4G - $12

Jenkins™
#2041 · 15"

Introduced: 7/3/2001
Retired: 2002
4G - $15

Jersey™
#8026 · black and white · 20"

Introduced: 1997
Retired: 1998
3G - $40

Jersey™
#8026 · brown and white · 20"

Introduced: 1997
Retired: 1997
3G - $40

Jeweled™
#10022 · 10"

Introduced: 12/29/2006
Current
4G - Current Retail Value

Jonah™
#7404 · 14"

Introduced: 12/27/2002
Current
4G - Current Retail Value

Josh™
#7101 · 24"

Introduced: 1994
Retired: 1996
2G - $75 ♥ 3G - $50

Jumbles™
#10005 · 18"

Introduced: 1/31/2005
Current
4G - Current Retail Value

Jumbo George™
#9008 · 48"

Introduced: 1991
Retired: 6/20/2001
2G - $100 ♥ 3G - $75

Jumbo PJ™
#9016 · white · 40"

Introduced: 1994
Retired: 1994
2G - $175

Jumbo PJ™
#9020 · brown · 40"

Introduced: 1992
Retired: 1998
2G - $100 ♥ 3G - $60

Jumbo Pumpkin™
#9017 · 40"

Introduced: 1995
Retired: 1996
3G - $75

Jumbo Rumples™
#9016 · 40"

Introduced: 1995
Retired: 1996
3G - $75

Jumbo Shaggington™
#9101 · 40"

Introduced: 7/3/2001
Retired: 12/2002
4G - $40

Jumbo Shaggy™
#9016 · gold · 40"

Introduced: 1992
Retired: 1993
2G - $85

Jumbo Shaggy™
#9017 · brown · 40"

Introduced: 1992
Retired: 1994
2G - $85

Jumbo Shaggy™
#9026 · 40"

Introduced: 1993
Retired: 1996
2G - $75

Kasey™
#5006 · brown · 13"

Introduced: 1989
Retired: 1989
2G - $100

Kasey™
#5006 · grey · 20"

Introduced: 1990
Retired: 1991
2G - $100

Kasha™
#1007

IMAGE UNAVAILABLE

Introduced: 1986
Retired: 1986
1G - $2,500

Kimchi™
#2003

IMAGE UNAVAILABLE

Introduced: 1986
Retired: 1986
1G - $2,500

King Ghidorah™
#5615 · 10"

Introduced: 11/1/2001
Retired: 8/5/2005
4G - $30

Kingly™
#7435 · 15"

Introduced: 12/28/2001
Retired: 5/2003
4G - $16

Kissed™
#80120 · 14"

Introduced: 5/30/2006
Current
4G - Current Retail Value

Kissycat™
#10013 · 10"

Introduced: 11/30/2005
Retired: 2/27/2007
4G - $11

Kit™
#10024 · 13"

Introduced: 1/31/2007
Current
4G - Current Retail Value

Kitty™
#1141 · 10"

Introduced: 6/28/2002
Retired: 12/30/2004
4G - $15

Kivu™
#7438 · 14"

Introduced: 6/28/2002
Retired: 12/30/2004
4G - $20

Kodi™
#20011 · 20"

Introduced: 9/30/2004
Retired: 11/23/2005
4G - $30

Laces™
#20016 · 17"

Introduced: 5/31/2005
Retired: 12/21/2006
4G - $16

Lacey™
#5121 · gold ribbon · 12"

Introduced: 6/28/2002
Retired: 2/19/2004
4G - $12

Lacey™
#5121 · with flag sweater · 12"

Introduced: Summer 2003
Retired: 2003
*Also holiday sweater 2003,
valentine sweater 2004*
4G - $14

Lagoon™
#5046 · 15"

Introduced: 12/28/2001
Retired: 1/8/2004
4G - $16

Large Curly™
#9019 · bear, blue sweater with
flowers · 26"

Introduced: 2000
Retired: 11/15/2001
4G - $25

Large Curly™
#9019 · bear, flag sweater

Introduced: 1998
Retired: 1999
Also LIMITED Store exclusive - $40.
2G - $60 ♥ 3G - $40

Large Curly™
#9003 · rabbit, tan · 24"

Introduced: 1994
Retired: 1997
2G - $60 ♥ 3G - $40

Large Curly™
#9007 · rabbit, white · 24"

Introduced: 1996
Retired: 1997
3G - $40

Large Curly™
#9018 · bear, brown plaid
ribbon · 26"

Introduced: 1992
Retired: 1997
2G - $60 ♥ 3G - $40

Large Curly™
#9019 · bear, blue plaid
ribbon · 26"

Introduced: 1992
Retired: 1998
2G - $60 ♥ 3G - $40

Large Curly™
#9019 · bear, blue sweater · 26"

Introduced: 2001
Retired: 11/15/2001
4G - $25

Large Curly™
#9019 · bear, moon and flower
sweater · 26"

Introduced: 2000
Retired: 11/15/2001
4G - $25

Large Curly™
#9019 · bear, stars and stripes
sweater · 26"

Introduced: Fall 1998
Retired: 11/15/2001
4G - $25

Large Ginger™
#9027 · 22"

Introduced: 1997
Retired: 1997
3G - $40

Large Harewood™
#80127 · 28"

Introduced: 1/31/2007
Retired: 3/27/2007
4G - $30

Large Honey™
#9021 · 26"

Introduced: 1992
Retired: 1994
2G - $75

Large Li-Li™
#9010 · 28"

Introduced: 7/3/2001
Retired: 9/23/2005
4G - $50

Large McGee™
#9005 · 26"

Introduced: 1992
Retired: 1997
2G - $65 ♥ 3G - $40

Large Moonbeam™
#9009 · 20"

Introduced: 1995
Retired: 1995
3G - $35

Large Paws™
#9004 · maple · 28"

Introduced: 6/30/2003
Retired: 12/29/2005
4G - $26

Large Paws™
#9029 · sable · 28"

Introduced: 1997
Retired: 1/2003
3G - $40

Large Paws™
#9030 · black · 28"

Introduced: 1997
Retired: 7/24/2000
3G - $40

Large Paws™
#9031 · white · 28"

Introduced: 1998
Retired: 3/24/2000
3G - $40

Large Petunia™
#9003 · 26"

Introduced: 1992
Retired: 1992
2G - $100

Large Ping Pong™
#9010 · 26"

Introduced: 1992
Retired: 1993
2G - $100

Large Pinstripes™
#70012 · 36"

Introduced: 1/1/2006
Current
4G - $40

Large PJ™
#9012 · brown · 24"

Introduced: 1992
Retired: 1992
2G - $80

Large PJ™
#9012 · brown · 26"

Introduced: 1993
Retired: 1998
2G - $70 ♥ 3G - $40

Large PJ™
#9014 · white · 26"

Introduced: 1994
Retired: 1994
2G - $100

Large Powder™
#9028 · 22"

Introduced: 1997
Retired: 1997
3G - $35

Large Pumpkin™
#9015 · 26"

Introduced: 1995
Retired: 1996
3G - $40

Large Rumples™
#9000 · gold with green or pink ribbon · 26"

Introduced: 1995
Retired: 1995
3G - $50

Large Rumples™
#9002 · beige · 26"

Introduced: 1995
Retired: 1996
Also pink nose and pink ribbon.
3G - $50

Large Rusty™
#9011 · 26"

Introduced: 1994
Retired: 1995
2G - $100 ♥ 3G - $50

Large Scruffy™
#9000 · gold bear · 28"

Introduced: 1992
Retired: 1993
2G - $100

Large Scruffy™
#9008 · gold bear · 26"

Introduced: 1992
Retired: 1992
2G - $100

Large Scruffy™
#9011 · gold dog · 26"

Introduced: 1992
Retired: 1993
2G - $100

Large Scruffy™
#9013 · cream bear · 28"

Introduced: 1992
Retired: 1992
2G - $100

Large Shaggington™
#9013 · 25"

Introduced: 7/3/2001
Retired: 12/2002
4G - $28

Large Shaggy™
#9014 · gold · 26"

Introduced: 1992
Retired: 1993
2G - $100

Large Shaggy™
#9015 · brown · 26"

Introduced: 1993
Retired: 1994
2G - $100

Large Shaggy™
#9025 · beige · 26"

Introduced: 1992
Retired: 1996
2G - $100 ♥ 3G - $50

Large Snowball™
#9009 · 26"

Introduced: 1992
Retired: 1993
2G - $100

Large Sparky™
#9002 · 26"

Introduced: 1992
Retired: 1993
2G - $100

Lazy™
#5008 · 20"

Introduced: 1995
Retired: 1996
3G - $40

Leo™
#7427 · 22"

Introduced: 1997
Retired: 1998
3G - $45

Leonard™
#56005 · 10"

Introduced: 12/1/2005
Current
4G - Current Retail Value

Lexie™
#10008 · 10"

Introduced: 6/30/2005
Current
4G - Current Retail Value

Licorice™
#1009 · 20"

Introduced: 1988
Retired: 1995
1G - $200 ♥ 2G - $100 ♥ 3G - $50

Licorice™
#1125 · 17"

Introduced: 1998
Retired: 1998
3G - $35

Lilac™
#5128 · 14"

Introduced: 12/31/2003
Retired: 12/30/2004
4G - $10

Lilacbeary™
#5314 · 15"

Introduced: 2000
Retired: 12/27/2001
4G - $13

Li-Li™
#5116 · 18"

Introduced: 7/3/2001
Retired: 2/19/2004
4G - $20

Lillie™
#8004 · 20"

Introduced: 1990
Retired: 1990
1G - $200

Lilypad™
#70004 · 14"

Introduced: 12/30/2004
Current
4G - Current Retail Value

Lovie™
#8001 · lays flat · 18"

Introduced: 1988
Retired: 1990
1G - $200

Lovie™
#8004 · stands on all fours · 20"

Introduced: 1991
Retired: 1993
2G - $75

Lovie™
#8019 · white, floppy · 20"

IMAGE UNAVAILABLE

Introduced: 1993
Retired: 1996
2G - $50 ♥ 3G - $35

Lovie™
#8027 · beige, floppy · 10"

Introduced: 1998
Retired: 1999
3G - $15

Lyric™
#10019 · 18"

Introduced: 6/30/2006
Current
4G - Current Retail Value

MacDougal™
#2048 · 14"

Introduced: 12/28/2001
Retired: 12/29/2005
4G - $12

Magee™
#5027 · 10"

Introduced: 1998
Retired: 11/22/2000
3G - $18

Maggie™
#1115 · in curled position · 22"

Introduced: 1996
Retired: 1998
3G - $40

Maggie™
#1115 · lays flat · 20"

Introduced: 1992
Retired: 1995
2G - $50 ♥ 3G - $35

Magilicuddy™
#50010 · 14"

Introduced: 1/1/2006
Retired: 8/25/2006
4G - $15

Mandarin™
#5201 · 13"

Introduced: 1996
Retired: 1997
Designed by Sally Winey.
3G - $30

Mango™
#7100 · white · 20"

Introduced: 1995
Retired: 1998
3G - $35

Mango™
#7102 · brown · 20"

Introduced: 1995
Retired: 1998
3G - $35

Max™
#2008 · white shaggy dog · 20"

Introduced: 1991
Retired: 1992
2G - $125

Max™
#2036 · Schnauser · 11"

Introduced: 8/31/2000
Retired: 6/15/2001
4G - $15

Max™
#3001 · white shaggy dog, no tongue · 20"

Introduced: 1989
Retired: 1989
1G - $300

Max™
#3001 · shaggy dog, tongue · 20"

IMAGE UNAVAILABLE

Introduced: 1990
Retired: 1990
1G - $300

McGee™
#5001 · brown · 14"

Introduced: 1991
Retired: 1997
Two muzzle versions.
2G - $60 ♥ 3G - $30

McGee™
#5001 · muzzle shaped like Blackie style 5003 · 13"

Introduced: 1988
Retired: 1990
1G - $200

Meadow™
#8037 · 15"

Introduced: 12/28/2001
Retired: 12/29/2005
4G - $11

Melville™
#70003 · 11"

Introduced: 10/29/2004
Current
4G - Current Retail Value

Melvin™
#7413 · 12"

Introduced: 12/27/2002
Retired: 12/29/2005
4G - $10

Memphis™
#2049 · 14"

Introduced: 12/28/2001
Retired: 6/23/2006
4G - $18

Meows™
#10012 · 10"

Introduced: 11/30/2005
Retired: 12/21/2006
4G - $10

Mercury™
#2060 · 16"

Introduced: 6/30/2005
Retired: 12/30/2004
4G - $18

Merribear™
#57002 · 14"

Introduced: 10/31/2006
Current
Carlton Cards/American Greetings exclusive.
4G - Current Retail Value

Merry™
#50003 · 13"

Introduced: 9/30/2004
Retired: 12/30/2004
4G - $10

Midnight™
#5009 · all black, stands on
all fours · 20"

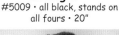

Introduced: 1990
Retired: 1990
1G - $200

Midnight™
#5009 · black and brown,
stands on all fours · 20"

IMAGE UNAVAILABLE

Introduced: 1991, 1993
Retired: 1993
2G - $100

Midnight™
#5101 · black and brown, lays on
its side · 13"

Introduced: 1996
Retired: 1996
3G - $40

Mischief™
#7000 · auburn · 18"

Introduced: 1990
Retired: 1991
Also #7000A: 1G - $200 ♥ 2G - $100
Also #7000A 1989-1989 1G $250
Also #7001 1992-1993 2G $100
1G - $200 ♥ 2G - $100

Mischief™
#7001 · white · 18"

Introduced: 1990
Retired: 1991
Also #7000 1989-1989 1G $250
Also #7000 1992-1993 2G $100
1G - $200 ♥ 2G - $200

Mischief™
#7000B · brown · 18"

IMAGE UNAVAILABLE

Introduced: 1989
Retired: 1989
1G - $250

Mischief™
#7002 · chocolate · 18"

Introduced: 1990
Retired: 1991
Also #7000C: 1989-1989 1G - $250
1G - $200 ♥ 2G - $100

Mischief™
#7414 · jointed · 21"

Introduced: 1996
Retired: 1997
Designed by Sally Winey.
3G - $40

Misty™
#7400 · no ribbon · 12"

Introduced: 1991
Retired: 1992
2G - $125

Misty™
#7400 · with ribbon · 14"

Introduced: 1993
Retired: 1994
2G - $175 ♥ 3G - $45

Misty™
#7431 · lays on its back · 11"

Introduced: 1998
Retired: 1999
3G - $25

Mitsy™
#20043 · 10"

Introduced: 12/29/2006
Current
4G - Current Retail Value

Mittens™
#1117 · gold striped · 12"

Introduced: 1993
Retired: 1994
2G - $100

Mittens™
#1118 · grey striped · 12"

Introduced: 1993
Retired: 1994
2G - $100 ♥ 3G - $30

Molasses™
#5125 · 15"

Introduced: 12/27/2002
Retired: 12/21/2006
4G - $16

Moonbeam™
#5009 · 14"

Introduced: 1995
Retired: 1995
3G - $30

Moondust™
#56004 · 13"

Introduced: 11/4/2005
Current
UK Harrods exclusive.
4G - Current Retail Value

Moonstruck™
#10020 · 13"

Introduced: 8/31/2006
Current
4G - Current Retail Value

Mootina™
#80000 · 15"

Introduced: 9/30/2004
Retired: 12/21/2006
4G - $16

Moppet™
#20036 · 10"

Introduced: 7/31/2006
Current
4G - Current Retail Value

Mortimer™
#7417 · 18"

Introduced: 1996
Retired: 1998
3G - $35

Mothra™
#5616 · 11"

Introduced: 12/1/2001
Retired: 2/2/2005
4G - $60

Mr. Flurries™
#80112 · 12"

Introduced: 9/30/2005
Retired: 1/8/2007
4G - $15

Muffet™
#10027 · 16"

Introduced: 3/30/2007
Current
4G - Current Retail Value

Muffin™
#2020 · 13"

Introduced: 1996
Retired: 1998
3G - $26

Mugsy™
#2052 · 13"

Introduced: 6/28/2002
Retired: 12/29/2005
4G - $15

Musher™
#2061 · 14"

Introduced: 6/30/2005
Retired: 6/23/2006
4G - $14

Mystery™
#1127 · 13"

Introduced: 2000
Retired:12/27/2001
4G - $15

Nibbles™
#8000 · brown · 9"

Introduced: 1994
Retired: 1999
3G - $20

Nibbles™
#8001 · white · 9"

Introduced: 1995
Retired: 1999
3G - $20

Nippey™
#2055 · 13"

Introduced: 12/27/2002
Retired: 12/30/2004
4G - $12

Nipsey™
#2057 · 20"

Introduced: 12/27/2002
Retired: 12/30/2004
4G - $20

Nutmeg™
#5013 · 18"

Introduced: 1996
Retired: 1997
3G - $35

Nuzzle™
#2042 · 13"

Introduced: 7/3/2001
Current
4G - Current Retail Value

Oasis™
#50000 · 14"

Introduced: 6/30/2004
Retired: 9/25/2006
4G - $10

O'Malley™
#1140 · 16"

Introduced: 6/28/2002
Retired: 12/30/2004
4G - $14

Omelet™
#8014 · 12"

Introduced: 9/30/2003
Retired: 6/23/2006
4G - $13

Onyx™
#1136 · 20"

Introduced: 1/1/2001
Retired: 2002
4G - $25

Opal™
#80105 · blue · 22"

Introduced: 11/30/2004
Retired: 7/25/2006
4G - $25

Opal™
#8101 · rainbow · 12"

Introduced: 6/30/2003
Retired: 7/25/2006
4G - $15

Orchard™
#80125 · 13"

Introduced: 1/31/2007
Current
4G - Current Retail Value

Oreo™
#5005 · crouching position · 20"

Introduced: 1994
Retired: 1996
2G - $100 ♥ 3G - $40

Oreo™
#5010 · stands on all fours · 20"

Introduced: 1990
Retired: 1991
1G - $200 ♥ 2G - $100

Oscar™
#2007

IMAGE UNAVAILABLE

Introduced: 1986
Retired: 1986
1G - $1,500

Otto™
#7417 · 20"

Introduced: 1993
Retired: 1994
2G - $150

Outback™
#70023 · 10"

Introduced: 6/29/2007
Current
4G - Current Retail Value

Papa PJ™
#9021 · 50"

Introduced: 1997
Retired: 1998
3G - $90

Papa Pumpkin™
#9023 · 50"

IMAGE UNAVAILABLE

Introduced: 1995
Retired: 1996
3G - $95

Papa Rumples™
#9022 · 50"

Introduced: 1995
Retired: 1996
2G - $250 ♥ 3G - $100

Papa Shaggy™
#9022 · gold · 50"

IMAGE UNAVAILABLE

Introduced: 1991
Retired: 1991
Also brown 50" 2G - $500
2G - $300

Papa Shaggy™
#9024 · beige · 50"

Introduced: 1994
Retired: 1996
2G - $300 ♥ 3G - $100

Patches™
#1114 · cat · 20"

Introduced: 1991
Retired: 1995
3G - $45

Patches™
#2003 · dog · 18"

Introduced: 1996
Retired: 7/24/2000
3G - $35

Patter™
#80113 · 11"

Introduced: 11/30/2005
Retired: 2/27/2007
4G - $10

Patti™
#1118 · 20"

Introduced: 1989
Retired: 1989
With or without ribbon.
1G - $200

Paws™
#5024 · sable · 18"

Introduced: 1997
Retired: 4/10/2000
3G - $35

Paws™
#5025 · black · 18"

Introduced: 1997
Retired: 3/14/2000
3G - $35

Paws™
#5026 · white · 18"

Introduced: 1998
Retired: 3/14/2000
3G - $35

Paws™
#5301 · maple · 18"

Introduced: 6/30/2003
Retired: 11/23/2005
4G - $20

Peaches™
#10016 · Himalayan · 17"

Introduced: 4/28/2006
Current
4G - Current Retail Value

Peaches™
#1003 · lays flat · 20"

Introduced: 1988
Retired: 1993
1G - $200 ♥ 2G - $100

Peaches™
#1003H · dark accents, lays flat, Himalayan · 20"

Introduced: 1988
Retired: 1990
1G - $1,500 ♥ 2G - $500

Peachy™
#1137 · 20"

Introduced: 7/3/2001
Retired: 12/2002
4G - $30

Pearl™
#1133 · 15"

Introduced: 8/31/2000
Retired: 12/27/2001
4G - $16

Pecos™
#70021 · 11"

Introduced: 1/31/2007
Current
4G - Current Retail Value

Peepers™
#8015 · 9"

Introduced: 1992
Retired: 1994
Also without feet 1991.
2G - $100

Penny™
#5039 · 12"

Introduced: 8/31/2000
Retired: 12/27/2001
4G - $12

Pepper™
#2024 · 12"

Introduced: 1997
Retired: 1999
3G - $30

Perkins™
#2034 · 15"

Introduced: 2000
Retired: 6/15/2001
4G - $20

Peter™
#8002 · 20"

Introduced: 1989
Retired: 1994
1G - $200 ♥ 2G - $100

Peter™
#8002 · jointed · 14"

Introduced: 1996
Retired: 1998
3G - $35

Peter™
#8020 · lop-eared · 15"

Introduced: 2000
Retired: 4/25/2000
4G - $20

Petunia™
#6001 · lays flat, pink polka dot ribbon · 20"

Introduced: 1989
Retired: 1990
1G - $200

Petunia™
#8008 · stands on all fours, blue ribbon · 20"

Introduced: 1993
Retired: 1993
2G - $100

Petunia™
#8008 · stands on all fours, pink ribbon · 20"

Introduced: 1992
Retired: 1992
Also red ribbon 1991 - 1991 2G - $100.
2G - $100

Petunia™
#8008 · stands on all fours, red checkered ribbon · 20"

Introduced: 1994
Retired: 1995
2G - $100 ♥ 3G - $50

414

Pierre™
#2004 · 10"

Introduced: 1995
Retired: 1996
3G - $20

Ping Pong™
#5005 · 13"

Introduced: 1989
Retired: 1990
Also 14": 2G - $60
1G - $200

Pinstripes™
#70011 · 12"

Introduced: 1/1/2006
Current
4G - Current Retail Value

Pinwheel™
#50019 · 14"

Introduced: 6/30/2006
Current
4G - Current Retail Value

Piston™
#7441 · 15"

Introduced: 6/30/2005
Current
4G - Current Retail Value

Pitter™
#80114 · 11"

Introduced: 11/30/2005
Retired: 2/27/2007
4G - $10

PJ™
#5200 · white · 18"

Introduced: 1994
Retired: 1994
2G - $100

PJ™
#5400 · brown · 36"

IMAGE UNAVAILABLE

Introduced: 1991
Retired: 1991
2G - $100

PJ™
#5400 · brown · 18"

Introduced: 1993
Retired: 1998
2G - $50 ♥ 3G - $35

PJ™
#5400 · brown · 22"

Introduced: 1991
Retired: 1992
2G - $100

Pokey™
#8015 · 19"

Introduced: 1996
Retired: 1997
3G - $35

Porridge™
#5054 · 14"

Introduced: 9/30/2003
Retired: 12/29/2005
4G - $15

Powder™
#5607 · 18"

Introduced: 1997
Retired: 1997
3G - $35

Prayer Bear™
#5600 · white · 14"

Introduced: 1992
Retired: 1994
2G - $75

Prayer Bear™
#5601 · yellow/gold · 14"

Introduced: 1992
Retired: 1993
2G - $75

Presents™
#20019 · 11"

Introduced: 9/30/2005
Retired: 1/8/2007
4G - $11

Presto™
#80107 · 8"

Introduced: 12/30/2004
Retired: 4/2007
4G - $10

Prissy™
#1128 · 13"

Introduced: 2000
Retired: 12/27/2001
4G - $18

Pudgy™
#5006 · 14"

Introduced: 1994
Retired: 1996
2G - $75 ▼ 3G - $30

Puffy™
#1003 · 15"

Introduced: 1996
Retired: 1997
3G - $30

Pumpkin™
#5304 · 18"

Introduced: 1995
Retired: 1998
3G - $35

Purplebeary™
#5313 · 14"

Introduced: 1999
Retired:2/01/2001
3G - $30

Purrecious™
#1142 · gold bow · 12"

Introduced: 11/27/2002
Retired: 10/25/2006
4G - $20

Purrecious™
#1142 · plaid bow · 12"

Introduced: 11/27/2002
Retired: 10/25/2006
4G - $18

Quackie™
#8033 · 12"

Introduced: 1/1/2001
Retired: 6/15/2001
4G - $11

Quake™
#70019 · 14"

Introduced: 12/29/2006
Current
4G - Current Retail Value

Rabble™
#20018 · 16"

Introduced: 6/30/2005
Current
4G - Current Retail Value

Rags™
#2035 · dog · 20"

Introduced: 8/31/2000
Retired: 12/27/2001
4G - $20

Rags™
#5102 · bear · 12"

Introduced: 1992
Retired: 1996
2G - $40 ♥ 3G - $28

Raindrops™
#50035 · 12"

Introduced: 6/29/2007
Current
4G - Current Retail Value

Raj™
#70041 · 18"

Introduced: 6/30/2006
Current
4G - Current Retail Value

Rascal™
#7001 · 16"

Introduced: 1994
Retired: 1998
2G - $75 ♥ 3G - $30

Razzmatazz
#5034 · red · 17"

Introduced: 2000
Retired: 6/20/2001
4G - $18

Razzmatazz
#5035 · blue · 17"

Introduced: 2000
Retired: 6/20/2001
4G - $18

Rebel™
#2058 · 14"

Introduced: 5/26/2004
Retired: 12/29/2005
4G - $15

Regent™
#70013 · 14"

Introduced: 6/30/2006
Current
4G - Current Retail Value

Rescue™
#2040 · 15"

Introduced: 1/1/2001
Retired: 8/25/2006
4G - $16

Ripples™
#2066 · 22"

Introduced: 12/31/2003
Retired: 9/23/2005
4G - $28

Rocker™
#75002 · 11"

Introduced: 6/30/2005
Retired: 3/7/2006
4G - $10

Roller™
#75004 · 10"

Introduced: 6/30/2005
Retired: 3/7/2006
4G - $10

Romancer™
#70018 · 16"

Introduced: 11/30/2006
Retired: 12/21/2006
4G - $15

Romeo™
#5310 · gold ribbon/I Love You · 14"

Introduced: 1999
Retired: 2001
3G - $30

Romeo™
#5310 · purple ribbon/Mothers Day · 14"

Introduced: 1998
Retired: 1998
3G - $30

Romeo™
#5310 · red ribbon · 14"

Introduced: 1998
Retired: 1998
3G - $30

Romper™
#2038 · 13"

Introduced: 1/1/2005
Retired
4G - $11

Roscoe™
#20050 · 11"

Introduced: 6/29/2007
Current
4G - Current Retail Value

Rosette™
#5120 · 14"

Introduced: 1/1/2001
Retired: 12/2003
4G - $15

Rosie™
#8003 · 20"

Introduced: 1990
Retired: 1994
1G - $300 ♥ 2G - $80

Rouge™
#5044 · 15"

Introduced: 1/1/2001
Retired: 9/13/2001
4G - $15

Ruffles™
#5014 · 12"

Introduced: 1995
Retired: 1995
3G - $20

Rufus™
#5015 · 18"

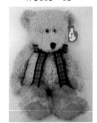

Introduced: 1993
Retired: 1997
2G - $75 ♥ 3G - $35

Rumbles™
#7412 · 17"

Introduced: 12/27/2002
Retired: 12/29/2005
4G - $25

Rumples™
#5002 · beige, burgundy
ribbon · 18"

Introduced: 1995
Retired: 1996
3G - $40

Rumples™
#5003 · gold, green ribbon · 18"

Introduced: 1995
Retired: 1995
3G - $40

Rusty™
#2011 · 20"

Introduced: 1992
Retired: 1996
2G - $75 ♥ 3G - $35

Sahara™
#7421 · floppy, gold chest,
long mane · 12"

Introduced: 1998
Retired: 12/27/2001
3G - $25

Sahara™
#7421 · sitting, gold chest,
long mane · 12"

Introduced: 1996
Retired: 1996
2G - $70 ♥ 3G - $25

Sahara™
#7421 · sitting, white chest,
short mane · 12"

Introduced: 1995
Retired: 1995
2G - $70 ♥ 3G - $25

Saint™
#5130 · 11"

Introduced: 6/30/2005
Retired: 11/23/2005
4G - $15

Sam™
#5010 · 18"

Introduced: 1995
Retired: 1996
3G - $35

Sandy™
#20015 · 17"

Introduced: 2/28/2005
Retired: 7/25/2006
4G - $18

Sarge™
#2003 · 20"

Introduced: 1994
Retired: 1995
2G - $75 ♥ 3G - $40

Schnapps™
#3000 · white dog · Unknown

IMAGE UNAVAILABLE

Introduced: 1986
Retired: 1986
1G - $2,000

Schultzie™
#2068 · 13"

Introduced: 12/31/2003
Retired: 12/29/2005
4G - $11

Scooter™
#2033 · 16"

Introduced: 2000
Retired: 12/29/2005
4G - $20

Scoundrel™
#20037 · 12"

Introduced: 7/31/2006
Current
4G - Current Retail Value

Scrapper™
#2056 · 13"

Introduced: 12/27/2002
Current
4G - Current Retail Value

Scraps™
#2047 · 20"

Introduced: 12/28/2001
Retired: 12/29/2005
4G - $20

Scratch™
#1117 · 15"

Introduced: 1996
Retired: 1997
3G - $30

Screech™
#1116 · 15"

Introduced: 1995
Retired: 1996
In 1996 this cat came WITH a collar.
2G - $70 ♥ 3G - $35

Scruffy™
#2000 · dog, cream, blue ribbon · 20"

Introduced: 1992
Retired: 1992
2G - $75

Scruffy™
#2000 · dog, white, red plaid ribbon · 20"

Introduced: 1993
Retired: 1996
2G - $75

Scruffy™
#2001 · dog, gold, red ribbon, singly ply tongue · 20"

Introduced: 1991
Retired: 1991
2G - $75

Scruffy™
#2001-1 · dog, gold, red ribbon, double ply stitched tongue · 20"

Introduced: 1992
Retired: 1994
3G - $45

Scruffy™
#5012 · bear, gold, jointed · 18"

Introduced: 1991
Retired: 1994
2G - $70

Scruffy™
#5013 · bear, cream · 18"

Introduced: 1992
Retired: 1992
3G - $40

Scruffy™
#5013 · bear, red gold, jointed · 18"

Introduced: 1995
Retired: 1995
2G - $75

Scrumptious™
#50022 · 10"

Introduced: 9/29/2006
Current
4G - Current Retail Value

Serena™
#80108 · 13"

Introduced: 12/30/2004
Retired: 4/5/2005
4G - $14

Serengeti™
#7425 · 13"

Introduced: 2000
Retired: 6/15/2001
4G - $22

Shadow™
#1112 · cat, lays flat · 20"

IMAGE UNAVAILABLE

Introduced: 1988
Retired: 1988
1G - $250

Shadow™
#1129 · cat, sitting · 13"

Introduced: 2000
Retired: 12/27/2001
4G - $12

Shadow™
#5011 · bear · 20"

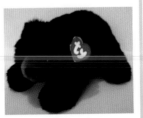

Introduced: 1994
Retired: 1996
2G - $60 ♥ 3G - $45

Shaggington™
#5117 · 18"

Introduced: 7/3/2001
Retired: 2002
4G - $20

Shaggy™
#5303 · gold · 24"

Introduced: 1993
Retired: 1993
2G - $85

Shaggy™
#5304 · brown · 18"

Introduced: 1992
Retired: 1994
2G - $75

Shaggy™
#5305 · beige · 18"

Introduced: 1993
Retired: 1996
2G - $75 ♥ 3G - $25

Shantou™
#20009 · 13"

Introduced: 12/30/2004
Current
4G - Current Retail Value

Sheriff™
#2039 · 13"

Introduced: 1/1/2001
Retired: 12/2003
4G - $15

Sherlock™
#1110 · black with white,
lays flat · 20"

Introduced: 1990
Retired: 1992
1G - $250 ♥ 2G - $125

Sherlock™
#2029 · Basset Hound · 12"

Introduced: 1998
Retired: 1998
3G - $25

Shivers™
#7419 · 9"

Introduced: 1993
Retired: 1994
2G - $150

Shredder™
#20044 · 11"

Introduced: 12/29/2006
Current
4G - Current Retail Value

Silky™
#1004 · 15"

Introduced: 1996
Retired: 1997
3G - $35

Skeeter™
#20039 · 14"

Introduced: 9/29/2006
Current
4G - Current Retail Value

Skimmer™
#7402 · 15"

Introduced: 12/27/2002
Retired: 12/21/2006
4G - $16

Skippy™
#2046 · 13"

Introduced: 3/6/2002
Retired: 12/29/2005
4G - $12

Skootch™
#5037 · 13"

Introduced: 8/31/2000
Retired: 6/20/2001
4G - $14

Slush™
#2045 · 13"

Introduced: 12/28/2001
Current
4G - Current Retail Value

Smokey™
#10017 · Himalayan · 17"

Introduced: 4/28/2006
Current
4G - Current Retail Value

Smokey™
#1005 · grey, lays flat · 20"

Introduced: 1988
Retired: 1993
1G - $1,200 ♥ 2G - $100

Smokey™
#1005H · grey w/dark accents, Himalayan · 20"

Introduced: 1988
Retired: 1988
1G - $1,200

Smokey™
#1005H · grey w/dark accents, Himalayan · 10" or 12"

IMAGE UNAVAILABLE

Introduced: 1986
Retired: 1987
1G - $1,200 ♥ 2G - $300 ♥ 1G - $125

Smokey™
#1130 · dark grey, lays flat · 16"

Introduced: 2000
Retired: 2002
4G - $15

Smokey™
#8016 · grey, sit up style · 19"

Introduced: 1996
Retired: 1997
3G - $45

Sniffles™
#2021 · 18"

Introduced: 1996
Retired: 1996
3G - $45

Sniffy™
#2043 · 20"

Introduced: 7/3/2001
Retired: 2002
4G - $25

Snow Angel™
#56000 · 12"

Introduced: 8/10/2004
Retired: 2/18/2005
Mitsukoshi Japan exclusive.
4G - $30

Snowball™
#2001 · cat · 13"

IMAGE UNAVAILABLE

Introduced: 1986
Retired: 1986
1G - $1,000

Snowball™
#5002 · bear, blue ribbon · 13"

Introduced: 1989
Retired: 1989
Also without ribbon.
1G - $250

Snowball™
#5002 · bear, red ribbon · 14"

Introduced: 1991
Retired: 1993
2G - $150

Snowball™
#5002 · bear, red ribbon · 13"

Introduced: 1990
Retired: 1990
1G - $250

Snowfort™
#50014 · 9"

Introduced: 1/31/2006
Retired: 12/21/2006
4G - $11

Socks™
#1116 · 12"

Introduced: 1993
Retired: 1994
2G - $200

Sofi™
#27001 · 9"

Introduced: 10/18/2005
Retired: 2/24/2006
Claire's Club exclusive.
4G - $10

Sophisticat™
#10021 · 17"

Introduced: 12/29/2006
Current
4G - Current Retail Value

Spanky™
#2010 · St. Bernard · 20"

Introduced: 1992
Retired: 1993
2G - $75

Spanky™
#2015 · cocker spaniel · 8"

Introduced: 1996
Retired: 1998
3G - $20

Sparkles™
#8100 · with multicolor mane and tail · 20"

Introduced: 1999
Retired: 5/24/2000
3G - $35

Sparkles™
#8100 · with pink mane and tail · 20"

Introduced: 1997
Retired: 1998
3G - $40

Sparky™
#2004 · sits · 20"

Introduced: 1990
Retired: 1993
1G - $275 ♥ 2G - $70

Sparky™
#2012 · lays flat · 20"

Introduced: 1994
Retired: 1995
3G - $45

Spice™
#1121 · cat · 17"

Introduced: 1998
Retired: 3/14/2000
3G - $30

Spice™
#5020 · bear · 18"

Introduced: 1996
Retired: 1997
3G - $40

Spout™
#7426 · floppy · 9"

Introduced: 1998
Retired: 4/20/2000
3G - $20

Spout™
#7426 · sitting · 9"

Introduced: 1996
Retired: 1997
3G - $20

Squirt™
#20007 · 9"

Introduced: 1/31/2005
Retired: 12/29/2005
4G - $12

Stardust™
#5617 · 12"

Introduced: 11/1/2003
Retired: 7/26/2004
UK Harrods exclusive.
4G - $30

Streaks™
#7439 · 15"

Introduced: 6/30/2005
Retired: 6/23/2006
4G - $16

Stretch™
#1131 · 14"

Introduced: 2000
Retired: 12/27/2001
4G - $15

Stubbs™
#20032 · 16"

Introduced: 6/30/2006
Current
4G - Current Retail Value

Sugar™
#1138 · cat, blue bow · 20"

Introduced: 4/30/2002
Retired: 5/25/2007
4G - $20

Sugar™
#1138 · cat, pink bow, feet and ears · 20"

Introduced: 12/1/2001
Retired: 12/27/2001
4G - $20

Sugar™
#5007 · bear · 14"

Introduced: 1995
Retired: 1995
3G - $35

Sugar™
#5008 · bear, stands on all fours · 20"

Introduced: 1990
Retired: 1990
Also 14" 1G - $125.
1G - $175

Sugarbeary™
#57000 · 14"

Introduced: 10/20/2006
Retired: 2/27/2007
4G - $14

Sugarcane™
#53002 · 12"

Introduced: 12/30/2004
Retired: 1/24/2007
4G - $11

Sugarcoat™
#50016 · 12"

Introduced: 6/30/2006
Current
4G - Current Retail Value

Sugarplum™
#5042 · 16"

Introduced: 1/1/2001
Retired: 2002
4G - $20

Sunny™
#2028 · 14"

Introduced: 1998
Retired: 1998
3G - $30

Sunset™
#50001 · 14"

Introduced: 6/30/2004
Retired: 7/25/2006
4G - $12

Super Arnold™
#9003 · 32"

Introduced: 1990
Retired: 1990
1G - $350

Super Buddy™
#9006 · 32"

Introduced: 1990
Retired: 1991
1G - $350

Super Chi-Chi™
#9004 · 52"

Introduced: 1989
Retired: 1989
1G - $400

Ty Classic®/Plush

Super Fritz™
#9002 · 36"

Introduced: 1989
Retired: 1989
1G - $350

Super George™
#9007 · 38"

Introduced: 1990
Retired: 1991
1G - $350

Super Jake™
#7002 · white · 16"

IMAGE UNAVAILABLE

Introduced: 1988
Retired: 1988
1G - $250

Super Jake™
#9001 · auburn · 55"

Introduced: 1989
Retired: 1989
1G - $400

Super Max™
#3002 · no tongue · 32"

Introduced: 1988
Retired: 1989
1G - $300

Super Max™
#3002 · with tongue · 32"

Introduced: 1990
Retired: 1990
2G - $250

Super Max™
#9001 · 26"

Introduced: 1991
Retired: 1992
2G - $250

Super McGee™
#9005 · 26"

Introduced: 1991
Retired: 1991
2G - $200

Super Petunia™
#9003 · no ribbon · 36"

Introduced: 1989
Retired: 1989
Also with ribbon, 32": 2G - $200.
1G - $350

Super Ping Pong™
#9010 · 26"

IMAGE UNAVAILABLE

Introduced: 1991
Retired: 1991
2G - $175

Super PJ™
#9012 · 24"

IMAGE UNAVAILABLE

Introduced: 1991
Retired: 1991
2G - $100

Super Schnapps™
#3002 · white dog

IMAGE UNAVAILABLE

Introduced: 1986
Retired: 1986
1G - $2,500

427

Super Scruffy™
#9000 · bear · 28"

IMAGE UNAVAILABLE

Introduced: 1991
Retired: 1991
2G - $300

Super Scruffy™
#9011 · dog · 32"

IMAGE UNAVAILABLE

Introduced: 1991
Retired: 1991
2G - $300

Super Snowball™
#9009 · 26"

Introduced: 1991
Retired: 1991
2G - $300

Super Sparky™
#9002 · 32"

Introduced: 1990
Retired: 1991
1G - $300 ♥ 2G - $150

Super Tygger™
#9004 · 32"

Introduced: 1990
Retired: 1991
1G - $400

Superdog™
#2058 · 14"

Introduced: 2/28/2003
Retired: 5/26/2004
4G - $13

Supersonic™
#70000 · 36"

Introduced: 6/30/2004
Current
4G - Current Retail Value

Sweeten™
#50024 · 13"

Introduced: 11/30/2006
Retired: 1/24/2007
4G - $10

Taffy™
#2014 · floppy · 12"

Introduced: 1998
Retired: 7/24/2000
Not available in Germany.
3G - $30

Taffy™
#2014 · sitting · 8"

Introduced: 1996
Retired: 1997
Not available in Germany.
3G - $20

Taffybeary™
#5315 · 15"

Introduced: 2000
Retired: 12/27/2001
3G - $25

Tandy™
#20045 · 13"

Introduced: 1/31/2007
Current
4G - Current Retail Value

Tango™
#7000 · white · 12"

Introduced: 1995
Retired: 1998
3G - $25

Tango™
#7002 · brown · 12"

Introduced: 1995
Retired: 1998
3G - $25

Tangy™
#10026 · 13"

Introduced: 1/31/2007
Current
4G - Current Retail Value

Tanner™
#2054 · 13"

Introduced: 10/31/2002
Retired: 12/30/2004
4G - $14

Tapioca™
#50025 · 10"

Introduced: 11/30/2006
Current
4G - Current Retail Value

Tart™
#10025 · 13"

Introduced: 1/31/2007
Current
4G - Current Retail Value

Teddybearsary™
#5050 · 15"

Introduced: 6/28/2002
Retired: 12/27/2002
4G - $16

Teensy™
#7437 · 20"

Introduced: 6/28/2002
Current
4G - Current Retail Value

Thatcher™
#80119 · 13"

Introduced: 1/1/2006
Retired: 6/23/2006
4G - $14

Theodore™
#5501 · 19"

Introduced: 1996
Retired: 1997
3G - $40

Thimbles™
#8038 · 14"

Introduced: 12/27/2002
Retired: 3/4/2004
4G - $15

Thomas™
#1139 · 15"

Introduced: 12/28/2001
Retired: 12/30/2004
4G - $20

Thunder™
#20040 · 15"

Introduced: 10/31/2006
Current
4G - Current Retail Value

Tidbit™
#2044 · 13"

Introduced: 12/28/2001
Retired: 12/21/2006
4G - $18

Timber™
#2002 · 20"

Introduced: 1994
Retired: 1998
2G - $100 ♥ 3G - $50

Tippi™
#20038 · 12"

Introduced: 12/29/2006
Current
4G - Current Retail Value

Toasty™
#50007 · 12"

Introduced: 9/30/2005
Retired: 12/21/2006
4G - $12

Toffee™
#2013 · shaggy · 20"

Introduced: 1993
Retired: 1999
2G - $50 ♥ 3G - $35

Toffee™
#2032 · soft terry · 20"

Introduced: 2000
Retired: 12/2002
4G - $20

Topanga™
#70002 · 14"

Introduced: 6/30/2004
Retired: 12/29/2005
4G - $12

Tornado™
#7405 · 15"

Introduced: 12/27/2002
Current
4G - Current Retail Value

Trails™
#80128 · 13"

Introduced: 4/30/2007
Current
4G - Current Retail Value

Truly Yours™
#5134 · 10"

Introduced: 12/31/2003
Retired: 2/24/2006
4G - $25

Tucker™
#2065 · 22"

Introduced: 12/31/2003
Retired: 11/23/2005
4G - $30

Tugger™
#20008 · 14"

Introduced: 12/30/2004
Current
4G - Current Retail Value

Tugs™
#2062 · 13"

Introduced: 6/30/2005
Retired: 12/29/2005
4G - $12

Tulip™
#8008 · 18"

Introduced: 1996
Retired: 1998
3G - $45

Tumbles™
#1008 · 17"

Introduced: 1996
Retired: 1997
3G - $50

Twiddle™
#70020 · 14"

Introduced: 12/29/2006
Current
4G - Current Retail Value

Twiggy™
#7422 · 23"

Introduced: 1991
Retired: 1996
2G - $75 ▼ 3G - $45

Twitcher™
#8036 · 17"

Introduced: 12/28/2001
Retired: 12/30/2004
4G - $18

Tygger™
#1120 · stands on all fours · 20"

Introduced: 1990
Retired: 1990
1G - $150 ▼ 2G - $60

Tygger™
#7420 · floppy · 20"

Introduced: 1991
Retired: 1991
2G - $55

Tygger™
#7420 · in crouching position · 20"

Introduced: 1994
Retired: 1998
2G - $40 ▼ 3G - $30

Tygger™
#7420 · standing · 20"

Introduced: 1992
Retired: 1993
2G - $45

Tygger™
#7421 · white, standing · 20"

Introduced: 1991
Retired: 1992
2G - $50

Tyler™
#27000 · 16"

Introduced: 10/20/2005
Retired: 1/26/2006
BonTon Elder Beerman exclusive.
4G - $15

Vanilla™
#5012 · 18"

Introduced: 1996
Retired: 1997
3G - $35

Wally™
#7423 · 12"

Introduced: 1992
Retired: 1993
2G - $100

Wally™
#7423-1 · 12"

IMAGE UNAVAILABLE

Introduced: 1996
Retired: 1996
3G - $25

Walnut™
#5124 · 13"

Introduced: 12/27/2002
Retired: 11/23/2005
4G - $12

Weensy™
#7446 · 36"

Introduced: 12/31/2003
Current
4G - Current Retail Value

Wentworth™
#50011 · 13"

Introduced: 1/1/2006
Retired: 12/21/2006
4G - $11

Whinnie™
#8006 · 20"

Introduced: 1994
Retired: 1995
2G - $55 ♥ 3G - $35

Whistles™
#50006 · 16"

Introduced: 6/30/2005
Retired: 12/21/2006
4G - $11

Willow™
#20021 · 13"

Introduced: 1/1/2006
Current
4G - Current Retail Value

Winston™
#2007 · 20"

Introduced: 1991
Retired: 1999
2G - $100 ♥ 3G - $40

Winthrop™
#5047 · 14"

Introduced: 12/28/2001
Retired: 1/8/2004
4G - $18

Woolly™
#8005 · 9"

Introduced: 1996
Retired: 1999
Not available in Germany.
3G - $22

Wuzzy™
#5202 · 13"

Introduced: 1996
Retired: 1997
3G - $40

Wynter™
#2064 · 16"

Introduced: 9/30/2003
Retired: 12/30/2004
4G - $15

Xio Lin™
#5316 · 16"

Introduced: 2/26/2004
Current
4G - Current Retail Value

Yappy™
#2016 · floppy · 12"

Introduced: 1998
Retired: 5/24/2000
3G - $20

Yappy™
#2016 · sitting · 8"

Introduced: 1996
Retired: 1997
3G - $20

Yesterbear™
#5028 · brown · 18"

Introduced: 2000
Retired: 6/20/2001
4G - $20

Yesterbear™
#5029 · cream · 18"

Introduced: 2000
Retired: 6/20/2001
4G - $20

Yesterbear™
#5030 · yellow · 18"

Introduced: 2000
Retired: 6/20/2001
4G - $20

Yodel™
#20035 · 32"

Introduced: 8/31/2006
Current
4G - Current Retail Value

Yodeler™
#20033 · 15"

Introduced: 8/31/2006
Current
4G - Current Retail Value

Yodels™
#20034 · 21"

Introduced: 8/31/2006
Current
4G - Current Retail Value

Yorkie™
#2006 · 20"

Introduced: 1991
Retired: 1996
2G - $75 ♥ 3G - $40

Yukon™
#7424 · 12"

Introduced: 1996
Retired: 1996
3G - $50

Zephyr™
#70024 · 16"

Introduced: 6/29/2007
Current
4G - Current Retail Value

Zulu™
#7421 · 20"

Introduced: 1994
Retired: 1994
2G - $175

NOTES

NOTES

PILLOW PALS™

Pillow Pals were the first Ty collection designed with babies in mind, but their sweet simplicity can appeal to all ages. First introduced in 1995, they continued until 1999, when Baby Ty came along. Some of the Pillow Pals were released first in one color and then later, in another. The eyes were embroidered for safety. The later Pillow Pals had larger eyes with a dash of white stitching for sparkle. The last releases changed from one or two solid colors to three and four more vibrant colors.

### Antlers™ #3028 · brown	### Antlers™ #3104 · green	### Ba Ba™ #3113 · purple

Introduced: 1998 Retired: 1998 Thank you God, for all I see, As the sun shines down on me. **2G - $13**	Introduced: 1999 Retired: 1999 Thank you God, for all I see, As the sun shines down on me. **2G - $20**	Introduced: 1999 Retired: 1999 Thank you God, for the sun and daylight, And for the twinkling stars, the moon and night. **2G - $13**
### Ba Ba™ #3008 · white	### Bruiser™ #3018	### Carrots™ #3101 · green

Introduced: 1997 Retired: 1998 Thank you God, for the sun and daylight, And for the twinkling stars, the moon and night. **1G - $20 ♥ 2G - $10**	Introduced: 1997 Retired: 1998 To From With Love **1G - $14 ♥ 2G - $10**	Introduced: 1999 Retired: 1999 All the families are special, big or small, Thank you for my family, I love them all **2G - $11**
### Carrots™ #3010 · peach	### Chewy™ #3105	### Clover™ #3020 · black eyed

Introduced: 1997 Retired: 1998 All the families are special, big or small, Thank you for my family, I love them all **1G - $13 ♥ 2G - $12**	Introduced: 1999 Retired: 1999 As we bow our heads to pray, Thankful for each busy day. **2G - $12**	Introduced: 1998 Retired: 1998 To From With Love **2G - $20**

Clover™
#3020 · bluish-grey eyed

Introduced: 1998
Retired: 1998
To From With Love
1G - $17 ♥ 2G - $10

Foxy™
#3022

Introduced: 1998
Retired: 1998
To From With Love
1G - $12 ♥ 2G - $11

Glide™
#3025

Introduced: 1998
Retired: 1998
To From With Love
1G - $12 ♥ 2G - $11

Huggy™
#3002 · blue ribbon

Introduced: 1995
Retired: 1997
To From With Love
1G - $11

Huggy™
#3002 · pink ribbon

Introduced: 1997
Retired: 1998
Help me to do what is right,
Watch over me day and night.
1G - $13

Huggy™
#3111 · yellow/red

Introduced: 1999
Retired: 1999
Help me to do what is right,
Watch over me day and night.
2G - $12

Kolala™
#3108

Introduced: 1999
Retired: 1999
Be with me as I climb a tree,
Be with me as I run free.
2G - $13

Meow™
#3011 · grey

Introduced: 1997
Retired: 1997
To From With Love
1G - $18

Meow™
#3107 · pink

Introduced: 1999
Retired: 1999
As the day ends and turns to night, Thank
you God, for each twinkling night.
2G - $10

Meow™
#3011 · tan

Introduced: 1997
Retired: 1998
As the day ends and turns to night, Thank
you God, for each twinkling night.
1G - $11 ♥ 2G - $10

Moo™
#3004

Introduced: 1995
Retired: 1998
God made the sky so high and blue,
And all the little creatures, too.
1G - $13 ♥ 2G - $11

Oink™
#3005

Introduced: 1995
Retired: 1998
To From With Love
1G - $13 ♥ 2G - $11

Paddles™
#3103 · green

Introduced: 1999
Retired: 1999
*God thank you for the sun and sea, And all
the things that are special to me.*
2G - $12

Paddles™
#3026 · fuschia

Introduced: 1998
Retired: 1998
*God thank you for the sun and sea, And all
the things that are special to me.*
2G - $11

Purr™
#3016

Introduced: 1997
Retired: 1998
To From With Love
1G - $14 ♥ 2G - $10

Red™
#3021

Introduced: 1998
Retired: 1998
To From With Love
1G - $11 ♥ 2G - $10

Ribbit™
#3006 · green

Introduced: 1995
Retired: 1996
To From With Love
1G - $30

Ribbit™
#3009 · green and yellow

Introduced: 1997
Retired: 1998
*God, please make my life a little light,
To help make the world a little bright.*
1G - $11 ♥ 2G - $10

Ribbit™
#3106 · red

Introduced: 1999
Retired: 1999
*God, please make my life a little light,
To help make the world a little bright.*
2G - $12

Rusty™
#3100

Introduced: 1999
Retired: 1999
*Thank you God for the sun and moon,
Thank you for my new raccoon.*
2G - $13

Sherbet™
#3027 · pastel ty dye

Introduced: 1998
Retired: 1998
*Dear God, be with me as I start my day,
Please watch over me during school and play.*
2G - $10

Sherbet™
#3112 · vivid ty dye

Introduced: 1999
Retired: 1999
*Dear God, be with me as I start my day,
Please watch over me during school and play.*
2G - $12

Snap™
#3015 · green and yellow

Introduced: 1997
Retired: 1998
To From With Love
2G - $10

Snap™
#3007 · pale yellow/brown
patterned shell

Introduced: 1995
Retired: 1996
To From With Love
1G - $45

Snap™
#3102 · ty dye shell

Introduced: 1999
Retired: 1999
Help me to be kind and sweet,
Help me to be clean and neat.
2G - $12

Snuggy™
#3001 · blue ribbon

Introduced: 1997
Retired: 1998
To From With Love
1G - $13

Snuggy™
#3001 · pink ribbon

Introduced: 1995
Retired: 1997
To From With Love
1G - $20

Sparkler™
#3115

Introduced: 1999
Retired: 1999
As I sleep and dream tonight,
Watch over the Stars and Stripes!
2G - $10

Speckles™
#3017

Introduced: 1997
Retired: 1998
To From With Love
1G - $11 ♥ 2G - $10

Spotty™
#3019

Introduced: 1998
Retired: 1998
To From With Love
1G - $18 ♥ 2G - $10

Squirt™
#3013 · pale blue with pink inner ears

Introduced: 1997
Retired: 1998
To From With Love
1G - $11

Squirt™
#3109 · pale teal blue with purple inner ears

Introduced: 1999
Retired: 1999
God loves the world and sky so blue,
So smile, God loves you too.
2G - $13 ♥ 2G - $10

Swinger™
#3110 · blue and yellow

Introduced: 1998
Retired: 1998
God, thank you for the flowers and trees,
And all the animals we get to see.
2G - $11

Swinger™
#3023 · brown

Introduced: 1998
Retired: 1998
God, thank you for the flowers and trees,
And all the animals we get to see.
1G - $11 ♥ 2G - $10

Tide™
#3024

Introduced: 1998
Retired: 1998
To From With Love
1G - $11 ♥ 2G - $10

Tubby™
#3012

Introduced: 1997
Retired: 1998
To From With Love
1G - $15 ♥ 2G - $13

Woof™
#3003 · brown

Introduced: 1995
Retired: 1998
To From With Love
1G - $11 ♥ 2G - $10

Woof™
#3114 · orange and yellow

Introduced: 1999
Retired: 1999
A good friend is the best thing to be,
God help me be one to those who need me.
2G - $10

Zulu™
#3014 · thick stripes

Introduced: 1997
Retired: 1998
Zulu was issued without a phrase.
1G - $13 ♥ 2G - $11

Zulu™
#3014 · thin stripes

Introduced: 1997
Retired: 1998
Zulu was issued without a phrase.
1G - $30

NOTES

NOTES

Little girls everywhere were happily surprised with the variety of Pinkys products that were released. Besides the Beanie Babies, there are purses, key-clips and larger size Pinkys.

Chic™
#40213

Introduced: 2/28/2005
Current
1G - Current Retail Value

Fab™
#40212

Introduced: 2/28/2005
Current
1G - Current Retail Value

Gloss™
#20013

Introduced: 2/28/2005
Retired: 12/31/2005
1G - $13

Hug Me!™
#75005

Introduced: 1/31/2006
Retired: 6/23/2006
1G - $6

Lil' Gloss™
#20014

Introduced: 2/28/2005
Retired: 12/31/2005
1G - $10

Love Me!™
#75007

Introduced: 1/31/2006
Retired
1G - Current Retail Value

Orchid™
#10007

Introduced: 2/28/2005
Retired: 12/21/2006
1G - $11

Paradise™
#20028

Introduced: 2/28/2006
Current
1G - Current Retail Value

Pinky Poo™ (large)
#20011

Introduced: 2/28/2005
Current
1G - Current Retail Value

Pinky's Pack™
#44073

Introduced: 8/26/2005
Current
*Pack includes Pinky Poo™ Key-clip, Baseball
Cap, T-shirt, Light Up Ballpoint Pen, and
Pinkys™ Tote Bag. Ty Store exclusive.*
Current Retail Value

Poodle Caboodle™
#40363

Introduced: 3/31/2006
Current
1G - Current Retail Value

Purrrse™
#40337

Introduced: 1/31/2006
Current
1G - Current Retail Value

Ratzo™ (large)
#70007

Introduced: 2/28/2005
Retired: 12/21/2006
1G - $8

Scribbly™
#20026

Introduced: 1/31/2006
Retired: 12/21/2006
1G - $9

Shimmers™
#53003

Introduced: 2/28/2005
Current
1G - Current Retail Value

Smooches™
#40303 · pink

Introduced: 10/31/2005
Current
1G - Current Retail Value

Smooches™
#40303 · red

Introduced: 10/31/2005
Current
1G - Current Retail Value

Squeeze Me!™
#75006

Introduced: 1/31/2006
Retired: 6/23/2006
1G - $6

Style™
#40284

Introduced: 10/31/2005
Current
1G - Current Retail Value

Sugarcat™
#10014

Introduced: 1/31/2006
Current
1G - Current Retail Value

Twinkles™
#20012

Introduced: 2/28/2005
Retired: 9/25/2006
1G - $10

PLUFFIES™

The miracle of a unique Ty fabric, Tylux, makes Pluffies softer than soft and kid friendly. Introduced in 2004, these squishable, cuddly friends can be loved forever, because they can be machine washed again and again.

Baseball™
#32098

Intoduced: 6/29/2007
Current
1G - Current Retail Value

Bashfully™
#32091

Intoduced: 1/31/2007
Current
1G - Current Retail Value

Basketball™
#32070

Intoduced: 2/28/2006
Current
1G - Current Retail Value

Beary Merry™
#32060

Intoduced: 9/30/2005
Retired: 12/29/2005
*ReIntroduced: 9/29/2006 and
ReRetired: 1/7/2007*
1G - $7

Bloose™
#32077

Intoduced: 6/30/2006
Current
1G - Current Retail Value

Bluebeary™
#3221

Intoduced: 6/28/2002
Retired: 1/8/2004
1G - $13

Candy Cane™
#32061

Intoduced: 9/30/2005
Retired: 12/29/2005
*ReIntroduced: 9/29/2006 and
ReRetired: 1/7/2007*
1G - $7

Castles™
#32093

Intoduced: 4/30/2007
Current
1G - Current Retail Value

Catnap™
#3233

Intoduced: 6/30/2003
Current
1G - Current Retail Value

444

Chomps™
#32066

Intoduced: 1/31/2006
Current
1G - Current Retail Value

Clomps™
#32073

Intoduced: 3/31/2006
Retired: 12/21/2006
1G - $7

Cloud™
#3223

Intoduced: 6/28/2002
Retired: 1/8/2004
1G - $18

Corkscrew™
#3231

Intoduced: 3/31/2003
Retired: 12/21/2006
1G - $8

Cruiser™
#3244

Intoduced: 3/30/2004
Retired: 5/24/2006
1G - $7

Dangles™
#3226

Intoduced: 3/31/2003
Current
1G - Current Retail Value

Dangles™ (large)
#32057

Intoduced: 1/31/2005
Current
1G - Current Retail Value

Dotters™
#32074

Intoduced: 6/30/2006
Current
1G - Current Retail Value

Flips™
#32097

Intoduced: 6/29/2007
Current
1G - Current Retail Value

Football™
#32068

Intoduced: 2/28/2006
Current
1G - Current Retail Value

Gallops™
#32065

Intoduced: 1/31/2006
Current
1G - Current Retail Value

Gilly™
#32087

Intoduced: 12/29/2006
Current
1G - Current Retail Value

Goodies™
#32050

Intoduced: 9/30/2004
Retired: 12/30/2004
1G - $7

Googly™
#3238

Intoduced: 12/30/2003
Current
1G - Current Retail Value

Gourdy™
#32059

Intoduced: 8/31/2005
Retired: 11/23/2005
1G - $7

Grazer™
#3230

Intoduced: 6/30/2003
Retired: 12/21/2006
1G - $8

Grins™
#3224

Intoduced: 6/28/2002
Retired: 12/21/2006
1G - $8

Growlers™
#32067

Intoduced: 1/31/2006
Current
1G - Current Retail Value

Harts™
#32085

Intoduced: 11/30/2006
Retired: 1/24/2007
1G - $9

Icebox™
#32051

Intoduced: 11/26/2004
Retired: 1/31/2005
Ty Store exclusive.
1G - $13

Jingles™
#32082

Intoduced: 9/29/2006
Retired: 12/21/2006
1G - $8

Lasso™
#3246

Intoduced: 3/30/2004
Retired: 11/23/2005
1G - $8

Leapers™
#32076

Intoduced: 6/30/2006
Current
1G - Current Retail Value

Lil' Icebox™
#32052

Intoduced: 11/26/2004
Retired: 1/31/2005
Ty Store exclusive.
1G - $9

Lovesy™
#32053

Intoduced: 11/30/2004
Retired: 8/25/2006
1G - $13

Lumpy™
#3235

Intoduced: 9/30/2003
Retired: 12/29/2005
1G - $9

Melton™
#3236

Intoduced: 9/30/2003
Retired: 1/9/2004
1G - $10

Merlin™
#32058

Intoduced: 8/31/2005
Retired: 11/23/2005
1G - $8

Merry Moose™
#32083

Intoduced: 9/29/2006
Retired: 12/21/2006
1G - $8

Milkers™
#32088

Intoduced: 12/29/2006
Current
1G - Current Retail Value

Mr. Snow™
#32080

Intoduced: 9/29/2006
Retired: 12/21/2006
1G - $9

Ms. Snow™
#32081

Intoduced: 9/29/2006
Retired: 12/21/2006
1G - $9

Munches™
#32086

Intoduced: 11/30/2006
Current
1G - Current Retail Value

Peppy™
#32099

Intoduced: 6/29/2007
Current
1G - Current Retail Value

Piggy™
#32089

Intoduced: 9/29/2006
Current
1G - Current Retail Value

Pinks™
#3220

Intoduced: 6/28/2002
Retired: 1/8/2004
1G - $13

Plopper™
#3225

Intoduced: 6/28/2002
Current
1G - Current Retail Value

Plumpkin™
#32049

Intoduced: 8/30/2004
Retired: 10/1/2004
ReIntroduced 8/31/05,
ReRetired 11/23/2005.
1G - $9

Pokey™
#3241

Intoduced: 12/30/2003
Retired: 10/25/2006
1G - $8

Pookie™
#3243

Intoduced: 3/30/2004
Retired: 12/29/2005
1G - $10

Pudder™
#3240

Intoduced: 12/30/2003
Retired: 12/21/2006
1G - $7

Puddles™
#3222

Intoduced: 6/28/2002
Current
1G - Current Retail Value

Puppers™
#3237

Intoduced: 9/30/2003
Current
1G - Current Retail Value

Purrz™
#3234

Intoduced: 6/30/2003
Current
1G - Current Retail Value

Quackies™
#32064

Intoduced: 12/30/2005
Retired: 5/24/2006
1G - $8

Shearly™
#3245

Intoduced: 3/30/2004
Retired: 4/21/2006
1G - $12

Slumbers™
#3227

Intoduced: 2/28/2003
Current
1G - Current Retail Value

Snackers™
#32063

Intoduced: 12/30/2005
Retired: 5/24/2006
1G - $8

448

Soccer Ball™
#32069

Intoduced: 2/28/2006
Current
1G - Current Retail Value

Stomps™
#32071

Intoduced: 3/31/2006
Current
1G - Current Retail Value

Sweetly™
#32084

Intoduced: 11/30/2006
Retired: 1/24/2007
1G - $8

Tinker™
#3239

Intoduced: 12/30/2003
Retired: 11/22/2006
1G - $7

Tiptop™
#32075

Intoduced: 6/30/2006
Current
1G - Current Retail Value

Towers™
#32047

Intoduced: 6/30/2004
Current
1G - Current Retail Value

Tromps™
#32072

Intoduced: 3/31/2006
Retired: 12/21/2006
1G - $8

Tubby™
#3232

Intoduced: 3/31/2003
Current
1G - Current Retail Value

Twitches™
#32090

Intoduced: 1/31/2007
Current
1G - Current Retail Value

Twitchy™
#3242

Intoduced: 1/30/2004
Retired: 12/29/2005
1G - $10

Waddles™
#32092

Intoduced: 1/31/2007
Current
1G - Current Retail Value

Whiffer™
#3228

Intoduced: 2/28/2003
Current
1G - Current Retail Value

Whiffer™ (large)
#32055

Intoduced: 1/31/2005
Retired: 10/25/2006
1G - $11

Windchill™
#32048

Intoduced: 9/30/2004
Retired: 11/19/2004
1G - $9

Winks™
#3229

Intoduced: 2/28/2003
Current
1G - Current Retail Value

Winks™ (extra-large)
#32054

Intoduced: 11/30/2004
Current
1G - Current Retail Value

Winks™ (large)
#32056

Intoduced: 1/31/2005
Retired: 6/23/2006
1G - $16

NOTES

Pluffies®

Ty created another original fabric in the development of the Punkies line. TyTips® is a spiky/prickly looking fabric that is actually as soft as silk. It has an amazing ability to stand on end and looks like nothing Ty has ever used before. These colorful animals are part fantasy and all fun.

Big Hugz™ (extra-large)
#0435

Introduced: 11/30/2004
Retired: 12/30/2004
1G - $50

Big Kiss™
#0445

Introduced: 11/30/2005
Retired: 2/24/2006
1G - $50

Big Siren™
#0450

Introduced: 11/30/2006
Retired: 12/21/2006
1G - $25

Bitty Kiss™
#0444

Introduced: 11/30/2005
Retired: 2/24/2006
1G - $11

Butters™
#0422

Introduced: 12/30/2003
Retired: 12/29/2005
1G - $8

Dominoes™
#0418

Introduced: 9/30/2003
Retired: 12/29/2005
1G - $8

Flair™
#0431

Introduced: 10/29/2004
Retired: 5/24/2006
1G - $7

Flame™
#0420

Introduced: 11/26/2003
Retired: 12/29/2005
1G - $8

Flipflop™
#0409

Introduced: 12/27/2002
Retired: 12/29/2005
1G - $7

Frizzy™
#0400

Introduced: 6/28/2002
Retired: 1/8/2004
1G - $10

Great Big Hugz™ (jumbo)
#0436

Introduced: 11/30/2004
Retired: 12/30/2004
1G - $200

Great Big Kiss™
#0446

Introduced: 11/30/2005
Retired: 2/24/2006
1G - $200

Hopscotch™
#0406

Introduced: 6/28/2002
Retired: 3/27/2006
1G - $7

Hugz™ (buddy size)
#0437

Introduced: 1/20/2005
Retired: 12/29/2005
American Greetings (USA)/Carlton Cards (Canada) exclusive.
1G - $20

Hugz™ (buddy size)
#0434

Introduced: 11/30/2004
Retired: 12/30/2004
1G - $17

Itty Bitty Kiss™
#0443

Introduced: 11/30/2005
Retired: 2/24/2006
1G - $7

Jolly Santa Claws™
#0440

Introduced: 9/30/2005
Retired: 12/29/2005
1G - $55

Kitty™
#0415

Introduced: 4/30/2003
Retired: 12/30/2004
1G - $9

Lil Hugz™
#0433 · pink

Introduced: 11/30/2004
Retired: 12/29/2005
1G - $12

Lil Hugz™
#0433 · white

Introduced: 11/30/2004
Retired: 12/29/2005
1G - $12

Lil Santa Claws™
#0442

Introduced: 9/30/2005
Retired: 12/29/2005
1G - $7

Lil' Siren™
#0447

Introduced: 11/30/2006
Retired: 1/24/2007
1G - $8

Mambo™
#0425

Introduced: 4/29/2004
Retired: 7/27/2005
1G - $7

Marbles™
#0423

Introduced: 12/30/2003
Retired: 12/29/2005
1G - $7

Pipsqueak™
#0411

Introduced: 12/27/2002
Retired: 12/30/2004
1G - $10

Polka Dot™
#0408

Introduced: 12/27/2002
Retired: 2/27/2005
1G - $7

Polka Dot™ (large)
#0429

Introduced: 10/29/2004
Retired: 9/23/2005
1G - $13

Rainbow™
#0401

Introduced: 6/28/2002
Retired: 1/8/2004
1G - $8

Santa Claws™
#0441

Introduced: 9/30/2005
Retired: 12/29/2005
1G - $11

Screamers™
#0438

Introduced: 8/31/2005
Retired: 11/23/2005
1G - $7

Shockers™
#0424

Introduced: 12/30/2003
Retired: 12/29/2005
1G - $7

Shreds™
#0405

Introduced: 6/28/2002
Retired: 5/24/2006
1G - $7

Shriekers™
#0439

Introduced: 8/31/2005
Retired: 11/23/2005
1G - $11

Siren™
#0449

Introduced: 11/30/2006
Retired: 1/24/2007
1G - $15

Sizzles™
#0407

Introduced: 11/27/2002
Retired: 1/8/2004
1G - $10

Skitters™
#0419

Introduced: 9/30/2003
Retired: 1/8/2004
1G - $9

Slim™
#0414

Introduced: 4/30/2003
Retired: 12/30/2004
1G - $8

Snort™
#0413

Introduced: 4/30/2003
Retired: 6/29/2005
1G - $7

Splash™
#0403

Introduced: 6/28/2002
Retired: 5/24/2006
1G - $7

Spookers™
#4401

Introduced: 9/27/2004
Retired: 11/1/2004
Ty Store exclusive.
1G - $11

Static™
#0416

Introduced: 9/30/2003
Retired: 12/29/2005
1G - $7

Swoosh™
#0427

Introduced: 4/29/2004
Retired: 6/29/2005
1G - $7

T-Bone™
#0410

Introduced: 12/27/2002
Retired: 1/8/2004
1G - $9

Topsy™
#0426

Introduced: 4/29/2004
Retired: 6/1/2005
1G - $7

Trapeze™
#0417

Introduced: 9/30/2003
Retired: 11/23/2005
1G - $7

Treetop™
#0412

Introduced: 4/30/2003
Retired: 3/27/2006
1G - $7

Tropics™
#0421

Introduced: 11/26/2003
Retired: 12/29/2005
1G - $7

Twizzles™
#0402

Introduced: 6/28/2002
Retired: 1/8/2004
1G - $9

Zapp™
#0428

Introduced: 4/29/2004
Retired: 11/2/2004
1G - $10

Zig-Zag™
#0404

Introduced: 6/28/2002
Retired: 5/24/2006
1G - $7

Zig-Zag™ (large)
#0430

Introduced: 10/29/2004
Retired: 5/24/2006
1G - $12

NOTES

NOTES

Alphabetical Index

Abbreviation Key

ANG	Angeline	JB	Jingle Beanies
AT	Attic Treasures	PK	Pinky's Beanie Babies
BB	Beanie Babies	PKO	Pinkys Others
BK	Beanie Kids	PL	Pluffies
BOP	Beanie Boppers	PP	Pillow Pals
BSK	Basket Beanies	PU	Punkies
BT	Baby Ty	TBB	Teenie Beanie Babies
BU	Beanie Buddies	TBOP	Teenie Boppers
BW	Bow Wow Beanies	TGIR	Ty Girlz
CL	Ty Classic/Plush	TGR	Ty Gear
HB	Halloweenie Beanies	VB	Valenteenie Beanies

458

Our Gift to You!

Here at Bangzoom we value your confidence in our collectors' guides, and we'd like to show our appreciation. So visit our web site right away and while quantities last, we will send you 4 free protectors for those precious Ty tags! There's no charge or future obligation to you.

1. Go to **www.bangzoom.com** and click on Bangzoom's "Contact Us" option, and a window will appear with an e-mail form.
2. In the "Subject" field, enter the words "Ty 3 FREE GIFT."
3. In the body of the e-mail, please provide the following information:

> Name
> Street Address
> City, State, and Zip Code
>
> Where you purchased our guide.
> We'd also like to know how you heard about us, but it's not a requirement.

4. Fill out any remaining fields in the form.
5. Submit the e-mail, and we will send your gift to you right away!

If you do not have computer access to our web site, you may request your gift by mail. Please send the requested information to the address below, or call us at 800-589-7333, ext. 108.

> Bangzoom Publishers
> Attn: Ty 3 Free Gift
> 14 Storrs Avenue
> Braintree, MA 02169